HARD
STUFF

▬

THE AUTOBIOGRAPHY OF
COLEMAN
YOUNG

HARD

STUFF

THE AUTOBIOGRAPHY OF

COLEMAN YOUNG

Coleman Young and
Lonnie Wheeler

Viking

To my mother, Ida Reese Young

VIKING
Published by the Penguin Group
Penguin Books USA Inc., 375 Hudson Street,
New York, New York 10014, U.S.A.
Penguin Books Ltd, 27 Wrights Lane,
London W8 5TZ, England
Penguin Books Australia Ltd, Ringwood,
Victoria, Australia
Penguin Books Canada Ltd, 10 Alcorn Avenue,
Toronto, Ontario, Canada M4V 3B2
Penguin Books (N.Z.) Ltd, 182–190 Wairau Road,
Auckland 10, New Zealand

Penguin Books Ltd, Registered Offices:
Harmondsworth, Middlesex, England

First published in 1994 by Viking Penguin,
a division of Penguin Books USA Inc.

1 3 5 7 9 10 8 6 4 2

Portions of this book first appeared in the *Detroit Free Press*.

Unless otherwise indicated, the photographs appearing in this book
are from Mr. Young's collection.

LIBRARY OF CONGRESS CATALOGING-IN-PUBLICATION DATA
Young, Coleman A.
Hard stuff: the autobiography of Coleman Young / Coleman Young with Lonnie Wheeler.
p. cm.
Includes index.
ISBN 0-670-84551-5
1. Young, Coleman A. 2. Mayors—Michigan—Detroit—Biography. 3. Detroit (Mich.)—Politics
and government. I. Wheeler, Lonnie. II. Title.
F474.D453Y68 1994
977.4'34—dc20
[B]   93-40731

Printed in the United States of America
Set in Postscript New Baskerville
Designed by Kathryn Parise

Acknowledgments

The authors would like to acknowledge the following people for enriching this project with their memories, perspectives, and selfless assistance:

Juanita Clark, Bernice Grier, Claud Young;

Dave Moore, Doug Fraser, Stanley Nowak, Sid Rosen, Wardell Polk, Alfonso Fuller, Bernie Klein, Bob VanderLaan, Peter Kelly, Charles Beckham, Arthur Johnson, Rose Ann McKean, Kirk Cheyfitz, Emmett Moten, Esther Shapiro, Harold Shapiro;

William Beckham, Walt Stecher, Marge Malarney, Ray Schultz, Dorothy Brodie, Pauline Wolf, Dolores Cooper, Mary Korn, Iris Ojeda, Pat Morefield, Bernice Carter;

With special thanks to Barbara Parker, David Black, and Nan Graham;

And deep gratitude to Bob Berg, whose files, recollections, insights, and unflagging helpfulness served as a support system for this otherwise daunting undertaking.

Contents

Introduction

The opinion has often been privately expressed—and Hugh Carey, the former governor of New York, once said it publicly—that if Coleman Young had been born white, he would have been President. Maybe. He certainly had the vision and the political talent. But after working with the man for more than two years on his autobiography, I sort of think, instead, that if Coleman Young had been born white, he would have been bored.

Being black, on the other hand, has kept his interest for a number of years now, and through several careers. Beyond all the details, it has pumped his veins with family tradition and filled his nostrils with the ways of the world; it has opened his eyes, set his jaw, burdened his shoulders, doubled his fists, and guided his feet to and through the office of mayor of Detroit, among other engaging stops. Over the decades, it would seem that the accumulated implications of the mayor's color have presented him with both an appropriate cause and a sufficient challenge, organizing a posse of his energies and calling out all of the political chutzpah that has ultimately come to characterize the legend of Coleman Alexander Young.

Actually, Young was born just a little less than half white, which is hardly unusual considering his roots in Alabama, where race mixing was a whispered but conspicuous custom. Nor does it have any particular bearing on this discussion, inasmuch as the white portion of the mayor's endowment has had a negligible influence on his identity, life, and career, which have been dominated instead by his slightly majority heritage. Issues pertaining to the black condition would inevitably and rather famously incline Young's performance as mayor.

The spontaneous endeavor to cope with the myriad, daunting manifestations of race has, along the way, prescribed his historical destiny as well as contemporary Detroit's, to the extent that Young's story is also his city's. In the American context, it is the consummate tale of black sovereignty. For twenty years, Coleman Young presided over and controversially personified the seismic demographic rearrangement that has made Detroit the nation's blackest big city (in both population and autonomy), hands down. In that time, no other figure embodied any other city in America in the manner that the mayor came to embody Detroit.

This carries with it extra significance because Detroit stands now for much more than the automobiles and sweet music that made it great. Due to its cutting-edge racial and socioeconomic makeup (more than three out of four residents of the city are black, and one out of three falls below the poverty line—both national highs), Detroit encompasses much that is salient and all that is urgent about urban America. In a country still fundamentally white, a black city stands self-consciously underdressed and frightfully isolated amid surroundings that it cannot assimilate, a third-world subcontinent within the greater society; a tangent and, to some, a terrifying culture.

A sense of social horror seems to overtake much of America when it contemplates a black city, drawing out racial anxieties that must be confronted if the nation is ever to truly become one under God, indivisible. Symbolically and specifically, Detroit is the problem that the country sorely needs to deal with at this moment. And it is for precisely that reason that America must also, belatedly, hear out Coleman Young. His chronicle is the one of essential relevance to the present condition, the metaphor that illuminates the black and urban predicaments with one incandescent life.

The full sweep of Coleman Young's saga envelops events that occurred long before he was even involved in it, when his relatives were fighting with white folks and dying at their hands in Alabama. He had not yet started school when the family migrated north along with other black pioneers who collectively redrew the American landscape, casting an urban society that would soon be fenced off from the more prosperous world around it. In Detroit, Young's life began to unfold in extravagantly colorful interludes, opening with backroom crap-table scenes on the fast streets of his Black Bottom neighborhood, then meandering through clandestine labor meetings in the shadows of the great automakers and rebellious strategy sessions in the black officers' quarters of the Army Air Corps. Viewed as a whole, Coleman Young's experience is that of a city boy moved by naked sensitivities and humanistic instincts toward a life's work, and that of a man whose private war with the system happened to go public when he became part of it thirty years ago. It is a documentary that moves beyond the black struggle to the black franchise. The big picture of Coleman Young reveals a battle-scarred radical whose personal history uniquely represents not only the black social history of modern Detroit but the last seven decades of black political history in the United States.

All the way down its kaleidoscopic path, Young's odyssey has been attended by circumstances that make the whole of it much greater than its episodes. He threw himself into the union movement, for instance, at a time when labor was breaking through the collective-bargaining barriers of the auto industry, and a time when blacks were breaking through the racial barriers of both the industry and the unions themselves. He was a Tuskegee Airman at a time when black officers—often at his urging and by his scheming—were rebelling audaciously against the Jim Crow customs of the armed services. He was a left-wing extremist and a recalcitrant witness when the House Un-American Activities Committee was persecuting his kind. He was a state senator when the great riot of 1967 ripped Detroit asunder. And he was Detroit's standard-bearing mayor during a period when white flight systematically looted, trashed, and imperiled his city.

A life so ideologically connected as Young's would inherently carry him into compelling company, and in the mayor's case those characters range from, among others, his poker-playing father to his Marxist barber to his local preacher-mentor to Paul Robeson and W.E.B. Du Bois and Walter Reuther and Henry Wallace and

Henry Ford II and Jimmy Carter and Jesse Jackson. And because he has lived so long on the front bumper of black history as it steers into contemporary urban America, Young's resonant voice narrates, in the pages ahead, a political and social commentary that traffics in the author's own chromatic background.

The voice, by the way, is a matter unto itself. Around Detroit, the mayor's speech patterns are legendary for their street qualities, to the extent that a small book of his unabridged quotations was published locally and sold briskly. For the purposes of this memoir, he gave considerable thought to the merits of authentically rendering that particular fashion of his, and ultimately decided to do so—with moderation—in the interest of stylistic integrity. The fact is, and Mayor Young is well aware of it, that his persona, however unceremonious, cannot be separated from his politics. It was his brass, after all, that brought him to Detroit's attention in the first place, on the occasion of his combative testimony before the House Un-American Activities Committee; and subsequently the mayor's profanity, although by no means contrived, has served as a sort of populist indulgence, reminding his constituents that he has never left where they reside.

Although he has occasionally reprimanded himself in public for swearing, the thing is, he believes in it. Young is a master of the spoken word, and he regards the spoken cuss word, if well timed and well chosen, as an invaluable player on the urban orator's semantic roster. His deployment of such words is neither indiscriminate nor haphazard, and he uses them in such a skillful way as to maximize their value. Versatility, in fact, is the chief attribute of his personal favorite, as the mayor explained once to an elderly Japanese interpreter during a trip to the Orient. When advised that some Japanese words have many meanings depending on the inflection with which they are articulated, the mayor replied, "Oh, yes, we have words like that in English, too—'motherfucker,' for instance." Another function of selective vocabulary that he particularly appreciates is its capacity for unsettling those whom he believes ought to be unsettled.

For the most part, Young has not been discouraged concerning his distinctive way of expressing himself. To wit, it has never compromised him at professional conferences or formal affairs, for which he has at his command a more traditional and equally eloquent manner of public speaking. (In this regard, Young describes himself as bilingual, a skill acquired by dint of an upbringing split between the indecorous leanings of his venturesome father and the more meticulous ways of his schoolteacher mother.) Even the assembled Baptists to whom he has personally carried his election campaigns seem to approve. At one Sunday stopover, he appealed to the congregation to pray for him to cease smoking and cursing, and the congregation answered that it would indeed put in a few good words about his cigarette habit, but as for the other, there were some folks who needed to be cussed out. And so the mayor has reason to feel that he has a mandate in this question. He will consequently write in the spirit in which he so notably talks, albeit with prior apologies to the clergy and any others who might be offended.

In any case, Young's reputation precedes him, and for the uninitiated who happen to call on the mayor at his office in the Manoogian Mansion, there is a revealing introduction on a placard at the corner of the desk. It is a nameplate inscribed with the letters M.F.I.C., which stand for much of what one needs to know about Coleman Young: Motherfucker In Charge. He considers himself to be all that the title implies—unholy, dangerous, accountable, and, above all, The Man.

The latter classification is the one that has caused him the most trouble over the years. The white establishment, which in Detroit is represented in great part by the suburban interests and their media mouthpieces, tends to be discomfited by the concept of a black man as The Man. This is perceived as encroachment upon territory already spoken for, a social trespass that many suburbanites not only apply to Coleman Young but extend generically to all of the black people who have unofficially annexed Detroit. The city's overwhelming color identification suggests to those white former Detroiters that it has been snatched from their dominion. The effect is a cold war over turf, not unlike the simmering stages of ethnic strife that has since boiled over in older regions of the world. Detroit's extreme situation is exacerbated by a lumpy racial composition that makes it the most segregated metropolitan area in America and fixes the attention of both sides on leaders and symbols. On that logistic, the parties agree. At the top of all the lists, in a burgundy velour sweat suit, working the phones in his second-floor office at the mayoral mansion on Dwight Street, is the M.F.I.C.

I don't recall that, in the time I've been involved in the research and writing of this book, I've come across a single soul from the vicinity of Detroit who might be called impartial on the matter of Coleman Young. It is rather common for suburban white people to despise him and say so. To those who do, he represents the element that chased them out of their native community and made it fearfully unfit to live in or visit. (This line of reasoning, of course, eschews the fact that discrimination long ago relegated the black people to poor pockets of the city that were subsequently plowed under by urban renewal and sliced up by the freeways built for decentralization, upon which they repaired to neighborhoods that the white people then elected to flee; and the fact, also, that, by virtue of creative development and concentrated effort, downtown Detroit happens to be a pretty nice and comparatively safe place to spend an evening, the city's former status as the murder capital of America lingering only in malignant, anachronistic reputation.) In a popular suburban view, as shared freely in social settings of two or more, the mayor is little more than a mean-spirited, race-baiting bully (an assessment unrespective of the fact that he has predicated his career, in both labor and public service, on the principle that racial unity is the best and only course by which the socioeconomic conditions of the nation can be meaningfully improved, and the fact that he has demonstrated this philosophy time and again through the formation of coalitions that have distinguished his mayoralty and through countless public appeals and speeches on the theme of racial and regional cooperation), and probably corrupt, as well (an opinion that persists in spite of the fact that federal authorities have literally hounded the man for more than fifty years—taking pictures, tailing, taping, tricking, trapping, etc.—in the desperate, relentless pursuit of an indictment, any indictment, and yet, after thousands of hours and millions of dollars and the best efforts of any number of highly motivated investigators, they haven't come up with a doggone one.)

On the other hand, the black people of the city, as a rule, swear by Young and made him the most repeatedly elected mayor in Detroit's history. The comment most often heard is that no other mayor, black or white, could have done for Detroit what Coleman Young has done. The litany includes normalizing the previously ugly relationship between the black community and the police; thwarting bankruptcy with an artful blend of brimstone and back scratching; persuading major auto companies to build in Detroit and then damning the obstacles to make it happen; restoring the riverfront; standing up to the suburbs; bringing internal respect to a beleaguered population that can't seem to get it from any other source; and generally, day in and day out, through crisis after crisis, controversy after controversy, beating the odds to pull the city—to say nothing of himself—through.

Although the two camps will never come to terms on the implications of Young's role in local history, nobody within his universe would dispute its prominence. The last twenty years have irrefutably been his, the only genuine question in that regard being whether the natural cycles of Detroit are responsible for the political legacy that is Coleman Young's or whether the mayor did the cycling himself. The respective positions, both evident to arguable degrees, would be (a) that regardless of who occupied the Manoogian Mansion, Detroit was headed swiftly and inevitably toward a numerically preponderant, politically dominant, and economically isolated black population, and (b) that Coleman Young put the pedal to the process.

In retrospect, it's apparent that Detroit's first black mayor was, in many respects, the preordained product of two centuries of local and national evolution. The independent schemes of destiny, however, while still on the scene in Young's Detroit, don't divorce him from his part in the past two decades. If white flight was a redefining fact of life in Detroit before Young assumed his office, he was a doorman to those with their bags already packed. There can be no doubt that the election of Coleman Young—his mere and formidable presence in office—blackened the complexion of the city.

Nonetheless, there is a very legitimate doubt about whether his administration has expressly operated to alienate Detroit's white population.

Viewed in a broad context, the theme of inevitability is one that makes the study of Detroit uniquely fascinating. In *The American Earthquake*—published in 1958, at the height of the city's automaking eminence—Edmund Wilson wrote that "Detroit is a simple, homogenous organism which has expanded to enormous size. You can see here, as it is impossible to do in a more varied and complex city, the whole structure of an industrial society." Detroit's was a cumulative development, constructed in layers of geographic and sociological responses. In its early days, the plight of the city was determined, as most are, by its location. Situated in the northern woods, on a river connecting the Great Lakes and separating two countries, Detroit became a town distinguished, in sequence, by lumber trade, by shipping, by its strategic positioning in commercial and international affairs, by the underground railroad, and by contraband. It consequently became, by the natural order, a town uncommonly driven by the political ramifications of its multiple identities. West of most other major cities in the new country and far from them, Detroit also became a place particularly concerned with transportation and a leading manufacturer of ships and railroad cars. As the centuries rolled over, all of the pertinent elements dramatically converged to make Detroit the automobile—and consequently the industrial—capital of America, if not the world; which in turn put the city at the center of the labor movement. In the meantime, Henry Ford's progressive five-dollar workday restructured the demographics of Detroit, stocking it with poor blacks and whites from the South and Eastern Europe and effectively manufacturing an American middle class. When the bombing of Pearl Harbor brought the United States into World War II a generation later, the nation logically turned to the automobile plants to build its heavy weapons, refashioning Detroit as "the Arsenal of Democracy." This predestined the expansion of Greater Detroit, for when the war was over, the federal government saw fit, for security and more subtle purposes, to decentralize the defense installments, building a network of highways intended to scatter the city. As the new white middle class, swelled by labor's gains, followed those highways to fresh suburban locations, blacks followed into the places they had left behind, drastically altering the racial and cultural constitution of the city, not to mention its tax base. Then the energy crisis belted Detroit in the gut, and rampant union wages landed telling blows to a complacent auto industry that had become much too careless. These mischievously mutable cycles of industry put Detroit on its back, with white folks tromping over it in their haste to get out of town. And that was about the time Coleman Young took over as mayor.

At the moment he did, in 1974, the proportion of white people in Detroit had dropped to half. The 1967 riot had accelerated the already rapid rate of white flight, and during Young's terms the Caucasian percentage of the city would be halved again. Of the 1.6 million white people who lived in Detroit just forty years ago, only two hundred thousand remain, a dizzying plummet of nearly ninety percent. This demographic metamorphosis has left the mayor in the uncommon position of simultaneously representing both a city and a race. While his antagonists have tediously complained that Young introduces race into every issue, the fact is, as a public servant with a manifest black constituency, he is duty bound to identify any prejudicial impositions upon the citizens under his charge. That's what big-city administration has essentially become in the segregated, suburban-oriented, two-nation modern society—the defense and promotion of the minority cause. As the unshrinking mayor of the city running point on this movement, Young is the prototype of the new-age urban official.

It is a role that he devours. In it, he has been able not only to vent his spleen and kick some conservative fanny, but to acquire and wield political influence in a measure that few other blacks have attained. It is not coincidental that two of the most notorious power brokers of his generation, former Chicago boss Richard Daley and black New York congressman Adam Clayton Powell, rank among the public servants whom Young most admires. He has openly envied Daley's autonomy over Chicago. And Powell, he has said, "was an arrogant son of a bitch. That's one of the reasons I loved him. Everyone had to deal with him. He took all the blows for having cracked citadels of racism that had never been challenged before, and he didn't back off of anybody." The quote could apply just as squarely to its source.

As the imperious, controversial Powell did a generation earlier, Young moves saucily in both the office and the trappings of power. His uninhibited expression of authority has no doubt hardened and multiplied his enemies, several of whom, over the years, have gone so far as to divulge their plans to terminate the mayor's life at the next opportunity. Most of the threats are shortstopped by his security staff before they reach him, and Young has come to regard them as part of the bargain of being who he has chosen to be. At any rate, his comportment has not been suppressed. On executive matters, he finds it stimulating to charge ahead unilaterally, even if it tosses him into the fire of public protest, such as when he took it upon himself to dig a large hole downtown and call it an arena, or when he leveled an old neighborhood for a Cadillac plant. Hesitation, Young figures, is the stuff of liberals (whom he regards as the pathetic counterfeits of real leftists like himself), and modesty is a luxury for those who can afford it by birthright. His mayoral lifestyle reflects this attitude, from his cultivated insularity to his sartorial refinement to his travel habits. When Young moved into the mayor's mansion, it was suggested that he surrender the traditional midnight-blue limousine that went with the office in order to show his constituents a common-man mentality, but he waved off such talk. "What would people think if Detroit's first black mayor went tooling down Woodward in a Rambler?" he asked, and then ordered a bigger limo.

Many perceive Young's administrative manner as imperial, and because of the hedges he has installed around his personal particulars, the media can't resist peeking in. The game annoys Young, but he has not been unwilling to use it to his advantage. He once returned from vacation with a bushy beard, figuring that two weeks was long enough to be out of the newspapers. After the *Detroit Free Press* ran an opinion poll on whether Young should retain his facial hair—eliciting one of its largest responses ever—the old hustler called his cousin and physician, Claud Young, and said, "Well, it's time to shave this motherfucker off."

In the main, however, media coverage in Detroit has not complemented the mayor's designs, and he considers his compliance with
their overtures to be strictly optional. Observing a broadened base
of prerogatives after twenty years in office, Young is not reluctant
to lecture the press in his own characteristic vernacular. On that
score, if it makes the reporters feel any better—and the mayor has
no particular interest in doing so—he addressed his staff in the
same disposition. "I've seen people come out of his office quiv-
ering," said Esther Shapiro, the city's director of consumer affairs
under Young and a longtime friend of his. "People are afraid of
him, and yet his secretary tells me he doesn't believe this. At the
same time, though, the people at City Hall really love him. There's
a tremendous feeling for him within these walls."

To a significant degree, Mayor Young's demeanor has to do with
being the M.F.I.C., and making sure everybody knows it. "As chairman of the Board of Police Commissioners," related Harold
Shapiro, Esther's husband and an old union crony of the mayor's,
"I had a serious problem with the police department and asked for
a meeting with the mayor. He called in the head of another department, a very important department that had to be involved in this
police problem. I found myself on opposite sides with the head of
this other department, and Coleman obviously supported my position. In the course of doing so, he went from Genesis to Revelation
and called this guy everything but a son of God. I have never seen
such vituperation. And yet the guy sat there and took it, and everybody understood that this was a momentary thing, that the guy's
job was not in danger—that this was just Coleman sounding off
and making himself vehemently clear on how he stood."

The Shapiros, possibly more than anyone else, have been privy
to the full spectrum of Coleman Young. They were there way back
at the first lustrous moment of his public life, when he was elected
to the executive board of the Wayne County CIO council in 1947,
breaking its color line. ("One night I got a phone call from Hal
telling me to get a babysitter and come on down to the Book
Cadillac because we were celebrating," remembers Esther. "Everybody was cheering, telling stories, carrying on. It was a tremendous
occasion—like getting the first black governor. And at the center

of it all was this tall, black, very elegant, very handsome man. That was how I met Coleman Young—on his night of triumph.") And they were also there just a few cruel, topsy-turvy years later, when his first marriage and his labor career had both been kicked out from under him. ("That was a very, very low period of his life," Esther says. "He had thrown himself into his work to the point that it probably cost him his marriage, and on top of that, he had nothing to show for all that he had done in the labor field. It seemed like everything he touched had turned against him. He would come into our house and flop down in a chair and say, 'What's wrong with me?' I vividly remember one of those days when Coleman's life was falling apart, a late fall day, cold and rainy and depressing, and as I was letting him in the door the balloon man went down the street. Our son, Mark, of course had to have a balloon, but balloons were a quarter and I told him no. So Coleman turned around and followed the man and bought Mark a balloon. I went in to make some coffee while Mark played on the floor and Coleman settled into his chair. He had a way of sitting sideways in the chair when he was relaxed, with one arm flung out, and there was a cigarette in his hand. Suddenly, boom, the cigarette hit the balloon and it popped. Mark looked up at Coleman with his big brown eyes filling with tears and said, 'Why did you do that?' I don't think Coleman uttered a word. He just put on his hat and coat, got in his car, and scoured the neighborhood until he found that vendor and bought another balloon for Mark.")

Although he is betrayed somewhat by the playful twinkle in his eyes and the uncontrollable bounce in his shoulders when he is amused (which is often), Young otherwise has gone to great lengths to keep his vulnerable side out of public view. It probably has something to do with Black Bottom machismo, which, to a lesser extent, has obscured his religious side as well. (Many will no doubt be startled to learn that it exists.) The mayor's religion, as such, is not indulged in the daily routine of the Manoogian Mansion; but when he travels, for instance, he has been known to remove the Gideon Bible from the drawer and interpret the characters on the pages with his own Coleman Young spin. "One night, about eleven o'clock, the phone rings and it's Coleman calling from Washington," says Claud Young. "He had been reading about David sending Bathsheba's husband to the front lines to have him killed, and he just called to kick it around. He said, 'That David was a bad son of a bitch, wasn't he?' "

As a mayoral candidate, Young traditionally made himself visible to the city's major black congregations in the months before an election, joining in the appropriate prayers and spirituals; and most of Detroit's political rallies have taken him to one church or another, where "Lift Every Voice and Sing" invariably follows the national anthem. He affects no piety on those occasions, however. Even from the pulpit, the M.F.I.C. jokes that he is building up credit for the rest of the year, when he sleeps in on Sundays. The truth is that Young considers his religion to be a private affair. As he explained once at New Bethel Church, pastored at the time by the locally renowned Reverend C. L. Franklin, Aretha's father, "I've never worn my religion on my sleeve. I'm a little bit suspicious of someone who talks about how religious they are. I believe that the basic concept of religion is to demonstrate your religion. People know who you are; you don't have to tell them. My religion is an impatient religion. I'm not any less a Christian because I want things to happen now. I want our children to reap better benefits than we have now. That's what religion is all about. My religion tells me that God helps those who help themselves. My religion tells me that ain't nobody going to do nothing for nobody until you do something for yourself. My religion tells me that it is proper to fall on your knees and pray, but once you are finished praying, get up off your knees and march forward. God didn't ask me to stay on my knees forever. He said, 'Just sit down there and pray and then get up and walk.' That is the religion that can move this city forward. Our God is a God of action, and Jesus Christ was an activist."

If Young's religious orientation defies a common categorization, it's certainly no harder to specify—and considerably less at issue— than his political bearing, which has taken on all the inevitable complications of years and reality. While committing his existence to a leftist's pursuit of a better society, Young has nonetheless broken with the liberals on countless matters of initiative and development. His radicalism—a nomenclature he much prefers to "liberalism"—often loops him back around to the conservative side, yielding sometimes to contemporary pragmatism and other times to old-fashioned values. On the issue of legalized gambling in Detroit, for instance, Young has determined that the economic implications supersede the higher-minded arguments. Yet on such questions as gays in the military and even women in the locker room, the warhorse radical surprisingly lines up as a traditionalist, deferring to social sensitivities he has forever lived with.

In the mayor's estimation, these positions in no way compromise his foremost devotion to the Bill of Rights. His life's work, in a nutshell, has been to see the American guarantees applied in full array without considerations of class and color, and the federal government's culpable negligence on that score has been at the front of Young's wearisome battle with it over the past half-century. For all of his iconoclastic eminence, and for every defiant syllable of his notoriously provocative rhetoric, Coleman Young has never wanted anything more than what has constitutionally been promised him and his city and his race—which, in the vicinity of Detroit, Michigan, have come to be perceived as essentially one and the same.

L.W.

HARD
STUFF

◼

THE AUTOBIOGRAPHY OF

COLEMAN
YOUNG

1

Echoes from Black Bottom

My earliest memory of Detroit is being awakened in the middle of the night—our first night in the city—by the bells of St. Joseph's Church, which stood just down the block from where we stayed, at my grandmother's house on Antietam Street. Although I failed, at the age of five, to fully appreciate the metaphor, the fact is that Black Bottom was like that during Prohibition, the sort of neighborhood that could be as lyrical as church chimes and at the same time keep you up at night with an assortment of commotion that was by no means restricted to the belfry.

For some whimsical reason, St. Joseph's has emerged out of context through the ensuing years, surviving as a relic of a resonant, colorful community whose demise was orchestrated by the public scourge known as urban renewal. Owing to the virulent postwar practices of the United States government, I grew up in a part of Detroit that doesn't exist anymore. In that general respect, Black Bottom has gone the way of the surrounding metropolis of its day, buried beneath the drifts of time and urban transformation. The few remaining shards attest to a once-thriving inner-city civilization that has been long lost.

This much is apparent: Detroit will never again be the city it once was. By virtue of compounded and confounded federal policies and of the unsympathetic cycles of social and industrial evolution—of such damn things as decentralization and white abandonment and the Toyota Corolla—Detroit will not revisit the

1

prosperity or eminence it once knew as the center and circumference of the automotive world. The auto industry is no longer willing or able to provide employment across the board for a city like mine, and there is one statistic that says about all there is to say on that subject. After World War II, one-half of all the cars in the world were built in Detroit. Now, Detroit makes one car out of every thousand. The days when the city could live off the auto industry are irretrievably gone, and they have taken with them the standards and artifacts of the old Detroit.

The popular way to explain the decline of Detroit—that is, the one so ardently talked up within certain white circles and the media, if I may risk being redundant—is to pin it all on me. The reasoning goes something like this: Detroit has had nothing but problems since the white people got the hell out, which goes to show that black people can't run anything by themselves, much less a major city, especially when it's in the hands of a hate-mongering mayor like the one who's been entrenched there for twenty goddamn years.

This, as one might imagine, is a school of thought to which I take exception, as the pages ahead will elaborate. But my personal reviews are only a footnote to a much more urgent theme relating to my city. While there can be no disputing that the traditional Detroit—as Motown and the Motor City, a model to the world, the soul and (with apologies to Chevrolet) the heartbeat of America—is a thing of the past, that much is merely the prologue. The real message lies in the fact that since 1914, when Henry Ford's futuristic production system and new-wage workday began to attract the multiracial, ethnic, huddled masses yearning to be gainfully employed, Detroit's special place in urban American history has been as its great indicator, a condensed, microcosmic, accelerated version of Everycity, U.S.A. Tocqueville noticed that about Detroit as far back as the early nineteenth century. In the evolutionary urban order, Detroit today has always been your town tomorrow. Superannuated as it may seem in this late segment of a swirling century, troubled and forsaken as the times have conspired to leave it, Detroit remains a surpassingly purposeful place, as important to the nation right now as it has ever been—maybe more so, because right now it is telling us that the cities are in trouble. Detroit is the advance warning system—the flashing red light and siren—for what could be a catastrophic urban meltdown, and the country had damn well better pay attention.

History has taught us that no civilization can survive the deterioration of its great cities, and it would be a grave mistake for America to be so pompous or unaware as to abide the urban crisis all around us. Detroit is screaming in our ears right now—in mine, anyway. For two or three terms, people asked me why I didn't just walk away from all the thanklessness that goes with being the mayor of Detroit—all the hopelessness and helplessness and hate and distortion and conflict and criticism and pain and despair—and until I decided that five terms was enough, I always answered the same way: Because there's too damn much to do. There's no other city in the world like Detroit and no predicament like Detroit's—not yet, that is—and consequently there has been no other mayor with a charge and a challenge like mine.

I might have felt differently about my burden in recent years if I thought that anybody else understood Detroit and its hardships as deeply as I do. But nobody else could understand, as I do, how the federal government has toyed wantonly with the fortunes of Detroit over a period of decades; how the suburbs have disassociated themselves from the problems of Detroit even as they have maneuvered to control our assets; how the press has been caught up in a program that indulges the suburban appetites at the expense of the city. For those parties and their influential collaborators, the enemy has consistently and seemingly forever been personified by me. For me to prematurely walk away not only would have represented a personal surrender but would have been tantamount, in my estimation, to giving up Detroit and turning it over to its assailants.

Let me say right off the top, as a warning to the reader, that I will now and often hereafter discuss the plight of Detroit in racial terms—not exclusively, of course, but at length. If you don't want to read about racism, close the book right now and let's agree to stay out of each other's lives. The risk I run in this respect—and it's one that can just be damned, as far as I'm concerned—is supplying material to my legion of antagonists who delight in referring to me as the flag-bearing racist of Detroit. This charge is deduced from my persistent habit of identifying racism as it impacts upon my life and city—by which reasoning, I might point out, a newspaper must be criminal for calling attention to crime. The only difference between reporting racism and reporting crime lies in the subjectivity of the offenses and the scope of the suspects; racists, unfortunately, don't leave fingerprints. Nearly everyone will admit to the presence of racism in our society, but, with the exception of some Klansmen and Skinheads and other racial zealots on the fringe, virtually no one will acknowledge his or her perpetration of it; it's always "Yes, yes, that's awful, but not me, not here." I attribute that more to ignorance than to denial. The racist mentality can be a subtle killer, a lot like high blood pressure in the way that you can have it and not know it.

Subtle or flagrant, the effect is much the same, and the unflagging incidence of racism in our midst has set the agenda for both my travail and Detroit's. As it was shaping my private resolve in the early part of the century, it was more significantly reconfiguring Detroit's demographic structure by driving black people up from the South and classifying the socioeconomics of the emerging city. In later years, racial intervention has been nothing less than definitive for Detroit, realigning it, undermining it, slicing it up, isolating it, condemning it, abusing it, ditching it, screwing it—and then, after the returns are in, insolently blaming its black leadership.

My critics are tired of hearing this sort of thing from me, I'm well aware. They hold me and my race rhetoric responsible for the anxious relationship that exists between Detroit and its suburbs, among other local tensions. But I refuse to accept responsibility for racism, because I am, in fact—as both a citizen and mayor—its sworn enemy and a lifelong victim of its machinations. To me, it's a pathetic commentary that I'm so roundly and vigorously indicted for racism when the truth is that I merely react to its assault. If a mugger grabs an old lady on the street and hits her upside the head, do we indict the old lady for screaming?

Regardless of the accumulated objections, I will not cease to make noise about racism—certainly not in these pages—because it will not be overthrown until there is a full awareness of its prevalence and devastation. In that context, racism and the urban problem are fitted together so precisely as to be effectively one, like overlapping pinwheels spinning together when either catches a breeze. As the symbol and spokesman for my city, I tend to get whirled around in the same zephyrs. In my part of the world, I've become synonymous—a code word—for Detroit, and in turn the name of Detroit is too commonly deployed with tacit racial connotations. When, for instance, a suburban Republican named Richard Headlee campaigned for governor in 1982 on the promise that he would put Coleman Young in his place, it was understood that he intended to promote the white interests and stick it to Detroit at every opportunity. I appreciated his candor and savored his defeat.

The interchangeable nature of racism and the urban predicament has been a recurring theme in modern America, and one whose popularity tends to rise and fall with the news. After the race-related riots of the late sixties, a presidential commission went to work on an enlightened urban report that would have improved millions of lives if only its belated release could have capitalized on the flurry of attention stirred by its cause. But it was to be lost in the malaise of Republican self-interest, which turned the nation's lenses away from the cities for most of two decades—actually, until Los Angeles cops were videotaped beating Rodney King and the place went berserk over their acquittal. We should have learned by now that we can't afford to shut off the camera. History and civil rights both need the footage.

I've learned also of history that it doesn't turn on a dime, or a tape, or a riot, or an election. In the sixties and seventies, I found myself every four years saying to myself and friends, in effect, "This is it. This is the fork in the road. This election will set our course for the future." But it doesn't work that way. We like to think that we're at the vortex of history, that all of the currents have joined at our heels, waiting for us to part the waters; but it's not like that.

There's no cosmic salvation, no miracle cure, no magic moment—only good and bad and politics. And time. The wheels of the gods drive slowly.

The wheels of America, meanwhile, tend to turn and drive in the other direction whenever they draw near to any sort of urban responsibility. This, to me, is a mighty curious thing. The question of the times surely has to do with why the inner-city problem has not been solemnly confronted—why it has not been at the top of the national agenda. It doesn't require the mayor of Detroit or any sort of political wizard to figure out that America's worst problems are largely city problems. While the federal government has fiddled around, crime and unemployment and dropout and infant mortality rates have burned themselves into the national superstructure. Our urban troubles have become ingrained to the point of characterizing the country's dark side. That would seem to make a no-brainer of domestic prioritizing, but the Republicans, in their several socially impaired administrations, never caught on to the concept.

I ought to make mention here, being an equal-opportunity mayor and in light of the foregoing, that the only thing I find as contemptible as a conservative establishment bigot is a bleeding-heart, pansy-ass liberal. Liberals talk as though they would change the world, but all of the things required to change the world are basically the things that liberals are not. Liberals are not radicals, by definition, and many of them are not capitalists, either. Liberals, whose currency is the impassioned harangue, nibble cheese and model the latest political fashions in front of each other while radicals and money are at work changing the world.

Bleeding-heart liberals operate under the ethereal premise that political correctness and economic development are mutually exclusive, when in fact they ought and need to be practiced in concert. The change I seek for the world around me is a radical one, and it will not be effected—I say this without apology to the liberals, who convulse over such pragmatism—without an economic foundation. It will not be effected without jobs. When you get right down to it, economics amounts to jobs. Equality is about jobs. Liberals, holier than profit, pontificate in terms of human rights; but in my opinion the primary human right is the economic right—the right to take home a check. Provide a citizen with a job, and everything else will fall into place. Honor the economic equality of a people, and they'll take care of education and housing and the social things themselves. That, right there, is the urban imperative.

True to its heritage, Detroit is positioned on the leading edge of this mandate which is so critical to the nation. If America rejects the vital demand for human rights and fails to meet the urban challenge—the challenge of economic equality, the challenge of Detroit—it will no longer be able to exist as a model of the free world. Like Detroit, it will no longer exist as we know it. The policy of urban indifference—human indifference—is a meandering backroad to a ghost society of cultural and economic ruin. It is the slow but sure path to internal division, rebellion, and all the familiar national tragedies of history. Indifferent to the lessons of Detroit, America would update the final scene of the Roman Empire, and do it for the same damn reasons.

We need to learn these things from modern Detroit: that its alienation from the society around it is, to a large degree, the specific predestined result of systematic disfranchisement imposed over the years by the multiple auspices of the federal government; and that the city's reentry into the socioeconomic mainstream must be gained by the same concerted methods. There is nothing accidental about modern Detroit. The cycles of industry and labor have authored it in part, but not without the domineering collaboration of the government. White flight, for instance, while attributable somewhat to the inevitable comings and goings of major companies, was preordained by the frenzied construction of superhighways leading out of the city and federal housing programs blatantly favoring the suburbs. Historically, federal policy toward black people has served the purpose of keeping them isolated, of reinforcing segregation by truncating their neighborhoods, thereby enabling white folks to get on with their lives unencumbered by the burdens of the lower class. In the same tradition by which black people have been systematically cut off from the basic rights and privileges that America would tout for its citizenry, so has Detroit. There's little distinction.

In the various phases of my life, I've crashed head-on into every hard place within the broad parameters of this organized disaffection. Its punishing civil effects virtually dictated my job description as mayor of Detroit; while on the personal level, the federal government, according to its own records—for which I'm most grateful, by the way—has been on my ass for more than fifty years, doing all it could to sabotage not only my private affairs but my military career, my labor career, and my political career, and persisting in its obsession even to the vicious detriment of my city. On that basis, I harbor no fondness or respect for my adversary whatsoever. At their declaration, the feds and I have been at war for every goddamn bit of my adult life; and if it seems sometimes that I relish the fight, well, I don't. I resent the hell out of it.

Believe me, I haven't ever wanted it this way. It's like what Rodney King said in the heat of the L.A. riot—can't we all just get along? I can think of no advantage to be gained by maintaining enemies in the government or the suburbs or the newspapers. Despite what the feds and many of my white critics seem to think, I've always preached and would prefer to practice cooperation, not conflict. My political consciousness was hatched at the neighborhood barbershop in Black Bottom, where the local radicals educated me with a dialogue that offered nothing about passivity or surrender but much about unity. As both a means and an end, unity—the coalition of races, classes, sectors, and political parties—has driven virtually every pursuit of my public life. I want no part of anything less.

Unity implies equality, by my definition, and equality cannot be meaningfully discussed in terms that don't presuppose economic parity. Understanding that, the radicals at the barbershop were concerned foremost with unity and equality in the workplace, and so am I. Jobs built Detroit, and only jobs will rebuild it. In that spirit, investment in the black and urban workplace is a matter of affirmative action on the economic front, and it's probably the single most important step the country must take to save not only black folks and the cities but America. Republican ignorance of this basic reality has assaulted our population centers and left us all in a state of crisis.

Somehow, though, Detroit, like St. Joseph's Church, has managed to survive the schemes to bring it down. It's a durable, remarkable town, and for that reason alone I retain a powerful faith in it. But I fear for it, too. I see contemporary Detroit—and by extension, contemporary America—the way Langston Hughes saw the dream deferred. Will it dry up like a raisin in the sun, or will it explode? If we don't get some economic satisfaction real soon in cities like Detroit, I'm afraid this goddamn urban situation is going to explode.

2

The Stiff-Legged
Mule

The white folks probably would have killed my father if we hadn't left Alabama. The situation had been building to that for a generation or two.

In the social order of the Deep South, the offense of my ancestors was that they were not intimidated by white people. This might have had something to do with the proximity of one to the other, which was immediate, the patriarch of the family being a wealthy landowner named Robert "Cap" Napier, whose father had come from Virginia and prospered on a plantation that had among its assets nearly eighty slaves. One of those, a mulatto named Sarah White, became Cap's unlawful wife during or just after the Civil War. Although it was anything but unusual in those days for white planters to father children with the black women who lived on their land, for the two to live together without pretense or shame was openly defiant, and pretty goddamn dangerous as well. That the Napiers were able to get away with it was a tribute to Cap's standing in the community and a legacy to their heirs. To me, the important thing was that they did it without compromise, moving not only Sarah into Cap's big cedar log house but her children, too. Napier gave his last name even to the kids whom Sarah had previously borne to a black or mulatto man from Virginia named Henry White, including a daughter named Virginia, my paternal grandmother.

Cap was respected all over Marengo County, and his funeral, just before the turn of the century, was a large affair held at the Episcopal church in Faunsdale, Alabama. The legend in our house was that my great-grandmother and my grandmother and her husband, Alex Young (from whom I received my middle name), and the rest of the family marched right into that church and took their seats in the front row, and none of the white people said a thing. In Marengo County, white people sat in church with black people about as often as they played polo with them, but everyone around there knew that Cap would be cursing in his grave if the service excluded his family. They also knew that the Youngs and the Napiers would tear that church down before they would be left standing in the back of it. That's the way they were.

Fighting bigots was a way of life for my predecessors. It was a costly one, too. Cap had left a vast amount of land to the family, but the white people of Marengo County found ways to take it over little by little. My grandmother had six sons, and collectively they managed to entangle themselves in legal and physical disputes on a regular basis, most often with the local types who resented or disrespected them. Each time, Sarah Napier would have to give up a piece of property as a white man's settlement. Any sort of trespass, real or contrived, was reason enough to grab some land. One of my uncles was a constable for Judge Hugo Black, later of the Supreme Court, and his job was to retrieve prisoners who tried to escape or violated parole. On one occasion, he found himself in a tight spot with a criminal who elected not to be hauled back to jail, and Uncle Bennie had to kill the guy. The prisoner was black, but the white authorities still didn't cotton to the idea of a black constable using a gun, and somehow or another, through the inexplicable realities of Alabama justice, that one ended up costing the Youngs five hundred acres. Before long, the land was all gone and the family had been cut down to a scale more befitting its color. I have an aunt who still lives near the old plantation; and not long ago, when one of my cousins was visiting in Faunsdale, she took him to a nearby farm, where a white man offered them figs and all sorts of fresh vegetables. Afterwards, my cousin commented on how nice the white fellow had been, and Aunt Gladys said, "He ought to be nice, all right. It's your land that he has."

Even without their land, the Youngs always made a decent living through various enterprises. My grandfather Young, the son of a probate judge named James Young and one of his slaves (of which the judge owned about twenty, although he was not a planter and lived within the town limits of Linden), was a barber who moved his family to the bigger town of Demopolis and hustled around to supplement his income any way he could. He owned a small market and, as a drayman, operated several wagons and mules, loading the wagons with wood and coal from the train and selling his goods from the yard of the family's one-story frame house. When his other businesses were slow, he would pull the night watchman shift at Webb's general store or guard the corn and cottonseed mill. But his reputation came from his barbecuing. When white churches or wealthy merchants or planters put on lavish weekend barbecues, they hired Grandpa Young to do the cooking. He would hustle up a wagon load of fresh pork, chicken, and turkey, haul it home and precook it until it was dropping off the bones, then mix it in with okra, celery, onions, and bushels of tomatoes. On the day of the picnic, he'd simmer the stew in a row of huge black kettles and dig a pit to barbecue a whole pig with an apple in its mouth. On a special occasion like the Fourth of July, he might serve as many as five hundred people. The way I've heard it, Grandpa Young put on the finest barbecues in Marengo County.

My grandmother could get around the kitchen a little herself. She ran a restaurant in Faunsdale, the only place in town that served both blacks and whites. Like most of the Youngs and Napiers, Grandma Young was so light-skinned and Anglo-featured—she had long, straight hair down to her waist—that she could have easily been mistaken for white by someone who didn't know her, which everybody in Faunsdale did. One afternoon a customer—no doubt from out of town—asked her why she served niggers in the restaurant, and her answer was, "Because *we're* niggers." The visitor said, "Don't get smart with me," to which my grandmother replied, "Don't you get smart with me, white man, or I'll whip your pants off!"—which she could and would have done. Like her husband, Grandmother Young was nobody to mess with. My grandfather once beat a white man with a cane of sugar for calling him a nigger.

My mother's family was of the same kind of stock. She handed down a story about an ancestor whose son was beaten by a white man. Knowing full well the consequences, the father carried his pistol to the white man's house and shot him dead, then returned home, loaded his guns, and barricaded the doors. The mob arrived on schedule and started shooting, then set fire to the house. My ancestor and his wife never came out—just stayed in that burning house, cursing the white people outside with their last breaths.

Now and then, though not often, someone in my family would choose an alternative to fighting, one of which was passing for white. A cousin of my father left Alabama for Boston, where he could easily pass, and became a very successful doctor. We didn't see much of him after that—if a man was passing for white, it wasn't a good idea to visit his black family—but we could have used him in Alabama. When my Uncle Walt had appendicitis, the only available surgeon was a white one who had it in for him for whatever reason it was that most of the white people there had it in for the Youngs. The doctor completed the appendectomy, but sewed up Uncle Walt with the surgical scissors still inside him—a development that none of the Youngs presumed to be accidental. My uncle died a few months later from the infection.

Tales like that seem remote nowadays, and perhaps apocryphal, but they hovered like death itself over my father's family. Since my father and his brothers were ambitious, more learned than most blacks in that part of the country, and not as obsequious—Daddy, in particular, was congenitally incapable of kissing anybody's ass— the white people regarded them as "crazy niggers" and kept a close eye on their activities. My father got their attention after he moved his family to Tuscaloosa, where I was born in 1918, because he sold and circulated black newspapers like the *Pittsburgh Courier* and the *Chicago Defender.* This was threatening to the good old boys, because it encouraged black people to read, for one thing, and in addition to that it put all sorts of northern ideas in their heads, such as voting and integrated schools and labor unions. One of my father's white friends—he didn't have many—was able to keep the lynch mob off his tail, but by and by the time came for the friend to move away from Tuscaloosa, at which point he advised Daddy to take his black ass and do the same. My father was a fighter, but he wasn't a fool. By then, we had no place to stay in Tuscaloosa, anyway, because around that time—around 1921—our house burned down. It seems like an incredible coincidence, but I honestly don't recall the KKK or the local rednecks being involved. I do remember sitting on a mattress in the front yard and watching the walls crumble in flames. That's one of the earliest memories of my life.

Another is my first encounter with the Klan. When we left Tuscaloosa, we stayed for a short while in Huntsville, where my uncle Stanley had a restaurant. As my mother was walking me to the restaurant one summer night, we crossed a street and all of a sudden a car came wheeling around the corner with men standing on the running boards wearing sheets. What made the scene so vivid to me was my mother's reaction. I sensed immediately that she was terrified. As she grabbed me up in her arms, I could feel her trembling.

While we were in Huntsville, my father, who pursued knowledge doggedly and always looked to better himself, took advantage of his World War I experience and the GI Bill to attend Alabama A&M, where he acquired expertise in tailoring. His brothers, although not college-educated, were trained in barbering and restaurant skills, and periodically Daddy joined them as they knocked around the South, plying their trade in the large hotels. A couple of my uncles had a fancy twelve-chair barbershop in Selma where they purportedly cut only white men's hair, although after it closed at night they would draw the curtains and bring in their black friends, taking perverse pleasure in the knowledge that it would horrify their white customers to think that the clippers and combs in their hair had previously been in black men's.

My father, among other hustles, also managed a barnstorming baseball team for a while, and he claimed that Satchel Paige pitched for him. He went so far as to say that the crooked finger on his left hand came from catching Paige with a primitive mitt, although between Satchel and Daddy the actual truth is hard to put your hands on. My recollections of that period aren't quite so epic. I remember backing into the searing brazier my mother used to heat her iron, leaving a scar that started behind my knee and over the years has moved down to my calf. I remember the junk man coming around with his jackass. I remember the outhouse. And I remember, on a rainy day in 1923, a dead mule lying in the mud by the railroad tracks, his feet sticking straight out like the legs of a kitchen table on its side, as our train pulled out of Alabama headed for the land of opportunity that they called Detroit.

A MIGRATION on the order of America's northern one could not possibly be preconceived. It was not as if all the black people in the South got together and decided that the best thing for the race was to pick up and repair en masse to the industrial cities of the Great Lakes region. Nor was it the persuasive influence of a great black leader, because, although there were some—W.E.B. Du Bois, the author and founder of the NAACP, was most prominent among them—they had no effective way to reach the poor and largely illiterate black masses of the South. And so, rather than an orchestrated, collective movement, the migration was a cataclysm of personal watersheds. It was the accumulation of generations of social degradation and economic despair, of lynchings and whippings and fires and rapes, of second-class citizenship and third-world living conditions, of the suffocating cycle of ignorance engendered by poverty and poverty engendered by ignorance, of helplessness, of ruthless planters cheating their sharecroppers at the autumn settlement, of subsistence-level jobs lost to the mechanical cotton picker, of mud floors, of trampled spirits, and, more than any one thing or institution or fact of life, of family histories. For virtually every man, woman, and child who escaped Alabama and Georgia and Mississippi for the south side of Chicago or the east side of Detroit, there was an ancestor, like mine, who died in flames, or an uncle, like mine, who was murdered for sport, or a father, like mine, who had used up his southern options.

At the turn of the century, Detroit had a small and stable black population, much of which was descended from former slaves who had been brought north as prisoners of the Indians generations before in territorial raids against Kentucky. But between 1910 and 1930, when the production of automobiles became an industry and Henry Ford breast-fed it with the irresistible wage of five dollars a day, the number of blacks in Detroit increased from 5,000 to 120,000. This would not have been so problematic had not Ford and the others attracted similar waves of Appalachians and Poles and Italians and assorted ethnic groups. The massive multicultural migration created a predictable crisis in housing, the principal victims, naturally, being the blacks. The Detroit Real Estate Board was forbidden to sell homes to blacks in white neighborhoods, and the inevitable result was an epidemic of overcrowding in the East Side Colored District, as it was called, which included the neighborhoods of Paradise Valley and Black Bottom, where I grew up. Although the housing was poor quality and overpopulated, rents in the black neighborhood were two or three times as high as those for comparable spaces in the white districts. And since blacks were traditionally the last hired and first fired, in order to pay the rent it was often necessary for two or three families to share a small apartment. Civilization has yet to produce a more reliable formula for a ghetto.

Black Bottom, which was not named for the color of its inhabitants but for the rich, dark soil on which the early settlers farmed, was in a transitional stage when my family arrived. It had long since passed from agrarian to urban, but by the early 1920s the neighborhood was in the process of turning over again, from European to black. In the meantime, for a decade or so it was completely and uniquely integrated.

When we first moved to Detroit, we lived with my maternal grandparents on Antietam Street between St. Aubin and the railroad tracks on a block that was less than half black. My grandfather Jones had been the first in the family to migrate to Detroit, in 1920, followed by my aunts and uncles a year later, my father in 1922, and then my mother and the rest of us the year after that. Together, the Youngs and the Joneses considerably increased the black population of our street, which at the time was an ethnic smorgasbord. Our house was next door to an Italian family, whose daughter, Polly, I frequently played with. There was a Syrian family down the street, a German grocery on the intersection—I can still smell the sour rye bread—and a Jewish delicatessen around the corner. Nearby, at St. Aubin and Gratiot, a German singing society occupied a building called Schiller Hall that exemplifies the many incarnations of Black Bottom. In the thirties, it became a union hall and a refuge for leftist political groups. In its most recent life, it has been owned by an order of black masons and used for a black credit union and barber school.

I don't recall an unusual amount of racial tension in the years Black Bottom was integrated, but the adversarial attitude was gathering ominously around the city as the new migrant groups staked their competing claims for social status, housing, and jobs. The very summer we moved to Detroit, there was a KKK initiation ceremony in which thousands became members in a single goddamn swoop. Most of them were factory workers from the South who suddenly found themselves threatened by blacks in a way that they had never been before. Later that summer, the Klan burned crosses right in front of City Hall. Michigan's KKK membership was the largest of any state in the country, nearly a million. At the same time, Poles were emigrating to Detroit in large numbers and jostling with the blacks at the bottom of the social order for jobs and housing, both of which were all too scarce. Those were formative years in Detroit. One cannot begin to grasp the dynamics of modern Detroit without understanding the forces that shaped it when I was a boy. The racial disposition that has come to define the city in recent decades is an inevitable legacy of a place and an industry that grew too big too fast.

In Black Bottom, a metamorphosis seemed to occur overnight. By the late twenties, the neighborhood was entirely black except for some of the merchants on St. Aubin and Hastings streets. The racial makeover was not the only one, though. Prohibition and, in turn, the Depression converted Black Bottom into a haven for hustlers of every stripe. In our neighborhood, Prohibition was a period of enthusiastic debauchery in which nothing on the street was what it seemed to be. After a few years at the Antietam house, our family settled on St. Aubin, where we were just a block or two away from a strip that offered all manner of illicit backroom sin. The local hat shop was a front for the biggest numbers operation on the east side. Dave Winslow made whiskey in the rear of his sweet shop.

If you were stupid enough to walk into Lonnie's shoe shine parlor and ask for a shine while the poker and blackjack games were going on—which was most of the day and night—you were liable to get your ass beaten. When I was about ten, I started sweeping floors and delivering suits for three bucks a week plus tips—which were considerable in those days—at Ike Portlock's tailor shop, where there was usually a crowd of men shooting craps in the back room. Ike kept as many as eight very large fellows on his payroll as bouncers and stick men. I wasn't allowed in the back most of the time; but in the coldest days of the winter, if we weren't pressing and the steam wasn't warming up the front, I was permitted to sit on a pile of wool samples by the potbellied stove, where I could peek over the shoulders of the craps players. Before I was out of grade school, I had learned the bar points (the bets you don't make), the difference between a three-way, a four-way, and a five-way point, and how to identify crooked dice by the way they rolled.

After a while, I was known at most of the card games around Black Bottom due to the fact that, as the oldest of five kids and my mother's chief deputy, I had the job of fetching my father or carrying home his winnings. If he saw me coming, Daddy would just empty his pockets and hand everything over, knowing, as we all did, that our bread money would turn to liquor and probably trouble if I didn't collect it first. My father, for all of his self-made education and instinctive dignity, was a chronic and peculiar kind of drinker who would lose himself in the alcoholic life for a while and then dry out for years at a time. He was also a frequent fighter and, most of all, an inveterate gambler. In addition to being a master contract bridge and whist player, William Coleman Young—Daddy went by his middle name—was unquestionably one of the best poker players in the city, known in all the back rooms as Rip or Eagle Eye or the Natural Truth or, if it wasn't a friendly game, Tricky Slim. All of the top players had nicknames—I remember Gabble Eyes and Hound Dog Red—but none of them could win money from my father.

My father's most lucrative game might have been the one he played regularly with the reporters and printers from the *News* and the *Free Press*. Every payday, they would gather in the back of a recreation building across from the post office, where Daddy worked. He would not have been allowed in the game if the other players had realized he was black, but although he never tried to pass for white—Daddy was too proud and ornery for that—he was not dark enough to jeopardize his seat at the table. Coming up with the stake was a trickier proposition, however. Fortunately, he had a friend in the wholesale stamp window at the post office. A lot of money rolled through that window, and at the end of every Friday the guy would give Daddy three hundred or four hundred dollars to take across the street. The return was generally about a hundred percent in six or eight hours.

Daddy spent many a night that way when he was supposed to be watching over the post office. If he couldn't make it to work, my brother George and I would cover for him. Other times, we'd drag him to the Federal Building, let him punch in, and then drop him onto a couch in one of the judge's chambers to sleep it off. When he woke up at about four A.M., he'd send us out to American Coney Island for a bag of hamburgers. But that is not to suggest that he cared nothing for his duties. One time Daddy caught a white man trying to rob a stamp machine at the post office and ordered him to halt. But the guy ran, upon which my father pursued him across Ford Street into an alley, where he proceeded to take a few potshots at the perpetrator with his .45. Fortunately for the crook, he spotted a couple of cops at the end of the alley on Congress Street, made a dash for it, and leaped into their arms. The arrest happened to be the first of the new year, and as a result the *Free Press* duly reported it. Daddy carried the clip around in his billfold for years afterward.

Before he went to work at the post office, my father held a job as a busheler—mending and altering clothes—at Sam's Cut Rate downtown. The position was based on the unspoken assumption that he was white. It wasn't the first time that Daddy's pale complexion had gained him entree where he would otherwise have been prohibited, and he was fortunate in that respect; but in other ways he considered his light skin to be a curse. Because of it, my father often heard white people say things that they wouldn't have knowingly said in the presence of a black man. It caused him to hate them uncommonly.

The prevailing bigotry at Sam's came to the surface one day when one of Daddy's friends from the neighborhood dropped by to visit. The moment the store managers realized that my father was black, he was fired. Eventually, he opened up his own dry cleaners and tailor shop, which was the place we moved into on St. Aubin. My mother ran the cleaners and my father did the tailoring between naps, poker games, and the post office. We had a couple of rooms in the back for a living area, but George and I slept in a bed behind the cases in the shop. My parents and my two younger sisters, Juanita and Bernice, slept in the apartment, and my little brother, Charles, bunked out where he could. In the winter we'd let him in with us, because he was like a little heater, but in the summertime he was on his own.

With all of the little enterprises we had going on, our family was never indigent. We did particularly well during Prohibition, which can be said for all of Black Bottom and Paradise Valley. I never saw such prosperity in the black community—hell, in the city—as there was then. The money was practically jumping from pocket to pocket in those days. If you weren't making any, you either weren't trying or were inhibited by an unusual code of lawfulness. There must have been fifteen dealers working every poker game and twenty more guys with jobs at the biggest numbers stations. The only people not on the hustle were mothers and preachers, although it was hardly unanimous in their cases, either. Even my grandmother—my mother's mother, who was still only a few blocks away after we moved out of her house—played policy, as it was called, which paid off on numbers mimeographed all over town in houses named after southern railroad lines, like the Yellow Dog. In the late twenties, policy gave way to the clearinghouse, which took its winning numbers from government banking transactions printed in the major newspapers. Since more papers carried race results, the basic numbers game eventually revolved around the winning combinations from tracks all over the country.

However the games were played, there was plenty of action to go around. All over the streets you'd see black guys with their pants neatly pressed and their fingernails manicured and their yellow leather shoes shined so bright it made you squint. Most of those guys came from the South, where their models for success were the highfalutin plantation owners, with their crisp clothes and smooth hands. The object was to remain unsullied by hard labor, and the young smartasses of Black Bottom seemed to have it knocked. Naturally, I aspired to be one of those fine gentlemen. I thought they had things all figured out. They were so sure of themselves that they'd sit along the street and make jokes when the buses came through to recruit men for the Ford plants. They'd laugh and point and shout things like "Bring the job to me! I want to see it!" They were even so brazen as to taunt the Ford men about having their wives while the husbands were off bolting bumpers. Their motto was "You feed 'em, we fuck 'em." I basically had two role models in those days—the hustlers, with their flashy clothes and money clips, and the Ford mules, as they were called, straggling home from work all dirty and sweaty and beat. To this day, it amazes me that I became a labor man.

That is not to say that I didn't follow after my father when I was young. I managed to pick up a little poker and a lot of guile from his expert example. One of his trades was bootleg whiskey, which he obtained from Canada and brokered to about half a dozen federal judges, to whom he had access in his position at the post office. It seemed as if Daddy couldn't make a dollar without tweaking the system along the way. Even his night watchman's job was something of a scam, because the chief doctor at the Veterans Administration Hospital was a friend who certified that my father had been disabled during World War I by an arthritic condition so bad that it prevented him from making his regular rounds, which is what enabled him to get away with playing poker and sleeping through his shift. It helped also that he was indispensible among the watchmen, the only one at the post office who understood mathematics well enough to schedule three shifts and fifteen guards.

I was not in my father's league as a hustler, but it wasn't for lack of trying. Along with several well-chosen friends, I had my own little bootleg business during Prohibition. The Detroit River, which separates the city from Windsor, Ontario, is a network of inlets and canals, which, when I was a boy, provided the cover and escape

routes for thousands of professional and amateur bootleggers. The
Hiram Walker distillery in Windsor was built where it is for the express purpose of accommodating the illicit transportation of its
products across the Detroit River. As the primary American distri-
bution center for Canadian whiskey, Detroit was the front door to
the United States. It was said that eighty-five percent of the Canadian liquor that came over the border during Prohibition passed
through Detroit, where the bootleg industry employed as many as
fifty thousand people—not to mention kids like me—and was second only to the manufacturing of automobiles. The unlawful con-
veyance of booze was so common that the Detroit Tunnel was
known locally as the Detroit Funnel. But the particular contraband
that interested my friends and me was the stuff that came over by
small boat. The Coast Guard patrolled the river constantly, and the
bootleggers had adopted the technique of smuggling small loads
that they could dump into the water at the first sign of the law. We
considered it no great misfortune that they often had to unload
just before they reached shore. Our job was to mark the spot and
then dive there first thing in the morning. Turning the whiskey
into cash was no problem: all over the city, there were literally
thousands of blind pigs—Prohibition saloons—that would buy our
booty. We were partial to Little Harry's Restaurant on Chene,
where we could knock on the back door, ask for Little Harry, and
walk away with twenty bucks for every fifth of Canadian. It was a
profitable operation, but we were compelled to retire prematurely
after one of our best swimmers got caught in the undercurrent and
drowned.

There were any number of safer ways to turn a buck, anyhow. I
worked out a deal with Dave Winslow, the confectioner, whereby
I'd pick up pint bottles at places like the poolroom across the street
and sell them to him for a penny apiece to use in his moonshine
operation. I made more money from him than I did from Ike
Portlock. After that, I graduated to the drugstore hustle. A fellow
in the drugstore would sneak me merchandise out the back door
at cost or thereabouts so that I could resell it for a profit as an independent wholesaler. In the store, cigarettes were thirteen cents a
pack, or two for a quarter, but I could buy them for five cents and

sell them for ten. If anybody saw anything they wanted from that store, they knew I could get it for them cheaper. There were no limitations. The mother of a friend of mine once wanted me to save her some money on a douche bag, but she didn't know how to ask me for it. She told me to look in the window and the third box from the right, or whatever, was what she wanted. I went to the store with my friend to check it out and there was this goddamn douche bag. Naturally, I couldn't complete the transaction without ragging my friend, realizing all the while that I was dangerously close to what we called "playing the dozens," which amounts to insulting someone's mother.

This sort of economic mischief was perpetrated during my grade-school years, a period in which my friends and I operated what we considered to be a theft ring. It started after the Mafia bombed a dry goods store in the neighborhood. We were among the first ones in there to help ourselves to the dry goods, coming away with a few changes of clothes, which we couldn't take home because our mothers would want to know where we had gotten them. So we stashed the stuff in an abandoned shack on a vacant lot, and every day after finishing up my work at Ike's tailor shop, I'd meet my friends at the shack, where we'd put on our "stealing clothes" and then make the rounds for a couple of hours before going home. Our gig was basically shoplifting, victimizing the local merchants with a little devious teamwork. For instance, two of us would walk into a store with some kind of curio, like a cigar in a glass tube, and one of us would ask two dollars for it even though it was only worth a dollar. Meanwhile, the other guy would quickly make his selections around the store, and if we distracted the merchant for just twenty seconds, we had him.

Hustling—including the legitimate kind—was a way of life for our family. My father earned fresh creamery butter by cutting the hair of a dairy farmer. I would often get up at four or five in the morning to stand in line for free bread at a bakery that had an arrangement with the welfare department. And I could always make a dollar on Saturday afternoon from a well-known black doctor in the neighborhood named Ossian Sweet.

Solemn and broad-shouldered, Dr. Sweet was renowned for a

highly publicized incident in which a white man had been shot and killed while standing in a mob outside the house into which the doctor had moved on a previously segregated street. (Ironically, the man from whom he had bought the house, at Garland and Charlevoix, was a light-skinned black man successfully passing for white.) Dr. Sweet had grown up in Florida, where he had been painfully familiar with the atrocities visited capriciously upon black people by white mobs—he was careful to wear a chauffeur's cap when he drove his fancy Marmon automobile through the South— and he was also aware that another black man had been run out of a nearby home just weeks earlier by a throng of thousands. It must have seemed to Dr. Sweet that the time had come to take his stand. As it was, he was already coping with discrimination in his profession. Even though he had studied medicine in Europe, he had no choice but to operate his own clinic, because white hospitals wouldn't hire him. For these reasons—and owing also, no doubt, to a palpable degree of fear pushed to its limit—Dr. Sweet made up his mind to defend his new home with guns, which he put in the hands of several friends and relatives. When the mob showed up and the incident escalated, a shot was fired from the house and a white man dropped in the street.

The entire Sweet party was charged with murder, and the case took on national proportions when Clarence Darrow was brought in as the defense attorney. Darrow was as brilliant as ever, but his client wasn't bad, either. On the witness stand, Dr. Sweet testified, "When I opened the door, I saw the mob and I realized that I was facing the same mob that has hounded my people throughout its entire history." The verdict was to be rendered by judge in the city Recorder's Court, presided over by Frank Murphy, who later became mayor, governor, and a Supreme Court justice—and the first man I ever saw with a hundred-dollar bill, which, to my astonishment, he placed in the collection plate at St. Mary's Church during the Depression. Murphy was famously sensitive, and courageous enough that Dr. Sweet and the others were acquitted. The defeated prosecutor later allowed that he was disadvantaged by the fact that "the colored people involved were so far superior to the white people involved." Of course, most of this was lost on me at the time, because it had taken place two years after we arrived in Detroit, when I was seven years old. All I knew was that I could pocket a dollar for going up to Dr. Sweet's office every Saturday—his clinic was over Ike Portlock's cleaners and crap game—and answering the telephone while he went to lunch with his lovely nurse, Miss Smith. It occurred to me that a dollar was an exceptional amount for a man to pay a kid for an hour or so of secretarial work, but it also occurred to me that Miss Smith was an exceptional lunch companion.

The money I took away from Dr. Sweet's office in an hour was half as much as I had made in a week of hard work in one of my more memorable summer jobs. It was at a lakeside cottage owned by two men named Thomas and Forsyth, who operated a prosperous haberdashery. When I was younger and delivering suits for Ike Portlock, I had met an insurance salesman named Al Frands, who knew Thomas and Forsyth and set up it for me to be their houseboy over the summer. My grandfather Young, who was up from Alabama to spend the summer with us, went out there with me to negotiate a deal. My grandfather was no Uncle Tom, but he was accustomed to Alabama-style bargaining between blacks and whites, and I came out of it with two dollars a week plus room and board. So I went out to Silver Lake, where I would get up at seven every morning to fix breakfast, do the cleaning, and work the lawn. I had to push a hand mower up all these damn terraces that led to the lake and weed two hundred feet of flower bed. But there was plenty of sunshine and fresh milk from the Jersey farm down the road. It was the only summer I can remember—and the following winter was the only winter—that I haven't had any colds or sinus trouble. When the summer was over, Thomas and Forsyth gave me the same sort of position I'd had with Ike, cleaning the store and delivering garments. I acquired a very thorough knowledge of downtown that way.

In my spare time, I made what I could shining shoes. For the most part, I only did shoes on Sunday, when I wasn't working for Thomas and Forsyth. My corner was Dubois and Mullett, where my father's cousin John Young eventually opened the original Young's Bar-B-Q. I'd set up there in the morning, catching everybody going to and from church, and when I made sixty cents I'd give fifteen cents to each of my brothers and sisters for the movies—a dime for the show and a nickel for popcorn. (Since my mother was always working at the shop and my father was generally occupied by re-freshment and poker, I was deputized over the children. I was the one who assembled their wagons at Christmas and talked to their teachers at school, and I was the one who had to climb the back-yard fence to pull Bernice away from the killer Dobermans next door. The neighbor fed his dogs gunpowder to make them mean, but Bernice, who was three or four at the time, didn't understand this and was hanging over the fence trying to play with them. They were reciprocating by snapping at her throat. I still have the tooth cut on my wrist to show for my efforts.) Anyway, after I had shined shoes for a few hours, all my brothers and sisters would line up with their hands out. After presenting them with their movie money, I'd turn back to the shoeshine stand to make some for myself. I might not make anything more, or I might make fifty cents, which I would use to buy my own way into the movies and all the food and popcorn I could carry. My plan was to sit off somewhere by myself so my brothers and sisters wouldn't bother me, but they'd show up wherever I was, begging. It didn't do them a bit of good.

My biggest payday of the year was probably Christmas Eve, when I'd work all day as a substitute clerk at the post office, sorting the mail until the last card was on its way, then hurry across the street to the recreation building, where a fellow named John Christie had a shoeshine stand with about twenty stalls. At John Christie's, I could shine for eight or nine hours without even straightening up. It didn't take much of that before I could identify a frog by the condition of his shoes and pants. A frog was a guy who didn't tip, and without fail it was somebody with old ratty shoes that hadn't been buffed in three months. He was getting a shine because he needed one, and not only was he going to stiff you, he was also go-ing to work you too damn hard and long. So I looked for the guys whose pants were neatly pressed and who were there because they had style and liked to show it.

The one job that I really wanted when I was young and never got was that of carrying ice into people's homes and apartments for their iceboxes. It paid well, but you had to grunt and sweat for your money, because the ice came in twenty-five- and fifty-pound blocks, and not many of the customers lived on the first floor. I was envious of the guys who were big and strong and lucky enough to work as icemen—especially one particularly strapping older boy named Joe Barrow. I knew Barrow from the Brewster Rec Center, where I'd seen him beating up on some of the local boxers, among whose number I liked to count myself. It had occurred to me about the time I was becoming a teenager that I might like to take after my uncle Buddy, whom Daddy had managed as a fighter and who had been a former sparring partner of Jack Johnson. Barrow was a more immediate role model, and although I never stepped into the ring with him, I stood up with some of the better boxers in the gym. On one memorable occasion, I landed a good blow to the chin of an opponent who was very highly regarded. There were usually girls around, and when I scored on this big fellow, they started chittering and giggling. With that, I tore into him, which was not prudent. The moment I hit the canvas, it was apparent that I didn't have a career in store for me like the Barrow boy, who later became known as Joe Louis.

Even after he was heavyweight champion and a folk hero to black people all over the country, Joe Louis still came back to Black Bottom and passed out dollar bills on the street corner. He usually did it after a big payday—after he'd beaten somebody like Max Schmeling or Max Baer or James Braddock. Everybody would gather around him, and the champ would dole out money according to his own system—the most for older men and friends, and on down the line. Since I was four years younger than Joe, I was probably a punk in his eyes. That made me a two-dollar man.

Louis also kept up his presence in the neighborhood by sponsoring a softball team, the Brown Bombers, that was the class of Black Bottom. The Brown Bombers gave us a sense of superiority in a neighborhood rivalry that was fierce. In our part of town, there was always a battle to establish hegemony—blacks against Italians, blacks against Mexicans, blacks and Italians against Mexicans and Irish, and so on. When push came to shove and the challenge came from the other part of town, all of the east side neighborhoods would band together to kick the shit out of the west side. There were never any weapons involved, but it was required that there be roughly a fight a day. It was also understood that there would be a large one after every softball game. If you played in another neighborhood and won—as the Brown Bombers always did—there was no getting away without an ass-whipping.

Because he was local, I don't think we fully realized what Louis meant to the black population of America. What mattered most to us—the thing that showed everybody in Black Bottom that he was still with us, more than handing out money or buying softball shirts—was that he hadn't given everything away to The Man. Even after he reached the top, Louis stuck with his black handlers from the old neighborhood. His principal manager was one of the Roxborough brothers, John, who ran the numbers game on the east side and was known as the richest black man in Detroit. The other Roxborough of local renown, Charles, was the first black legislator in Michigan. You couldn't beat those connections.

Charles Roxborough was the first of a long line of state and federal officials from our neighborhood. In retrospect, it was no coincidence that Black Bottom was the birthing room of black politics in the city and the state. Between the unions and the bread lines and the bootlegging and the general bandying-about of civic concerns, the east side was an ideological orgy. During the Depression especially, somebody was nearly always standing on a soapbox in front of the soup kitchen I passed on the way to school, bellowing about Marx or revolution. Politics in Black Bottom, though, unlike in other black neighborhoods, was more than rhetoric. Our district was politically operational, thanks mostly to the local undertaker, Charles C. Diggs, who owned a large funeral home just across the street from our shop on St. Aubin and also ran an insurance business, which was the basis of his political machine. The insurance company had about a hundred agents who went door to door selling policies and carrying the partisan message. In effect, Diggs's salesmen were agents for the first Democratic organization in the black communities of Detroit and Michigan. Until then, blacks had always voted Republican, a tradition that went back to Abraham Lincoln. Roxborough was a Republican. But Diggs succeeded him as state senator from the Third District, and virtually all of the black legislators from that time on—including Diggs's son, Charlie, Jr., the congressman—were Democrats.

I picked up some useful political lessons from Diggs, Sr.—many that are still applicable today—but my early civics classes were actually conducted in the two-chair barbershop of a self-educated Marxist and pontificator extraordinaire named Haywood Maben. Maben referred to himself as a dialectician and to his forensic agenda as dialectical materialism, which meant that he argued about economic systems. In his whiskey tenor, he would take off on day-long diatribes about unionism and unity between the races, invariably attracting a crowd of the more thoughtful men of the neighborhood, among whom was John Conyers, Sr., father of the current congressman. Occasionally, somebody would purchase a haircut, but if you weren't in the market for a political quarrel, you didn't happen into Maben's. Most of the regulars shared the same basic ideology—essentially, trade unionism with a liberal dose of communism—but there was plenty of room for disagreement concerning the fine points, which made for damn provocative conversation. One of the standard debates was over who was the greatest leader: Booker T. Washington, Frederick Douglass, and W.E.B. Du Bois. As you might expect, there were not a lot of conservative, no-resistance, nonpolitical Booker T. Washingtonians in the barbershop crowd (an exception being the cobbler next door, who had attended Tuskegee Institute, which Washington founded), and consequently there was little chance that I would become one. I was a good ten years younger than anybody else there and wasn't precocious enough to contribute much, but I soaked it all up. The fellows saw to it that I was receiving a proper education.

That's more than I can say for most of the schools I attended. I went to public grade schools until my father, upon meeting a white man at the post office who treated him like an equal and happened to be Catholic, converted to Catholicism. Daddy and Mother took catechism at Sts. Peter and Paul's Church on Jefferson, after which all of the kids were baptized and enrolled at St. Mary's in Greektown, which was in the process of becoming the first Catholic school in Detroit to admit blacks. St. Mary's was an outstanding school and I flourished there, making straight A's in the eighth grade, which placed me among the top ten parochial students in Detroit and was supposed to qualify me for a scholarship to one of the city's best Catholic high schools. But when I showed up to enroll in the fall, the brother looked at me and said, "What are you, Japanese?" I said, "No, brother, I'm colored." He tore up the application right in my face.

It was during that period that I became acquainted with racial discrimination at the personal level. Among other activities, I was involved in the Boy Scout troop we started at St. Mary's—the Beaver Patrol—and went pretty quickly through the ranks as patrol leader, senior patrol leader, and then the strategic position of junior assistant scoutmaster, which is the only thing under the scoutmaster. Everything sailed along just fine until that point, but when I became junior assistant scoutmaster, they broke up the troop—just dissolved the damn thing. I guess it was better to have no troop than one led by a black boy. It seems peculiar that discrimination would hover in the shadows and then leap out all of a sudden like that, but that had been the pattern historically—it becomes an issue about the time the boys and girls are old enough to start noticing each other.

That summer, our class scheduled an eighth-grade graduation party at a local amusement park known as Boblo, which is still located on an island in the Detroit River. As we were loading the boat to take us to Boblo, one of the guides jerked the cap off my head to check out my hair and officiously informed me that black children were not permitted at the park. Despite my Boy Scout experience and all of the things I'd heard from my father and other black adults, I honestly wasn't prepared for that. And I was never quite the same person again. My sister Juanita must have been as taken aback as I was, because to this day she refuses to go to Boblo.

From that time on, I was increasingly sensitive to the dynamics and heritage of race. Whenever a black speaker came to town—as when A. Philip Randolph of the Brotherhood of Sleeping Car Porters appeared at Bethel African Methodist Episcopal Church as part of its lecture series—I was there. Although Randolph was too conservative for my tastes, the evenings at Bethel AME and the influence of men like my father and Haywood Maben instilled in me a sense of ethnic awareness that inevitably sent me careening into the white authorities of my world. At Eastern High School, for instance, which I attended after being shunned by the Catholic school (about ten or twelve black students had to raise hell even to go to Eastern, and after we left, the door was slammed on blacks and nailed shut), we were taught American history out of a book by Samuel Beard. When we got to Reconstruction, Beard more or less justified the forcible suppression of black liberties and even the presence of the KKK by depicting ex-slaves as stupid, lazy, thoroughly lacking in morals, and utterly unable to fashion a life for themselves. That clanged in my head, because the black people I knew were nothing like Beard's descriptions. I wrote something to that effect on the paper we had to do and received a C for my efforts. I wasn't accustomed to receiving anything but A's and an occasional B, and was piqued. Indirectly, though, it was the best thing that ever happened to me at school, because it sent me straight to the public library. I'd always spent part of my Saturdays at the library, riding down on my skate box—a two-by-four screwed to an old skate, with a handle sticking up like a scooter—but I usually came home with adventure books by Zane Grey and James Fenimore Cooper and Arthur Conan Doyle. This time, I got my hands on a little volume by Du Bois—*The Souls of Black Folk*—that changed my entire pattern of thinking. For a long time thereafter, I read almost nothing but black history and philosophy.

Among other things, Du Bois made me realize that my experience was different from his and other American blacks' only in the names, dates, and places. He wrote about the time he was in a New England grade school with white classmates—much like I had been at St. Mary's—and a gangly white girl looked at him in a cold, superior way that suggested he didn't even exist. It was only a fleeting moment, but it was a turning point in Du Bois's life, because it was the moment in which he first shuddered with the realization that he was different—inferior—in the eyes of white people.

Du Bois was the first author I'd ever read who made sense in a way that related to my own life. He gave me words that I could live by, and did and still do. He wrote, for instance:

One ever feels his two-ness,—an American, a Negro; two souls, two thoughts, two unreconciled strivings; two warring ideals in one dark body, whose dogged strength alone keeps it from being torn asunder. The history of the American Negro is the history of this strife—the longing to attain self-conscious manhood, to merge his double self into a better and truer self. In this merging he wishes neither of the older selves to be lost. He would not Africanize America, for America has too much to teach the world and Africa. He would not bleach his Negro soul in a flood of white Americanism, for he knows that Negro blood has a message for the world. He simply wishes to make it possible for a man to be both a Negro and an American, without being cursed or spit upon by his fellows, without having doors of Opportunity closed roughly in his face.

As much as anything I've read or come across in the last half a century, those words have endowed me with a guiding philosophy as both a man and a public official.

Because of the world that Du Bois opened up, I can say that I'm as bookish as most of the college people I know, even though I didn't make it that far. I certainly planned on going to college and thought that I would. My mother, who was fastidiously attentive toward her children's academics, had graduated from Stillman College in Tuscaloosa before becoming a teacher, and my father, in addition to his college background in the trades, was highly self-educated (and made it a point to read at least one newspaper a day, front to back), all of which made me scholastically fit. In fact, I had thought I had qualified for a college scholarship or two. Late in my senior year the principal at Eastern High informed me that since I had placed second in my class (which I lorded over my schoolmates insufferably, constantly reminding them that my grades had been achieved without the benefit of studying), I was entitled to select one of the partial grants—two to the University of Michigan and two to City College of Detroit—that were offered annually to the top four students in the school. I told him that I chose Michigan. Traditionally, part of the Michigan package was a job that would be arranged by one of Eastern's alums. But when I reported to the principal that summer to catch up on the specifics, he asked me, "Have you gotten a job?" I replied that it was my understanding that the job would be taken care of. He said there must have been a misunderstanding, because nothing had been lined up for me. Knowing that I was unlikely to find an equal-opportunity employer on my own in the village of Ann Arbor and that I couldn't meet my remaining costs without one, I advised the principal that I would consequently accept one of the City College scholarships. He said that they had already been taken. I was out of luck. Later, I heard that the same thing had happened to a black student the year before.

I encountered a similar kind of misunderstanding one Christmas when a priest at St. Mary's recommended me for a seasonal job at Crowley's downtown department store. I received a postcard from Crowley's telling me to come down for training as a sales clerk. There were about fifty or sixty high school students there, and after a session in which the sales manager taught us how to write up CODs and that sort of thing, he took us in the elevator to the various floors where our departments were located. I was headed down to men's clothing on the second floor, but as we got off the elevator on the fourth floor, the sales manager—I still remember his name, a Mr. Nielsen—looked at me and then blanched, as if it just dawned on him that there had been a colossal fuck-up. I guess, in the crowd of kids, he hadn't noticed before that I was black. Well, he never dropped me off on the second floor. He carried me all the way down to the basement, turned me over to the black man who was head custodian, and said, "Give this boy a job." The custodian knew my family and he was embarrassed by the situation, which he quickly surmised. Thinking he was doing me a favor, he elected not to put a mop in my hands, but instead gave me this ridiculous sky-blue doorman suit with gold buttons and epaulets and boots about ten sizes too big and a goddamn Napoleon hat. Crowley's used doormen to direct traffic during the Christmas rush, and I wouldn't have minded the job if it hadn't been for that silly uniform. Sure enough, I no sooner assumed my post than a bunch of gals that I'd been looking at in school came strolling by. I was supposed to be some bigshot scholar, and here I was in Napoleon's hat and Paul Bunyan's boots. Naturally, they broke up laughing. I ripped that motherfucker off, threw it down, and quit right there.

I never could pretend to be what I wasn't, a fact that came into play later when I was invited to a fraternity dance at one of the elite (that's pronounced EE-light) churches where everybody was light-skinned and attempted to be very civilized. I had a girlfriend, more or less—a neighborhood girl named Mary Kelly, whose stepfather owned City Hatters—but elected to go to the fraternity bash unencumbered. I wasn't sure that the dance was Mary's kind of place, considering that she was the only girl I knew who was my equal in the art of profanity. Actually, that quaint quality was just one of several things that endeared me to Mary. Another was that there was no shortage of food at her house, where I could place myself in the company not only of the effervescent Miss Kelly but of all the hot dogs and tamales and blackberry wine I could handle.

For this particular occasion, however, I preferred the companionship of my Black Bottom buddy Frank Saunders. Frank was a very adept dancer, although his type of dancing was not the sort they did at the ee-light church. Black socialites favored ballroom dancing, very elegant and refined, and when they really got to partying hard, they tended to dance like white folks, jumping up and down a lot. None of that bore any resemblance to the way they danced on Hastings Street, where Frank had made his reputation. When I took Frank into that fraternity party, he practically turned the place upside down. All of the girls wanted to dance with him, and he was more than willing to accommodate them. While Frank was drawing a crowd on the floor, I was making time on the sidelines, inviting various society girls to step outside for a little nip of the blackberry wine (which probably came from Mary's house) I'd stashed in the snow. The only problem was that the other fellows at the party didn't cotton to this too much. They had been looking for a reason to toss Frank out of there from the beginning, anyway, because his skin was too dark for their circles, and all of this inevitably resulted in some spirited scuffling. We tore up that damn fraternity dance, which goes down as my final foray into black "society."

At any rate, I was more in sync with the rhythm of the streets. I'd do anything for a few bucks, including some of the sporting pastimes at which my father had excelled, and eventually I attained the status of a nickname: Big Time Red. The "Red" part had to do with my coloring, as many of our nicknames did, and the "Big Time" part came by way of a late-teenage incident in which I suppose I exercised a conspicuous mastery of Black Bottom economics. I was in the poolroom one day when a guy came around to put a sign in the window about a show that was bringing forty French girls to a hall on Hastings Street. I told the guy I could sell a lot of tickets for him on my side of town, so he turned over to me the concession for all of Black Bottom. The tickets were seventy-five cents, and I must have sold five hundred of them. The night of the show, I was supposed to turn in my proceeds, but the fellows taking the money seemed pretty busy, and I hadn't settled up yet when I noticed that it was past starting time and the customers were stomping their feet and yelling for the girls. Then I noticed that the promoter had quietly taken his leave. There were still about five ticket sellers at the windows with money in their hands, so I stepped behind the counter and started collecting it as if I knew what I was doing. My sidekick, Frank, was working with me, and we knew it would be nip-and-tuck to get out of there with our hides before everybody figured out what was going on. I told Frank to locate an exit for me and let me know the exact moment to hit it. About ten minutes later, when it was obvious that the girls weren't going to show and the customers were beginning to plot their revenge, we jumped out the second-floor window and literally hit the ground running.

Most of my questionable shenanigans in those years were executed in the company of Frank, who could have made the same statement about me. As a rule, we were able to two-step out of trouble, but we were always aware that, whether we were guilty or innocent, the law was keeping a hard eye on us from behind. To black people in Detroit, a cop was someone to fear. Frank and I found that out one night when we were walking home from a movie on Woodward Avenue. We were laughing about something as we started across the street, and about that time a car slowed down as it went past and a guy shouted out the window, "Hey, niggers, next time you'll get knocked on your ass!" Being the levelheaded type that I've always been, I replied, "Fuck you, motherfucker." When I said that, two white cops jumped out of the car and grabbed me. I said, "Hey, you can't hit me—I'm a minor!" It worked that time, but you could never be sure. Our standing rule was never to turn your back when a cop called out at you—make them shoot you in the front so they couldn't say that you were fleeing arrest.

The custom in the Detroit Police Department—as in many other northern industrial cities—was to place ads in southern newspapers for law-enforcement officers who were experienced in "handling coloreds." Detroit's force was populated by a high percentage of Appalachians who seemed to welcome any excuse to bust some black heads. In an eighteen-month period in the mid-1920s, twenty-five black people were killed by policemen in Detroit as opposed to three in New York, which had twice the black population. It was common for Detroit policemen to rout blacks who were standing around in groups, and often they would take a black man—virtually at random—to a sandpile by the river and beat him savagely. In the thirties, the cop we most feared in Black Bottom was a huge man named Blondie Hayes, who would kick down doors and claim that his search warrant was the size-fifteen shoe on his right foot. Even the few black officers on the force were generally hired for their willingness to exercise brutality on other blacks. That was an age-old southern convention dating back to the days of slavery.

Jaundiced as it was, most of us understood that the disposition of the police force was merely symptomatic of the basic racial attitude of the government at large—local, state, and especially federal. In all of its forms, the government made clear that its policy toward black folks was predicated on containment. The purpose was to keep them in their place, and it was done without apology. The concerns of black people simply made no impression on the government. During the Depression, when Detroit was "the capital of the jobless" and the black community was the capital of Detroit's jobless, the public welfare commissioner, a reputed gentleman named Dr. Blain, responded to petitions on behalf of the east side by saying, "Let's not worry so much about a few Hastings Street pickaninnies and start worrying more about the white taxpayers."

It seemed to me and my mostly adult acquaintances that the only ones who gave a damn about the concerns of us pickaninnies were the Communists and Franklin D. Roosevelt. The local Communists were doing things that made a tangible difference to many in the black community, like storming the welfare offices when shoes and shirts and assistance checks were slow in coming, and moving people back into apartments that carpetbagging landlords had thrown them out of. They talked about equality between all people, which was something that the United States Constitution also made mention of, although its executors seemed acutely unimpressed by the fact. Until FDR.

Roosevelt was the first President in my lifetime to administer what amounted to an urban policy. It was actually a Depression policy, but the effect was much the same, because it addressed the social problems brought on by the unemployment and poverty so predominant in the cities. Roosevelt's New Deal represented a concept toward which the recent Republican administrations showed nothing but disdain—the idea that everyone is entitled to a livelihood and that in difficult circumstances, it is the government's responsibility to step forward as the employer of last resort. That was the basis of the Civilian Conservation Corps and the Works Progress Administration, which provided not only jobs but jobs that improved the natural resources and the infrastructure of the country while at the same time providing the work force with an immeasurable sense of dignity and self-esteem. Under the WPA, the government not only hired laborers but, through branches like the Federal Writers Project and the Federal Arts Project, offered a contributing outlet for skilled people as well. The New Deal simultaneously rebuilt the country's economy and morale. One cannot be addressed without regard for the other.

From where I viewed things, though, the best thing about Roosevelt's recovery programs was that they were equally accessible to blacks and whites. Most of my friends got jobs with the CCC, but I was ineligible because of my father's government position with the post office. Thanks to his talent for hustling up money—through his job and other habitual means—we came through the Depression comparatively well. On Saturday nights, Daddy often showed up with corned beef and fresh roasted peanuts, on which we would feast while arguing politics around the kitchen table. His efforts were complemented by those of my resourceful mother, Ida, who could conjure up a meal out of most anything. She would take a sassafras root, for example, and drop it in water to make tea, which she would serve with biscuits and butter for dinner. Then, after most people would throw away the root, she boiled it again and again, supplementing the sassafras with sugar and powdered Pet milk. But not everybody in the neighborhood had it so good. I saw many men and families broken down by their inability to earn a living—some of them very close to home. My grandmother Jones—we called her Mama, because when we moved to Detroit she considered herself too young to be called Grandma— happened to be a very good cook and was able to sell barbecue and baked goods and homemade mayonnaise out of her house; but my grandfather was unequipped to adapt as well to the hard times. He contracted lung disease while working at American Copper and Brass around 1930–31, was laid off, and never regained his job, his health, or his pride. Papa had worked hard all of his life, and it damn near broke his heart to be economically impotent as other people around him made a living, however meager. He did what he could. He and Mama picked up rags in the alley and found various odd jobs so that my aunt and her children, who lived with them, would not have to eat in the soup kitchen; but I truly believe that the absence of steady work is what killed him.

Indirectly, though, while it brought on the demise of many good men, the Depression also gave life to Black Bottom. The social and economic conditions, brutal and unpitying as they were, animated the neighborhood over matters like housing and unions and communism and the Ford Motor Company. For answers—for salvation—people turned to church and politics. In many cases, the two were symbiotic. Every pastor had a political position, and every address had multiple purposes. Maben's barbershop was a left-wing caucus in the afternoon, and the nights were for meetings held in private houses behind drawn curtains. It was a climate very conducive to the nurturing of young radicals.

3

The War at Home

By the thirties, the erstwhile hotshots of Hastings Street and
Black Bottom, their attitudes adjusted by the material circumstances, were no longer strutting their stuff in front of the Ford
mules but searching for ways to catch on with the company. They
were desperate, and Henry Ford, a wily old bird, was not above taking advantage of the situation.

There were many in the black community who regarded the old
man as a benefactor, inasmuch as he was the only one hiring them
in significant numbers—he was, in fact, a paternal figure for the
masses he employed—but the people in my crowd were of a more
skeptical predilection. We realized that Ford had his own good reasons for maintaining a presence in our neighborhood. He used
black men to do the jobs that white men didn't want, like laboring
in the foundry or duco work—spray painting—which was well
known to be fatal to people who did it for a few years. And at the
same time, Ford knew damn well that black workers were his strike
insurance. The white workers had to think twice about forming a
union and walking out on their jobs when the old man had thousands of hungry blacks at his beck and call. Chrysler used this strategy during the Dodge Main strike in 1939, sending in blacks as
strikebreakers. In fact, taking their cue from Henry Ford, all the
auto companies recognized the advantage of playing the races
against each other, a practice that created palpable tension between black and white workers throughout the industry.

In this and other ways, Henry Ford had the black community exactly where he wanted it. Most of the black people in Detroit had migrated from the South in search of a job, and to be at the mercy of The Man, as they were in the case of Ford, was a way of life to which the majority were grudgingly resigned. Among the conspicuous exceptions were the radicals at Maben's barbershop, who recognized that there was no future for black workers in any system that separated them from white workers; that, in effect, there was no such thing as separate but equal. That sort of reasoning made a union man out of me. It was obvious to me that the workingman, black or white, had no strength, no security, no hope without unity. It was also obvious to me that the cause of the workingman and the cause of the black man were one and the same. We sure as hell weren't going to make it on a large scale as professionals and captains of industry. Bear in mind, this was a decade before there was even a black ballplayer in the big leagues.

By a very young age, I had already rejected the notion that white people would grant us full citizenship on religious or moral or constitutional principles. In order for any substantial segment of white society to join our struggle, there would have to be a compelling economic reason—a self-interest—and the union was it. Although some of them were too bigoted to acknowledge it, other white workers realized that it was fruitless for them to form a labor union that excluded blacks, because in that scenario there would always be the threat of black strikebreakers. For the first time, I could see that by dint of the labor unions, white people ought and might be willing to fight for equal rights in behalf of *their* best interests, not ours. That made it all fall into place for me. It also encouraged me to enroll at Ford's apprentice school.

Since the option of college was effectively closed off to me, I signed up in 1936 to be an electrical apprentice. The minimum age to work in the plant was eighteen, but you could start in the apprentice program at seventeen and nine months, which I did. On your eighteenth birthday, after three months of training and testing, you could go into the plant as an apprentice within the trade you had selected and attend the school at night. Most of the preliminary academic work was mathematics—basically algebra—which I handled easily. In fact, I averaged a flat 100 on the tests.

There was only one other fellow in the electrical program who was up for graduation at the same time—a guy named Hamilton who averaged about 68. But Hamilton was white and his father was a foreman at the plant, and since there was only one electrician's job available, I was dispatched to the assembly line. After that experience, you might say that I was pretty damn ripe for the union.

The United Auto Workers had been formed in 1935 and made its mark early in 1937 when it won a contract with General Motors after the great sitdown strike in Flint. Not coincidentally, the victory occurred shortly after Frank Murphy, the judge who had presided over the Ossian Sweet case, was elected governor. Murphy was known to be very liberal on rights issues, and when GM asked him to order the pickets off private property and call in the National Guard to carry out the order, Murphy crossed them up by sending in the Guard to keep the peace and protect the strikers. The company's hands were tied, which meant that finally, after years of furtive backgrounding, the union had achieved collective bargaining with one of the major automakers.

That historic triumph was quickly followed by another, at Chrysler. But even as legal and public momentum shifted toward the union, everyone knew that the major battle of the campaign still lay ahead. Henry Ford had vowed that hell would freeze over before he would negotiate with a labor union. And he hired Harry Bennett to keep hell's heat turned up.

Those who take exception to my frequent use of the term "motherfucker" have obviously never encountered anyone like Harry Bennett. He was an ex-sailor, ex-boxer, and all-purpose badass who served as Ford's security chief, closest confidant, and bouncer against the union. Under the euphemistic heading of the Service Department, Bennett recruited a gang of ex-cons and wrestlers and assorted goons who, disguised as workers, were paid to spy on and intimidate union sympathizers. Needless to say, I was included in the ranks of the latter. Like the rest of us, though, I thought it advisable not to go public with my political orientation. At Ford, job security was tenuous enough without personally insulting the old man, which is what he considered any talk about collective bargaining. The union didn't mean squat without a job. The first order of business was to stay in the plant, and there were a few fundamental ways to do this. One was to buy a Ford, preferably from Henry's cousin on West Fort. As long as you owed Mr. Ford on West Fort, the odds were that you wouldn't be laid off. I couldn't afford a car, but that wasn't the only way to owe the man. Another was to run up a bill with Ford Hospital. I managed to pick up an eye infection which put me in debt to the hospital for a couple hundred bucks. Sure enough, I wasn't laid off when Ford cut back his work force. Instead, I was eventually fired.

They fired me for fighting, which I suppose was the best reason to be fired. One of Bennett's thugs apparently picked me out as a union man, and one day, when he was working across from me on the rolling machine, he started to come at me with a readily discernible intent to inflict pain. He was a big son of a bitch, like most of Bennett's men, and my immediate priority was to prevent him from laying one of his large hands on my person and messing up the face that been representing me rather well with the young ladies of Black Bottom. So I picked up the steel rod that I'd been using to unjam my machine and brought it down on top of his head. It stretched him across the conveyer belt, which in turn carried him to an open rail car that was filled with steel shavings. He was pretty cut up, but all right. I, on the other hand, was unemployed.

Out on the street and angry at the world, there was still a struggle going on inside me between adult responsibilities and the street life. I had not yet abandoned my fundamental hooliganism. I hung around the pool hall and hustled wherever I could, but I was in transition, screwing less and no longer stealing. I got a job as a cook in the Veterans Administration Hospital in Allen Park and another in a dry cleaning plant, but my most important work was with a labor-oriented civil rights organization called the National Negro Congress that was active in the thirties and forties. It was through the NNC that I met the man I regard as my mentor and role model, the Reverend Charles Hill.

The longtime pastor at Hartford Avenue Baptist Church, Reverend Hill was an old-time hellfire preacher whose moral convictions carried him to the presidency of the Michigan branch of the NNC. The NNC provided a progressive forum for black working people, and it naturally acquired a political accent, but it was Reverend Hill's simple passion and courage that drove the organization and inspired young ideological upstarts like me. I was generally teetering on the edge of trouble in those years, and I have to give Reverend Hill the credit for steering me into the life of social activism. From the barbershop I got the attitude. From Reverend Hill I got the leadership.

Reverend Hill was the first Detroit minister who had the guts to stand up to Henry Ford. As a vital part of his employment strategy, Ford supported local churches of various ethnic persuasions with donations and jobs. This was vintage Ford, because it not only made the clergymen and their congregations beholden to him, but also pitted the churches against each other, a tactic he used famously and with obvious relish throughout his career. Carrying this maneuver to its full extent, he even had separate personnel directors for each ethnic community—one Italian, one Polish, one Arabic, one black, etc. In the black community, his satrap was Don Marshall, who lived less than a hundred yards from Maben's barbershop and taught Sunday school at St. Matthew's Episcopal Church. Ford contributed to St. Matthew's and visited there once a year, which made a terrific impression on the congregation and the pastor, Father Daniels. If Father Daniels or Reverend Bradby of Second Baptist recommended one of his church members for a job at Ford, Don Marshall could see to it. It was Marshall, actually, who had arranged my job at Ford, in deference to the fact that he was a neighbor of ours and Mrs. Marshall had become good friends with my mother by taking Don's cleaning to our tailor shop.

Whatever his motive, the bottom line was that Henry Ford presented a much friendlier posture to the black community than any of the other major employers. He invited George Washington Carver to his home. He financed an all-black village called Inkster. He also bankrolled the Republican Party in the black community, which is where the quid pro quo came in. If they were to be his employees and beneficiaries, Ford expected the people of Black Bottom and Paradise Valley to vote Republican—and even more important, he expected them to banish all notions about a labor union. At a church meeting in 1936, after the political tide had turned in black communities around the country—the Democrats had gained favor by supporting unions—Don Marshall said to the congregation, "My employer, he was disappointed when he saw the returns from Negro districts—twenty to one Democratic!" Ford's disappointment was not something that it behooved the auto workers to incur.

For the most part, Ford was up-front about his disposition toward union organizers. When A. Philip Randolph was invited to speak at Bethel AME, Ford advised the church members in his employ that they would be fired if Randolph appeared in their edifice. Randolph spoke, and they were fired. Because of Ford's far-reaching influence, the clergymen of the black community were fearful that their churches would be foreclosed if their members supported the union. Reverend Hill was the exception to this rule. He not only encouraged union membership among his congregation but opened his facility to the organizers of Ford Local 600, which was founded at Hartford Baptist and eventually became the largest local in the world. At one point, Ford wrote Reverend Hill directly to say that if he continued to use his church for union meetings, members on his payroll would be terminated. In his own pious way, Reverend Hill told Ford to go to hell.

The contributions of reputable figures like Reverend Hill and Frank Murphy (not to mention FDR, who, as the first President to show sympathy toward industrial workers, emboldened them with his memorable comment that if he were a workingman, he would join a union) cannot be underestimated in the labor struggle, because at that time it was considered by many to be a Communist cause. Undeniably, the Communist Party was very influential in organizing industrial unions at a grass-roots level, particularly in Detroit, and it dominated the UAW's left wing, to which I gravitated. I knew the party line backwards and forwards from Maben's barbershop, and while I didn't agree with all of it, I didn't give a damn who I was associated with on the side of equal opportunity. At the time, the Communists and Reverend Hill were about the only ones doing anything about discrimination. Hell, I would have teamed up with Satan if he could have assured me that I'd have all the working privileges of a white man.

There was very little middle ground in Detroit in those days. Colorful fascists like Father Coughlin and the Reverend Gerald L.K. Smith rallied the right. The KKK had plenty of political clout—their candidate was actually elected mayor in the late twenties—and its violent arm, the Black Legion, wrought racial terror with virtual impunity. One social extreme always invites another, and consequently Detroit became a battlefront of left versus right. I enlisted in the fray as secretary of the Detroit chapter of the NNC.

Through the NNC, I was able to stay in touch with the UAW campaign without holding a job at one of the auto plants. As Reverend Hill and I saw it at the time, the Ford Motor Company was the battleground for the civil rights movement whether you worked for it or not. Consequently, we stayed as close to the Ford situation as we could. I only wish that I had been at the Miller Road overpass leading to the River Rouge plant in May of 1937 when Harry Bennett fucked up.

A contingent of UAW people, including future international president Walter Reuther, was at the plant to hand out leaflets—a very common and ordinary routine—when Bennett met them at the overpass with a mob of his goons and perpetrated a bloody mass mugging. Violence was not a new technique for Bennett, but this time he made the stupid mistake of beating people up in front of newspaper photographers. His boss, playing all the ethnic and paternal angles, had been hoping to keep public sentiment on his side, but that was impossible after the Battle of the Overpass, which became a turning point in labor history. Henry Ford had lost his leverage with the working people of Detroit.

As a testament to the arrogance of the Ford Motor Company, it saw no immediate need to back off from its systematic terrorism in union affairs. Over the next four years, there was a fairly steady pattern of minor strikes and skirmishes before things heated up in 1940, when we began to smell victory. As the picketing intensified, Bennett brought in boatloads of musclemen from Cleveland and Pittsburgh and Chicago, running them right up the River Rouge and into the plant, their express purpose being to work over the pickets at gates 4 and 9. Since they had nothing to do but fight and get ready to fight, Bennett's thugs spent most of their time in the plant grinding down steel rods into two-handed swords. Our mission as defenders of the protest was to strike fast and stay clear of the swords. So we would put a thin line of young, agile guys out front holding picket signs—that was where I came in—while everybody else stayed behind the fence tossing over rocks like mortars. When the rocks started finding their marks, we'd drop our signs and hop over the fence. Occasionally, there was some hand-to-hand combat, but it wasn't much more serious than a baseball fight. When a few people did get hurt one time and Ford fired twenty-three workers for union activity, the courts ruled that the company had to desist in its union bashing and rehire the twenty-three.

With everything else failing, Ford turned to its time-tested tactic of racial division. During the famous strike of 1941, Bennett hired southern blacks for the Service Department and had them sit down inside the plant to resemble union activists. Then he charged that the sitdown was a scheme of Communist terrorists who were sabotaging tools and dies that were vital to the manufacturing of aircraft parts. He may as well have announced to the public that the men inside were using American flags as toilet paper. Don Marshall was placed in charge of the alleged strikers, but, under pressure from the black community—which knew that the black workers were being used to undermine the protest—he rebelled and tried to lead them out of the plant. White Service Department thugs forced them back inside, and a race riot might have broken out if Charles Diggs and Reverend Hill hadn't arrived on the scene. After calming the crowd at River Rouge, Diggs and Reverend Hill spoke on the radio with Diggs's colleague in the state senate, a Polish union man named Stanley Nowak, appealing for racial unity. Unity was Reverend Hill's currency, and it has always been mine.

I saw firsthand the power of racial cooperation when Reverend Hill, knowing that victory or defeat for Local 600—the River Rouge plant—would rest with the black vote, arranged for Paul Robeson to speak at Cadillac Square in behalf of the union. Robeson was greeted by a cheering, irrepressible swarm of people, black and white, many of them Ford workers who showed up wearing masks to conceal their identity. Shortly thereafter, the union was voted in and Ford capitulated. To everyone's astonishment, the old man agreed to the most liberal contract the UAW had entered into. Among other conditions, it stipulated that Bennett's servicemen had to wear uniforms so the workers would know who the hell they were.

WITH VICTORY ON the labor front, I followed Reverend Hill into the battle over housing. To combat the inflated rents and substandard conditions of many of the apartments in Black Bottom and Paradise Valley, the NNC staged rent strikes, in which a bloc of tenants would withhold their rent money until adjustments or improvements were made in the property. The rent strike was an aggressive tactic for the times, requiring considerable vigilance, and it was during one of them that I learned a valuable lesson.

A ladies' club had provided me with an office and a secretary to administer this particular strike, and since it happened that the secretary was single and quite companionable, the two of us disappeared into the city for the weekend. When I surfaced again on Monday, one of the old union hands, Pete Perry, informed me that the strike had been broken while I was off satisfying my urges. "Son," he said, "the human race is perpetually involved in two separate struggles—the class struggle and the ass struggle. If you want to make a difference in this world, it's important not to get your struggles mixed up."

In June of 1941, the class struggle came to a head when the Detroit Housing Commission selected two sites for housing projects, one in a black neighborhood and one in a white. Despite a local real estate policy prohibiting the alteration of a neighborhood's racial characteristics through the construction of public housing, the federal government vetoed the dual sites and substituted a single location at Nevada and Fenelon streets, a principally white neighborhood. It also designated the two-hundred-unit project for black occupancy and named it Sojourner Truth in honor of the feminist, abolitionist former slave whose dauntless efforts rallied Michigan behind Lincoln during the Civil War. Not surprisingly, there was a full-scale rebellion in the white community, led by Congressman Rudolph Tenerowicz. Succumbing to the pressure, Washington suddenly reversed itself in the early days of 1942, declaring that Sojourner Truth would indeed house white families and that there was no suitable site available in the city of Detroit for a black project.

When the government's turnabout was announced, it activated a left-wing, black-white coalition headed by Reverend Hill and the Reverend Horace White, for which I was appointed full-time secretary. Initially, our protest focused expressly on the fact that the feds had reneged on their pledge to the black community. But in the course of the campaign, we incidentally flushed out a roll call of racist and right-wing interest groups that had been covertly lobbying the government from the time it first announced the project. The unfettered activities of these pressure groups, whose ranks included everything from the KKK to Polish community clubs to local civic organizations to neighborhood real estate committees, eventually led to a grand jury investigation (the results of which were never made public) of a possible conspiracy to prevent black tenants from occupying their apartments. Meanwhile, as the conflict accelerated, Sojourner Truth became a microcosm of all the indigenous issues that plagued and divided Detroit—the severe housing shortage, the competition between blacks and immigrants, the polarizing agendas of the left wing and the right, and the chronic urban insensitivity of the United States government.

Reverend Hill's typically high-ground position was to send a letter to the Polish community, which essentially stood to inherit the project if it were to be taken from the blacks. "We are in the same boat together," he wrote. It was a reaffirmation of the very theme—unity—that he'd preached during the union struggle. Reverend Hill instinctively recognized that a divided Detroit was a self-destructive Detroit. Meanwhile, the government, which seemed to be working from the other extreme, exacerbated the situation by vacillating, turning the project back to black a month after it first changed its mind. The last day of February was finally established as the date for blacks to begin moving into the project, but when they tried, they were met by thousands of white protesters, armed and hooded. Bricks were thrown, knives were brandished, and, as always, crosses were burned. It was a hot news story that had the whole nation watching to see if the white people of Detroit would succeed in using violence to keep black people out of homes they'd already leased and paid on. If we lost Sojourner Truth, it would be open season on the black residents of every community in the country.

Even without a legal or moral leg to stand on, the whites managed to hold justice hostage for a couple of months. It was late April before anybody actually moved in, and when they did, it was under the protection of federal troops and state and local police. By that time, I was in basic training.

IN OUR NEIGHBORHOOD, only fools went off to war. And the only fools were me and my brother George.

There were numerous ways to flunk your physical, and everybody we knew used one or another. I certainly wasn't above it, but I didn't think it was necessary. A couple years before, I'd spent a month in Herman Kiefer Hospital for a congenital respiratory problem I've had all my life. At first, they diagnosed it as tuberculosis. This was before the advent of penicillin or sulfa to treat TB, and the only known cure was rest and fresh air. Most people with TB could expect to spend at least three years in the hospital. It was a grim existence. They'd even take your matches so you couldn't smoke, which is how I acquired the invaluable skill of being able to divide a match head in half with a razor blade to make two matches out of one. The only thing to look forward to was going to the sun room, where you could gaze out across the courtyard to the women's side of the hospital. Each guy would pick out a girlfriend over there and write messages to her, using the window glass to form the letters. The prospect of playing out my love life across a hospital courtyard was nearly enough to break my spirit. I was just starting to work up a good depression when they decided that I didn't have TB after all. But I had all the symptoms, so they had to call it something. One doctor said I had chronic bronchitis and another said

I had nonspecific pneumonitis, which is an inflammation of the lungs. When it came time to report for our physicals, I never dreamed that the Army would take some poor fucker with chronic bronchitis and/or nonspecific pneumonitis.

I'd been working in the post office on a Sunday, distributing fourth- and fifth-class mail, when the news came that Pearl Harbor had been bombed. There were several young guys working with me, and we figured we'd all get a call from the draft board within a month or two, which we did. What I hadn't figured on was getting fired first.

Several months after passing the civil service exam, I had started at the post office on a six-month probation basis. While I was there, I edited a union newspaper and attempted to organize a local of the United Public Workers. Meanwhile, before the probation period was over I was required to pass a scheme—a sorting test. My scheme, 31st Street, required some preparation that I, in my preoccupation with the union cause and the Sojourner Truth affair, did not take seriously enough. It was common, although not mandatory, for the government to give an employee three tries to pass, and I succeeded in failing twice. But instead of getting a third chance, I was fired the week after Christmas, 1941, five months and twenty-nine days into my probation. It didn't take much imagination to link my dismissal to my interest in the union. I was not devastated by the development, however, because it enabled me to give full attention to the Sojourner Truth campaign—for a little while, anyway. Within two months, I was back in the employ of the government.

If I'd known that the Army would have so little respect for chronic bronchitis and/or nonspecific pneumonitis, I almost certainly would have tried one of the usual tricks at my physical examination, such as swallowing a bar of laundry soap, which made your blood pressure rise, or talking crazy against the government, which I suspect I could have managed convincingly enough. By no means was I enamored of the idea of fighting for a country in which I was not afforded full citizenship. The fellows at Maben's had also made me wary of America's imperialist tendencies, and in the company of my radical friends I'd participated in antiwar demonstrations in

New York and Chicago, where our motto was "The Yanks ain't coming!"

My square brother George, who didn't share my enthusiasm for antiestablishment politics, played it straight with the draft board, and when the time came to hear the results of the exam, nobody was surprised to hear his name called. Poor George, I thought. There were about fifty of us there waiting to see who would be drafted, and we'd heard through the grapevine that they'd taken only two. About ten minutes later, they called my name. My friends disowned me on the spot. It was humiliating—a hell of a note for a guy called Big Time Red.

In late February of 1942, George and I reported in thigh-deep snow to Fort Custer in Battle Creek, Michigan. After a few days of orientation, they put us on a meandering train that four days later pulled up at Fort McClellan in Alabama. Although I suspect now that we zigzagged in order to pick up black soldiers and keep the train segregated in the Army tradition I would come to know so well, at the time I accepted the explanation that our indirect course was calculated to confuse the enemy. I was willing, at that point, to allow the Army the benefit of the doubt. In fact, despite my humbling induction, in the interest of self-preservation I intended to give the Army my best shot. At the same time, I was hoping that if I behaved myself, George and I could stay together.

That plan fell apart quickly one day when we took a twenty-five-mile hike in a pouring rain. George had arthritis, and toward the end of the day his leg was hurting so badly that another soldier and I carried him along. When the hike was over, we had to dig slit trenches to sleep in. George was in no shape to dig, and as he was lying on the ground, a captain spotted him, leapt from his jeep, and rushed over to cuss him out. Then they shipped George to another base. I wanted to go with him, but they wouldn't allow it, and we were separated for most of the rest of the war.

I had depended on George for companionship and perspective, both at home and in the Army, and it wasn't easy for me to push ahead without him, completely cut off from my family for the first time. I might have gotten over it easier if I'd had access to the distractions of Hastings Street, but things were considerably different in Anniston, Alabama. It was located in a dry county, which made it a bonanza for bootleggers. I was unaccustomed to being on the consumer end of the bootleg business. If that wasn't bad enough, wearing a uniform was like having "sucker" written across your chest. One night, about nine o'clock, a kid came up and offered me a pint of rotgut whiskey for eight bucks. It was stuff I could buy in Detroit for seventy-five cents. As a man of the streets, I was highly insulted, and told the kid to beat it. About midnight, the same kid came around again and, things being what they were, I told him I'd take that pint now. He said, "Okay, but it's ten bucks." He had me.

Although it seems like a complete reversal of character, I actually fared better on the base. Within ninety days I had made corporal and been assigned to the infantry, and was such a model soldier that they kept me around for another three months as an instructor. The last hitch at Fort McClellan was pretty slow, however, and I used the time to bone up on the fundamentals required to be a "shithouse lawyer," which is a soldier who studies military regulations in search of loopholes and technicalities. My accomplice in this pursuit was the first sergeant, and the first opportunity to apply our unofficially acquired expertise came when I noticed that the black soldiers were presenting themselves very obsequiously—in the southern tradition—when they went in before the captain to ask for weekend passes. The captain was a farmer from somewhere in cotton country, and not a bad guy as white southerners went, but it helped if you did a little shucking and winging when you asked him for something. If you scratched your head and shuffled your feet and looked down at the floor, you were sure to get your pass. The first sergeant and I didn't care much for that, though, because we considered it Uncle Toming, and we came upon a regulation that got us thinking. If a soldier is armed, he can keep his hat on in the presence of an officer, even inside a building, which makes sense because it leaves his hands free to handle the weapon. He is considered armed if he has a cartridge belt or a bayonet belt, which our men had. So we advised them to keep their helmets on when they stood before the captain. We also drew a line in the captain's office about six or eight feet from his desk and suggested to the men that they stay behind that line. Actually, we told them that if they went over the line it was their ass, because they would get their pass to town but then they would have to come back and face us. The idea was that if they stayed behind the line, they had to speak up in order to be heard. And since they were farther away, they could pretty much look the captain in the eye. Like most of the shithouse lawyering we undertook on behalf of the black troops, it was a matter of building up some self-esteem, which was a new experience for the guys from the South. They liked it. At the same time, it shocked the hell out of that captain. The men were drawing that cracker right out of his seat. They were getting their passes, besides.

We also took advantage of the Army regulation requiring an exchange of salutes between military men. The military courtesy is that the junior officer recognizes the senior officer and the senior officer returns the salute. So I told my men to salute sharply whenever they spotted one of the senior officers in the vicinity. They would start lining up when they eyed one coming from a block away. By the time the officer made it through the gauntlet, he could barely get his hand up to his temple.

Any latrine barrister worth his regulation book will manage to keep himself relatively clear of trouble, and after the minimum six months, I was a buck sergeant and an officer candidate at Infantry Training School, Fort Benning, Georgia. There was little time for extracurriculars at Fort Benning, and in another ninety days—as quickly as you could make it—I was proud to be Second Lieutenant Coleman A. Young of the United States Army, ready for action. I was not destined for action, however. There were only about a dozen blacks in my class of about 150, and none of us was included when half the graduates were sent directly into battle in North Africa. Actually, it was a break for us, because the white boys who went were green troops and suffered very high casualties. But it was also a revealing glimpse of the segregationist mentality that would be my enemy for the next three years.

While the white soldiers were representing our country on the front, I was sent to Camp Breckinridge near the tough coal-mining town of Morganfield in western Kentucky, where the War Department was setting up the 370th Infantry Regiment as part of its second black infantry division, the 92nd, also known as the Buffalo Division. The first one, the 93rd, had trained at Fort Huachuca in Arizona and was in the process of being shipped to the South Pacific.

As it turned out, the 93rd was scattered all over the islands but never fought in combat. The operative theory in the War Department was that blacks were not adequate soldiers, because they lacked courage and were too stupid to master the intricacies of modern warfare. And while I won't waste space here elaborating on what I think of that premise, it's certainly true that many blacks entered the Army woefully deficient in soldiering skills because of their lack of education and job training. In order to deal with the complicated automatic rifles and machine guns that were used in the infantry, it was necessary to be able to read and have some rudimentary understanding of how things worked mechanically. It was nearly impossible to take soldiers with no education and teach them quickly how to fire a mortar or disassemble a weapon. They could ultimately be taught, and in fact they learned damn well, but it could not be done expediently with the kind of troops they were sending us. In the South, many of the recruiting offices had been drafting blacks without any physicals or testing. They might get an order to draft, say, twenty whites and twenty blacks, and would fill their quota without taking the trouble to examine the blacks. In addition, many blacks could dodge the draft if they had any connections at all through their employers. As a result, the ones inducted were often those with the least wherewithal and fewest qualifications. We had a guy in our outfit who was blind in one eye and another whose left leg was two inches shorter than his right. Of course, they had to be discharged, but you had to wonder how in the world they got that far in the first place. The black divisions were assigned the most uneducated, least prepared troops in the entire Army. It took three months to teach some of our men how to sign their names on the payroll. From where I stood, it looked like the Army was trying like hell to doom us to failure. At the same time, some of the most qualified and capable soldiers were relegated to pressing pants and shining shoes for the officers.

That sort of thing became increasingly noticeable to me the longer I stayed at Breckinridge, and after a while it got my rebellious dander up. Since there were only black troops in my platoon, I took it upon myself to enhance their senses of self-worth by whatever methods I could devise. At the firing range, for instance, my job was to supply my men with ball ammunition and then, when they were finished shooting, search them for what they didn't use, because soldiers were not permitted to carry ammunition. I made it clear to the guys that I would discharge my duties by frisking them upon their departure from the range, but also advised them that their M-1 rifles made them equal to anything that walked the earth, and anybody who had an M-1 and nothing to put in it was a goddamn fool. I didn't want to know how they did it, but most of them found ways to conceal their ammunition. The colonel was a good old boy from Mississippi, and when he caught wind that there were armed black infantrymen in his ranks, he whipped me out of there posthaste and placed me in charge of his MP platoon.

Mine were the only black MPs in the area, and we were not empowered to arrest white folks. On top of that, we were the only MPs who were not permitted to carry guns. As an officer, I was graciously allowed to have a pistol, but I was the only one armed in the whole damn command. You could say that we were ineffectual. I was at the sheriff's office in Morganfield one night when a call came in with the information that a bunch of black miners were beating up a bunch of black soldiers, as the miners in those parts, both black and white, were apparently wont to do in defense of their women and turf. Before I could gather up my men and rush to the aid of the infantrymen, the sheriff ordered me to sit tight and wait for another call from the miners advising that it was safe for him and us to come on over. That sheriff had learned long before not to mess with miners, and to my amazement, he wasn't about to budge until he got their go-ahead. He was successful in convincing me that my unarmed little MP platoon would have been dead meat.

I felt degraded by the MP command and in general was becoming increasingly disgusted with the way the Army operated. As the racial offenses picked away at my sensibilities, I finally decided that there was no use soldiering in America's kind of army. Sitting in my office at the MP station one afternoon, my mood turned darker and darker until it sucked me into the drastic measure of sitting down at the typewriter and writing the first and only poem of my life. It was about the contradiction of a Jim Crow army in a four-freedom war, as it was known. I thought my poem was pretty damn good, so I reproduced it on carbon and got up in the middle of the night to stick it in the white officers' mail slots. When they found that poem waiting for them in the morning, you could hear their rebel yells all over the base.

Before noon, the base commander had called together all of the black officers to let us know that he was extremely disturbed by the literature that was circulating around the camp, because it suggested that the black soldiers were not happy, which was apparently a possibility he'd never before considered. He said that the author was obviously a sensitive, educated man—which immediately removed me from suspicion—and that if he would come forward, the Army would give him an opportunity to resign his commission and would facilitate his honorable discharge. Having learned early on that skepticism is the better part of trust in matters pertaining to The Man, I declined the general's generous offer and shut the hell up. But I wasn't the same soldier anymore. I had serious reservations about defending a country so committed to the perpetuation of racism, although I would have willingly gone overseas and fought with the Buffalo Division if the black soldiers had been treated with some degree of human dignity.

The poem incident blew over without repercussion, but I wasn't long for Breckinridge, anyway. In the spring of 1943, my infantry division was packed off to Fort Huachuca, where the entire Buffalo Division was being assembled for final training before going overseas. In addition to three infantry regiments, there were four artillery battalions, three tank companies, and a signal corps that included my brother, George. We weren't able to see much of each other, but it helped my morale just to know that George was on the same base.

Fort Huachuca was in a remote Old West location south of Tucson, ten miles from Tombstone and surrounded by landmarks like the bullet holes where some character like Mad Jack shot some other character like One-Eyed Slim. Although the military realities were still very discouraging, I enjoyed the atmosphere in Arizona, and also the company. One of my fellow officers was a friend from the post office in Detroit, Robert Millender—I called him Lucky—whose presence would recur in my career. Another was a very bright guy from back home named John Simmons, whose brother, LeBron, had been president of the Detroit chapter of the National Negro Congress. John was one of the most qualified men in the infantry, with a master's degree and a doctorate from the University of Michigan, but his political activities had caught the attention of the FBI, which had seen to it that he was assigned to menial chores throughout his Army hitch. It was a travesty for a guy like John Simmons to be shining shoes, so Lucky Millender and I searched the regulations to find something more suitable for him. To our delight, we came upon an obscure position still on the books from the colonial wars known as artificer—a soldier who repaired flint locks. The fact that the position still existed was the ultimate in Army bureaucracy—I wonder if we're still paying for it—but in the meantime, John Simmons was happy to wash the boot black off his hands and serve his country as assistant artificer of the Buffalo Division.

Frankly, though, I was a little more concerned about myself than I was about John. Being at Huachuca meant that I had to seriously contemplate the possibility of going to the front. But even so, I couldn't allow myself to be consumed by the prospect of Europe or North Africa or the South Pacific, because I had enlisted in a private war that was being fought on a different front. My sights were trained on Jim Crow, and I dug my foxhole wherever my orders took me.

I would estimate that this predisposition put me in the majority at Huachuca. Most of the men there, like me, had been training on what we called the southern front, and we were not in the mood to take any more of the Army's plantation attitude. There was damn near an open rebellion. The men simply refused to go along with the Jim Crow operating procedures, and the Army's response was to arrange a visit by the big gun, B. O. Davis, Sr., the only black general in the Army and a heel-clicking military man from top to bottom. Officially, B.O., Sr., was there to represent the inspector general's office and hear our grievances. Unofficially, he was there to kick ass and give us new, improved outlooks on military service. He wasn't the least bit interested in our grievances, but he was very interested in letting us know how fortunate we were to be fighting in the greatest army in the world. He advised us of all that he had overcome to make general, which obviously was a hell of a lot, and summed it up by saying, "I'm your color, but not your kind." We gave a big "Amen" to that and held the gate open for the general on his way out. When we heard that he would be back for another visit, we planned a little surprise on his behalf. We were waiting for him in the mess hall the day he made his second big entrance, and when we removed our hats and stood up to greet him, we were all sporting handkerchiefs on our heads (a handkerchief on the head being a symbol for Uncle Tom). It was not a memorably clever scheme, but it had the intended effect. He stormed out of there and caught the next plane for Washington, and that was the last we saw of General B.O. Davis, Sr.

While I was at Huachuca, though, I was introduced to another adversary from the government who would dog me much longer than General Davis. I actually don't recall if the fellows who called me in were from the FBI or from Army Intelligence, but at any rate, their questions were based on information that the FBI had compiled on me back in Detroit. It surprised the hell out of me, because here I was a few minutes from Mexico, training infantry soldiers in a desert that was once the stomping ground of Geronimo, and they were asking me about some meeting I had allegedly attended on Maple Street in Dearborn. I was not even aware of a Maple Street in Dearborn, although Maben the barber lived on Maple Street in Detroit, and I might have gone to a union meeting at his house when we were trying to organize Ford, which was none of their damn business anyway. I accordingly informed my inquisitors that I had never attended any meeting on Maple Street in Dearborn.

The FBI was becoming very interested not only in me but in any soldier who might have had a background in what they called "subversive activities," which were loosely defined as attending any meeting or rally at which could be found others suspected of sub-versive activities. Theoretically, one Communist in a city like De-troit could implicate a circle of hundreds. And if you were black and knew white people—especially European immigrants—you went right to the top of the list of suspects. Shortly after I left Fort Benning, the government started yanking suspected radicals right off the stage during graduation ceremonies there. I was fortunate to have graduated from Officer Candidate School before the FBI had a chance to organize its records, but the Bureau caught up with me soon enough. By the time I left the infantry—after my stint at Fort Huachuca—it was apparent that they had it in for me.

My transfer to the Air Corps was made for the most practical of reasons. Blacks were finally being accepted as paratroopers and pi-lots under Public Law 18, which specifically mandated that the Air Corps train black pilots, and it didn't escape my attention that ei-ther job paid nearly double what I earned in the infantry. Airmen also slept in beds, a luxury that infantrymen didn't have on the front, and ate on tables with tablecloths. With all these things to consider, I couldn't persuade myself to opt for an infantry assign-ment in Italy, which was where the 92nd was being deployed. The Buffalo Division would ultimately become the most renowned black fighting force in the Army, but I was about to join another group every bit as distinguished—the famous Tuskegee Airmen.

After applying for both pilot and paratrooper training, I was ac-cepted for the former at Tuskegee Institute in Alabama. With the passage of Public Law 18, Tuskegee had been chosen as a training site because the Air Corps had no independent facility for blacks and it was unthinkable to train black and white airmen together. The chief of the Air Corps, General Henry Arnold, had said, "Ne-gro pilots cannot be used in our present Air Corps units, since this would result in having Negro officers serving over white enlisted men, an impossible social situation." Tuskegee provided a handy solution to that problem, permitting us to study at the college cam-pus and use adjacent Moton Field as our air base.

Despite my feelings about fighting for the United States, I quickly grew enamored of the idea of flying a B-25 over Germany and dropping bombs on those superior Aryan motherfuckers. Actually, I wouldn't be dropping bombs, because we were training to form a pursuit squadron, but I didn't let the details stop me from dreaming. The FBI took care of that job.

When I arrived at Tuskegee, I found out quickly that one of the most hated men on the post was a tall black staff sergeant, assistant to the provost marshal in charge of the MPs. The cadets distrusted him because he had set himself up as the point man with the local bootlegger and was screwing with the whiskey supply, but I could appreciate that sort of enterprise—which was no coincidence, because the staff sergeant, whose name was Hayes Porter, happened to be a friend of mine from Detroit with whom I'd worked closely in trying to organize Ford and the like. I'd been on the base for only three days when Hayes came scratching at my window late at night and told me to meet him outside. He was petrified, because, for starters, he knew he wasn't supposed to be in the bachelor officers' quarters, and also because he was in the process of tampering with government information. But we were old accomplices, and he had something he felt he needed to show me. So he led me to the outfield of the baseball diamond and handed me a teletype he'd copied in the provost marshal's office. It was a message from the FBI office in Birmingham warning the provost marshal that I was a subversive and dangerous character who should be watched closely. Hayes might have thought that since we had common backgrounds, whatever implicated me implicated him, but he was nevertheless taking a big risk on my behalf. After I read the copy, he burned it and buried the ashes in the outfield.

I wasn't yet aware of the thorough and unscrupulous manner in which the FBI would mess with somebody's life, so I continued earnestly in my training, still intent on flying against the Nazis and getting the most out of my time. Unlike some of the other posts I'd been on, there was surprisingly much to do at Tuskegee. That is to say, women and booze were within our reach—within mine, anyway. I should probably point out here that in my relatively short stay in the military, I demonstrated a rather famous ability to ferret out women where there seemed to be no women—sort of like finding water in the desert. In this enterprise, my 1941 green Chevrolet coupe, to which I referred as the Green Hornet, was a valuable

THE WAR AT HOME

sidekick. As a former Boy Scout and a young soldier who prided himself on preparedness, I made it a point to travel with a blanket in the car, keeping it folded into a square, readily available for an emergency picnic or whatever. At Tuskegee, where the pursuit of female companionship was greatly simplified by the presence of young coeds on the campus, it reached the point that the girls would see me coming and pantomime folding a blanket into a square.

The booze was actually harder to come by than the women at Tuskegee, due to the earnest efforts of the local sheriff. We bought our liquor at a store in Union Springs until we realized that the owner was calling the sheriff after we left with our license numbers and details of our purchases. The sheriff would arrest us in town, hold our booze and our cars, and charge us the exact amount of money we had in our wallets to buy our cars back. To get around him, we started filing flight plans for Atlanta and dropping in on some nearby liquor store to load up. The enlisted men didn't have the benefit of that option, so they would commandeer the assistant provost marshal's Buick Roadmaster and try to elude the sheriff by weaving over backroads to the base. He was usually on their tail as they arrived. They would honk their horns when they drew close to the compound, and the MPs would swing the gate open, then close it in a rush as the sheriff came squealing to a stop, lights flashing.

Although I never exactly warmed to Alabama hospitality, I must confess here to perpetuating an apocryphal story about urinating over my birthplace while on a training flight out of Tuskegee. Much as I take pleasure in the idea, that never really happened. If it had, my target would have actually been the flight school itself, and the deed would have been done just before I left the damn place.

Toward the end of our training, we were required to make a series of solo flights that would determine our success or failure as cadets. For our first solo, the Army sent in a white lieutenant to give us a test flight consisting of some stalls and spins and three or four landings. It was no big deal. I handled everything easily—or so I thought—and when we were done, the lieutenant son of a bitch told me I was washed out. I had never failed any kind of a test in my life—except the post office sorting test, which I had blown off—and I didn't know whether to be crushed or angry or bewildered. I still hadn't figured out what had happened at Tuskegee when several years later, back in Detroit, I ran into Hayes Porter and he told me that my failure had nothing to do with my flying: orders to wash me out had come straight from the FBI in Birmingham. It wouldn't have mattered if I'd been Lindbergh; my ass had to go. To this day, I'm not clear on what threat I posed to the country as a pursuit pilot.

Apparently deciding that I was a better risk handling ammunition than airplanes, the Air Corps reassigned me to Tyndall Field in Panama City, Florida, for bombardier training and over-the-water gunnery. It might have been a satisfactory second chance, except that whatever heart I had for that kind of soldiering—and I still hadn't given up the hope of raising hell over German air space—was stomped upon once again by the United States Army as soon as I unpacked my gear.

There had never been any blacks at Tyndall Field, where, in common with all the other southern military bases, the basic problem was housing. Most often, it was handled by dividing a base with railroad tracks on the order of a small southern town. Squadron C, composed of black orderlies and mess hall attendants, would be situated on the wrong side of the tracks, with its own barracks, mess hall, PX, and recreation facility. At Tyndall Field, this indignity was elevated to the next level, with the black enlisted men banished to tents pitched on the baseball field. The cadets were moved into the barracks, and the half-dozen of us who were officers slept in the sergeant's quarters at the end of the barracks. Everyone ate together, although the food was so bad that many of the men went to the mess hall only to sign in so they could be paid at the end of the month.

All of this put me in an angry mood for most of the time I was at Tyndall Field, and it didn't necessarily help to get off the base and into the Florida Panhandle. I was on a bus in Panama City one time, holding on to a strap in the back, when I heard the driver call out, "Coon Town!" I was just about to lunge forward and do something stupid when an old black lady next to me said, "Calm down, son, that's what they call it here." Actually, Coon Town was my stop. There was a young lady there who was able, thankfully, to assuage my agonies.

Unfortunately, I couldn't take her back to the compound with me. The housing situation there was blatantly discriminatory to the extent of violating virtually every regulation regarding the privileges of officers and cadets. Soon enough, the ire of the black officers was provoked to the point of protest. We frequently held meetings at night to plot broad strategy and specific mischief, but just as frequently the brass would somehow know all about our meetings by seven the next morning. In search of the stool pigeons, I arranged about ten separate meetings and gave them different agendas to see which ones were reported. The security system was not infallible, but we were able to pull off some minor devilment, which, while momentarily satisfying, did not enhance our bargaining position in the matter of living conditions.

When it was evident that we were getting nowhere in the big picture, I initiated what would soon become a steady correspondence with the Army's inspector general. The letter I sent to him was signed by all of the black officers and cadets on the base, and it constituted an insurrection that, for all we knew, might be punishable by death if the case fell under the purview of the military reactionaries who seemed so prevalent in the upper echelons. But I was counting on the rigid reflexes of the Army machine, which, if tapped in a certain spot, would automatically respond a certain way. Sure enough, the inspector general showed up just before our graduation, and for a vindicating couple of days the black and white cadets slept in the same cadet headquarters, although they were still separated by the configuration of the building.

From Tyndall Field I was transferred to Midland Field in Texas, where it was immediately apparent that our small triumph in Panama City had no implications beyond the Panhandle. In order to keep us apart from the white officers at Midland, the black officers were put in the visiting officers' quarters, which, while insulting our rank and personal dignity, actually enabled us to live more aristocratically than the top brass. The VOQ had sixteen two-room suites, and since they wouldn't put anyone else in with the seven of

us, we took two suites apiece and lounged around that place like
sultans. But at the same time, we were prohibited from entering
the officers' club. It was also made clear to us that we would be
washed out of the bombardier training program if we even looked
sideways at one of the WACs stationed on the base, although I did
manage to make the close acquaintance of the only black lieutenant among them. But that diverting exception did not right the
wrongs being inflicted upon us, so I dispatched a note to my pen
pal the inspector general, who hustled down to read the riot act.
About three weeks before we graduated from Midland, we were admitted to the officers' club. Taking it like the classic military man
and Texan that he was, the post commander called all the officers
together and said, for the benefit of the white officers, "I may not
like this and you may not like this, but these are orders. These
[black] officers will be treated as officers. They will have full access
to all privileges, and nobody will fuck with them. Is that clear?"

Having been denied graduation from Tuskegee for reasons I
didn't yet understand, I was eager to get the full experience out of
the ceremonies at Midland. And since I seemed to be on a roll as
a shithouse lawyer, I scoured the Army regulations and, lo and be-
hold, discovered that, as the second lieutenant with the most seniority, I was entitled to lead the graduation procession. This was
not the way the ceremony had been organized, which was a little
complication that delayed the graduation for a couple of hours as
the commanders and attending brass examined the records to determine the proper sequence. Meanwhile, the last train pulled out
of Midland. That was not my problem, though, because I had my
Chevy, and inasmuch as I was the first one to be graduated, I was
out of there before most of the guys were off the platform. Although they never expressed their gratitude to me personally, I'm
sure the other fellows enjoyed their extra day in the heart of Texas.

The cadets became officers upon their graduation from Midland, and a group of about fifty officers was assigned to Godman
Field in Kentucky. En route, we were held over for a while at
Atterbury Field near Indianapolis, where I convinced about thirty
of the men to take advantage of the regulation that said officers
were free to leave the base if they had no orders to the contrary. So

we all went home for a week. I headed back to Detroit with a friend named Alfonso Fuller, the only problem being that on the return trip, we hit a blizzard in Huntington, Indiana, which made us late and put us in jeopardy of a violation. As it was, though, the commanders were preoccupied by their astonishment over the unprecedented phenomenon of thirty officers AWOL at the same time under the protection of military regulations.

Godman Field, whose memory we would hold close in the years ahead, was located near Louisville and adjacent to Fort Knox. This proved handy for the white officers, who could avail themselves of the Fort Knox officers' club—as guests—and leave the Godman Field officers' club to the black officers. It was an uncommon bit of shithouse lawyering on the part of the brass, and according to the regulations, they had us. But then they pushed it. Word got out that they were going to commandeer the Godman Field officers' club and relegate us to the service club. They even confiscated a treasury that we'd been accumulating in order to buy ourselves a grand piano and other amenities for the officers' club. We dug our trenches right there and swore that they wouldn't take away our officers' club this time.

The rage of the black officers had been building up at Godman Field even before our group arrived, much as it had on military bases all around the country, about which I stayed informed by word of mouth—officers transferring from various locations—and by reading the *Pittsburgh Courier* or other black newspapers whenever I could get my hands on one. (I also monitored the progress of the war with my short-wave radio, on which I was able to pick up transmissions from Europe and Japan. Years later, in Detroit during the Korean War, I used the same short-wave to pick up English broadcasts from Korea, which gave me the battlefront news about half a day ahead of the American media reports. After receiving my Korean update in private, I would sit down with my friends, spread a map across the table, and predict the strategy for the next twenty-four hours. My buddies thought I was some sort of military genius until they caught me one afternoon at Belle Isle, our local island park, lying on a towel with my radio to my ear.)

While disenchantment with the Jim Crow Army was universal

among the black divisions, the climate at Godman Field was uncommonly tense, attributable in large part to the unsubtle leadership of the commanding officer, a thundering segregationist named Colonel Robert Selway, who served under another celebrated bigot, General Frank O. D. Hunter. The two of them had been at the center of a major racial controversy at Selfridge Field near Detroit before being transferred to Godman, and they were apparently undaunted. The hatred of Selway was so intense that—rumor had it—some of the black mechanics had plotted to kill him by stuffing tissue paper into the fuel line of his plane to make it sputter and die while he was in the air. The plan allegedly failed when the plane shut down before it got off the ground. The black airmen had also written a letter to President Roosevelt and signed it covertly at night, the message being that they would proudly give their lives defending a country that granted them equal rights as citizens and soldiers. Many of them were frustrated over having been bypassed for promotions while less qualified white officers sped by them up the ladder. They were also fed up with the inadequate flying facilities at Godman—short runways and insufficient hangar space—while crucial acreage was occupied by a polo field they couldn't use. Nor did it help their morale to notice that the Fort Knox MPs had tanks at their disposal. As a way of escaping the oppression of the post, the black pilots had taken up the practice of flying weekend missions while the Nat King Cole show was on the radio and sky-dancing to the music, eight B-25s dipping their wings in unison to the beat of "The Vine Street Jump" and "The King Cole Blues."

It didn't take long for me to get into the spirit of Godman Field. I had a reputation by then, anyway, and after a couple months of making noise about the officers' club, I was removed from my squadron and placed in a reserve training unit, which was where they put malcontents and fuckups. Most of us fell into that category, but they had to draw the line somewhere. As it turned out, my time in the RTU was well spent. I got involved in a good-sized crap game one weekend, the results of which made me the proud new owner of a 1941 navy blue Buick convertible with a white top and red leather upholstery. That same night, while I was at the base trading on my Black Bottom skills, a fellow officer and Detroiter named Wardell Polk was chasing girls around the Louisville projects in my Green Hornet. Wardell wouldn't give the damn thing a rest, and before the night was out he had wrecked it beyond repair. The Buick filled in nicely, until my kid brother, Charles, totaled it a few years later in Detroit.

As military officers, we were basically in a holding pattern at Godman Field. Our arrival from Midland had expanded the 477th Bombardment Group, whereupon the Army commenced moving it squadron by squadron to Freeman Field outside Seymour, Indiana. Naturally, since we in the RTU were the leading troublemakers, our squadron was the last to go. In the meantime, there was a steady flow of traffic between the two posts, and as a result, the black officers at Godman had been hearing for months about the disagreeable situation at Freeman, where the infamous Colonel Selway had taken command. When the initial wave of the 477th arrived in Seymour around the first of March, 1945, the men noticed that signs quickly went up in most of the restaurants and stores declaring, Colored Will Not Be Served. This effectively confined the black officers to the base, where they were also prohibited in white men's places. Selway and his accomplices had designated the officers' club for white officers only and were using our Godman Field treasury to prepare the noncommissioned officers' club for black officers (we called it Uncle Tom's Cabin) and the service club for noncoms.

Before our squadron was transferred to Freeman Field, a few of the second lieutenants from the 477th had dropped in at the white officers' club to see what would happen. As they were sitting around the tables and playing the slot machines, the club officer wandered over and said, "We can't serve you boys in here." The black officers left without incident, and Selway responded to all inquiries by saying that there was no racial problem on his post. At the same time, however, the colonel and his minions were at work devising a way to legally segregate the club. Segregated traditions had been superseding official regulations all over the country, and the commanders at Freeman Field were hell-bent to somehow make that practice stick. General Hunter was reported to have said, "I'd be delighted for them [the black officers] to commit enough actions so that I can court-martial them." His and Selway's mission was to manufacture a violation. As it was, they knew they couldn't court-martial an officer simply for entering an officers' club because of Army Regulation 210-10, which stated that "on every post there shall be an officers' club in a Government building . . . open to all officers of the post."

To assist in the technicalities of the matter, Selway called in a representative of the inspector general's office, who informed the colonel that the intruding black officers had been well coached and had not done anything that would constitute insubordination. Putting their heads together to contrive an order that would close the legal ground between segregation and court-martial, the brass came up with one called "Assignment of Buildings and Areas at Freeman Field," at the heart of which were instructions that various buildings on the base, including the officers' club, would be available to instructors only, and certain others, including the service club, would be set aside for trainees. Then it listed all of the officers on the base along with their designations as instructors or trainees. In a remarkable coincidence, all of the instructors were white and all of the trainees were black. There were black flight surgeons with twenty years of medical practice serving as trainees to white interns. To enforce the order, Selway directed the provost marshal to station MPs at the doors of all instructor buildings. At the same time, guns were taken away from the black troops.

With no forum on the post for their protests, the "trainees" had written the *Pittsburgh Courier* to request an NAACP investigation of Selway and the Freeman Field command. Meanwhile, in our capacity as the last of the 477th remaining at Godman Field—and as an innately rebellious group of men—Squadron E of the 118th Administrative Unit had been carefully planning an assault on the white officers' club as soon as we arrived at Freeman Field. We were well aware that it was a radical and risky proposition. My job was to convince the men to get arrested, and most of them were angry enough to do it. We realized that we would need public support if we were going to tangle with the United States Army on its own turf, and so our next step was to quietly alert some of the black media that there might be an incident. On April 5, the *Indianapolis Recorder* sent a reporter to Freeman Field to be on the scene if something happened, but Selway and his men became suspicious and barred him from the base. The commanders feared, with good reason, that they would have enough on their hands that day. In a matter of hours, the rest of the infamous 118th was due.

Most of the squadron was transferring up by train, but I had my car and went on ahead to do some reconnaissance. The first thing I noticed was all the MPs with .45s at their hips. But we'd been expecting as much, and by the time the others arrived, we were ready to make our move. The plan was not to storm the club but for black officers to enter in orderly groups of two or four and circulate for a while, play some Ping-Pong and pool, then leave and allow more small groups to follow. The first wave, of which I was not a part, arrived at the club around 8:30 P.M. They were met at the door by a white first lieutenant, Joseph Rogers, who instructed them that they were not to enter. One of the black lieutenants, Roger Terry, pushed through Rogers and told him to get out of the way so that he could go in and be arrested. A few others followed Terry, and Rogers declared that they were all under arrest. He also reminded them that failure to obey a direct order before witnesses in a time of war could be punishable by death. They still didn't budge, and a short while later my group joined them inside the club. I sat down at the bar and ordered a drink, upon which the bartender said that the club didn't serve trainees. I inquired as to how he knew I was a trainee and he answered that the membership list included no coloreds.

Group by group, we continued to crash the club that night and the next day, and Selway's men continued to arrest every one of us, until there were sixty-nine black officers incarcerated in quarters. The charge was willful disobedience, but Selway and Hunter tried their best to expand it to include mutiny, sedition, and conspiracy. Legal clerks swooped down on the base to prepare charges and possible court-martial proceedings. That process took a turn when another representative from the inspector general's office arrived and advised the commanders that the instructor-trainee order was not clear enough to guarantee punishable violations and that a new one should be prepared. Numbered 85-2, which any black officer at Freeman Field in 1945 will recall vividly, its subject was "Assignment of Housing, Messing, and Recreational Facilities for Officers, Flight Officers, and Warrant Officers." Substantively, it was not much different from the previous order, the new twist being that every officer on the base was required to initial the order to certify that he had read and understood it. Except for additional charges against Terry and two others for their forcible entry into the club, legal restraints against the rest of us were dropped when the new order was issued, and we were released.

Rather than posting the new order, as was the custom, the brass had all the black officers on the base come into the post headquarters one at a time and sign it in the presence of several commanding officers. Selway would ask if we had read and understood the new assignment, then direct our squadron commanders to order us to sign our names to it. Failure to do so would constitute willful disobedience before witnesses in a time of war, which brought the prospect of a death penalty into the picture. They knocked off about sixty of us that way before we came up with a strategy. Since they summoned us in alphabetically, I had the advantage of being at the end of the line, and about the time they reached the G's I remembered an Army regulation that was essentially the military equivalent of the Fifth Amendment. I hastily advised the men to go before the commanders in a very military, courteous fashion, saying "Yes, sir" all the way until it came time to sign the order. Then we would say that we could not sign 85-2 out of fear that it might incriminate us.

The men stuck gamely to the plan. When we refused to place our initials on their order, the commanders repeated it and gave us second and third chances. When we still didn't sign, they placed us under arrest. Amazingly, 101 men refused to sign Order 85-2 despite arrest and the possibility of the death penalty. It was even more amazing to me that not one of them ever snitched on any of us who organized the rebellion.

When word got out that 101 black officers had been arrested, there was nearly a full-scale mutiny on the base. The black troops refused to gas the airplanes or carry out the basic daily operations of the post. And since we had little to do while restricted to quarters, there was plenty of time to define and refine our course of action. To that end, I wrote a statement of our position and submitted it to the pertinent parties, including Selway and, of course, the press. It read:

> Undersigned felt and feels that to have signed an endorsement signifying that he understood the regulation in question as required by paragraph 6 thereof would have constituted a false official statement, inasmuch as undersigned did not, and does not, understand the cited regulation. Such an act would not only have, in itself, rendered the undersigned liable to trial by a general court-martial; it would have done violence to the conscience of the undersigned; it would have constituted moral conduct less than that requested of an officer and a gentleman in the Army of the United States. To have signed a statement to the effect that the undersigned had read but did not understand the document would have been a half-truth, and certainly would not have effected compliance with the written order contained in paragraph 6 of the cited regulation. Such an act would have constituted moral "weaseling" and would have been no less contemptible or dishonest than to have signed the statement in full. To have affixed a signature to the document without further comment would have been equally dishonest. . . . Hence, any course of action available to the undersigned other than one of manifest moral dishonesty would have rendered him liable to trial by general courts-martial. Knowing this full well, undersigned in consonance with his conscience could only decline to sign the document. . . . For the record, undersigned wishes to indicate . . . his unshakable belief that racial bias is fascistic, un-American, and directly contrary to the ideas for which he is willing to fight and die. There is no officer in the Army who is willing to fight harder or more honorably for his country than the undersigned.

Selway was unimpressed. A day or two later, he ordered us to pack and assemble by the runway. As we walked out, we saw a fleet of C-47s awaiting us with their engines running and, next to them, wagons for our baggage. The commander of our unit, a smartass white captain out of New York who obviously knew something we didn't, was lining us up and singing a popular Duke Ellington song that included the line "Bring enough clothes for three days." We had no idea where in the hell we were being taken, although, judging by all the MPs holding carbines, we were pretty confident that it wasn't anywhere we might volunteer to go. For me and most of the men along that runway, it was probably the most frightening moment of the war.

Less than an hour later, we were back at a familiar place, except that things there were noticeably different. We could see that beyond the MPs who met us in battle array, barbed wire had been strung around the black officers' quarters of Godman Field and the yard had been covered with spotlights. The other major difference was the squadron of orderlies assigned to us. Being involved, as it was, in a dispute over the privileges of black officers, the Army couldn't very well deny our right to orderlies, even though it had been doing so all along. Consequently, we had our beds made and shoes shined while imprisoned behind barbed wire, through which we could see German prisoners of war walking freely about the grounds, picking up an occasional cigarette butt. It would have been militarily proper for the Germans to assist us as orderlies, but the Army couldn't countenance the idea of white men—even Nazi soldiers who had been killing Jews and Americans—cooking and cleaning for black men.

As it turned out, the orderlies were our contact with the outside world—especially the sergeant commanding the outfit, whom I knew from the poolroom on St. Aubin. He was one of the first guys I saw there, and he immediately told me not to worry, because he'd take care of me, which he did. There was also a cadet from Detroit who could type about as fast as I could talk, and he banged out letters that I dictated to the *Pittsburgh Courier,* the *Baltimore Afro-American,* Eleanor Roosevelt, and Judge Hastings, the civilian secretary of war. The sergeant, and sometimes I, would in turn sneak our seditious mail to Chappie James, the famous pilot who later became the first black four-star general, by slipping it to him through the barbed-wire fence. Chappie was the courier for the daily communications between Freeman and Godman fields and the East Coast bases and the War Department. We knew that Chappie was coming through on his end, because we received an encouraging reply from Mrs. Roosevelt, who had the power and will to do more for civil rights than anyone else in the country. At the time, though, she had other things on her mind, because the President was fatally ill.

We were still imprisoned at Godman Field when FDR died on April 12. Although I was a great admirer of Roosevelt, I remember only the selfish feeling that we were screwed because we had lost an invaluable ally and, more pertinently, had been bounced off the front page. We believed that publicity had become crucial to our cause, because without public pressure we would be subject to the mercy of the Army, which had the death penalty at its disposal. Deep down, I didn't really believe the authorities could get away with that; but on the other hand, we knew for a fact that there was sentiment in the upper echelons to have us court-martialed and shot, and there was sufficient reason to be uneasy about the prospects of military justice. In the absence of publicity, Godman Field seemed not unlike the secluded cellblock of a small-town southern sheriff. When we wrote a letter to the commanders asking to retain Thurgood Marshall as our legal representative, we received one back saying that since we had not been charged, there was no need for legal representation. We realized later that the letter was placed on the record of every officer who signed it—a fact that came to light when many of us applied for government or civil service jobs in later years and were told there was material in our files indicating that we were uncooperative toward authority.

Authority, for its part, seemed uncommonly diligent toward us. An investigator who identified himself as being with the inspector general's office questioned us in an encompassing manner that suggested he might be gathering information for the FBI. My roommate—or should I say "cellmate"—at Godman Field, my Detroit friend Wardell Polk, was curiously asked by the alleged inspector general's man about having once signed a petition to put the Communist Party on the ballot. In ensuing years, Polk, myself, and many more of the 101 arrested officers had periodic brushes with the FBI—specifically, inquiries about communism, many of which were predicated on nothing more than a suspicion of un-Americanism tracing back to our military careers.

Isolated as we were at Godman Field, we really had no inkling of what forces were at work determining our fate. Our rage toward the Army was exceeded only by our anxiety over what it might do to us. We knew what Hunter and Selway wanted to do; but fortunately, clearer heads prevailed, and on April 20 the War Department overrode our commanders and released all of us but the three involved in the entryway incident. Two of them—Marsden Thompson and Shirley Clinton—were acquitted, and Roger Terry had fifty dollars docked from his paycheck over the next three months.

To crown our victory, the Army relieved Selway and Hunter of their command. With no officer remaining at Godman Field higher than the rank of captain, we had the virtual run of it. But after a month or two of merrymaking, the Army put a halt to our mirth by announcing that the new post commander would be none other than Colonel B. O. Davis, Jr., whose father some of us had become so memorably acquainted with at Fort Huachuca. B.O., Jr., was a West Point man—the first black to enter the academy in fifty years—and, as the only black colonel in the Air Corps, was every bit as military as his father. We called him the West Point Uncle Tom. But he was a hell of a soldier and flier, having returned in triumph from action with the 332nd Fighter Group in Italy, for which he was generously decorated. The word was that Davis was coming to Godman Field to take command of a joint division that included both the 477th and the 332nd, marking the first and the last time that the Air Corps ever saw fit to combine a bomber group and a fighter group. That charade notwithstanding, it was apparent to us that B.O., Jr., was coming in to put the fear of God into the black troublemakers. There was also the distinct possibility that he might take pleasure in getting even with some of those who had humiliated his father at Huachuca. I'd heard for a fact that he had my name and I was to be one of his main objectives, whatever those objectives were. My plan was not to find out.

Among the shithouse lawyers with whom I consulted at Godman

Field were a couple of notable Philadelphians, one being William "Bumps" Coleman, the future secretary of transportation under Nixon and Ford, and the other a loquacious preacher named Slick Nick. In the matter of my personal situation, relative to both the Army and B.O. Davis, Jr., we concurred that I had no respectable option but to tender a letter of resignation. I was in the swing of writing letters, anyway, and proceeded to knock out about five pages—in stilted military third person—of charges and complaints of racism in the Army, concluding with my offer of resignation. This, of course, was not a prudent or an effective strategy. For the Army to honor my petition would have been tantamount to a virtual endorsement of my accusations. It elected not to do that.

Going back to the drawing board, I was once again extremely fortunate that the 477th never seemed to run short of Detroiters. Another fellow from home, Gene Savage, happened to be in charge of the administrative offices on the post and consented to help me search the Air Corps installations around the country for one that would take me as a transfer. Time was of the essence, because it was imperative that I get the hell out of there before Davis arrived. The ticket was celestial navigation. I was already a bombardier navigator, but celestial navigation was the most advanced form that the Army taught, and it required a thirteen-month program, graduation from which was the equivalent of a college degree. Perfect. I was accepted to study celestial navigation at Selman Field in Louisiana and drove away from Godman Field just as Colonel Davis was driving in. I saluted him smartly and grinned. Although he had never met me and probably didn't know who I was, he got the message and saluted back, sans grin.

There were a few dozen second lieutenants and flight officers from our division who felt the way I did about a future at Godman Field. Savage's research was of special interest to them, as well, and we arrived in Louisiana together in the heat of summer. When we received our first paychecks at Selman Field, we all noticed that the Army was quick to deduct our officers' dues even though it was still delinquent in opening up the officers' club. We'd thought that battle was behind us—a foolish underestimation of Jim Crow's tenacity and depth. I was learning that discrimination, unlike the war, would not come to an abrupt and spectacular end. It was a relentless opponent that would have to be fought daily, tirelessly, and for the rest of our lives. It was certainly not confined to the Army, as we discovered when we ventured off Selman Field into the city of Monroe, where many of the black officers chose to eat chicken tamales sold out of street wagons as a way of avoiding restaurants like the Red Onion, where blacks and whites stared at each other from facing counters.

We had no legal recourse in town, but back at the base we set about to go through the drill once again. We met with the commanders to protest—fruitlessly—and I was in the process of writing my customary letter to the inspector general when Hiroshima blew up. Nagasaki was wiped out three days later, and within a week the war was over.

We were all grateful for the restoration of peace, but to the black airmen, the victory wasn't really ours. We immediately began plotting a way to capitalize on V-J Day and register a triumph of our own. Knowing that the white officers would be whooping it up in the officers' club, we figured we might be able to walk right in without a fuss, inasmuch as nobody would want to begrudge our celebration and start a racial fight on such a glorious night for the red, white, and blue. The officers' club was built into a square block, with four entrances, and our plan was to send a half-dozen men into each entrance about thirty seconds apart. We managed to get thirty or forty men into the club that way without incident. The evening proceeded wonderfully. Black and white officers sang and partied together. A colonel from Mississippi, feeling very good, put his arm around me and offered me a glass of champagne, which under the circumstances I thought best to decline. We stayed about half an hour, then left quietly without a cross word having been spoken.

By late morning, however, the white officers had sobered up and come calling. My friend the Mississippi colonel let us know that our violation was unpardonable and that the only thing saving us from a court-martial was their embarrassment over the whole scenario. He gave us two choices—to sign up for another eighteen-month stint or be discharged immediately. Most of us declined the opportunity to think it over for a few hours and, choking back our smiles, humbly opted for the discharge.

The Army's procedure for discharge was to send men home in the general order of points they had earned through various types of duty served, with a heavy emphasis on action overseas. I had forty-seven points, which was the most in my outfit but not nearly enough to put me near the front of the list—or so I thought. To our great and grand surprise, however, practically the whole lot of us were ordered to ship out immediately, ahead of guys with a hundred or two hundred points. And whereas the normal routine was to assign soldiers to the base nearest their home for processing, we were dispatched off to Maxwell Field in Alabama—the closest post to Selman Field—in order to get us the hell out of the Air Corps as soon as possible.

As expeditiously as our discharges were arranged, there was still a checkpoint system to be observed. Each of us had to pass through more than a dozen stations, where we filled out papers and signed off before we could move on to the next one. At one of the stations, we were required to register as reserve officers, which was something I had absolutely no intention of becoming. So I deliberately screwed up the paperwork, signing on line 8 where it said line 18, etc. It got me through the station, but about a month after I returned to Detroit I started getting mail from the Army reserve with new papers to fill out. After five or six sets of papers, I guess they gave up on me. My brother George, ever the straight arrow, completed his reserve stint and was discharged as a major. But I preferred not to set foot on a military base again, and because I never served in the reserve—or maybe because I never filled out the papers correctly—I wasn't officially discharged in the eyes of the Army until 1950, which I didn't realize until I read it in my FBI file a few years ago. The file included a surprising number of details about my discharge process, as well as letters concerning me from the Air Corps to J. Edgar Hoover.

Officially discharged or not, the bottom line for me on December 23, 1945, was that I was out of the Army and raring to return to civilian life, disappointed only that I had to check out of the fight that remained to be fully won on the southern front. Within a matter of months, however, the War Department issued Memorandum 450-50, which made it explicit that racial discrimination would no longer be practiced in the armed forces. It was a great day for those of us who had put ourselves on the line at Freeman Field. We knew that we had made a hell of a difference; but we also knew that the struggle wasn't over. The policies of segregation still held forth.

Three years later, I was engaged in another battle of what, to me, was the same war—this time on the labor front—when the news came out that President Truman had issued Executive Order 9981:

> It is essential that there be maintained in the Armed Services of the United States the highest standards of democracy, with equality of treatment and opportunity for all persons in the Armed Services without regard to race. . . . [There] shall be created in the National Military Establishment an advisory committee to be known as the President's Committee on Equality of Treatment and Opportunity in the Armed Services. . . . [The] committee is authorized . . . to examine into the rules, procedures, and practices of the Armed Services . . . [and] to determine in what respect such rules, procedures and practices may be altered or improved with a view to carrying out the policy of this order.

When asked if his order meant the end of segregation in all branches of the United States military service, Truman said "Yes."

4

The Infamous Wayne County CIO

When I got back home, the family had moved out of the tailor shop to a house on Harding, and George, my longtime roommate, was about to marry and take his own place, which meant that I would have a room to myself for the first time in my life. Free of the Jim Crow Army and back on my turf, I was impatient about the possibilities ahead and eager to make my mark in Detroit, which had been turned on its side while I was away and seemed to be waiting for me to set it straight. I had not yet decided exactly how I would do that, however, and was biding my time, reacquainting myself with the city and working in the tailor shop to stay busy, when my mother called me there one day and, with no explanation, ordered me to come home immediately. As I walked through the door, I stopped short and swallowed hard. There, waiting staunchly with my mother—four hands on four hips—was someone I'd known well in my former days as a Tuskegee Airman.

Although most of my liaisons at Tuskegee had been entered into with playful coeds, one of the girls—shall we say, Vera—was a lovely and vivacious nurse who would surrender nothing of herself without a foregoing promise of matrimony. That was against my principles; but being in a weakened condition because of the military circumstances, I put in a call to my sister Juanita. Mother frequently described Juanita as my willing confederate, a fact of which I was once again able to take advantage. I asked Juanita to chance by Engass Jeweler, where I had an account, and acquire for me the cheapest engagement ring available. The ring arrived in the mail a week or two later, and I gallantly proffered it to Vera with the attendant proposal, whereupon she became more congenial. I did all of this with the assumption that, like most of the gals around there, Vera would latch onto another soldier as soon as I was shipped out—a development that would enable me to launch into a diatribe of righteous indignation and call the whole thing off. After I was dispatched to Panama City and points beyond, I regularly checked back through my spy system to see whether Vera's betrayal had indeed occurred. I began to anticipate this scenario with accelerated interest when I was in Louisiana for celestial navigation and had occasion to use the ring act with another young lady—shall we say Stella—who was also beautiful and vivacious and had a deep southern accent that obviously impaired my judgment. Before my military career was over, Juanita had fetched me three or four rings.

It was Vera who awaited me with my mother. Though my spies had failed to catch her in the clutches of another airman, I had mistakenly calculated that she simply had carried out her subsequent romances with skillful discretion. But this wasn't the case: Vera was still wearing my cut-rate ring, determined to hold me to the bargain it represented. It was a sticky situation, the most fearful aspect being my mother. In previous predicaments, I had generally been able to lie my way out of Mother's disfavor, but in this matter she was standing squarely with my alleged fiancée. Unmoved by my stammering, she threw me out of the house and gave my room to Vera, who stuck it out for a full two weeks before she had to return to work in Alabama. Once Mother began speaking to me again, I thought I was home free—until Stella showed up a month or two later. Her southern guile notwithstanding, Stella lacked the perspicacity to take her case up with Mrs. Young, for which I'm thankful to this day.

Although I was not in concert with her unflinching schoolteacher morals, I appreciated the saintly qualities of my mother, as did all those who knew her, and considered her to be practically perfect. If anyone in the neighborhood was struggling and in need of a meal, the door to Mrs. Young's house was always open. Quick to comfort and slow to condemn—except in matters of my social life—she was especially faithful and long-suffering when it came to my father. In addition to her endless domestic duties, Mother could be counted on to open and close the tailor shop while Daddy—if he was there at all—hosted poker games in the back. Though I sympathized with her, I remained amused by my father's carryings-on until I was at a party one evening and inquired about a particularly attractive woman across the room. I was told that she was my old man's stuff.

Mother's health was erratic around this time, which led my brothers and me to the conclusion that she was fretting about my father's womanizing. So we decided to do something about it. Being the oldest, I was the spokesman. We went to Daddy at the tailor shop, where he slept, and I said that Mother was sick and might die over worrying about him and the way he was fucking around, so we were going to take him out. I told him flat-out that we were going to kill him. We were pretty intense about it, but he was a cagey old fox and he didn't say anything. We had hardly made it down the street before he was on the phone talking to our mother. "Ida, do you know what our boys said to me?" Then he weaved this tale about how shocked he was to be threatened by his own sons. My mother immediately summoned all three of us to the house on Harding and read us the riot act. She ordered us to get down to the shop right away and apologize to our father, which we did, hats in hand.

Although it was several years later, Mother ended up dying before he did. My brothers and I could never get over the notion that his catting around might have had something to do with it, so one night, after George and I had been drinking, we went to see the old man. He was in bed, which was not a customary place for him to be at night, but we felt like talking, so we got him up and went into the kitchen, sat around the table at which we used to shell peanuts and discuss politics—my father could recite the voting records of judges and congressmen most people had never heard of—passed around a few bottles of beer, and spoke our minds. I'm not sure if we'd ever been in a situation where my father was the only sober one, but he was mostly just listening while George and I rattled on. George was in worse shape than I was, and in the course of the conversation he unwittingly referred to my father as a son of a bitch. It was not said in hostility, but my father was programmed to act when he heard those words. Without wasting a moment, he grabbed the beer bottle and cracked it on George's head. The cuts turned out to be only superficial, but they were bloody and bad-looking, and the sight of George provoked me to respond out of reflex, too. I jumped out of my chair, grabbed Daddy by the chest, and shoved him against the wall. That slowed the action down a little, and when we all had a chance to realize what was going on, I came to my senses and let him go. The important thing at that point was to get George to a hospital. I rushed him there, and when he walked in all bloody and cut up, they wouldn't admit him. I had to argue like hell just to get George treated.

We never spoke about that moment again, but I think Daddy and George and I understood each other—and ourselves—a little better after that night. As much as I resented him sometimes, I think I've always realized that, except for the evolving circumstances in which we were sensitized, I wasn't and still am not much different from my father. I could also see that in many ways, he was a later version of his father.

My grandfather Young spent one of his last summers in Detroit, drinking whiskey and wine, puffing on his corncob pipe, and educating me in racial realities with his Deep South parables. From observing him and my father, I have to wonder if the biggest difference in the generations might not be that each succeeding one takes itself a little more seriously. Grandfather Young, for instance, fought discrimination with his wits and his fists for most of his ninety-two years, but he never let the struggle assume such grave proportions that it stood in the way of more basic matters, like populating Alabama—he must have had twenty kids with his three wives, of which my grandmother was the last—or a good bottle of hooch. When I knew him well, in his late eighties, he drank a quart of hard liquor every day, and I never saw him stagger. I gladly indulged Grandpa Young by taking him to an Italian confectionary where I occasionally worked and where they served whiskey and made dago red wine in the basement. He told us that he had to sit down there watching the presser—with liquid refreshment and cinnamon cookies—because, he swore, the presser was stealing. Cleaning the basement at the end of one summer, I came upon an empty quart bottle of Sunnybrook whiskey for every day the old man had spent in Detroit.

When I was old enough to begin contemplating the dynamics of labor unions, it was one of Grandpa Young's Alabama tales that illustrated for me the fundamental racial dilemma inherent in collective bargaining. The way we had it figured at Maben's barbershop, racial unity in organized labor was the only way for blacks or whites to gain any leverage in the workplace. For the white man, however, the notion of rubbing shoulders with black men, while to his economic advantage, required him to surrender his sacred myth of superiority—as I clearly understood when my grandfather told me the story of the honey dippers.

In the old South, honey dippers were the men who drove the shit wagons and had the job of cleaning outhouses, which was done by removing buckets that had been placed in the holes or, where there were no buckets, dipping out the waste with cups. Often, honey dippers came in pairs, one black and one white, the black one doing the dipping and the white one driving the mule team. When the black dipper had a bucket of shit, he would hand it up to the white driver, who would fill the wagon with buckets to be hauled out to the dump. In one instance, however—according to my grandfather—the driver suddenly had a change of heart and said to the dipper, "Tom, get up here in this wagon." So Tom sat in the wagon and the white guy proceeded to hand him the bucket. When Tom's curiosity finally got the better of him and he asked why they had swapped jobs, the white fellow told him, "I ain't gonna have no nigger handing me no shit."

My grandfather's folksy lesson, taken in the context of his time and place, still applies to the here and now, and it helped prepare me for the union meetings which became the focal point of my life soon after I returned home from the Air Corps. Although the same radicals were still arguing with the same fascists, much had changed in Detroit during the war. For one thing, I was able to eat in the downtown Coney Island chili parlor for the first time. For another, the union that I had been fired from the post office for trying to organize had been organized. Although I was sorry to miss the vote by which the union was approved—just as I had missed the Battle of the Overpass and the occupation of Sojourner Truth—I was honored that my efforts were appreciated. When I was home on leave from the Army in 1944, I had attended a meeting of the Wayne County Congress of Industrial Organizations council at Paradise Theatre Hall and was asked to step onto the stage. Remembering my efforts with the National Negro Congress and the postal union, the host introduced me as "one of ours" and said (I can quote him only because it was duly reported in my FBI file), "He will be back with us and will go far. Watch him, and remember."

The biggest change in the city, though, went well beyond local customs and politics. It was a discernible shift in consciousness that had been brought on in part by one of the worst race riots in American history. The Detroit riot of 1943 was the most violent since St. Louis in 1914, which happened to be the year that Henry Ford kick-started Detroit when his five-dollar workday touched off the wave of migration from the South and Eastern Europe. In the intervening period, which included the influx of wartime workers attracted by the defense factories, Detroit's black population had risen from about six thousand to two hundred thousand. This compositional change in the city was attended by the predictable tensions, most of which were played out in the Sojourner Truth affair of 1941 and 1942. In the aftermath of Sojourner Truth, there was another major breakout of racial enmity early in 1943, when twenty thousand white workers went on strike at Packard to protest the company's upgrading of black employees.

It was obvious that gasoline had been splashing on the city for years, and it was finally set off in the summer of '43 by a senseless fight between blacks and whites—many of the latter being sailors from the nearby Naval Armory—on Belle Isle, the recreational park located across a bridge from the city's east side. False rumors circulated after the Belle Isle melee, and bloody racial incidents broke out all over Paradise Valley and Woodward Avenue, where whites overturned and burned automobiles driven by blacks and pulled blacks off trolley cars and beat them in the streets. Of the thirty-four lives that were lost, twenty-three were black. And while there is no disputing that the 1943 episode was a race riot in nature—as opposed to the more infamous uprising in the hot summer of 1967, which I regard as a community rebellion against the police department—there is also no question that the police presence was an exacerbating influence. The police killed seventeen rioters during the 1943 disturbance, every one of them black—despite the fact that most of the fighting was in black neighborhoods which the residents were endeavoring to defend, or on Woodward Avenue, where isolated blacks on their way home from work were trapped by merciless white mobs. A Detroit police lieutenant shrugged off his department's casual slaughter of black suspects by explaining, "If you locked them up, they just ate free. If you shot them, they didn't have to worry anymore." Two-thirds of the arrests were of blacks, even while whites were perpetrating unrequited violence on the main street of the city and in the immediate proximity of City Hall. Thurgood Marshall, investigating the riot as counsel for the NAACP, concluded that the police department used "persuasion" against white rioters and "the ultimate in force" against blacks.

I could sense in 1946 that with a riot and a war behind them—with welts on their backs and family members in their graves—the average citizens of Black Bottom and Paradise Valley were no longer willing to fall in line with the old southern ways to which they'd traditionally been resigned. This was most apparent in the union movement, which more and more blacks were eager to join. By the late forties, the labor challenge was no longer organizing the emboldened black workers but enlisting the whites who had fought them on Woodward Avenue and the Belle Isle bridge.

By nature, a union is able to survive only in a climate of unity, and such a climate was quite evidently not prevailing in Detroit. Many of the employers were doing their best to keep it that way, fostering a deep division between the races by telling white workers that they would be denigrating themselves if they associated with blacks. The result was that, as my grandfather might say, the city was full of honey dippers who would sink their elbows in shit before they would take any from the black men at their sides—although there were many who recognized the mutual advantages of new ways.

The racial situation in the workplace was profoundly complicated by the return of white servicemen from the war. The war had marked a high point for black and also women workers, who, by virtue of the white manpower shortage, occupied jobs that had previously been unattainable. Especially in Detroit, where wartime employment swelled as the automaking facilities were converted into defense plants—so vital was the city's role as the nation's manufacturer of arms that it was known as "the Arsenal of Democracy"—the veterans' homecoming created a major upheaval in the job market. There were simply more people than jobs, a condition to which industrial Detroit was unaccustomed. Black and women workers were of course anxious to hold on to the gains secured during the war, while white GIs understandably maintained that their prewar working experience should be honored as "superseniority," superseding that of the wartime help. The issue of superseniority was a principal point of contention between the left and right wings of the union movement.

I officially reentered this divided arena through the United Public Workers. Although I'd been fired from the post office before the war, my veteran status put me in better stead after I returned, and I got hired back—albeit without my seniority, super- or otherwise, which proved to be costly when I requested a leave to work for the union that had belatedly been established in my absence. Denied the privilege of devoting all my time to the union, I dabbled on the side in the union newspaper, which printed a comment from me to the effect that I found my post office supervisor to be curiously reminiscent of Hitler. I was gone after two months.

I continued working with the union, however, and took on a job as an organizer for the hospital and garbage workers. Since our contract was newly won and unrefined, we were basically a seat-of-the-pants organization. For instance, we had not yet won the right to have the employer deduct union dues from the workers' paychecks and forward the money to the union, an inconvenience that left the collection duties to the stewards and made it problematic to sustain an operating balance. The logistical complications fostered union leaders like Louis Beatty, head of the incinerator local. Alert to the possibilities of his position, Louis provided a full gamut of personal services, which made him something of a neighborhood banker, available at all times for check cashing and moneylending. You could borrow five bucks from Louis and pay him six next week. He arranged for the subforeman to hand him all the paychecks, which he would gladly cash for twenty-five cents each. If one of the fellows owed Louis money, as many of them generally did, it was prudent for him to have the check cashed on the spot so that Louis could be repaid. Louis had a racket going, but he was what we considered a good, strong union man. His shop reelected him numerous times.

Weak as we basically were, the union nevertheless reserved the ability to strike, an option that I was not especially reluctant to recommend. When garbage Local 183 was stalled in its contract negotiations, my advice was to wait until summer and then take the offensive—literally. In those days, garbage was collected in shallow-bed trucks and covered with a tarp to be hauled away. Before the strike, we filled twenty trucks with garbage and drove them to a remote location, Erskine Yard, to let them ripen in the midsummer sun for a week or so with the tarps off. Then we staged a rally at City Hall, which we climaxed by bringing in the trucks, parking them on all sides of the building, and tossing the keys down the sewer. The new contract was expediently resolved after that. I'm not sure that a more effective strike strategy has ever been devised.

The UPW was a member in good standing of the Wayne County chapter of the CIO, an enormous outfit organized by labor luminary John L. Lewis, who later headed the United Mine Workers. Wayne County's three hundred thousand CIO members also included, among others, auto workers, leather workers, electrical workers, and machinists. Ours was the most radical of all the chapters in the state, and possibly in the country. The Michigan CIO as a whole was famously conservative, following the lead of Walter Reuther, who was elected UAW president in 1946 but gained absolute control of the union in 1947 when his caucus swept the top four international offices. By campaigning vigorously against Communist and other leftist influences in the UAW-CIO, Reuther deftly enlisted the partnership of most white unionists and the federal government. This omnipotent coalition put bull's-eyes on the backs of those who didn't fit the profile. In the eyes of Walter Reuther, J. Edgar Hoover, and the redneck on the stamping machine, anyone who espoused such things as equal opportunity or affirmative action was a dangerous radical, otherwise known as a Communist—or in FBI lingo, a subversive.

To the extent that the government and unions believed that the Communist Party had a voice in the policymaking of the Wayne County CIO, they were right. To the extent that they believed we were all party members, they were wrong. To the degree that they believed we were a threat to the United States Constitution, they were ridiculous. And to the extreme that they went to gather evidence concerning our personal thoughts and associations, they were unforgivable.

In the beginning, it was amusing. We knew our phone lines were tapped, so we carried on our conversations as if J. Edgar himself were smoking a cigar under the bed. We also knew that the FBI's bidding was being done in the city by the witch-hunt wing of the Detroit Police Department, known as the Red Squad. The two officers generally assigned to worrisome community gatherings were a comic pair named Ike and Mike, whom we all recognized and had a little fun with. After a while, Ike and Mike stopped trying to conceal themselves. They would walk into a meeting and take a seat in the front row, or stay out in their car writing down our license numbers in order to get a complete list of those attending. They were particularly conspicuous at Sunday picnics, which was where working people tended to congregate. The local Communists showed up at most of the picnics for recruiting and political purposes— much like the local Democrats and Republicans—the upshot being that anyone with a basket of chicken might have had a Red Squad file identifying him or her as a possible subversive and dangerous character. Inasmuch as the neighborhood and church committees were also composed principally of working people, the Communists commonly circulated among the Poles and Jews and blacks, which meant that Ike and Mike attended a lot of bake sales and choir practices. It got to the point that we felt snubbed if we had a get-together of some sort and Ike and Mike weren't there.

While I was constantly aware of government surveillance after returning from military duty, I hadn't realized that they were on to me before the war until the staff sergeant opened my eyes that night at Tuskegee. Years later, when I received copies of my FBI and Red Squad files, I learned that the FBI had first put in a request for the local police to monitor my activities in the fall of 1941, when I was involved with the Sojourner Truth dispute. Their first couple of entries provided a revealing portent of the laughable incompetence that would characterize the government's tracking of me in the years ahead. The initial report identifies Coleman Young as an officer with the National Negro Congress, which I was, but lists my real name as William C. Young, which was actually my father, who was also called Coleman. The next entry indicates that I spoke at a Lenin Memorial meeting—which was actually a Sojourner Truth rally—at the Mirror Ballroom and quotes me as saying, "So journey truth has been taken away from us . . ." Obviously, they didn't have a clue.

As we found out later, a sizable percentage of the alleged Communists in our circles were actually government stool pigeons. Some of them were clever—I still don't know who they all were— and some were hilariously inept. When I was with the UPW, I sat in on a hearing held for the president of the garbage local, a fellow named Tom Coleman, who was accused of being a member of a Communist cell of city employees. One of the witnesses was a stool pigeon who testified that he had attended a Communist cell meeting with Tom Coleman and some other fellow and Coleman Young. He was asked first to point out Tom Coleman, who was sitting at the front table with his attorney, and then to point out Coleman Young. There were about a hundred people in the room, and this motherfucker, whom I had never seen before, was looking all around desperately while his advisers and counsel were whispering in his damn ear. Finally he pointed straight at a *Detroit Free Press* reporter named Collins George, a very straightlaced fellow from

Philadelphia. Collins George practically turned white when the guy fingered him, and the room just rolled. In the end, though, Tom Coleman was fired anyway. It didn't take much.

In its misguided zeal to rid the country of "subversives," the government didn't give a damn whose life it trampled upon. In 1947, I was running the campaign to get Reverend Hill elected to Detroit's Common Council when it came out that his son, Charlie, a reserve captain in the Air Corps, had been arrested and charged with disloyalty to the Army. His alleged crime—which he denied— was reading the *Daily Worker,* a Communist newspaper. The fact is that Charlie Hill was a good soldier who never had a radical thought in his life and they were fucking with him because he was assisting in his father's Common Council campaign. Ultimately, the charges against Charlie were dropped and he was cleared with an apology, but the damage to both him and his father had been done.

Reverend Hill was an old-fashioned Bible-thumping preacher whose only political concern was making things right in the sight of the Lord, and it was mind-boggling to me that the United States government would be so afraid of a man who was so good and decent. The government's obsession with Communists naturally trickled down to the conservative press, which suspected that everybody left of General MacArthur was a Russian agent. During the campaign, one local newspaper wrote, "The average voter little suspects that lurking behind the 'Reverend' is one of the most active communist-front figures in all America." For lack of a better idea, I had to wonder if they meant me.

The establishment's anxiety over Reverend Hill undoubtedly had something to do with the fact that his candidacy represented a broad left-wing coalition, which I'd helped piece together and was extremely proud of. Although Common Council candidates were elected individually on an at-large basis, Reverend Hill had broken from tradition by campaigning on an unofficial ticket with labor leader Stanley Nowak. A slight, sincere man with a thick Polish accent, Nowak was also a state senator who years before had been indicted for being both a Communist and an anarchist—a puzzling paradox—and for withholding that information when he was naturalized. The charges were so absurd that they ultimately had to be dropped.

By pooling their resources and endorsing each other during the campaign, Nowak and Reverend Hill attracted a considerable number of votes from each other's natural constituencies, although both fell short in the November election. When they again ran jointly two years later, the Detroit newspapers reported during the campaign that Nowak was soon to be the object of denaturalization proceedings because of alleged subversive activities. No charges were forthcoming that time, however, and the source of the bogus story, immigration director E. E. Adcock, eventually acknowledged that he had no hard evidence against the senator, just "impressions." Despite the damning press, Nowak and Reverend Hill made another strong showing, only to lose by a margin as scant as the immigration director's credibility.

I truly believed that our coalition ticket strategy might make Reverend Hill the first black on Common Council (in fact, I still think it's an intriguing concept, although nobody has ever picked up on it), and my confidence was a little shaken by the results of the 1947 election. But not much. The fact is, I was on a roll that year. In January, I had married a tall, long-haired, fashionable young lady named Marion McClellan, who, in the beginning, didn't seem to mind the fact that I was so damn concerned about everybody else making a decent wage, I overlooked the necessity of doing it myself. Or maybe she thought I was going to be the next John L. Lewis. I never bothered with such lofty ambitions, but the fact is that my future in the labor universe looked pretty damn good that spring, when I scored the first real triumph of my union life.

After the war, there was a renewed effort in the left wing of the CIO to press forward with the unsuccessful wartime attempt to elect a black to a full-time position. Traditionally, blacks in the union movement had served only as advisers or titular vice-presidents with part-time duties and no policymaking authority. George Crockett, a civil rights attorney with a Washington background, was the black representative on the UAW staff, chairing the Fair Employment Practices Committee, which investigated allegations of discrimination. In the Wayne County CIO, a vice-presidency was held by a feisty black aluminum worker named Hodges Mason. While both of them did what they could to elevate the black presence in organized labor, they were severely impaired by the perfunctory nature of their positions. Many of us believed that the time was right to break through with a full-time black officer at the state level of the CIO, and there was considerable lobbying to that effect at the 1947 state convention in Grand Rapids.

The first order of business for the left caucus was to nominate a sympathetic candidate as state president. The choice was Doug Fraser, the president of the UAW's DeSoto local, who, although conservative in his effort to banish Communists from the union, was a strong advocate of black leadership. That was a start. I made the seconding speech for Fraser's nomination and pursued the endorsement for secretary-treasurer, but the caucus eschewed my candidacy in favor of the left-progressive alternative, Barney Hopkins. I realized that our slate had a better chance with Hopkins and had no chance at all with a divided caucus, so I fell in line behind him, telling the convention, "Unity is the only agent that will solve our grave problems." In the back of my mind, I was also thinking about being a candidate for the new executive position we hoped to create for a black. That possibility was dimmed when Fraser was beaten by incumbent Gus Scholle, a right-wing Reutherite from the glassblowers' union.

We weren't ready to surrender the fight for a black executive, however; and as so many of them in those days did, it turned into a screaming, brawling convention. Our left-wing caucus managed to make a little headway on broad racial policies, passing resolutions to oppose discrimination in restaurants and support fair-employment legislation, but the floor was rigid in its opposition to the new administrative position for a black. The issue evolved into a political free-for-all. Radicals stormed the stage, carrying signs and shouting slogans, while Gus Scholle pounded his gavel in vain. The only way to control a CIO convention was literally to take over the platform, and I had a scheme to do that. The president of my union, the United Public Workers, was a firebrand named Yale Stuart, who had lost an arm in the Spanish Civil War. Knowing that Scholle had a short fuse, I figured that if we could get Yale Stuart up on the stage next to him, and if, in all the confusion, Stuart would somehow bump into Scholle or jostle him, Gus might take a poke at Stuart, which would most likely turn the convention against him for picking on a one-armed man. And I'll be damned if it didn't almost work. We worked our way up on the stage with a mass of people, and when we got close to the podium, I sort of pushed Yale into Gus. Sure enough, Gus turned and pulled his fist back to hit Yale, but—according to what he told me later—he stopped short when he caught a glimpse of me over Yale's shoulder and noticed my shitass grin. I obviously didn't have my father's talent for a poker face. Anyway, Gus said, "You motherfucker, you!" and walked away. On such momentous trivia does history turn. I'm certain that if we had carried the platform that night, Walter Reuther would never have been able to assume autocratic control of the UAW. Without a groundswell for our new executive position, however, we had little chance of converting the Reutherites. Shelton Tappes and Hodges Mason spoke on behalf of our proposal; but, doomed by Scholle's reelection, it was defeated without much of a hearing.

We had known all along that we had a better chance of getting a black position added to the Wayne County board. The county convention, held at the CIO offices in the basement of the Huffman Building on Woodward, followed the state by a few weeks, and the left-wing caucus was ready with an amendment written by Nat Ganley, head of UAW Local 155, the foremost union constitutionalist in Detroit and one of the movement's few open Communists. We were optimistic about gaining the new post— director of organization—but the initiative would have to be undertaken in two phases. First, the constitution had to be changed in order to add the third executive. If that could be won, the election would follow.

Not surprisingly, the conservatives greeted our amendment proposal with charges of reverse discrimination. Reuther, who had steadfastly opposed a black executive position ever since the concept was first brought before the UAW in 1943—George Crockett's job with the Fair Employment Practices Committee was the compromise from that debate—insisted that it would polarize the union along racial lines. But Reuther knew that the Wayne County convention wasn't the time or place to dig his trench, and accordingly the right-wing arguments were passionless. With the left-wing lobby being impressively represented by Doug Fraser and Harold Shapiro, an articulate Fur and Leather Workers leader, the amendment passed enthusiastically, and the executive council was increased to three members.

Without the amendment, we would have had little chance of electing a black to the board. The two existing positions were held down by a couple of union warhorses and considerable characters named Sam Sage and Tracy Doll, both of whom were popular figures at the county level. Sam, whom the community knew well as the voice of the CIO radio show, was a maverick electrician who believed in the therapeutic value of fasting once or twice a year and was quite taken with the notion that he could realize the benefits of exercise by sitting in an electrically charged chair and receiving stimulation to increase his heartbeat. His wife was always afraid that Sam was going to electrocute himself, and one night he damn near did—when he crawled out of that chair, his eyebrows were singed. Everybody got a chuckle out of Sam's eccentricities, but a couple of years ago I had to stop and look twice when I saw an advertisement for a sedentary exercise machine that looked a hell of a lot like Sam's chair. Tracy Doll, meanwhile, was a little more down-to-earth, and a man of unwavering principle. He was not a Communist, but believed firmly enough in the First Amendment to fight against the prohibition of Communists in the union, a position that eventually hurt him politically and personally. Both Sam and Tracy were friendly toward the agenda of the black caucus, and we preferred not to run athwart of them.

With the way opened for a new black official, the battle was joined over the selection of the person to fill it. The black caucus felt that it was crucial for us, rather than the left-wing caucus at large, to choose the left-wing candidate. By doing so, black unionists would gain vital leverage within the larger caucus, and consequently the county organization. The black caucus had never, on its own, put a candidate or a proposal before the floor. This was the time; the question was who.

Many of us, myself included, had assumed that the candidate would be Hodges Mason, the titular, part-time vice-president. In fact, it had occurred to me that the new position might have been designed expressly to make Hodges full-time. What I hadn't realized was that, while I was away in the Army, Hodges had made a lot of enemies and established a reputation as a mean motherfucker. Many in the black caucus felt that if Hodges were to be the candidate, we'd lose the slot. They preferred somebody who hadn't alienated so many people—somebody, for instance, who'd been off in the Army for four years. Considering also that I had earned some stripes from the struggle to establish the same position at the state convention, the choice was fairly brainless. Hodges will never believe that I wasn't a part of the selection process and never campaigned for the job; he's still out there giving me hell every chance he gets. I felt awkward about shutting him out, but that wasn't enough to stop me from accepting the nomination, which pitted me against the conservative candidate, Alex Fuller, a steelworker over whom I was elected by a vote of four to one.

A wild celebration ensued at the Book Cadillac Hotel, where I found myself in an unfamiliar position as the center of attention. The effect was not disagreeable, however, and I recall having the impression that the events of that evening were placing me in the mainstream of a great struggle that was taking on greater proportions daily. I could only assume at the time that mine would be a long and eventful association with the union movement.

T HE INTERLUDE of 1947 and 1948 might have been the most volatile, stimulating, highly charged moment of twentieth-century American politics, as well as, in my estimation, the last hurrah for the radical left. The electricity, as usual, was generated by the Communist presence in the labor movement. The Communists constituted the most uninhibited political force behind the racial revolution occurring within the major unions, and as a result I had only a few quarrels with them in the abstract.

My more germane reservations about the party had to do with its organizational rigidity, which conflicted with my billet as an outspoken advocate for freedom of expression. But I was in total support of the constitutional right of any citizen to affiliate as he saw fit, about which the same could not be said of the United States government. The federal position was clearly stated by the 1947 Taft-Hartley Act, which required Communist Party members to disavow their memberships in order to remain in labor unions.

Taft-Hartley was a colossal triumph for Walter Reuther, a landmark in his dogged campaign to rid the UAW-CIO of a left-wing element. Michigan handed Reuther and the conservatives a bonus when it took Taft-Hartley a step further with the Callahan Act, which required "subversives" to register as foreign agents and labor unions to make their records public. Unwilling to accept the troubling fact that such un-American legislation could hold forth in America, the Wayne County CIO promptly took aim at Callahan and Taft-Hartley. My first substantial duty in my new county office was to drum up enough signatures to put the repeal of the Callahan Act on the ballot.

The symbolic events of the period seemed to congregate at Detroit's enormous Labor Day parades down Woodward Avenue, and in 1947 the parade was characterized by labor's split over Taft-Hartley. Reuther led the strutting UAW brigade, and farther down the line was a string of Wayne County CIO floats decorated with crepe-paper protests against Taft-Hartley and the Callahan Act. In the 1948 parade, the left wing was led by Progressive Party presidential candidate Henry Wallace, but his presence was overshadowed by that of President Truman, who kicked off his campaign by addressing the huge crowd at Cadillac Square. The breach within the CIO was on public display that afternoon, as the Reuther caucus paraded to the square behind Truman while the leftists and Progressives peeled off in another direction to rally in behalf of Henry Wallace. (I was left to keep order while Sam Sage was busy squabbling over who should get to drive the revolutionary Tucker automobile that was part of our procession.)

Although the Wayne County CIO was not officially associated with the Wallace campaign, our obvious preference for his third-party candidacy was regarded as insubordination and put us at odds with the parent UAW-CIO, which had endorsed Truman and expected its affiliations to do the same. In his confirmed tradition, Reuther had impugned the motives of the Progressive Party by falsely publicizing it as a Communist front, when in fact it had been formed by Wallace when he realized that his New Deal policies would not be accommodated by the Democratic Party. Wallace was a reform-minded liberal who had been secretary of agriculture— like his father and grandfather—and then Vice-President to FDR before falling into disfavor with the administration and being re- placed on the 1944 ticket by Harry Truman. Under Truman, Wal- lace served briefly as secretary of commerce, which proved to be an untenable assignment for a labor-oriented politician entirely unsympathetic to big business. Wallace's vision of economic re- form was described in his book *Sixty Million Jobs,* in which he advo- cated a massive government program to ensure full employment. When he organized the Progressive Party as a vehicle for carrying out his program, he immediately became the presidential favorite of several large unions, including the steelworkers.

I jumped into the Wallace movement as a Progressive Party can- didate for the state senate. To this day, it remains the biggest polit- ical mistake of my life. I say that not in terms of ideology, to which I owed first consideration, but with grudging respect to the reali- ties of the day. My limb was sawed off, and it took me fifteen years to rehabilitate my position with the Democratic Party.

In retrospect, it's apparent that the Progressive Party was ill-fated from the beginning. I should have realized what we were up against when we set about to finance the Wallace campaign. Our initial fund-raiser was so large and promising that we held it at Olympia Stadium, the home of the Red Wings; but it seemed that for every- one willing to give to Wallace, there was somebody just as willing to take. Being in charge of security at the stadium rally, I had unex- pected difficulty collecting the money from the collectors, one of whom escaped with the contributions of an entire row of seats.

Like the Progressive Party and virtually everything else I associat- ed myself with in those days, the Callahan Act repeal campaign was a noble and lost cause. Although we collected more than enough signatures in two weeks, the secretary of state refused to certify our referendum petition, which meant that the repeal was never placed on the ballot. Even so, our efforts were not altogether in vain, because they put the Wayne County Council in motion politically and expanded our horizon.

Because of the activism of our CIO council and the swirl of action around the Progressive Party, it seemed as if Detroit were the center of the radical universe in those days. It was a second home, for instance, to the likes of Paul Robeson, the famous baritone, actor, football player, and activist, who sang at Reverend Hill's church when he came to town and attended evening meetings at many of our houses. One night, when there was a session planned at the Grosse Pointe Park residence of Sid Rosen, the state treasurer for the Progressive Party, Robeson arrived late, only to learn that Sid's six-year-old son had been trying his best to stay awake so that he could meet the great singer. When he heard this, Robeson tiptoed up to the boy's bedroom, and seconds later the Broadway version of "Old Man River" was booming through the house.

Another visitor was Benjamin Davis—not to be confused with my military friends Benjamin O. Davis, Sr. and Jr.—who spoke at the Greater Macedonia Baptist Church about his experience as the first black councilman in New York. As might be expected, Ike and Mike et al. filed the event as a Communist rally because of Davis's political persuasion. The police and the FBI both operated by a simple rule of thumb for that type of affair—incrimination by association. The advocates of change in whose circles I traveled found it curious that the government snoops lumped us all together as Communists/subversives and failed to recognize our individual discrepancies, because, in fact, we represented a myriad of political and social affiliations that had to be superseded if we were to pull together an effectual left-wing coalition. At any of our get-togethers, there were likely to be Progressives and Communists and Trotskyites and Socialists and Jews and Baptists and Catholics and Poles and Italians, for starters—and, of course, varying proportions of blacks and whites.

It was around that period that I began pushing the slogan "Black and White Unite to Fight." If there has been a prevailing theme to all my efforts of the past six decades, it has been the paramount importance of racial unity in addressing the country's socioeconomic problems. My ambitions as a union official were scarcely different from my ambitions as a mayor—to raise the American standard of citizenship, with particular attention given to those who most need it. In unions or cities or nations, that cannot be accomplished without a common willingness to leave behind personal differences for the greater good.

At my urging, the Wayne County Council broadened its scope in an effort to become an all-purpose vehicle for social change in the near and far community. That meant sticking our noses into countless places where others thought we didn't belong, such as the public establishments of downtown Detroit, many of which were still segregated. We protested that the Graystone Ballroom only allowed blacks on Monday nights. We protested that Negro League teams could not play games at Briggs Stadium, where the Tigers played, and that the Tigers had not signed any black players—unlike their rivals the Cleveland Indians, who won the 1948 pennant with Satchel Paige and my favorite player, Larry Doby. We could have picketed any number of restaurants that refused to serve blacks but chose the Barlum Towers (now the Cadillac Towers) coffee shop. After two or three days, the Barlum finally consented to offer us a table for lunch. I went in and ordered with three or four others—a couple of them white—but elected not to eat my food. I'd too often heard my father and his brothers tell tales from their restaurant days about the various misdeeds they had visited upon the food of the white folks who had fucked them over at one time or another, which included spitting on it and dipping in certain of their private parts. Having won the battle of the Barlum, I just paid for my lunch and chatted with my friends while they ate. I didn't even drink the water.

We also took an interest in the perils that black homeowners were encountering when they dared move into white neighborhoods. When two black families bought houses in Corktown, a working-class enclave within the shadow of Briggs Stadium, they were greeted by a mob of about two thousand whites who blockaded the area, stoned the houses, broke windows, dumped garbage, burned crosses, and patrolled the streets in KKK robes. One strange man sat in a hearse wearing a sheet, with a blue light shining on him, whatever the hell that meant. The incident received a lot of attention, and at one of our regular Wayne County CIO meetings, somebody suggested that we pass a resolution to raise some money for these families. Resolution, hell, I said—we ought to go out there and demonstrate. I thought it was important to make a show of solidarity within the labor movement. So under cover of darkness, about a half-dozen of us, black and white, stole into one of the houses, armed with shotguns. We had plenty of muscle available to handle the situation with force, but that would have probably set off another riot like the one less than five years before. Our plan, instead, was to secure the houses, then fix them up. That's the kind of demonstration that demonstrates something. I figured that if black and white union leaders worked together out in the open to paint and repair the houses, it not only would increase their value—which was the antithesis of what was expected when black people moved into a white neighborhood—but would make a statement that if anybody was going to fuck with black homeowners, they would be fucking with the entire trade union membership of Wayne County.

It was a solid plan, the tricky part being what to do if the mob tried to spoil the party. Our anxieties were confirmed at about midnight, when several of them stormed the porch of the house we occupied. It would have been helpful to identify the motherfuckers for our own edification—we weren't so naive as to think that the police would be interested—but we weren't able to get a look at their faces. After we kicked open the door and racked back our shotguns, we saw nothing but asses. The situation cooled off considerably after that. The next day, we put union leaders out there on ladders with paint brushes in their hands, making sure that the white ones were the most visible. We wanted it clear that this wasn't a black program, it was a solidarity program. When those black people settled into their new homes, it was an outstanding example of what could be accomplished by black and white unity.

In our efforts to save the world, we also found ourselves walking pickets on numerous occasions, such as the winter strike at the Square D electrical plant. A picket line generally implied that policemen would be present, often on horses, which they employed skillfully in the management of crowds, maneuvering the animals so as to lean their hind quarters against the overmatched demonstrators and thereby reconfigure the scene. This was frustrating to the pickets, but not indefensible. I happened to have a friend who was able to supply me with a large number of ball bearings during the Square D strike, which I divided between my pockets and those of my accomplice Dave Moore. I was fortunate also that another friend on hand, John Bell, could always be counted on to have a cigar burning. After Dave and I dropped ball bearings into the snow, where they couldn't be seen, I borrowed John's cigar and discreetly applied the warm end to the nearest horse's ass. This triggered a chain reaction of slipping and sliding that sent several policemen off their trusty steeds and onto the cold, hard pavement, whereupon, in a great show of cooperation and sympathy, I stood back and shouted for everybody to please remain calm and do what the officers said. It didn't precipitate a speedier end to the strike, but it was damn good for morale.

Given our unstinting enthusiasm for righting wrongs, the Wayne CIO often flew solo in those days. As has consistently been the case over the past half-century, however, we could depend on the police to periodically screw up in such a way as to rally the greater black community and various subdivisions of the left to join our efforts. That was what happened in 1948, when a fifteen-year-old black kid named Leon Mosely was shot in the back as he tried to escape police in a stolen car. At no point did the boy threaten the safety of the officers, who were consequently not authorized to employ deadly force. This understandably aroused the citizens, who formed a protest committee and gathered for a demonstration march of thousands that started at St. John's AME, where the funeral was held, stretched for more than a mile on St. Aubin, and paraded past police headquarters to the steps of the old City Hall on Woodward. Tracy Doll, George Crockett, Stanley Nowak, and Henry Wallace all spoke, as did I, whom Red Squad intelligence identified as "by far the most radical and malicious speaker of the evening." This kind description was undoubtedly based on the fact that I had demanded the killing officer be sent to prison and suggested that the real murderer was police commissioner Harry Toy.

Harry Toy was one of my favorite subjects that summer, he being
the master detective who had ordered a mass arrest of liberals and
subversives (a matter of rounding up the usual suspects) in the un-
solved assassination attempt on Walter Reuther in the spring. I was
fortunate to be clear of suspicion in that one, since I was engaged
at the time in the typical trench warfare between the left and right
wings of the Wayne County Council, for which Ike and Mike et al.
could probably vouch. The meeting that night was at the tool-and-
die local, and as we gathered near the back on the way out, someone ran up and reported in hushed tones that Walter had been
shot. I immediately asked if he'd been killed. When I heard that he
hadn't, I replied, in my typically diplomatic manner, "Too bad they
didn't kill the motherfucker," moving several in the immediate vicinity to fisticuffs. I suppose I've earned the hatred I've engendered over the years from the conservatives—particularly Reuther,
who would make me pay dearly before the year was out. In the
meantime, though, Toy was going around arresting people he didn't
like, which prompted me to lead a delegation to the district attorney
and request—to no avail, of course—that the commissioner be
indicted.

The anticlimactic conclusions so common to my various young-
radical adventures were only insignificantly discouraging, the operative thing being that I reveled in the trouble I now had the license
to cause for those who had it coming. I was feeling pretty bold in
those days, walking with a rebel swagger, full of ideological passion
and enough righteous indignation to take on the world. Unfortunately, my nemesis was not as amorphous as that; it was Walter
Reuther. There was none worthier. In all my years in public life and
politics, I've never known a man who better understood power and
how to use it. In retrospect, I find it much easier to respect Reuther
now that I don't have to cross his path.

It helped Reuther, of course, to have the Justice Department at
his side as a red-baiting bedfellow. Anticommunism, in fact, was the
path he had taken to power. Reuther had shrewdly capitalized on
his and the government's common Communist paranoia in his
death-match battle with liberal George Addes to gain control of
the UAW. Knowing that power would accrue to the larger caucus,

Addes and the liberals had attempted to tip the membership in their favor by merging with the left-wing Farm Equipment Workers union. FE agreed to Addes's proposal, but only if given highly placed executive positions within the UAW and preposterous guarantees of autonomy. Meanwhile, as the liberals were scrapping over the bone, Reuther kicked our asses with charges that the farm union was dominated by Communists. When the merger was inevitably voted down, it cleared the way for Reuther's clean sweep of the UAW executive offices, after which he swallowed up the farm union anyway in cooperation with the FBI, which put several of FE's left-wing leaders in jail as anti-American subversives. He also promptly fired George Crockett and Maurice Sugar, the leftist who had been the UAW's influential legal counsel.

Reuther was not reluctant to take advantage of all the anti-Red fervor at his disposal. He worked hand-in-glove with the FBI and other branches of the government's witch-hunting conglomerate, such as the House Un-American Activities Committee, which was becoming a national force well in advance of Senator Joe McCarthy's ignoble crusades. Like McCarthy, and even the likes of Ronald Reagan, Reuther gained popular favor by appealing to his constituents' more primitive instincts, such as fear, hatred, distrust, and bigotry. It was no coincidence that the Reuther camp, while including in its ranks many of the best and the brightest (some of my most valued friends were Reutherites), also embraced most of the perverse and backward elements in the union, such as the gangsters and Klansmen. A master politician who was a CIO international vice-president as well as UAW president, Reuther was blithely able to maintain a civil rights facade by opposing blatant discrimination in several unions, even as he held fast against affirmative action. His fundamental skepticism regarding the capabilities of blacks was exposed when he rejected the concept of a black position on the UAW executive board by asking, "Supposing you elect a man that is not competent to do the kind of job you want done on the minorities problem?" It was a question he never posed in relation to white executives.

Because organized labor inherently represented a proletarian movement, Reuther's deceivingly liberal public image made it maddeningly difficult for his antagonists to draw blood by attacking him from the left. But many labor activists, blacks in particular, had come into unionism through a Marxist rearing, from which perspective Reuther embodied the establishment. Ironically, Reuther's comparative conservatism betrayed a socialist upbringing straight out of Eugene Debs. As young men, he and his brother, Victor, had moved to Gorki to work at an auto plant and immerse themselves in the Russian system. It might, in fact, have been suspicions about his own Americanism and political orientation that drove Reuther to the right.

In the relentless effort to purge the union movement of Communists—and simultaneously wipe out the opposition—Reuther scored big in 1948, when his campaign to rid the CIO of subversive unions netted thirteen scalps, including the United Public Workers. Not content until he had remade American labor in his own image and silenced every whisper of dissent, he then turned his attention to the recalcitrant Wayne County Council.

Through his minion Adolph Germer, Reuther had already begun the process of eradicating us by impounding our assets and freezing our bank account. We had some extra money in the petty cash account, so I raced to the bank and pulled that out to use as operating expenses. It kept us afloat for a while, but by the time of the county convention in September, at the tool-and-die local on the west side, we were so hand-to-mouth that I was paying off our workers behind the stage with twenty-dollar bills until I ran out of them, at which point my sergeant-at-arms threatened to kick my ass. We did not acknowledge our premature demise, however, and assembled for the 1948 convention still in defiance of the international with our support of Henry Wallace and our political independence in general. As a result, the dispute over credentials was predictably impassioned, one point of contention being that the conservative delegates were allowed to participate in the convention by making impromptu per capita payments instead of the monthly installments required by the CIO constitution.

Generally, it took a day or two of the convention just to settle the issue of who would receive credentials in order to vote. Since the union was divided into highly partisan caucuses, every caucus fought like hell to have its members recognized as official delegates. This time, our left-wing caucus stationed two men at the bottom of the stairway leading to the credentials room—a keg-chested Cossack named Alex Semion and a six-foot-eight, three-hundred-pound black guy named Brooches Godfrey. I saw Alex and Brooches defend that stairway against thirty or forty men trying to muscle their way up to get credentials. Meanwhile, at a caucus meeting, one of our guys vowed, "Before we let these bastards take our convention, there will be blood flowing on the convention floor." A few minutes later there was a commotion outside, and we sent somebody to see what was happening. He returned with a knowing look on his face and said, "I've come to report to you that blood has flowed on the floor." One of our men had been hit in the mouth, but one of theirs was lying in a heap, with Alex Semion standing over him.

The partisan maneuvering had roared on eventfully for a full three days when out of the blue, with the vote on credentials impending, Adolph Germer grabbed the microphone and announced that, by the power vested in him by the international CIO, he was declaring a rump convention. The party was officially over. With that, he took the Reutherites to another hall and they held their own convention.

Less than half of the delegates followed Germer, but the numbers didn't matter. The Wayne County Council had been rendered null and void by a CIO dictatorship, and there wasn't a damn thing we could do about it.

5

That Word Is "Negro"

Having contributed generously to the demise of the Wayne County Council, I took stock and determined to commit my unsparing wiles to the Progressive Party foremost. The results, though longer in developing, were ultimately the same.

We should have gotten the message when we were hammered at the polls in 1948, but I surmise that radicals of my stripe and Henry Wallace's are injudiciously optimistic by definition. So I stuck with the party's quixotic platform for another four years, signing on as executive director for Michigan and carrying various banners for the isolated left. The political ferment of Detroit ensured that there would continue to be forums for those of us who had been disenfranchised by the CIO. If anything, the city's ideological profile was higher than ever. In 1949, Pete Seeger sang for a biracial activist organization called the Civil Rights Congress, Paul Robeson lectured at the Forest Club on the constitutional rights of Negro citizens, and my personal black-consciousness pedagogue, the great W.E.B. Du Bois himself, spoke at the Music Hall about colonialism in Africa. After his address, I visited Du Bois backstage and received a private lesson on the white man's self-aggrandizing distortion of African civilization. Then we repaired, as usual, to Reverend Hill's basement, singing and scheming into the early morning.

I ran Reverend Hill's campaign for Common Council again that year, another pause in a long and winding career path of nonpaying positions. My occupation was civil rights, and I freelanced for any number of employers—conscience, God (whom I consulted primarily for political purposes), and the Progressive Party, to name a few—depending on who called that day. Most of my CIO pals were in the same position, and since we were locked out of labor causes, we had to satisfy our activist urges in other ways. Although I had forgotten this until reminded by a Red Squad report—discrimination was so common in downtown Detroit that a single incident wouldn't stand out in my memory any more than a bad joke—the police were called on us at a lunch counter on Michigan Avenue one day when two of my white friends wouldn't accept or pay for their food after the restaurant refused to serve me. We continued to challenge white-only establishments, but after a while that sort of thing became routine. We needed special cases to get our juices flowing, such as when the city ordered newsstands to stop selling subversive literature, i.e., the *Daily Worker.*

The cause célèbre of 1949, however, was the federal indictment in New York of a dozen American Communists, the case being popularly known as the Foley Square Trials. The defendants were charged in violation of the Smith Act of 1940, which declared that it was unlawful to advocate—or to belong to any group that advocated—the forceful overthrow of the United States government. Eleven of the twelve were convicted on the basis of conspiracy, the reality being that, since there was no evidence of a revolutionary plot in the works, their crime was that of conspiring to conspire. From where I stood, and still stand, that was an egregious violation of the First Amendment and tantamount to thought control—a federal regulation of private political beliefs, otherwise known as fascism. The court's position was that the ideology of the Communist Party, as established and practiced in the Soviet Union, constituted sufficient grounds to convict the defendants of representing a clear and present danger to the government. No criminal action was committed at any of the meetings in which the evidence was gathered for their prosecution. The Foley Square eleven were essentially guilty of practicing democracy.

Needless to say, this didn't play well in my corner of Detroit. Several of those convicted—including Ben Davis and Carl Winter, the highest-ranking Communist in Michigan—were familiar figures to us, as was George Crockett, the Detroit attorney who served four months in prison for contempt of court during the Foley Square proceedings. A coalition of protest took up the case when Nat Ganley of the Communist Party, Jack Raskin of the Civil Rights Congress, and I, representing the Progressive Party, presided over a rally to free the Foley bunch. But it proved to be another united effort in futility. The Supreme Court ultimately upheld the constitutionality of the Smith Act, which says quite a bit about where our government was at mid-century.

As it became increasingly obvious that the full-time practice of left-wing politics was an occupationally tenuous proposition, I set about in 1950 to get a real job. The first place any able-bodied Detroit man looked for work was the Ford Motor Company, from which I'd already been fired once. So I lied about that and got hired onto the night shift of Ford's Pressed Steel plant at River Rouge. I didn't mind the hours, because it meant I could pick up Cleveland baseball games, with Doby and Luke Easter, on my Zenith Transoceanic before I punched in. But I had another problem—actually, two. If the company found me out, I would be summarily dismissed; and if the union found me out, I would be summarily fucked. I was more concerned about the union— particularly after I headed to the lunch wagon one night about three A.M. and caught a glimpse down the hall of a rotten right-wing UAW bastard named Henry Mackey. I saw him before he saw me and quickly ducked behind a machine. After a few seconds I peeked around, and that motherfucker was standing there scratching his head as if he thought he'd seen something but wasn't sure. Finally, he went on, but I knew I couldn't come that way again. I subsequently took my lunch in the boxcar where I worked.

In fact, to keep out of sight, I stayed in the boxcar for the whole shift, which meant that I had the worst job in the building. After fenders and hoods came out of the presses, oily-slick and razor-sharp, they were placed on a conveyor that carried them to the boxcars to be stacked and shipped to other plants for filing down, finishing, painting, and assembling. We wore gloves with metal cleats and heavy leather aprons to keep from being sliced up, but even so, nobody wanted to handle that lethal steel any more than necessary. One guy would hand a piece on to the next guy until it reached the boxcar and finally the last man, who worked up high trying to keep the stacks straight and not slip on the grease. That was me. Everybody else drew straws to see who had to be in the boxcar, but I volunteered for it every night. The other guys would say, "Hey, this motherfucker's crazy—he wants all the shitty jobs." But they would bring me my lunch, fight for me, do whatever I wanted, as long as I stayed in that damn boxcar. I was the most popular guy on the job.

One morning, when I got off work around seven, I came out gate 4 and ran into an old union crony named Jimmy Watts, who later became my public works director. He was surprised to see me, and asked, "What are you doing—passing out leaflets again?" Jimmy was a decent guy, but after being kicked out of the CIO I couldn't trust anybody in the union, so I said, "Yeah, passing out leaflets." That was the last time I used gate 4. From then on, I'd walk all the way around to gate 9 or gate 10 to come and go where nobody else would be. I took every precaution and made sure that I was never absent or late, knowing that if I could pass my ninety-day probation period, I could get UAW protection in the event the company tried to fire me. I was proud of myself for steering clear of trouble and thought I had it made, but it turned out that I was only fooling myself. After eighty-nine days, the labor relations director of the plant called me over and informed me that I was gone. When I asked why, he said he didn't have to give a reason why as long as I was still on probation. Apparently I hadn't escaped the notice of Henry Mackey, as I had thought, and the word had gotten around. I told him we both knew goddamn well that I had done my job and been cooperative and was there every fucking day, so what the hell was going on? "Look," he said, "don't bullshit me. This came right from the top, which means that you know a hell of a lot more than I do about what's going on." When I got back to my station and told the foreman what had happened, he was as angry as I was. He went right to the labor relations man and said, "What the hell are you doing to me? You tell me you want more production and then you fire my best man for no goddamn reason!" The foreman was told to shut up or he'd be fired, too.

With that, I went to Dodge and got a job in the foundry. They had a carryall to take people from the employment office and drop them off at the various buildings, and by the time we arrived at the foundry—not fifteen minutes after I'd been hired—there was a guy waiting for me as I climbed out of the carryall, shaking his head. The information, whatever it was, had come over the teletype. The upshot was, I couldn't work anywhere in the automobile industry.

Upon hearing of my predicament, my friend Hal Shapiro of the Fur and Leather Workers managed to find employment for me at Schwayder Brothers in Ecorse, which manufactured Samsonite luggage and chairs and card tables. Hal explained to King Schwayder that I was being jacked around or blacklisted or whatever for my political activities, and Schwayder consented to do Hal a favor and take me on. My job was operating the machine that cut out the tabletops. I thought the skills required were within my range of capabilities, but twenty-nine days later—the union contract carried a one-month probationary period—I was laid off. Since the plant operated on a seasonal basis, I assumed that was the reason they were letting me go; but when I went back for my paycheck, I was surprised to see that they were hiring people. So Hal stormed into the plant and looked up the foreman, who assured him that my work had met their standards. Then he talked to the plant manager, who said that if he wanted any more information he had to talk to King Schwayder, because they both knew what was happening and there was nothing he could say or do. At that point, Hal and I realized that the blacklist circulated beyond the offices of the UAW. I was being hung out to dry by the Justice Department of the United States government.

Seeing that there was no use in venturing into the mainstream, I pulled back and took refuge among my own. Jack Raskin and I opened a dry cleaner on Livernois, hoping that there was a living to be made on the shirts and slacks of Progressives and Communists and the assorted dialectical ideologues who frequented Haywood Maben's barbershop. I've heard people say that they couldn't get their pants back because we were always arguing about Wallace or Truman or Du Bois or Doby or whatever, but I think that's bullshit. I was a hell of a spotter. It's just that there wasn't much of a call for politically enlightened spotters in those days. So I tried teaching a night class on labor, seeing as how I'd been such a roaring success in the movement. Then I washed walls for a while with a guy named Max Chait. I was in low cotton.

As is often the case when things go badly outside the home, they were going badly inside, too. The times were harder on Marion than on me, because we were being assessed heavily for *my* principles. I at least had my conscience—which didn't do a damn thing for Marion when she suffered complications from her pregnancy and sat hemorrhaging on a bench in the hospital lobby for an hour and a half while I raced around town trying to borrow or beg $150. We couldn't get her checked in on time, and because of that, I'm confident, she lost the baby.

I have to take responsibility for what happened with Marion and the baby—I was neither an attentive husband nor a good provider—but at the same time I can't let the federal government off the hook. I can't dismiss the memory of how deeply and relentlessly the FBI fucked with people's lives in those days. I wasn't privy to the pillaging of Hollywood, where actors and directors were being blacklisted; but in my world, I saw Robeson reduced to playing union halls, stripped of his popularity by the condemnation of the press and government, and Du Bois chased off to Africa, where he ultimately died in exile. Nearer to home, I saw a dear man like Sid Rosen driven out of his jewelry business in Grosse Pointe Park by damning newspaper and FBI persecution, even as he was spending his last dollars taking care of his wife's mother, who was dying of cancer.

Even nearer to home, I found out firsthand that the government had no trace of respect for a person's family. In its efforts to get to me, the FBI approached my straight-arrow brother George and told him that the situation between Marion and me was so ugly that she had threatened to kill me. To give their story some credibility, they said that she was going to do it with a Beretta, an Italian pistol that George had given to me as a gift after the war; they must have known about the Beretta from taping our conversations. George swallowed it hard. One night, at the family home on Harding, he signaled me to come upstairs with him to the third-floor attic. All the way up there, he was glancing back over his shoulder as if afraid somebody was watching or listening. I couldn't help laughing, which infuriated George, because this was serious business to him. George had a job at the post office—he eventually worked his way up to assistant postmaster—and was in jeopardy of losing it if the government thought that it could intimidate or punish me through him.

They pulled the same routine on my father, with very different results. When he was getting off from his night shift in the Federal Building early one morning, an FBI agent walked up and asked him to step into the Bureau office on the ninth floor, where he was subjected to a battery of questions about my political activities. My father said that he had no control over me, because when a son became twenty-one he became a man with his own ideas and his own life. The FBI guy must have persisted, because something made my father say "God damn it!" and reach for his .45. They escorted him out of the building and didn't bother him again.

Nearly everyone on the far left had a story or two about FBI harassment. There didn't seem to be a level low enough for those pricks to stoop to, and with enemies licensed and unscrupulous as that, we stuck close to our friends. Hal and Esther Shapiro's house was a second home to me and others, a place to talk politics and drink beer late into the night without Ike and Mike. On one occasion, as I recall, Esther excused herself to go to bed, and a few hours later Hal and I had the poor judgment to wake her up and ask for breakfast, which prompted her to throw us both out of the house. She also tossed me out once for making fun of a friend of hers whom I didn't consider to be sufficiently virile. We were young.

Through it all, we had a pretty damn good time together for a battered group of political misfits, which says something about misery and company. We went to the same houses, the same picnics, the same fund-raisers, and the same black-and-tans (integrated clubs) on John R, which, as a nightlife district, had become a poor imitation of Paradise Valley thirty years before. There was an unusual number of interracial marriages among our crowd. But most important, for all of our social, ethnic, and ideological differences, we shared the same preoccupation with the plight of the working class—in particular, the black working class. Given that the company consisted largely of those who had been purged from the CIO, and given that most of us still believed unshakably in the radical changes required within the American labor force to effect equal opportunity, it was inevitable that we would organize again. Not only in Detroit but around the country, there was a deep void inside those who had been members of the thirteen left-wing unions Walter Reuther had cut adrift.

After three years of restless disfranchisement, the leftist labor movement was reincarnated—smaller, peskier, and more focused than ever—on October 27, 1951, as the National Negro Labor Council. The charter meeting was held in Cincinnati, with Paul Robeson singing and the NNLC dedicating itself to two basic goals: attaining jobs for blacks in places where we had previously been excluded, such as banks, airlines, and department stores; and winning executive positions for blacks within labor and trade unions, on the order of my short-lived stint on the Wayne County Council. William Hood of UAW Local 600 was elected NNLC president, I was elected executive secretary, and council headquarters—i.e., my desk and phone—were set up on Grand River in Detroit.

The first order of business was establishing branches in major cities around the country, which we accomplished at a dizzying pace. Our approach was to encourage the formation of black caucuses within various unions and use them as nuclei around which to attract white support in the creation of NNLC chapters. We drew regional and national leadership from a wide range of cooperative left-wing unions, such as the longshoremen and the electrical workers and the fur and leather workers. Some of our recruiting procedures—as well as our methods of protest—were later adopted by Martin Luther King, Jr., as part of the formula for the civil rights movement. They worked for us. We quickly swelled to twenty-two ambitious chapters, prompting many to speculate that our membership and scope would soon exceed that of the NAACP, which was being sucked in by the treacherous anti-Red whirlpool and closing its ranks to those who would pursue civil rights from the far left.

Although we were not at cross-purposes with the NAACP, we considered its agenda to be a little too genteel for our designs. There was no disguising the fact that we were a hell-raising outfit, operating on the premise that the struggle for jobs had to be carried forward with the tactics of mass protest, such as picketing, boycotts, and national campaigns. It was a matter of introducing union methods to the pursuit of social equality.

The specific civil right to which the NNLC dedicated itself was economic liberation. Intent upon creating a hundred thousand jobs in our first year, we concentrated initially on the South, attempting to break down Jim Crow standards in a campaign we called Operation Dixie. Recognizing this—and our agenda in general—as a formidable and troublesome task, we placed a quote from Frederick Douglass at the top of our letterhead: "Without struggle, there is no progress." We struggled; and gradually, systematically, we made progress. For a time, we fixed our attention on the discriminatory Louisville plants of Ford and General Electric. As a result, both companies increased their numbers of black employees in Louisville, Ford complying after the UAW began to investigate the hiring policies there and GE responding to a demonstration in front of its New York headquarters in which we distributed a hundred thousand copies of a pamphlet called "Give Us This Day Our Daily Bread." We also organized a booming NNLC chapter at an R. J. Reynolds tobacco plant in North Carolina.

Whenever possible, it behooved us to wage our battles in public view, capitalizing on the embarrassment of the large companies to whom we carried the campaign. This strategy proved unfortunate for the likes of American Airlines, which had the bad luck to be located in close proximity to the Cleveland hotel at which our 1952 convention was held. American's discriminatory employment practices were standard for the industry, but this did not dissuade me from calling them to the attention of the NNLC membership, upon which the whole damn convention poured out into the street. There were nearly two thousand of us, and we immobilized downtown Cleveland, which of course attracted the media, which of course is what we wanted.

Although American was a deserving target and our action was successful, we typically placed top priority on companies that merchandised in black communities. The most visible was Sears, Roebuck, which, located as it was in central cities, attracted black and working-class customers who would be most inclined to honor our picket lines. We commenced to picket in Detroit, Chicago, Los Angeles, and San Francisco, and soon thereafter scored our first nationwide triumph as black janitors and maintenance people in Sears stores all around the country were upgraded to clerks and cashiers. Woolworth's was slower to respond—its southern branches would be more famously integrated in the early sixties—but we made some headway. When we applied pressure to a Woolworth's store in Chicago, the manager announced that hell would freeze over before he would hire black women clerks (echoes of Henry Ford), then had to swallow his words when our boycott cut into his sales by more than eighty percent.

Meanwhile, there was plenty of hell to be raised in our immediate vicinity. Hood and I met with Ford officials and persuaded them to hire black clerical workers for the first time. We also made inroads at Big Bear Markets and Sam's Cut Rate, the latter being a delicious victory for me in light of my father's rude dismissal from there. A concerted campaign was directed at Bank of the Commonwealth, one of whose branches was located adjacent to a thriving black business district. Naturally, many of the black businessmen banked there, and they were loath to cross the picket line in order to make their deposits. This pressure-forced a meeting with the president of the bank, a drawling Frenchman from Mississippi who invited us to discuss the matter in his office downtown. When I explained that all we asked was for the bank to employ blacks as clerks and tellers, he replied, "If we hire black men for positions like that, the next thing you know they'll want to marry white women." I told him we were looking for employment applications, not marriage licenses, a possibility that he considered and finally accepted. Against all of his inbred southern instincts, he then proceeded, pragmatically, to break the bank's color line.

These small and large successes were among numerous signs of the NNLC's impact on the labor front, the most telling of which might have been the sharp reaction to us from the rest of the movement. We were obviously the bad boys of labor. James Carey, the secretary-treasurer of the CIO, assailed the NNLC as "a tool of the Soviet Union." And of course Walter Reuther had much to say about us. In a gratuitous UAW press release, the union membership and the general public were warned by Reuther that "the Detroit Negro Labor Council actually works against the best interest of all the American people by attempting to destroy genuine civil rights movements and increasing inter-group tension. . . . During the last year the Detroit Council has sabotaged the sincere and genuine efforts of a Detroit citizens' committee, including the CIO, the NAACP and other liberal groups, to bring about the enactment of a local fair employment practices ordinance." The latter comment was made in reference to the NNLC's protests over the union's inadequate Fair Employment Practice Committees legislation, which we regarded as a token attempt to appease the black interests. It also riled Reuther that we continued to push for black representation on the UAW executive board. Since I was the NNLC's point man on these issues and its only full-time administrator, Reuther was obviously referring to me when he further charged that "the man is acting as an individual. . . ." Lest anyone still not get the picture, he concluded that "the UAW-CIO does not support in any way either the Detroit council or the formation of the national group."

Thus repudiated by Walter Reuther, we knew we were on the right track.

BY 1952, the House Un-American Activities Committee had taken its act on the road, seeking out stool pigeons from coast to coast in the gallant, patriotic pursuit of red-blooded subversives. Naturally, Detroit was on the itinerary.

The HUAC, as intended, had been blazing a trail of terror through the country. Taking the offensive against the alleged Communist/Soviet/subversive forces it suspected to be covertly operating within government and industry, the committee was bent on bringing to bear the full, unchecked authority of its office in a sacrosanct crusade to expose un-American activities and their advocates. This translated to intimidation with impunity, a smear campaign whose awful power could be manifested in the mere naming of names.

The effect on those fingered in the hearings was devastating; yet it had little, if anything, to do with the reliability of the testimony. Many of the witnesses were untrained informants paid to bring names before the committee, while others were trembling unionists eager to say whatever the disquieting United States congressmen wanted to hear. The hearings had no judicial relevance, but this was of little solace to those who had been fired, beaten, and hung in effigy at their factories. To appear before the committee was so unnerving that Langston Hughes, the standard-bearing black poet, had been frightened into refuting one of his most famous works, a surrender that shamed him to the point of leaving the country.

When it was learned that the committee was carrying its inquisition to Detroit at the end of February, Hal and Esther Shapiro set up cots in their living room for friends who were hiding from subpoenas. One morning, their five-year-old son came downstairs for breakfast, rubbed his eyes, and matter-of-factly asked Esther, "Who do we know that's in jail today?" Even in advance of the public hearings, stool pigeons had been meeting privately with government agents to rat on the radicals of their close or distant acquaintance. While the informants remained anonymous, the names of the accused made it into the newspapers. A few days before the hearings, John Cherveny, a white auto worker and student activist at Wayne State University, had been threatened with a noose by his UAW co-workers after it was reported that he was under investigation by the committee.

Those subpoenaed to testify at the hearings—whose ranks included me and a fair share of the people I knew best—could never be certain whether they would be grilled about their own activities or their friends' or both. It was a common and simple strategy for a witness to invoke the Fifth Amendment as a defense against incriminating himself, but the protection of others was a trickier proposition, as the committee well knew. Against the advice of George Crockett, my attorney, I made up my mind to attack that problem with the First Amendment, asserting that any inquiry into my or another's ideological positions was a violation of my or his freedom of speech and privacy of political beliefs. Crockett, who after being dismissed by Reuther had made history by becoming the first black lawyer in a prestigious white law firm, was not the retreating type, and I respected his opinion that it was sufficient—and safer—to hide behind the Fifth; but I wasn't hiding from those bastards. I wanted them to come and get me.

Stanley Nowak, the state senator and Reverend Hill's Common Council running mate, was the first witness scheduled to testify in Detroit, but he was ill and did not appear. NNLC president William Hood was next, which made it obvious to me that the Labor Council was of major interest to the committee. Most of the witnesses were addressed initially by the committee's counsel, a Virginian named Frank Tavenner, who started off with Hood by asking when and where he was born. Hood replied, "I was born in 1910, but I categorically refuse to tell you where I was born. My father and mother are still in Georgia. I will write the name to the committee. My uncle was killed by a mob. I don't want them persecuted. I talked with my mother already and the hysteria created [in their] Georgia city . . . With my father in business and my sister a schoolteacher in Georgia, I don't want them persecuted or to have reprisals as the result of my behavior in the city of Detroit."

Later in the hearing, Tavenner read what he alleged to be Hood's Communist Party registration number for 1947, to which Hood responded by charging, "That's a damn lie." Although one might presume that evidence as hard and tangible as a registration card would be rather unimpeachable, I had no difficulty in believing Hood. My own experience in that area has shown the government to be capable of producing some very specious data in regard to registration cards. For instance, one of my FBI reports suggested that I had filled out a party card under an assumed name in 1946, at the same time indicating that I had been a party member for six years—in which case, why would I be filling out a new card?

Following Hood was Reverend Hill, who, in addition to his activist history, was president of the Detroit chapter of the NNLC. George Crockett was also his attorney, and the Reverend took Crockett's advice so seriously that he might have set a record by using the Fifth Amendment forty-nine times. Undaunted, the committee continued to press him with questions about his affiliations and associations until finally my mentor explained himself in a way that spoke for all of us. "I have been interested in primarily one thing," he said, "and that is discrimination, segregation, the second-class citizenship that my people suffer. And as long as I live, until it is eradicated from this American society, I will accept the cooperation of anybody who wants to make America the land of the free and the home of the brave."

I couldn't have said it better myself, although I tried like hell the next day. My testimony was on February 28, and I'd done my homework. Since the hearing was supposed to be about un-American activities, I'd kept that theme in mind as I conducted a little research into the high tribunal before which I had been summoned. It didn't surprise me a bit to find out that none of those congressmen had a goddamn thing to be proud of in terms of public service, and given their personal histories, I was incensed that they would have the nerve to question anyone else's Americanism. I thought this to be particularly true of the motherfucker from Georgia who headed the committee, Congressmen John Wood. I took the trouble to investigate his district and discovered that while over half of it was black, less than two percent of the blacks in his constituency had been allowed to vote. Given this, and the poll tax and the lynchings and the Jim Crow laws that had come to characterize the South, my attitude was, Why should I take any crap off this son of a bitch from Georgia? If they wanted to talk about my radical politics, hell, there's nothing as radical as the Constitution and the Bill of Rights. I was ready to take them on.

While I was shadow-boxing in my mind, the committee opened in a deceptively conciliatory posture. "Mr. Young," said Tavenner at the outset, "I want to state to you in advance of questioning you that the investigators of the committee have not produced or presented any evidence of Communist Party membership on your part. The purpose in asking you to come here is to inquire into the activities of some of the organizations with which you have been connected. . . ."

There was also something I wanted to state to him in advance. I told Tavenner that I was before him not of my own prerogative but because I had been subpoenaed. Knowing that I would shortly be assuming the offensive, I wanted to make it clear in advance that I was doing so only in response to the committee and its questions. "I can only state," I said, "that in being interviewed and being asked questions, that I hope that I will be allowed to react fully to those questions, and not be expected to react only in such a manner that this committee may desire me. In other words, I might have answers you might not like. You called me here to testify; I am prepared to testify. But I would like to know from you if I shall be allowed to respond to your questions fully and in my own way."

Tavenner replied that he would have no objections to my answers as long as they were responsive to the questions. Then, having carefully assured me right off the bat that the committee had no reason to link me to the Communist Party, he asked, "Are you now a member of the Communist Party?"

The bell had rung. "I refuse to answer that question," I said, "relying upon my rights under the Fifth Amendment and in light of the fact that to answer such a question, before such a committee, would be, in my opinion, a violation of my rights under the First Amendment, which provides for freedom of speech, sanctity, and privacy of political beliefs. . . . And further, since I have no purpose of being here as a stool pigeon, I am not prepared to give any information on any of my associates or political thoughts."

Despite Crockett's skepticism, I was operating under the theory that I could use the amendments as a couplet, sallying forth with the First and then holding up the Fifth in order to draw back and take cover. But I had to be careful about saying too much. The application of the Fifth Amendment, as I understood it, was that once a witness used the Fifth to close off a particular field of questioning, the committee couldn't enter that field. But once he answered a question in a certain area, he surrendered his Fifth Amendment privileges on that subject and had to respond to all related questions. It was a risky plan, but my strategy was to dance around and keep the bastards off balance—to dazzle them with my footwork, get in some good licks, then put up my guard by taking the Fifth.

"Have you been a member of the Communist Party?"

"For the same reason, I refuse to answer that question."

"You told us," said Tavenner in his plantation dialect, "you were the executive secretary of the National Niggra Congress—"

"That word is 'Negro,' not 'Niggra.' "

"I said 'Negro.' I think you are mistaken."

"I hope I am. Speak more clearly."

With that, I flushed out my friend from Georgia. "I will appreciate it if you will not argue with counsel," Wood said.

"It isn't my purpose to argue," I replied. "As a Negro, I resent the slurring of the name of my race."

The hearings were as big as the damn World Series in Detroit, and they were broadcast live on radio, which meant that the whole city heard me reprimand the government counselor. Over the next few weeks, and over the years, this was the exchange that people seemed to remember and repeat about my testimony. I suppose it got their attention because of the unexpected defiance, and that's fine. I meant to be defiant. I thought it was important to show the country and those self-righteous congressional sons of bitches that people like me wouldn't be intimidated any longer. But my mission that day was not to thumb my nose at Washington bigshots or to clarify their pronunciation of "Negro." I was there to have it out over the issue of un-Americanism. To hit back, absorb the blows, and keep coming. If I could score some style points along the way, so much the better.

But I could not afford to be reckless, which is what the committee wanted me to be. Knowing that I wouldn't stay on my feet if I walked into their best punches, I shuffled and ducked by refusing to answer any question about any organization that was already on the committee's subversive list. That included Reverend Hill's National Negro Congress, for which I'd been an officer before the war.

Tavenner: "Your position is that to answer any question with relation to your connection with the National Negro Congress might tend to incriminate you. Is that your position?"

"The National Negro Congress, as I understand it, has been labeled by not only the Justice Department but by this committee, which also labeled the National Association for the Advancement of Colored People as subversive, and I don't intend to discuss any organization that properly or improperly has been designated by your or any other committee as subversive."

Actually, the NAACP was not on the official subversive list, but it had been referred to in that manner by a former committee member. As we argued the technicalities of that point, the Republican congressman from Michigan, Charles Potter, broke in by saying, "We are here to find out the extent of the Communist activities in this area. You are in a position to help and aid, if you will, but the attitude you are taking is uncooperative to such an investigation."

"I am not here to fight in any un-American activities," I said, "because I consider the denial of the right to vote to large numbers of people all over the South un-American. . . ."

Tavenner: "Do you consider the activities of the Communist Party un-American?"

"I consider the activities of this committee, as it cites people for allegedly being a Communist, as un-American activities."

Tavenner: "Are you acquainted with any of the activities of the Communist Party in the city of Detroit?"

"I meant to make it clear that I consider any questions that deal with my political beliefs or with the beliefs of people I may or may not have been associated with a violation of my rights under the Fifth Amendment and an invasion of my privacy guaranteed me under the First Amendment."

Tavenner: "I asked you no question regarding your individual beliefs. I asked if you knew of any activities of the Communist Party in your community which might be of some assistance to this committee in its investigation of un-American activities. I understood from your statement you would like to help us."

"You have me mixed up with a stool pigeon."

Potter: "I have never heard of anybody stooling in the Boy Scouts."

"I was a member of that organization."

Potter: "I don't think they are proud of it today."

"I will let the Scouts decide that."

Tavenner was still determined to get me to talk about the National Negro Congress, and I was determined not to. However, I offered to supply information about the organization I administered at that moment, the National Negro Labor Council, which had not been placed on a subversive list—a condition that the committee apparently considered to be only temporary: it was trying to establish that the NNLC was actually an extension of the earlier NNC and consequently deserving of the same government classification as a subversive organization. I was bobbing and weaving to have the NNLC evaluated on its own purposes and merits. An exchange of semantics and fine points ensued, prompting the impatient congressman from Georgia to point out, "This is not a vaudeville here. This is serious business." Grateful for that sober revelation, I proceeded to read the preamble of the NNLC into the testimony.

Wood: "I want you to answer in what way the preamble you read of the National Niggra Labor Council differs, if any, in respect to the National Niggra Congress."

I might have let it pass this time had they not pushed me by asking the same goddamn thing over and over despite my repeated insistence that I would not answer any question relating to any organization on their list. "I would inform you also," I said to the congressman, "the word is 'Negro.' "

Wood: "I am sorry. If I made a different pronouncement of it, it is due to my inability to use the language any better than I do. I am trying to use it properly."

"It may be due to your southern background."

Wood: "I am not ashamed of my southern background. For your information, out of the 112 Negro votes cast in the last election in the little village from which I come, I got 112 of them. That ought to be a complete answer of that. Now, will you answer the question?"

"You are through with it now? Is that it?"

Wood: "I don't know."

"I happen to know, in Georgia, Negro people are prevented from voting by virtue of terror, intimidation, and lynchings. It is my contention you would not be in Congress today if it were not for the legal restrictions on voting on the part of my people."

Wood: "I happen to know that is a deliberate false statement on your part."

"My statement is on the record."

Wood: "Mine is, too."

To the best of my knowledge, my testimony was marking the first time anyone had turned the tables on the committee, and it put its smug archconservatives on the defensive. I wasn't about to back off. When they accused me of only selectively answering their questions, I accused them of only selectively investigating un-American activities—meaning that they had paid no attention to the unconstitutional atrocities of the South.

"At the moment," Wood responded, "we are investigating un-American activities we are asking you about and have been asking you about. Do you plan to answer them?"

"I consider it an un-American activity to pry into a person's private thoughts, to pry into a person's associates. I consider that an un-American activity."

"Is that your reason for not answering?"

"I am unwilling to engage in un-American activities."

Refusing to take no answer for an answer, the committee persisted in bombarding me with questions I wouldn't consider honoring. "Sir," I said finally to one of Tavenner's tiresome interrogations, "I have explained to you my refusal to answer such questions. I think it would be quite foolish on my part, in view of the hysteria stirred up by this committee, in view of the many bills having to do with people's political associations, etc., to indicate to you on any question any information which might amount to testifying against myself. Therefore, under the Fifth Amendment, I refuse to answer."

"If there is any hysteria in this country," replied Potter, "it is generated by people like yourself, and not by this committee."

Now, that made me angry. "Congressman," I said, "neither me or none of my friends were out at the plant the other day brandishing a rope in the face of John Cherveny. I can assure you I have had no part in the hanging or bombing of Negroes in the South.

THAT WORD IS "NEGRO"

I have not been responsible for firing a person from his job for what I think are his beliefs, or what somebody thinks he believes in, and things of that sort. That is the hysteria that has been swept up by this committee."

"Today, there are fourteen thousand casualties in Korea testifying to this fact of hysteria you so blandly mention," retorted Potter, who was also angry, "which is a cold-blooded conspiracy, which is killing American boys; and you, as members of the Communist Party of the United States, are just as much a part of the international conspiracy as the Communists in North Korea who are killing men there."

The longer we went on, the more puzzled I became over Tavenner's opening assertion that the committee did not regard me as a Communist. Potter directly contradicted Tavenner in the course of his feckless Korean parable, and in general the committee went to great length to portray me at least as a Communist sympathizer, which was sufficiently damning in their eyes. Despite my status as a global menace and murderer, as brought to attention by the levelheaded legislator from Michigan, the committee's principal interest in me seemed to pertain to the meetings I had attended—the one with New Yorker Benjamin Davis was brought up, as might have been expected—and the candidates I supported. I maintained that I favored the candidates who best represented my goals and those of my community.

"Is that regardless of whether or not he was elected on the Communist Party ticket, as a part of the Communist Party movement, if you knew it to be such?" Tavenner asked.

"Well . . . I would think that Negro people would be more interested in what a given candidate's program might happen to be, and what he was going to do to improve the conditions of Negro people, than [in] any label tagged on him by such a committee as yourselves and others."

". . . Therefore, if the Communist Party carried out its avowed objectives, its avowed program of working through mass organization—that is, by selecting groups of people and appealing to the particular items which that group is interested in, and organizing them as a Communist front organization—because that's what those organizations are—you would support such a thing, knowing that it is a Communist front organization?"

"You can—"

"Is that the sense and sum and substance of what you told us?"

"You can draw the substance and sum you wish from my last answer, but under the Fifth Amendment, I am not answering any question dealing with the Communist Party, and, I think, for pretty obvious reasons."

"You state you would sustain anyone who took a position which was favorable to the particular thing you were interested in?"

"When I go to the ballot box, as of now, I have privacy. I vote as I see fit. Are you trying to invade the privacy of my ballot box?"

"Not at all," Tavenner said.

"I don't see why you ask these questions."

"It is a very important question."

"You asked me how I vote."

"It is a very important matter to determine to what extent the Communists, through Communist front organizations, are endeavoring to injure the economics of this area, the religion of this area, and, in fact, the whole political structure as we know it in this country."

"Well, I leave that to you."

The committee undertook that solemn responsibility with conspicuous relish. There was some disagreement within the left wing as to whether the government was legitimately concerned with American communism or was simply using it as a hammer to crush the radical elements of the union movement, which were perceived as incompatible with the existing power structure; but from where I sat, if the government wasn't concerned about Communist and particularly Soviet influences in America, it went to a hell of a lot of trouble to make it seem that way.

To wit, the Soviet threat was the basis of a protracted cross-examination to which I was subjected by Congressman Donald Jackson of California.

"You said that there is a whole lot wrong with all the world," Jackson said.

I responded by saying that I was interested in the United States, not the whole world.

"Let us not lose freedom—"

"That is the point, Mr. Jackson. I am fighting for freedom myself."

"So am I. Let us not lose individual freedom and human dignity by sacrificing to an order of things which has filled concentration camps to overflowing. If you think of the lot of the Negro, who has in eighty-some-odd years come forward to a much better position—"

"Mr. Jackson," I interrupted, "we are not going to wait eighty or more years, I will tell you that."

"Neither are the Communists. They say they are going to overthrow the government by force and violence and effect all the changes immediately."

"If you are telling me to wait eighty years, I will tell you that I am not prepared to wait and neither are the Negroes."

"Neither is the Communist Party."

"I am speaking for the Negro people and for myself. Are you speaking for the Communist Party?" I couldn't resist that one.

"I am speaking *of* the Communist Party."

"I thought you were speaking *for* the Communist Party."

That little repartee concluded my visit with Congressman Jackson, leaving one final fox trot with my amiable neighbor Congressman Potter, who moments before had charged me with giving aid not only to the North Koreans but also to the Red Chinese by simple virtue of my political disposition. This time, he played a Russian number.

"As you well know," Potter said, "the Communist International as dictated from Soviet Russia is probably the most stringent form of totalitarian government in the world today. In case—and God forbid that it ever happens—but in case the Soviet Union should attack the United States, would you serve as readily to defend our country in case of such eventuality as you did during the last war?"

"As I told you, Congressman, nobody has had to question the patriotism, the military valor of the Negro people. We have fought in every war."

"I am not talking about the Negro people. I am talking about you."

"I am coming to me. I am a part of the Negro people. I fought in the last war, and I would unhesitatingly take up arms against anybody that attacks this country. In the same manner, I am now in the process of fighting against what I consider to be attacks and discrimination against my people. I am fighting against un-American activities such as lynchings and denial of the vote. I am dedicated to that fight, and I don't think I have to apologize or explain it to anybody, my position on that."

"Mr. Young, you have many, many groups in this country that have the same purpose as you are sponsoring here," Potter informed me. "Let me tell you this—the thing that you claim is your objective will not be accomplished by men like yourself."

"That is your opinion."

"Absolutely that is my opinion, and that is all."

I was finished, but the committee wasn't finished with me. The star witness the next day was a kindly grandmother named Bereniece Baldwin, who had been the office secretary at the Communist Party district headquarters. It turned out that the sweet Mrs. Baldwin was an FBI stooge who, to the committee's great pleasure, eagerly rattled off a long recitation of Detroit Communists. When my name came before her, she said that I was "a regular visitor" to the Communist offices. "It seemed he had various problems that came up with the Progressive Party, and he would want to take [them] up with the leaders of the Communist Party. He held many meetings there." To me, this suggested that I had been gathering intelligence from those who had already been through some of the mine fields that lay ahead for the Progressive Party. To the HUAC, it seemed to imply that I was Stalin's right-hand man.

The reality of the day was that anyone who took an active interest in the plight of black people was naturally drawn toward the Communist Party—not as a member, necessarily, but at least as a friend and ally, owing to the fact that the Communists historically had been out front in the struggle for civil rights. The prevailing paranoia about communism was consequently translated into a paranoia about civil rights—although, in retrospect, it is difficult to say which was the predominant phobia. It seemed that the government was unable to make any distinction between civil rights and communism, and by extension, between civil rights and subversion. As a result, the operative federal credo was the paradoxical and alarmingly unconstitutional notion that the struggle for equality was inherently un-American. For black people, that was the basic problem: the quest for civil rights—liberty, justice, equality, and happiness for all—was un-American in the eyes of the United States government. It was all but impossible for a black person to avoid the Communist label as long as he or she advocated civil rights with any degree of vigor. By the standard of Congress and the Justice Department, the two were married.

Enforcement of this rabid position depended primarily upon the investigative offices of J. Edgar Hoover, whose apparent contention it was that every liberal labor leader as well was inherently Communist. This represented a double whammy when linked with Hoover's legendary loathing of black rabble-rousers. His first major assignment as a young FBI director produced the trumped-up charges that led to the imprisonment and eventual deportation in 1927 of Marcus Garvey, controversial founder of the Universal Negro Improvement Association; and in a way, Hoover stayed on the same damn case—the persecution of those who would organize black citizens in the pursuit of what was rightfully theirs—for the rest of his seemingly eternal career, substituting new names and faces through the years. The heroine of my Army years, Eleanor Roosevelt, had one of the fattest FBI files, documenting her subversive activities on behalf of civil rights.

The Bureau, like most organizations, reflected its leader. It seemed to be interested in black people only insofar as it could place us in a Communist context, real or contrived, and dogged us relentlessly to that end. I hadn't realized the depth of the FBI's concern about me until I read one of the early reports in my file, involving an organizing meeting for UAW Local 600. The names of four of the people at the meeting were blacked out on the report, which suggested that they were FBI informants. The thing is, there were only five people there. Apparently, I was the only mother-fucker at the meeting who wasn't on the FBI payroll. I guess I was being heavily covered.

The Bureau's reliance on paid informants caused a considerable amount of unwarranted trouble for a considerable number of people, and it played havoc with the veracity of FBI evidence. With money at stake, it was all too common for informants to make up fanciful stories to justify their own existence. A hell of a lot of what they reported was pure fiction, and the percentage of fabrication was likely to be higher if the individual being investigated happened to be out in the forefront. Since I tended to be everywhere talking to everybody, the informants knew that it delighted their superiors to receive a report on me, which might not have been so abominable but for the Bureau's enthusiasm for embracing bogus information as fact. Some damn stool pigeon on the fringes of the movement would declare that half the Progressive Party was Communist, and that would serve as the official estimate until a better one came along.

When Hal Shapiro testified before the HUAC, he was jolted by a blindside blitz of FBI methodology. Near the end of the hearing, Tavenner said that he had information from a friendly witness named Michaelson that Hal was the treasurer of the Downriver Club of the Ford section of the Communist Party. Knowing that if he told the committee he had never heard of the Downriver Club of the Ford section of the Communist Party—which he hadn't—he could be indicted for perjury because the FBI informer had reported to the contrary, Hal grudgingly opted to take the Fifth. Meanwhile, as he debated with Tavenner and tried to recall who the hell Michaelson was, the picture came into focus. Michaelson was a bit player who had hung out at the Civil Rights Congress, which had its offices on the same floor as Hal's fur and leather local. Hal vaguely remembered that one day, as he was walking down the hall, Michaelson approached and handed him two bucks or so. Hal asked what it was for, and Michaelson said something like "You know" and walked away. Hal figured the guy just made a mistake, maybe believing he had borrowed a couple of dollars, and never thought about it again until he was on the hot seat in front of the congressional committee, at which time he suddenly realized that Michaelson had been setting him up as treasurer of the Downriver Club of the Ford section of the Communist Party—which name the informant apparently made up—by paying him dues.

For all the dastardly things that they did, I've never known anyone in the FBI to show any conscience in regard to either their procedures or the hell we were put through. I always had the feeling, though, that the FBI knew that we knew what was going on. I remember, after my HUAC hearing, getting into the elevator at the Federal Building with a few of my friends—probably George Crockett and Hal and Dave Moore of Local 600—at the same time as John Bugas, a former FBI honcho who had become the president of Ford, many of whose executives attended the hearings with a vested interest. I was in a snarly mood, grumbling about this motherfucker and that son of a bitch and what I would do to that other bastard if I ever caught him, all the while staring right at Bugas. Correctly sensing that he was in unfriendly company, Bugas just held up his hands and said, "Look, fellas, I had no part of this. I just came down here to observe." I can't say positively that the erstwhile fed was disavowing the committee's tactics, but I prefer to think that he was. In our relationship with the FBI, we had to savor the small moments.

Although I couldn't have known it as I rode down that elevator, the un-American hearing that had put me in such a combative temper would ultimately come to represent a much larger moment. It emerged as a symbol for the committee's Detroit stopover, which as I viewed it marked the beginning of the end of the HUAC. The public had been getting a little fed up with the congressmen's churlish bullying, and it didn't take much of a shove to put them on their heels. After Detroit, they carried their act to Chicago, where they were kicked in the ass a little more. Rather than cowering before the committee, people all over the country began to question the credentials of its members and the implicit un-Americanism of its very existence.

This is not to imply that redbaiting had been swiftly vanquished as a favorite pastime, as I found out a week or so after the hearings. I accompanied John Cherveny on a soapbox appearance at his

Wayne State campus, where we were met by a crowd of about four hundred hecklers, many of them athletes, who, as a group, were notorious for bringing muscle to the right wing. As we spoke, the students shouted us down with Communist epithets and sang "Back to Moscow" to the tune of "The Volga Boatman." The moment Cherveny stopped talking, he was handed a summons to appear before the HUAC, which would be reconvening in Detroit after a ten-day recess.

By contrast, in the friendlier environment of the east side I felt like Joe Louis home from a title fight. People called out my name as I walked down the street, and small crowds gathered when I stopped. Guys patted my back in the barbershop. Someone even made a phonograph record of my testimony before the committee, and it was the biggest hit in my part of town. I was a fucking hero. Strange as it all seemed, though—to be on top, that is, after taking so many kicks in the head—I understood what was happening. It was a vicarious thing. I had said words that the people of Black Bottom had dreamed all their lives of saying to a southern white man. I had talked back to the plantation boss and gotten away with it. I had stood up to the landlord and told off the foreman. I had spoken for all of them, and they were standing a little taller.

A group of citizens even asked me to run again for the state senate, this time as a Democrat instead of a Progressive; but I declined. I had this idealistic notion that I could accomplish more through the National Negro Labor Council.

ONE OF THE ADVANTAGES we enjoyed at the NNLC was having Paul Robeson on our side. He had remained a towering figure among black entertainers despite the pernicious State Department persecution that caused him to lose most of the mainstream audience he'd won over when he was playing in *Show Boat* and *All God's Chillun Got Wings*.

In the spring of 1952—shortly after the HUAC hearings in Detroit—we sponsored a national tour by Robeson in an effort to raise money for several civil rights organizations and elevate the NNLC to a national position of leadership in the black community.

Robeson created a stir wherever he went, and his courage inspired other performers to stand up and join him in song and purpose. Staunch in his role as the musical martyr, however, Robeson understood that this was not always a prudent move on their part. I recall, for instance, when we staged a rally across the river from Harlem and Harry Belafonte showed up to support Paul and the movement. At the time, Belafonte was just starting out as a traditional, Bing Crosby type of crooner, not having hit his stride by returning to the songs of his native Jamaica. But he had developed a social conscience, and I happened to be in the wings that night when Harry told Paul that he was going out on the stage to sing. As imposing as he was in stature, both physical and professional, Robeson was a teddy bear of a man, and he kindly advised Belafonte not to go out there, knowing that such an appearance could abort a young singer's career before it really started. "You don't need to do that to prove your support of me," Paul said. It was the benevolent thing to do, but also the practical thing, because Paul recognized that a performer's influence cannot exceed his fame. Harry cried, but he took Robeson's advice.

It might have been during the same trip—or perhaps a year or two later—that I stayed at the Hotel Theresa in Harlem, which was not far from a ribs joint owned by Sidney Poitier, who was already well regarded as an actor but was struggling to find steady work in the industry. I phoned out for ribs, and about half an hour later I heard a knock on the door and opened it to find Sidney Poitier standing there with my dinner. I was no damn celebrity, so you can be sure that Sidney wasn't coming to see me. He was just making a buck by running ribs, which gives you an idea how tough it was in those days for guys like him and Belafonte.

Virtually every black entertainer suffered, somehow, from the political climate, including some of the greatest talents the country has ever seen. Billie Holiday's accumulated troubles drove her to a premature death, which I could see coming when she performed one evening on Woodward Avenue. I don't know what she had been taking for her depression, but by the time she got to the theater she could barely stand. She was mentally alert, though, and as we talked backstage it was obvious that Billie was a militant supporter of black causes. I don't recall the particulars of the incident we were concerned with at the moment, but it was some criminal case involving young black men in the South, and it engaged her sympathy. When the time came for her to go onto the stage, we practically had to lead her to the microphone. Beads of perspiration were popping out on her forehead, and I remember wondering how in the hell she would be able to hold herself together. But when the spotlight came on, she faced the audience squarely and spoke for a few minutes in behalf of the situation we'd discussed backstage, then poured out all of her pain and anguish into the most beautiful, plaintive voice I've ever heard. I can still feel the chill that went through me when she sang "Strange Fruit."

Our big hitter, though, was always Robeson. He sang and spoke at our clubs and our churches, at our banquets and our rallies, and even at Reverend Hill's thirty-third pastoral anniversary in 1953. Robeson felt so much at home in Detroit that he celebrated his birthday there. But even in our town, he could never afford to get too comfortable. For him, the issue of the day was not only occupational ostracism but personal safety. There had been attempts on Paul's life, and we went to great lengths to see that no harm would befall him in Detroit or in his travels for the NNLC. I was in charge of security, and everybody else was a bodyguard. Dave Moore, my slight but feisty friend, likes to tell about the time several of us escorted Robeson to the airport during a particularly delicate period. We felt we had to protect Paul at all costs, not only from hate mongers but also from the FBI, which we knew was shadowing him. On the way to the airport, we noticed an FBI car that kept passing us, slowing down, and passing us again. Then, as we walked into the terminal, we spotted about four burly agents. So I assigned one of us to each of them until the only pair left was Dave and some guy about twice his size. Moore said, "Damn, couldn't you find a smaller guy to give me?" I told him, "Your fucking name is David, isn't it? Well, there's Goliath."

At the NNLC's 1953 convention in Chicago, at which Robeson spoke and I delivered the keynote address, we stayed in a black hotel owned by a former Harlem Globetrotter named Sonny Boswell. Sonny was a good guy, but I had a suspicion that something peculiar was going on in the hotel, and when I pressured him about it, he walked me into the suite where I was staying, took a picture off the wall, pulled out the screw that was holding it up, and showed me a small radio cell encased in a plastic plug that came out with the screw. Then he took me out to the hall and explained that agents from the FBI had bugged every damn room in the place and were taping our conversations at some central point. They were also examining everything we threw away. That got me wondering whether they had also wiretapped our previous conventions.

It was apparent then, if we didn't know it already, that the government would do whatever it had to in order to bring down the NNLC. Sure enough, midway through 1953, the attorney general, Herbert Brownell, placed us on the list of subversive organizations that he was compiling under Eisenhower's Loyalty Order, another manifestation of the McCarthy fervor. In its *Guide to Subversive Organizations and Publications*, the Justice Department wrote us up this way:

> One of the Communist fronts currently active in seeking to deceive American Negroes into serving the Communist cause is the National Negro Labor Council . . . formally founded at a conference held in Cincinnati, Ohio, October 27, 1951, under the direction of leading Negro Communists in the United States, such as Abner Berry, Sam W. Parks, and Coleman A. Young. According to the latest available information, Young is the present National executive secretary of the organization, from which post he controls and directs NNLC activities.

I don't know whether it's possible for anyone outside the movement, and removed by so many years, to appreciate the full extent of our frustration during this period. It wasn't the persecution that tore at us so much as the misrepresentation. We didn't give a hoot about subversion, or inversion, or perversion, or any damn version they could dream up. All we cared about was black folks getting what should be coming to us. Why was that so hard for those motherfuckers to understand? The fact that the government would not enable us to assemble and organize for that simple purpose was nothing more than a federal extension of the southern-styled, bullwhip, night-rider, Jim Crow, back-of-the-bus, time-honored and systematic oppression of black people that had gotten us into this fix in the first place.

I prepared a press release:

> The NNLC unequivocally rejects, and has officially protested, the recent action of the Attorney General when he saw fit to publicly label the NNLC as a subversive organization. . . . This arrogant and presumptuously undemocratic action on the part of the Attorney General is another example of the reckless manner in which the Eisenhower Administration is stepping up the assault on the basic democratic rights of the American people. . . . The Attorney General no doubt seeks to do what the Un-American Activities Committee in many hearings failed to do; namely, to intimidate the leadership of the NNLC with the overworked smear and fear technique. Moreover, this is an open attempt to intimidate and beat down the rising freedom struggle of the Negro people in America and their demands for full freedom now.

Well aware of whose highly dubious information had led to the attorney general's action, I also whipped up a letter to my friends at the FBI, referring to their "Gestapo-like" tactics and asking, "By what right have you imposed your secret concept of subversiveness, without giving us the public hearings demanded by us?"

Inclusion on the subversive list meant that the members of the NNLC were regarded as virtual agents of Russia—a stigma sufficient to get many of them fired from their jobs. Not content to screw up one life at a time, the FBI also managed on occasion to get our members' friends fired. It was not uncommon for an agent or stool pigeon to covertly follow our members around and take photographs of them chatting with friends and acquaintances, then show the pictures to the friends' employers, who, horrified to see their employees conversing with subversives from the NNLC, would dismiss them on the spot.

The worst person in the NNLC to be caught talking to was the

This picture is for my detractors—and my friends, for that matter—who have a hard time believing that I could ever be adorable.

My mother, a schoolteacher in Alabama, a working woman in Detroit, and an angel all the while, brought a sense of decorum and refinement to the Young household.

I was saddened when my brother George was transferred away from my side during basic training in 1942, but he and my sister Juanita cheered me up by visiting when I was a buck sergeant at Fort Benning, Georgia.

Having just been graduated from Eastern High School in 1935, shortly after my seventeenth birthday (I was a year younger than most of my class-mates, due to a double promotion in elementary school), I was about to embark on an adventurous post-adolescent career as Big Time Red. I was also continuing my informal but stirring education under the disputa-tious political philosophers at Haywood Maben's barbershop.

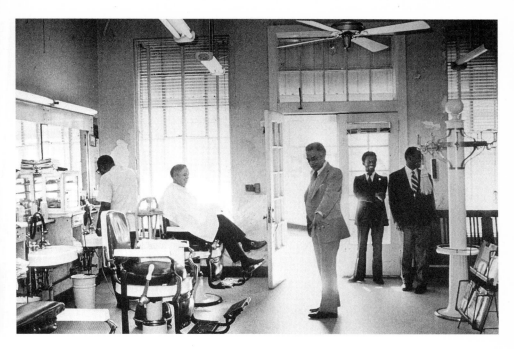

On a trip to Alabama in 1977, I visited the barbershop in Tuscaloosa where my father worked before he was run out of town for selling black newspapers. (*Detroit Free Press*)

In the fall of 1942, I'd just arrived at Fort Breckinridge as a newly commissioned second lieutenant in the infantry. Later, I transferred to the Air Corps and did my pilot training at Tuskegee Institute in Alabama.

There are hundreds of thousands of people in Detroit and in labor unions around the country who regarded former UAW president Walter Reuther as a great man. To me and those of us on the disfranchised left, which he purged from the industrial union movement in 1948, he was a great adversary. (Walter Reuther, *Detroit Free Press*)

In 1948, I made the grave political mistake of aligning with the Progressive Party and actively supporting Henry Wallace *(right)* for President. Here we conduct a campaign radio broadcast over Detroit station WJLB. Well-known attorney Maurice Sugar is second from the left.

My father *(standing, center)* doesn't look like such a mean son of a bitch, does he? He was particularly proud on the evening in 1964 when my brother George, assistant postmaster of Detroit, was honored as the city's federal executive of the year. *From left to right, back row:* my Black Bottom friend Mary Kelly; my nieces Claudia Young-Hill and Sidni Jacobs; myself; my father, William Coleman Young; my brother Charles; his wife, Muriel; my sister Bernice Grier; and her daughter Antonia Davis-Curry. *Front row:* Fritz Young, son of my cousin Dr. Claud Young; Elizabeth Young, my brother George's wife; and George.

On February 28, 1952, I swore to the Congressmen of the House Un-American Activities Committee that I would tell the truth, and by God, I did. They didn't much like it. (*Detroit Free Press*)

Office Memorandum · UNITED STATES GOVERNMENT

TO : DIRECTOR, FBI
DATE: April 19, 1954

FROM : SAC, DETROIT

SUBJECT:

      Remy letter dated February 4, 1954.

      YOUNG was contacted at the Willow Run Airport on April 9, 1954 by SA   with SA   protecting the security of the interviewer.

      YOUNG was very cordial and shook hands with SA He was about to send a telegram and SA   asked him if he would have time for "a coffee" when he finished. YOUNG said sure and SA waited until YOUNG had sent the telegram. When YOUNG and SA were walking toward the cafeteria YOUNG asked where he met SA before. When he realized that he was talking to the Bureau he suddenly seemed paralyzed, and finally stuttered "we have nothing to talk about." SA   replied "why not, we are both working for the same thing," and YOUNG seemed taken back again. After a brief pause he said "we have different approaches, I don't want to be bothered now," and rapidly walked away. SA made no attempt to follow him as he seemed quite upset and somewhat antagonistic.

      say that there is something wrong with COLEMAN these days and it is impossible to talk to him about the Party.

      It appears to SA   that this man is a dangerous individual and should be one of the first to be picked up in an emergency and one of the first to be considered for future prosecution.

You can see here that the FBI has always had a high opinion of me. (Provided by *Detroit News*)

The National Negro Labor Council's 1952 convention was held in Cleveland, which was bad news for American Airlines. Most of the companies we picketed, however, were retailers (such as Woolworth's and Sears and Roebuck) located in neighborhoods where black people shopped. My accomplices here were NNLC officers Jerry Boyd and Sam Parks.

After the devastation of urban renewal, Black Bottom, as portrayed in this 1957 photograph, was only a run-down relic of its former self. (*Detroit Free Press*)

Certain so-called liberals have been uneasy with the fact that I've actively conducted business over the years with the monied establishment. But the capitalists are the ones who can build things, and development means jobs for a city like Detroit. I don't suppose it's possible to cavort with capitalists more conspicuous than David Rockefeller *(left)* and Henry Ford II, pictured here as Rockefeller announced in late 1978 that he would build two towers adjacent to the Renaissance Center, which was developed by Hank the Deuce.

This *is* Motown, after all. If only I could sing worth a damn, we could have been the Five Tops. The Four *(from left)* are Renaldo Obie Benson, Duke Fakir, Levi Stubbs, and Lawrence Payton.

The surprise was on the trick-or-treaters when I greeted them at the door of the Manoogian Mansion one Halloween with Muhammad Ali.

Jimmy Carter, brilliant and sensitive, was a President whom I could do business with; and I often and eagerly did, much to the good fortune of Detroit. Until Bill Clinton was elected in 1992, Carter was the last President with even the rumor of an urban policy.

Do you think it was easy to raze this neighborhood for a Cadillac plant? Or to push the right buttons to rewrite eminent domain and put in motion the largest urban condemnation in the nation's history? Believe me, every twist and turn of the Poletown drama was hard stuff. But major industrial redevelopment was absolutely necessary for the economic survival of Detroit. On the day in 1993 when I announced I would not seek a sixth term as mayor, the General Motors plant that rose up on this site resumed its second shift, which means that Detroit is once again buckling down to the kind of work that made it great. (*Detroit Free Press*)

Rosa Parks, who struck a famous blow for civil rights in 1955 by refusing to relinquish her seat to a white man on a Montgomery bus, also helped make history in Detroit when she championed the 1981 referendum to increase the city income tax as a means of staving off financial disaster. Its passage marked one of the city's finest moments. (Mary Schoeder, *Detroit Free Press*)

I wonder if I'm the only big-city mayor to be arrested in three cities outside of his own. There was my military arrest in Seymour, Indiana, for crashing the white officers' quarters; in Dearborn, Michigan, for passing out leaflets; and here, in 1985 in the nation's capital, outside the South African embassy, for protesting apartheid. (William Archie, *Detroit Free Press*)

Jesse Jackson and I have not always agreed, but we have plenty of common ground upon which to talk.

My conservative antagonists had a field day with my remark, in answer to the question of whether I would support more stringent gun controls for Detroit, that I would not consider disarming the city as long as we were surrounded by hostile suburbs. This handbill was distributed in 1986 by a right-wing lobbying group and reproduced in the *Detroit Free Press*.

On the June day of the filing deadline for the 1993 mayoral race, I announced to Detroit that five terms and twenty years were enough. It was time to move on. (Craig Fujii, *Detroit Free Press*)

executive secretary. Although Hoover, Brownell, and company were obviously intent upon subduing the NNLC and containing its influence, their interest in the organization just as obviously had something to do with me. I was a growing problem to the government. The Republican Party newspaper, *Human Events*, referred to me as "possibly the most hostile, adroit, and evasive witness ever to confront a Congressional committee inquiring into Communist activities in the U.S." The FBI was even more flattering, devoting twenty-five pages to my life story in the form of a report to the director, and promoting me in their pecking order. According to a communication to Hoover from the special agent in charge, Detroit, "It's felt that the Subject's present degree of activity warrants his being classified as a Key Figure in the Detroit Division, and he is therefore being put on the Key Figure list."

Although the operative issues were civil rights and politics, my lifestyle no doubt contributed to the FBI's curiosity about me. I traveled incessantly for the NNLC, a circumstance that carried troublesome implications not only for my political profile but also for my marriage. Nobody ever mistook me and Marion for Ozzie and Harriet, and we finally divorced in 1954, childless. After that, I shared a house on Crane with an easterner named Jim Jackson, whom the Justice Department had indicted as a Communist; but I was seldom there. When I had a few days off in town, I liked to disappear into the neighborhoods to play some cards and chase some gals, having by this time mastered the art of separating the class struggle and the ass struggle. However, I had not mastered five-card stud to the extent that my father had, though poker was more cordial to me than craps or blackjack. I've had a few big evenings in my time—the blue convertible comes to mind, as do Army evenings in general—but I was not of the professional caliber that my bloodline might suggest. Nor was I in my father's class as a drinker, despite my periodic enthusiasm.

I was generally able to keep up with the accoutrements I required personally, such as clothes and cars. My good fortune in the sartorial line was chancing upon some sort of women's society store in Grosse Pointe that sold clothes for charity, its inventory deriving from the estates of the recently deceased local barons. Being familiar with fabrics from my background as a tailor and cleaner, I knew that I was getting six-hundred-dollar suits for twenty bucks. With a few repairs and tucks from my sewing machine, I stayed sharp by wearing the cashmeres and gabardines of dead men. Quality clothes were important to me, because if I was going to be on the road for several days and could take only one suit, it had to be a good one that wouldn't show the wear. I also carried a gabardine trench coat with a zip-out lining that could double as a bathrobe. In the matter of cars, however, it wasn't quite as easy to economize, so I usually bought my new ones when I hit the numbers, which seemed to be about every three to five years. I've always considered it a necessity to have a new car and decent clothes. Some people might regard this as a middle-class affectation, but if they do, fuck 'em.

The quality of my personal trappings did not escape the notice of the local FBI, which reported in 1954 that "close and continuous attention has been given to the situation surrounding Coleman Young. . . . Information received through contacts . . . indicates, as has been felt from the beginning, that Coleman Young is interested in money and the Negro rather than the Communist Party." While this was an uncharacteristically moderate judgment for the FBI, the rest of the report reverted to form. "Some persons," it said, "were suspicious Subject had connections with the Government because he was able to afford a new car, wears the best of clothes, and travels around the country." In one giant leap of improbability, the feds managed to kill off my Communist persona and reincarnate me as a government agent.

Actually, the duplicity implied in the report reflected an internal disagreement about my activities. During the same period, another Bureau agent referred to me as a high-level "continental courier" for the Communist Party, that conclusion having been shrewdly deduced from the fact that I traveled a lot. I first became aware of the debate within the Bureau when I returned from a trip in 1954 and found a long letter wedged above the sun visor of my car at Willow Run Airport. It was from an FBI agent, informing me that there was a sharp difference of opinion about my political identity within the Bureau offices, one school subscribing to the theory that I was a subversive, card-carrying member of the Communist Party, and the other speculating that I was a Communist dissenter for whom the party had plans that could be injurious. The author described himself as a member of the latter group and went so far as to suggest that he was in a position to help me out financially if I was interested in a cooperative arrangement. He also noted that he would be getting in touch with me in the near future.

While turning my stomach, the whole affair also amused and baffled me, because, in addition to the absurdity of my being a government informer, I found it equally unimaginable—and still do—that anyone, much less an organization with the resources and alleged know-how of the FBI, could spy on my everyday activities and expressions of thought and still entertain serious concerns that I was interested in something, anything, that was opposed to fundamental American freedom. What's more, the feds knew me to be a conspicuous capitalist. I remain puzzled as to how they could add all that together and come up with a diabolical un-American subversive. As for the Communist part, I will not do them or anybody else the service here of either denying or affirming it. The thing that matters is a person's program, not his label. Fuck the labels. I refuse to answer questions about labels. I refused to answer those questions for the Un-American Activities Committee, I refused for the FBI, and I'm sure as hell not going to gratuitously answer them now. What I've done is my testimony.

The sequel to the Willow Run letter came some time later when I was at the airport waiting for a plane and stopped at one of those machines that sold a million dollars' worth of insurance for a quarter, which I could never pass up. I was filling out the form when a guy in a jacket and baseball cap walked up to me, said "Hi, Coleman," and extended his hand. From my work with the NNLC and the labor movement in general, I knew more people than I could remember, so I figured he was some union guy I had met along the way. I told him we could grab a cup of coffee as soon as I was finished. But something made me suspicious, and as we headed down the corridor I asked him, "Where in the hell do I know you from?" He said, "If I told you, you wouldn't like it." Before I could pursue it further, he took off about how my activities were jeopardizing my father's and brother's jobs. "You son of a bitch," I said. "You're from the FBI." I reached for the guy, grabbed him by the collar, and as he pulled away and fell out of my grasp, I swung and clipped him on the chin. I happened to know a lot of the airport redcaps and baggage handlers from the pool-room on St. Aubin—specifically, a guy named Tommy and several of his cousins, who were paid so well they kept the jobs in the family—and by this time several of them had come to my aid, with their hands on their pockets as though they had knives in there. Tommy said, "Who is that motherfucker, Coleman? Is he fucking with you?" I said, "Yeah, he is, and he's the goddamn FBI." When I mentioned "FBI," they all just kind of said "Oh," pulled their hands away from their damn pockets, and slinked off. I caught up with Tommy later at the pool hall, but that's another story.

Years later, when I read about the airport meeting in my FBI file, I was revisited by the memory of that goddamn fed trying to lure me into his confidence by portraying himself (in the letter) as one of the few friends I had in the Bureau. Then he wrote this in his report of our brief encounter: "When he realized he was talking to the Bureau he suddenly seemed paralyzed, and finally stuttered 'we have nothing to talk about' and walked away. . . . He seemed quite upset and somewhat antagonistic. . . . It appears to SA [Special Agent] that this man is a dangerous individual and should be one of the first to be picked up in an emergency and one of the first to be considered for prosecution."

At the time, what infuriated me most about the incident was that the FBI would continue to hold my family accountable for my business; but I should have expected as much, knowing that ethics made no impression upon certain agents of the government. One of their common tactics was to plant the seed of dissension and see if anything came up, which they did in 1955 by concocting a story about employees at the NNLC being upset over my hiring of a pretty secretary named Nadine Drake—an interesting observation in that aside from me and Nadine, the NNLC didn't have any employees. I had two responses. As a precaution, I conducted security checks within the NNLC to see if we could uncover any FBI leaks or snitches. And I married Nadine.

Nadine was a politically minded woman who involved herself deeply with our agenda. She marched on numerous picket lines with me, and also happened to be on hand later that year when we collected donations in front of Ford's River Rouge plant in Dearborn for Operation Dixie. Dearborn was the most notoriously bigoted town in the Detroit area (its motto was "Keep Our City Clean," which everyone understood as a reference to racial purity), an example of its racial hospitality being the mounted policeman who watched us closely as we worked, petting his jet-black stallion on the neck while he stared straight at me and purred, "Whoa, Nigger . . . easy, Nigger . . . good horse, Nigger." The cops finally confiscated our money can—which contained, as I recall, sixty-five cents—and carted me off to jail. They didn't arrest me; they just put me behind bars and held me there for five or six hours, until Nadine and the NNLC could arrange my release. In the meantime, my cellmate was a black guy who was being held for a ticket violation. He had his paycheck in his pocket, but they wouldn't let him go to the bank to cash it and pay off the ticket. So when I was freed, I took the guy's check and brought back the money—which, needless to say, did not enhance my relationship with the Dearborn authorities.

We had worthier antagonists than those Dearborn bastards, however—or at least larger ones. The federal government was coming at the NNLC from every angle, pursuing even the chummy approach. For example, Hal Shapiro was walking out of a union meeting one day when a fellow came up to him and stuck out his hand. After shaking, the guy introduced himself as representing the FBI and said cordially that he wished to discuss a few things, to which Hal responded by wiping his hand on his trousers and telling the agent to go fuck himself. The ensuing FBI report noted all the interpersonal particulars, including Hal's language and the fact that he wiped off his hand.

Despite the government's transparent efforts to get friendly with many of us, we had known that the council was on thin ice from the moment it was placed on the attorney general's list of subversive organizations. Finally, late in 1955, a deputy U.S. marshal showed up at our door with torches and gasoline in the form of an order to register with the Subversive Activities Control Board—which I referred to as the Negro Activities Control Board—as a Communist front. Compliance entailed turning over our membership list. This, of course, constituted an egregious invasion of privacy. Moreover, we knew, and the Justice Department knew, that turning over our membership list would result in the mass firing of many of our five thousand NNLC members nationwide, a large number of whom were prominent union leaders. I refused to surrender it.

That meant, effectively, that the party was over. My daddy had taught me when to fold 'em, and this was the time. We stalled the legal process for as long as we could, but in April of 1956 I called the NNLC officers and members to a meeting at the Carlton Plaza Hotel in Detroit, the purpose being to make me the council's sole executor and the repository for its records. NNLC and union leaders from all over the country were there, and they poured out their declarations of undying support, which I knew was bullshit and they knew was bullshit and ultimately proved to be bullshit. Their support, dying or undying, was easily offered in light of the fact that there wasn't a damn thing we could do. We just hugged and lied for a while, then went grimly about the business of dissolving.

It was one of the few times in my adult life that I cried. I remember Dave Moore telling me, "Man, those tears of sorrow you're shedding now will someday be tears of joy." I thought, Shit.

The next day, I burned all the records.

6

Urban Passages

We never locked our doors when we lived in Black Bottom. By face, family, name or nickname, everybody knew everybody else and embraced the responsibility of looking after one another in a neighborly way, notwithstanding some flagrant differences in lifestyle and agenda. The churches and blind pigs shouldered each other tolerantly in our community—which brings to mind a local fellow we all knew affectionately as Too Too.

I'm not certain whether Too Too got his nickname because he was too black or too ugly or too tough or drank too much or smoked too damn much marijuana, in addition to which he also gambled too much and stayed up too late, as he did one Saturday night, stumbling out half-senseless onto Joseph Campau Street on Sunday morning. On his way home, or wherever he was going, Too Too teetered past his church and decided that it might be worthwhile to pay a visit. Given his immediate past, he also figured it might be in his best interest to put twenty dollars on the collection plate. The preacher, taking note of this, asked if Brother Too Too would like to follow up on his generosity with a few inspiring words, which Too Too was only too happy to do. "Brothers and sisters," he said, more or less, "I'm here to tell you that the music in this church is truly beautiful. I've heard a lot of choirs in my day, but that senior choir is the singingest motherfucking choir I ever heard." The congregation gasped in unison, the preacher and the old ladies putting their hands together and wailing, "Lord, give him strength!"

I loved that old neighborhood. Inevitably, the black neighborhoods were more diverse and fascinating than the white ones, because, by the impositions of segregation, they took in a vast range of social and economic types within the race. As one of the largest and boomingest black neighborhoods in the North, Black Bottom was a thrilling convergence of people, a wonderfully versatile and self-contained society. It was degenerate, but not without a lofty level of compassion. It was isolated, but sustained by its own passion. It was uneducated, but teeming with ideas. It was crowded, but clean. It was poor, for the most part, but it was fine.

When he had the world by the tail, Joe Louis was proud to buy his mother a beautiful place on McDougall, just a few blocks from ours on St. Aubin. You had it made if you had a place on McDougall. But most of us were satisfied just to have a place. Even in the worst times, Black Bottom was never a tenement community; we were house-and-yard people. Our values had to do with turf. Throughout the fifties, Detroit had more black homeowners and more black-owned businesses than any other city in America.

Looking back, I can see that Black Bottom had everything but a fighting chance. Not unlike the NNLC, it was red-tagged by the government as a sort of Yankee Doodle sacrifice, a trespasser upon somebody's sacred bureaucratic vision of America, a sociological trouble spot for which the keepers of the dream had no real solution but to lay it waste. Its demolition was an early step in a multilevel national response to the wartime and postwar migration of blacks to the northern industrial belt. Detroit was a pilot case in this massive campaign, which encompassed several phases and went by many names. The part that claimed Black Bottom was called urban renewal.

I could see it coming—everybody could—when I returned home after the war. Nobody really understood the dramatic and lasting implications of what was happening, but it was obviously something big. The city was being profoundly restructured, owing in large part to the fact that it had been the center of the wartime defense industry, the so-called Arsenal of Democracy. In deference to the red scare, the Cold War, and the Russians' acquisition of the atom bomb, and mobilized by Churchill's famous Iron Curtain speech at Fulton, Missouri, in 1946—in which the ex–prime minister spoke of the rapidly widening "Soviet sphere" and the Communist effort "to obtain totalitarian control" on the global level—the government had undertaken an emergency-speed policy of decentralization, breaking up and scattering the city of Detroit to mitigate its vulnerability. That translated forthwith into superhighways. More of them were built through Detroit than through any other city.

Most of us looked upon the new highways as a quicker way to get to work. Their debilitating effect on the city may have been perceived by the oracles among us, but not by anybody in my immediate circles. We were more concerned about the distant rumbling of bulldozers headed to the vicinity of St. Aubin Street. There was something in the works called the Detroit Plan; and, generally speaking, any plan with a name like that meant that somebody had thought up another way to screw black people.

The Detroit Plan was introduced in 1946 as a city-wide urban renewal blueprint for slum clearance, which was tantamount to the evacuation of blacks from a given area. As it pertained to Black Bottom and Paradise Valley, the plan called for existing homes and businesses to be leveled and replaced by a development known as the Gratiot Site, which consisted of more than a hundred acres northeast of the business district, including but not confined to the new east-side corridor for I-75, which ran smack down Hastings Street. Although the initial scheme called for the Gratiot Site to be devoted to new residences for blacks, the housing was to be privately developed. This proved a contradiction of themes, a depressing condition that was worsened by the offices of Albert Cobo.

When Cobo was elected mayor in 1949, he adamantly promoted the private aspects of urban renewal, emphasizing, however, the clearance and private development of the area at the expense of public housing. Simultaneously, he effected draconian cutbacks in the original scope of the Detroit Plan, reducing the number of designated sites from twelve to two while eliminating all of the vacant and outlying tracts upon which the project had been largely predicated. His obvious priority was to wipe out the lower east side. All the while, there was an obligatory battle of dueling commissions over the ultimate nature of the new units on the Gratiot Site, but the final disposition was predictably mainstream. The reality was that no private developer would come forward to build low-cost housing for blacks.

Meanwhile, the bulldozers moved ahead without waiting for the politicians and capitalists. My father's tailor shop was plowed under in 1950. Maben's barbershop bit the dust a little while later. Ours was the first neighborhood to be eliminated, with long stretches of stores and houses being demolished seemingly at random. The swath of destruction was broad and frightfully unpredictable. It took every nearby structure that meant anything to me, with the exception of St. Joseph's Church on my grandmother's street. So whimsical was the system of slum clearance that while some blocks were rubbed out, others, on streets like Chene and Joseph Campau, remained untouched. But even then the devastation was inescapable. Just the rumor of urban renewal was enough to ruin an area. Businesses would flee, and the remaining landlords were told by government officials that any improvements they made in their properties would not be considered in the ultimate settlements. It was a repeating pattern that we referred to as "blight by announcement."

Black Bottom lay in ruins for six years before the first new building went up. Eventually, it was rebuilt as Lafayette Park, a middle-class townhouse complex intended, naively, as integrated housing. Of the first two hundred families to move in, eight were black. All the while, the housing shortage in Detroit was so acute that 330,000 new units were built around the city during the 1950s; but that was of little consolation to the bursting black community, to whom fewer than ten thousand were available. At the same time, plans for a federal housing project on the St. Aubin extension, formulated in 1949, sat dormant until they were finally abandoned in 1960. By then, more than ten thousand buildings had been demolished on the east side, forty thousand people had been displaced, and Black Bottom was long gone.

Chased from their homes and community, the refugees from the east side poured into the previously smaller black enclave in a west side neighborhood that had been predominantly Jewish. As the

Jews resettled in the northwest clutches of the city, tides of blacks moved in behind them around Twelfth Street, many crossing over from Black Bottom and many more coming up from the South to work in the auto plants, which were producing at record levels in the mid-fifties and whose huge employment capacity had created the housing crisis in the first place. Landlords doubled their rents for the black tenants, who, because of their lesser earning power, packed their apartments fourfold in order to afford them. One stretch of a street called Blaine, near Twelfth, became home to more people than any other block in America. Within a few years, the entire Twelfth Street community was one of the most densely populated areas in the country, an impoverished, underequipped, irritable, and desperate neighborhood that trebled the problems of Black Bottom while inheriting little of its charisma.

I'm often reminded of a boy named Joey, who, to me, symbolized the tragedy of Black Bottom's removal to Twelfth Street. Joey was in his late teens, a giant of a fellow with the mind of about a second grader. Everybody in Black Bottom knew him, and when he would approach us, as he often did, to beg for nickels and dimes to buy candy, we would either give him the money or admonish him to get home before we told his grandmother what he was up to. Like everybody else, Joey and his family lost their home in Black Bottom and had to relocate to one of the unfamiliar blocks on the other side of town. Of course, Joey's habits didn't change, and when he walked up to a stranger on Twelfth Street one day to beg for candy money, the man thought he was being mugged and, terrified by Joey's size, shot him dead on the spot.

Nadine and I integrated a street called Collingwood between Twelfth and Woodrow Wilson. We had a one-bedroom apartment that had previously rented for $45 a month but was raised to $21 a week for blacks—twice as much. When the building was white, it had a white caretaker and his wife who received free rent and $150 a month to keep the place in working order and tidy. When the blacks moved in, the landlord fired the white couple and hired a black guy for nothing but free rent, which meant that he had to work at the foundry to make a living and wasn't available for maintenance. I once asked the landlord to paint our apartment, which needed it sorely, and the son of a bitch gave me three gallons of paint. But I couldn't complain too much, because the conditions there were much better than they were on Blaine or Pingree.

In addition to reconfiguring the neighborhoods, the war seemed to have a ripple effect that washed over Detroit street by street and person by person in the ensuing years, leaving hardly a single aspect of the city untouched. The auto industry, turning from its defense responsibilities, went bonkers for a while, then crescendoed and started its slow fade in the last half of the fifties, during which time several of the manufacturers lost valuable government contracts they had come to depend on and were unable to restore their positions in the car market, leading to the closure of the Packard and Hudson plants. New competition from foreign automakers like Volkswagen and Renault, in a portent of things to come, also made a major impact, causing mergers and cutbacks throughout the area. Chrysler, the city's biggest employer, began to drastically reduce its payroll, from 130,000 in the peak years to 50,000 at the end of the decade.

But while the city was scaling back economically, the great migration from the South wasn't over yet. Detroit was still the seat of the nation's biggest industry, and black families continued to pour into a community that was rapidly losing jobs. The black population of Detroit jumped from three hundred thousand to nearly half a million during the fifties, a startling increase of approximately two-thirds. By 1958, city-wide unemployment hit twenty percent. The neon lights began to flicker out along the used-car midway of Livernois, signaling an end to a period of great prosperity in Detroit, in which the black community had never really shared anyway.

The upshot of it all was that the city's white elements—the people, the money, the jobs—were beginning to find their way out of town. This was a process that the government was only too happy to expedite. It had big plans. Its postwar urban program, decentralization, was like a starting gun for the frantic scramble that would come to be known as white flight and would reshape Detroit into the unique socioeconomic phenomenon that it remains today.

Ostensibly, decentralization was a military mechanism, adver-

tised to make the defense industry less susceptible to wholesale nu-
clear destruction. There were obvious and legitimate arguments
on this behalf. But at the same time, the breaking-up of Detroit
represented a powerful and multifaceted social movement that
served to strand the black community in a city of endangered resources. I'll never accept the notion that the federal government
wasn't aware of what it was doing to us. Segregation didn't have a
goddamn thing to do with defense, except that the two could be
served together, which was a delicious prospect to whoever was
holding the spoon. I tend to see decentralization as a big chocolate
sundae that the policymakers just couldn't resist. If defense was the
ice cream, racial isolation smothered it in chocolate sauce. The
whipped topping was profit. There was a hell of a lot of money to
be made from the whole process.

The first step in decentralization was federally assisted industrial
relocation—the government, in effect, paying for auto/defense
plants to get out of the city. It began with Chrysler's move to
Twinsburg, Ohio, near Cleveland. Chrysler employees were given
the option to relocate along with the plant, and many of them did,
removing a significant number of union members from Detroit in
addition to jobs. Other plants followed in the same direction,
along the Lake Erie shore. Of the four hundred thousand manufacturing jobs that sustained and defined Detroit at its industrial
peak, a staggering three hundred thousand have left in the ensuing forty years—a statistic that, by itself, goes a hell of a long way toward explaining the city's economic troubles since World War II.

The second phase of the postwar federal program called for
facilitating decentralization by stepping up the pace of superhighway construction, which had gotten under way in Detroit during
the war. The first freeway in America, a short connector called the
Davison Expressway, was built through Highland Park to access the
Chrysler plant and headquarters in 1942. Even before that, Detroit
had a history of pioneering in road development. The world's first
concrete pavement was a one-mile section of Woodward Avenue
completed in the northern part of the city in 1909. Two years later,
the first painted center line appeared on Seven Mile Road. In
1927, Woodward became the first intercity superhighway when it

was expanded to eight lanes from Detroit to Pontiac. But the Davison Expressway, localized and inauspicious as it was, marked the beginning of a feverish and cataclysmic period of freeway construction in Detroit.

Before the war was over, an expressway had been built from downtown past River Rouge to the Willow Run bomber plant. When that road was completed, it was Interstate 94, known in the city as the Edsel Ford Freeway. In 1950, the John Lodge Freeway was dug north-south on the west side of downtown to connect the Davison to the Edsel Ford and also the Fisher Freeway, which became part of I-75. A mile away on the east side, at the edge of old Black Bottom, the Chrysler Freeway extended 75 north along what used to be Hastings Street, created a western buffer for the new Lafayette Park, and wiped out what was left of Paradise Valley. On the other side of the city, the Jeffries Freeway, part of I-96, swept through the northwest communities en route to Lansing.

The emphasis on freeway construction after the war was not limited to Detroit, but nowhere else was it administered with the same reckless abandon, and nowhere else did it carve up and mortify a municipality as it did Detroit. Cities like Chicago and Pittsburgh, benefiting from Detroit's example, later insisted that their new expressways occupy courses far removed from the major arteries, circumventing the inner cities and neighborhoods. It was learned from Detroit that severing a city's heart leads to critical economic complications. It entails digging an enormous ditch into the urban landscape, scattering homes and businesses that provide a tax base, and truncating communities that atrophy and die as a consequence. For Detroit, the fallout from the urban highway craze was nothing short of devastating, undermining not only its community essence but its very population base. Since 1950, when 1.8 million people lived in Detroit, the city has lost very nearly half its population.

For the suburbs, on the other hand, the freeway system was an umbilical cord. The swift new highways not only accommodated an exodus from the city; they invited it. Realizing this, Hudson's department store, the commercial anchor of downtown Detroit, started the country's first shopping center by putting up a store on vacant land just beyond Eight Mile Road—the city's northern border—in 1954, and then another one a little farther east in a cornfield. There were few significant suburbs at that point, but once the highways and shopping centers were built, as in *Field of Dreams* the people came. Over the decade of the fifties, the population of suburban Detroit increased by an incredible million. And in a reversal of social history, in which people have traditionally followed the jobs, this time the jobs followed the people. While the industrial plants were leaving Detroit at a crippling clip, the number of manufacturing establishments in the state and the metropolitan area jumped by fifty percent in the twenty years following the war. Over the same period, Detroit's share of the total Michigan payroll shriveled to half its original proportion.

All of this outward migration created a financial windfall for the owners of construction companies and real estate firms. The realtors in particular played greedily upon the anxieties and eagerness fostered by the changing demographics. As the uprooted blacks integrated new neighborhoods, the realty companies were poised and ready to work both ends of the recurring process known as blockbusting.

Blockbusting is one of those field-study social phenomena that give us naked glimpses of human nature. Its patterns reveal that, traditionally and with remarkable regularity, white residents will remain in their homes until the second or third black family moves onto their block. National statistics show that the tolerable level of black occupancy is about eight percent, and that very few whites will stay in a neighborhood that is twelve percent black. This standard runs roughly parallel to the southern guideline for racial identity, in which one drop of black blood makes a person black. Must be damn powerful blood.

As applied to Detroit's transitional neighborhoods of the fifties and sixties, the dynamics of blockbusting constituted a dream scenario for realtors. At times, it required nothing more than the dropping of a hint or a mere mention of the dirty word—"integration"—to make frantic whites flee their old neighborhoods. Capitalizing on the double-sided panic, realtors were able to gouge displaced black home buyers—getting twenty thousand dollars for houses worth about seven thousand—by taking advantage of their desperate situations, then make a quick suburban sale to the white family that was horrified over the prospect of the block turning black. After that white family was gone, the next one was even more anxious to get the hell out.

The Federal Housing Authority further penalized the black homebuyers by offering loans for new housing only, none of which was being built within the limits of Detroit. As the third step in the nationwide process of decentralization, this effectively racist policy stimulated the adolescent suburbs and sucked life out of moribund inner cities like that of Detroit, whose circulation had already been cut off by the destructive separatist policies of Mayor Cobo. Cobo's agenda was to isolate and contain Detroit's advancing black population, which the federal housing and highway programs allowed him to do. There was little alternative for blacks but to overpopulate the older, white-abandoned parts of town, and overpay for the privilege. In this endeavor, the mayor had the strong support of Detroit's white population. To get elected in the first place, Cobo had defeated liberal Democrat George Edwards by virtue of white unionists breaking rank with the UAW, which endorsed Edwards. It should be noted, consequently, that his segregationist administration was an honest reflection of his constituency.

By the end of Cobo's second and last term, however, Detroit's political complexion had changed considerably. That year, 1957, William Patrick was elected as the city's first black councilman, succeeding where Reverend Hill had been unable to. By 1960, blacks accounted for twenty-nine percent of the city's population, wielding nearly twice the voting influence they had held ten years before. This was a movement, perhaps, that the authors of decentralization had not foreseen. Or had they?

I WAS ACCUSTOMED to being out of a job, but this time I was also out of ideas. The auto companies wouldn't touch me, the union had kicked me out, my political party had failed, my labor organization had been outlawed, and the FBI was all over my ass. My second marriage wasn't so damn hot, either.

On top of all that, I owed the IRS. As part of the NNLC dissolution arrangement, I had agreed to personally assume the council's financial obligations, which amounted to several thousand dollars of payroll deductions that we hadn't submitted. Since nobody stepped forward to help me out—despite their oaths of undying loyalty—I had to give the government eighty dollars a week for the next few years until the debt was covered. In better days, I might have seen irony in the difficulty of doing this—scraping up eighty bucks every week for the folks who had eliminated my job—but irony was a luxury that, like everything else, I couldn't afford. I had to find a way to make the money.

Of the half-dozen or so jobs I had over the next few years, the best may have been driving a taxi. I didn't make much money at it, but, if nothing else, I kept up with the shifting currents of the city and came to know it well. I preferred to think of myself as an entrepreneur, however, and dropped everything to produce a black yellow pages, which earned me less money than driving the taxi. I also tried lugging meat for a while, which was the first job I ever had to quit because I couldn't handle it physically. The work entailed taking a side of beef off a hook and loading it into a truck. The sides weighed up to 550 pounds, and the only way to handle them was to put your shoulder into the hollow of the shoulder of beef and find a balance point, then stay in your crouch and walk it to the truck. It wasn't too bad until the time came to stack that motherfucker.

The veterans on the job wore composition shoes that helped them on the cold cement and the slippery polished steel of the truck floors, but I didn't have any composition shoes or the money to buy them. They weren't my style, anyway. I wore what I had, which did not go unnoticed by the other fellows, who asked me, "Hey, where'd you get those damn pimp shoes?" They took bets on how long I'd last, and it turned out that they had me pegged pretty well. My breaking point came one day when I didn't balance the beef quite right and went down to my knees. I had slipped with one of those mothers a couple of times before and nearly ruptured myself trying to manhandle it, so this time I didn't try. I just dropped my load and left it there. Of course, being unequal to the task, I had to salvage my manhood, so I went into my bravado act. I said,

"They can take this fucking job and stick it up their ass," and stormed off. I think I gained a little respect with the boys for the way I quit, which at least did something for my ego.

It did nothing for my marriage or my landlord or the IRS, however. I was self-destructing. A psychiatrist would have probably told me that I couldn't keep a job because, deep down, I didn't want to keep a job. Which I didn't—not that kind of job, anyway. I needed a cause. I needed to rally people, to organize something, to scream at somebody, to stir up some trouble. Basically, I needed to do what I'd been doing all my life.

I still hung out with my radical friends, but that only seemed to bring out my blues. Mostly, I was in the business of soliciting sympathy from people like Hal and Esther Shapiro, whose tolerance I tried severely. One hot summer day, Esther was chattering about going to the beach and having to be careful about getting sunburned when I snapped at her by saying, "I have troubles of my own, Esther, and I'm sorry, but right now I cannot concern myself with the special problems of white people." I guess I was a prick when I was depressed.

My father tried to shake me out of my funk by reminding me that I couldn't change the world overnight, which I knew for damn sure. My brother Charles—who, as the most mechanical and pragmatic member of the family, was the least likely to offer political counsel—pointed out that the ideological pendulum would eventually swing the other way, and when it did, I would be greater than I ever imagined. He was right in the sense that I sure as hell couldn't imagine it.

Things picked up a little bit—economically, at least—when I got a job with a chain of dry cleaners owned by a political friend named Nate Chalnick. I managed One-Hour Cleaners on Woodward and Chase Cleaners in Harper Woods, did my share of spotting, and picked up a little extra money by repairing cleaning machines. I still hadn't managed to pay off the NNLC tax debt, which the IRS recouped by appropriating an extra cut of my earnings right off my paycheck. It was reassuring to know that I was not being neglected by the government. In fact, there were at least two departments on my case, as I realized one afternoon in 1959 when an FBI agent walked into One-Hour Cleaners and said that he was in a position to help me. It was an old line that I'd heard before. I told him I wasn't interested in any proposition the FBI could offer and showed him the door without any further discussion.

Later that year, my mother died. Then Nadine and I were divorced, although we'd been off and on for some time. She first left me one day while I was at work. Unsuspecting, I came home to find neighbors standing around my house. I figured out what had happened as I walked up to the door and an older lady said, "Poor boy." Nadine had taken off with the furniture, leaving me a bed, a chair, and my books. She came back a short while later when she found out she was pregnant, knowing that I wanted a child as much as she did and thinking that perhaps we could make it as a family. In the meantime, though, she had parceled out our belongings to various family members, and everywhere I went with her I kept bumping into my goddamn furniture—which, incidentally, I never got back. I never really got Nadine back, either. Once again, my marriage collapsed under the strain of a tragic birth incident. This time, we lost the baby when it came out breeched. There was nothing left to keep us together, and not long after that Nadine left for California.

Floundering, and realizing that the only thing capable of pulling me out of my despair was a good jolt of politics, I ran for Common Council in 1960, only to lose badly in the primary. But I made a decent showing on the east side, which was enough to resuscitate my spirits. In the process, I came upon an issue that I could carry to the community.

In my campaign for council, I had spoken in broad leftist terms about peace and civil rights and taxation, but I struck a nerve when I lashed out against police practices and called for the commissioner to step down. The antipathy between the police and the black community had been historic in Detroit, and Cobo's successor as mayor, Louis Miriani, had undertaken what he called a war on crime, which was essentially a program to harass black people in the streets. Officers in the Twelfth Street area patrolled in what were referred to as Big Four cruisers, featuring a uniformed driver and three plainclothesmen armed with shotguns, machine guns, and tear gas. It was common for police cars to pull up randomly next to a group of blacks on the sidewalk and search every one of them. A minor traffic violation was a sure way for a black man to get searched. The Detroit NAACP conducted an analysis of racial complaints against police and found that officers routinely advised black citizens to "say 'yes sir' and 'no sir' when answering a white man." If blacks weren't deferential to the cop's satisfaction, he would attempt to put them in their place with familiar phrases like "I can see that you are one of those smart niggers."

I'd like to think that my harangue against police activities was instrumental in the defeat of Miriani in 1961 and the election of a young Kennedy-style liberal named Jerome Cavanagh. Black voters turned out in big numbers, for the first time playing a significant part in the mayoral election process. Understanding where his support came from and thereby the importance of a less militant police commissioner, Cavanagh appointed George Edwards, whom Cobo had defeated to become mayor. Reflecting upon the state of Detroit police in later years, Edwards said, "My job was to teach the police they didn't have a constitutional right to beat up Negroes on arrest."

While old habits died hard in the police department, Detroit politics in general took on a new sensitivity under Cavanagh. He was an active player in the War on Poverty, at the same time working to reverse the decline of the central business district by brisk office construction. Cavanagh's progressiveness cracked open a window of opportunity for Detroit. This was especially promising in 1961, when a ray of light emanated from Lansing. That was the year when, for the first time in half a century, Michigan staged a convention to review and revise the state constitution.

Encouraged by my failed bid for Common Council, I filed as a Constitutional Convention candidate from the Ninth District, which was on the east side. At the time, I had an apartment on Whitney, which was on the west side, but was staying with my old high school girlfriend, Mary Kelly, at her Ninth District house on McDougall. My two addresses soon developed into a major campaign controversy, which I suspect would have amounted to nothing if I had been an unthreatening candidate or a white conservative. In fact, George Romney, then the retiring president of American Motors, was a Con-Con candidate and had four goddamn addresses, including one in Florida. If the issue was where did I really live, well, where the fuck did *he* live?

For a political unknown, I managed to pull together an impressive coalition of enemies while running for Con-Con. The newspapers, the Democratic Party, and the AFL-CIO all staunchly opposed my candidacy, the latter two endorsing former state senator Anthony Wilkowski, who had served a prison term for vote fraud and was denied his seat in Lansing when reelected. Despite this broad repudiation, however, I placed first among twenty-five candidates in the primary, a showing that under normal circumstances would have ensured my election. But labor still withheld its endorsement, the Democratic Party rejected me in favor of a write-in candidate, and the newspapers went on at length in a blatant attempt to discredit me.

In reality, the stink over my addresses was nothing more than an excuse to attack my credibility as a candidate. The *Free Press* was zealous in its editorials against me ("When Young won in the primary the Democratic organization was horrified at the thought of his going up to Con-Con wearing the party label. We share, doubled in spades, its opinion of Young," it wrote, referring to me as "a distressingly sorry prospect as an occupant of a Constitutional Convention chair"); and the *News* would start front-page stories about the residency controversy, then, after a few paragraphs, leave that subject entirely and launch into a lengthy discussion of my alleged Communist connections. It would overtly denounce me on grounds that I had been linked to "subversive" organizations and cite my appearance before the House Un-American Activities Committee, quoting Congressman Potter charging me with being a Communist and the hecklers at Wayne State doing the same.

I wrote a letter to the editor, Martin Hayden, after one particularly slanted article, and when I received no response even after phoning, I went down to the *News* to confront him. It was late in the day, and I was told that Hayden had already left. So I took the opportunity to meander through the building; and as I was looking around the editorial offices and the press room, I couldn't help noticing the total absence of blacks. I did stumble upon a couple of black men mopping the floor in the lobby, and when I asked how many blacks worked in the building, they said, "You're looking at 'em." So I went home and wrote the *News* another missive, which I published myself this time and circulated around the Ninth District as a campaign-style newsletter. It was also reprinted in the *Michigan Chronicle*, a black-oriented newspaper serving the Detroit area.

An Open Letter from Coleman A. Young
to the Detroit News

Gentlemen:

Thanks to the copious and constant attention of the *Detroit News*, the entire state of Michigan must be aware by now that I, Coleman A. Young, am a Democratic candidate for Con-Con in the 9th Representative District.

I would like to take this opportunity to get a few facts straight. The question of my two addresses, as raised by the *News*, is a phony question which, as everyone knows, will not stand up in any court.

To question a candidate's address is to question his integrity, and it is interesting to note that of all the Con-Con candidates with multiple addresses, the *News* saw fit to raise questions around only two, both of whom happen to be Negroes.

As for subversive activities, I have not even been accused, much less convicted, of any crime whatsoever, political or otherwise. . . . In fact, it takes a special brand of self-righteous and sanctimonious gall for a publication that is not only Republican and anti-labor, but also lily-white, to suddenly begin to pass out free advice, and with a straight face, to Democratic, working-class, and Negro voters!

The *News* is obviously dissatisfied with the democratic process as exercised by the voters of the 9th District, where I received top vote in a field of 25 candidates. . . . It should be obvious from the above that the *Detroit News* enters the 9th Representative District Con-Con picture with neither clean hands nor pure motives. For the benefit of the *News* and all concerned I would like to reiterate my determination to fight for a state constitution that will return the control of our state government to the people.

. . . I hereby serve public notice that I will fight for the type of state constitution that will force the *Detroit News* to hire some Negroes.

Shortly thereafter—and, I assume, due in part to the pressure I brought to bear—the *News* did hire its first black reporter, Bill Matney, who later became the first black national reporter for NBC.

Of more immediate concern to me, however, was a complaint brought to the Wayne County prosecutor by my Republican opponent, Joseph Powers, over the residency issue. In a decision that received far less media coverage than the hullabaloo that preceded it, the prosecutor ruled that I did indeed legitimately maintain two addresses and was thereby eligible to participate in the runoff election. Having by that time received more publicity than one could ever wish for while pursuing such a position, I proceeded to win handily, finishing with four thousand two hundred votes to a thousand for Powers and three hundred for the Democratic write-in, Charmie Currie.

In Lansing, I was placed on the taxation and finance committee, which was not my first choice but as much as I could expect from a Republican-dominated convention. The anointed star of Con-Con was Romney, the Lee Iacocca of his day, who was on his way to becoming governor and had bigger aspirations than that. Before long, I became disenchanted with the agenda we were following and wrote to my constituents that "the convention is being used as a platform and vehicle for the buildup of George Romney, the next Republican candidate for governor, who has a longer-range objective of the White House itself. This has resulted in a Birch Society–blessed allegiance within the Republican Party with the Big Business forces and with conservative rural forces. . . . [The] basic approach of this Con-Con convention seems to be, 'What is good for General Motors is good for Michigan.' "

I was a spirited nemesis of the constitution that was ultimately adopted by the convention, but fundamentally pleased to have participated in the process. There is no better education in government than studying and dissecting a constitution, and it was an experience that greatly informed my political perspective. Along the way, I was proud to accomplish a few things for the state—most significantly, writing the first version of the provision that established the Civil Rights Commission and, together with Con-Con delegate Daisy Elliott of Detroit, introducing it at the convention. When the commission was put in place as part of the revised constitution approved by voters in 1963, the CRC became (and remains) the only one in the country mandated by state law.

My involvement at Con-Con seemed to persuade a few people in Detroit and the Democratic Party that I didn't have horns; and with that going for me, I ran in 1962 for the state legislature, losing to white incumbent Richard Guzowski by four votes from more than five thousand cast. It was a good performance, but five votes shy of a living. It was also the last time I lost an election.

Even without a public office in which to serve, I figured, at least, to have gained a little respectability as a job applicant, which I then became for the Municipal Credit Union League on the recommendation of an old union friend, Sam Karsman, who managed the league's insurance division. I was close to being hired when information about my radical past trickled down from the UAW. I found it interesting that this highly sensitive and confidential material— hell, I couldn't even get my own FBI records at the time—would make the rounds in such a comprehensive manner. Fortunately, Karsman and Bob Vanderbeek, the president of League Life, didn't see a subversive side to my preoccupation with social equality, and, given my promising scores on the credit union's aptitude test, were courageous enough to take me on in spite of the implications.

I was given a territory way up in no-man's-land, around the Lake Michigan towns of Muskegon and Ludington on the western edge of the state, where the natives were unaccustomed to doing business with a black person. My mission was to sell our family group insurance, which offered policyholders full coverage for fifty cents a week. Our package eliminated the middleman, and as a result it was so cheap I could have sold it in my sleep. I preferred to sell it over steak dinner, however, which I did again and again until I was the leading salesman in the company and set all sorts of records. We marketed the group insurance to the credit unions within local unions at five hundred and six hundred a clip, the only obstacle being competition from our rival, the Credit Union National Association. The big showdown with CUNA finally came at the Newspaper Guild, where they sent in their top two or three salesmen and League Life sent me. Sharpened by the streets of Black Bottom and the convention floors of the labor movement, I was not somebody to fuck with in a shootout; I never lost one. Within a year or so, I was placed in charge of the company's family group division.

After so many years of tilting at things bigger than me, I was at last in the clear and on my way to relative prosperity. Not only did I have a good income for the first time in about a decade, but my position with the credit union had reinstated me as a member of the CIO, which had merged with the American Federation of Labor. What's more, the FBI, preoccupied with the emergence of Malcolm X, Martin Luther King, and the civil rights movement in the South, apparently had me on the back burner. The atmosphere around me had lightened so distinctly by 1964 that I was actually hired as a union rep by my old adversary Gus Scholle, who was president of the Michigan AFL-CIO. I was back in the thick of the movement.

In the meantime, the movement had been doing all right with me in the thin of it. Although the NNLC could not be equaled as an agency of pragmatic activism, a few black labor organizations, local and national, worked diligently to carry on. A longtime local union figure, Horace Sheffield, administered the Detroit Association of Black Organizations; and the former head of the NNLC's Chicago branch, Charlie Hayes, who later became a congressman, was a principal founder of an NNLC descendant called the Coalition of Black Trade Unionists. But the most influential of our successors was the Trade Union Leadership Council, whose leaders included Buddy Battle, the second husband of my first wife. The TULC represented a small triumph for me and my crowd in the sense that it was conceived by Reuther as a political accommodation to the people and purposes that had been served by the NNLC. It represented a larger triumph in the sense that it flourished under a charter very similar to the NNLC's and grew to a membership of thirteen thousand. The TULC was not doomed by opposition from Reuther, as we had been, owing to the fact that its

key figures were UAW men and loyal to their throne. For that obvious reason, I was never involved in its operations; instead, I attempted, without sufficient resources, to recreate the NNLC in the
form of MANTU, the Michigan Association of Negro Trade Unionists.

MANTU enabled me, at least, to stay abreast of the times, over
which civil rights were beginning to take hold. Although the ven-
ues and slogans were new to those of us who had been pulling duty
on the industrial front, I felt like a veteran of the civil rights movement to the extent that, unlike many in labor and political circles,
I considered it and the union movement to be the same. For my
purposes, they were in pursuit of the same things—empowerment,
leverage, franchise, first-class citizenship, getting what we earned.
Most white unionists, in particular, preferred to separate the movements, which is why so many of the rest of us had fallen out of favor
in the labor arena. Ultimately, the inability to achieve our goals
through the union movement gave rise in part to the sovereign life
of the civil rights movement.

It was industry—the unique concentration of it—that had created the environment for Detroit's political consciousness in the
first place, attracting the ambitious needy and manufacturing a labor society that fostered the city's multisided left. From perspectives such as William Coleman Young's house and Haywood
Maben's barbershop and the insurgent wing of the Wayne County
CIO, the struggle for workers' rights forever included those of the
civil variety. Consequently, although the great movement of the
sixties is historically regarded as a southern endeavor, Detroit enlisted in it early—long before 1963, when, two months in advance
of the March on Washington and at the invitation of the Reverend
C. L. Franklin, Martin Luther King visited the city to call attention
to the twentieth anniversary of the 1943 Detroit race riot by leading a Walk to Freedom march of 125,000 down Woodward Avenue, with another 125,000 looking on. In his speech to a packed
house at Cobo Hall, King declared that the Walk to Freedom,
which was climaxed by the original rendition of his "I Have a
Dream" speech, was the largest civil rights demonstration in the nation's history.

The memory of the '43 riot was a convenient excuse to bring King to town, but hardly a gratuitous one. Despite the rearrangement of the city and the increasing awareness of racial injustice, basic conditions in Detroit hadn't changed very damn much in two decades except for the fact that a lot more black people were being screwed. Blacks were served in more restaurants, and a few had better working positions; but the labor gains were largely nullified by the evacuation of jobs. The impact of the Supreme Court's landmark 1954 decision in *Brown* vs. *Board of Education* had been severely mitigated by the city's residential segregation, as occasioned by urban renewal and decentralization. The operative reality was that the vast majority of Detroit's blacks still lived in a separate, second-class society. And the black community's relationship with local police—government's representatives on the street—still reflected the bitter, horrific enmity that had proven so tragic in the summer of 1943.

Despite George Edwards's efforts to wean his officers from the club and the gun, the deep-seated southern mentality still prevailed in the Detroit Police Department. Edwards finally gave up the task and resigned in 1963, the year of the celebrated slaying of a famous local prostitute known as Saint Cynthia. At six feet and nearly two hundred pounds, Saint Cynthia had become a landmark around Twelfth Street, which had assumed Hastings Street's old role as Detroit's avenue of iniquity. Thinking perhaps to make an example of her, policemen rushed Cynthia one night when they saw money in her hand. Not about to be taken easily, she slashed one cop with a knife while others shot her in the back and stomach. The officers, in keeping with Detroit tradition, were not punished for the incident.

In the case of Saint Cynthia, as in scores of others, a complaint had been filed with the police department by the local NAACP. Over a period of four years immediately prior to the establishment of the Michigan Civil Rights Commission in 1963, the Detroit PD investigated more than 170 complaints of brutality against blacks, finding officers to be free of fault on every occasion but one. Thereafter, the regulations set forth in the Civil Rights Commission made a significant difference, with thirty-one complaints—

nearly a third of those filed—being upheld in the first two years of its existence.

By this time, I was beginning to view the police issue as the rallying point within the black community—which Detroit, by and large, was on the way to becoming. As late as 1964, under the comparatively liberal administration of Jerome Cavanagh, blacks accounted for only four percent of the police department despite startling gains in the city's population, which was now approximately one-third black. It was apparent that the situation would not tangibly improve until decisions were being made by black officials, a realization that led me to a personal predicament. Common sense told me it would be damn foolish to even think about leaving behind the most secure, most lucrative job I'd ever had. But inasmuch as my senses have never been characterized as common, I entered the race for state senate in the Fourth District, the lower east side.

Among the political lessons I'd learned was that one of the few issues consistently more important than police in the minds of black voters—if not the only one—is religion. In this regard, I was not a candidate with strong credentials. My piety, however, was exceeded by my appreciation of the same in others. From observing the influence of legendary local ministers like Reverend Hill and Reverend Bradby and Reverend White and Reverend C. L. Franklin—a preacher's preacher and a singer to whom his daughter Aretha was at best an equal—I'd come to the conclusion that the vocal support of the collective clergy would represent a formidable political base. I went straight to the Baptist Pastors Council and quickly became a front-runner in my own mind, if nobody else's.

The newspapers and party officials might have been skeptical about my electability, but apparently the FBI took me seriously as a candidate. The progressive Great Society consciousness of the Kennedy and Johnson administrations must have made little impression upon the FBI, because a special assistant within the Bureau went to the trouble of sending a memo to Lyndon Johnson informing the President that I was running for the state senate. At the time, only seventy of the elected public servants at all levels of government in the United States were black, and I had to wonder if the President received a memo every time one of them, or any black candidate, had filed for office.

Basil Brown of Detroit was the only black legislator in the Michigan State Senate before the 1964 elections. He gained a roommate when I defeated Nelis Saunders by roughly two to one, thereby effecting a career change that would prove to be much more permanent than I had anticipated. I was forty-six at the time, and after switching occupations every couple of years since I was a teenager, I couldn't have contemplated the notion that, when the legislature convened, I would be setting out on three decades in public office. I did, however, attach a high level of esteem to my new station. When I first ventured into the neighborhood barbershop after my election and was greeted in the customary manner— "Hey, motherfucker!"—I turned to my offender, eyed him gravely, and set the record straight. "From now on," I said, "it's *Senator* Motherfucker."

Basil and I shared a place in Lansing with a couple of gutsy white Democrats from Detroit who possessed the self-assurance to be unconcerned about the taint of associating with a black radical like me: a labor advocate named Stanley Novak (not to be confused with Stanley Nowak, who had previously represented the same district) and Roger Craig, a progressive-minded attorney. We bought a house on McPherson Street that we called Mother McPherson's, and proceeded to appoint it with a sauna and various other amenities. We even landscaped the damn place, if you will. After Roger was defeated, leaving three of us, Charlie Zollar, a millionaire bowtie Republican from Benton Harbor and a hell of a guy, gave us three dwarf apple trees that we put in the backyard and named Fucked Up, A Little Fucked Up, and All Fucked Up. We planted them too close together, however, and then argued over which one was All Fucked Up.

Politically, we all stayed under the same roof on most issues, although there were a few touchy subjects on which Novak's Polish constituency pulled him in another direction. Open housing was one of those. It was the hottest topic in Detroit when I took my seat in the senate, the city's Common Council having soundly defeated an open-housing ordinance that would have abolished the systematic discrimination that held forth; and it was also the hottest topic at Mother McPherson's. Craig and I were in the forefront of the open-housing campaign, and many of the advocates around the state hung out or stayed at our place, much to the irritation of Novak, who came home one night grumbling loudly about all the hippies we had been taking in. About that time, one of our guests emerged from the sauna, wearing only a towel. Novak, a devout Catholic, pointed to the visitor as exactly the sort of unwelcome intruder he was talking about—a charge over which he turned scarlet when our friend changed into his priest's collar.

The housing situation was principally a Detroit problem, its sticking point being articulated by a member of the Homeowners Council and Realty Board who explained segregation by saying that "the Negro is not suitable for the place in society which he is trying to push into." Knowing the city as I did, I thought it best to pursue the matter on the state level, backing an open-housing law that would require Detroit's compliance. Brown, of course, was an ardent advocate of the bill—which was ultimately passed—but Novak reluctantly opposed it. When someone asked how he could be against open housing when he lived with two black men, Novak replied, "Oh, I can live *with* them. I just don't want to live *next* to them."

The priority I placed on open housing was a response to sentiments I'd picked up from my constituents at one of my regular district meetings. In addition to keeping the clergy involved in the lawmaking process, which I regarded as the political equivalent of saying my prayers (I reported to the various ministers regularly and convened all of them for an annual conference), I made it a point to hold monthly public sessions for the voters, conferring between meetings with an executive board and committee chairmen established within the constituency. That way, the citizens of the district were assured that their views and concerns had a forum at the state level. It beats the hell out of me why other state- and federal-level public servants didn't and don't do something similar to stay in touch with the community—in the interest of both their legislative and career agendas—but I've never known any who did. In addition to what they did for me at election time, I found those get-togethers to be terrifically informative and fundamental to my work in Lansing. Each conference focused on a topic such as housing, education, recreation, economic development, or law enforcement. Damn near half the district would turn out for the law enforcement panel, which confirmed my belief that while housing was an urgent concern, police brutality was the most chronic, threatening malady the city had to deal with.

The police problem went much deeper than brutality. At its core was the basic attitude that the police were not there to serve the citizens of the black community, but to beat them back; not to protect them, but to discipline them; not to comfort them, but to contain them. Detroit's cops were essentially prison guards, operating under the assumption that the people within their jurisdiction were criminally dangerous and should be forcibly quarantined from mainstream society. The police mentality was to keep the damn blacks away from the white folks at all costs, and what they did to themselves was their problem. Consequently, the neighborhood badasses—there was no shortage of thugs, crooks, and drug dealers—were an uncontested menace to the immediate community.

I received numerous letters from constituents complaining that the cops had been completely unresponsive to their problems. The police made no pretense of being on the side of the black people on their beats, and the attitude was not so subtle as to be restricted to poor folks, private company, and back streets. In 1966, policemen engaged a group of black student activists on Kercheval Avenue on the east side, and the resulting disturbance, known as the Kercheval Incident, stirred fears that the national riot epidemic was about to reach Detroit. The events of that summer are vivid to me, because I had just completed my senatorial campaign for the primary election and was pulling back to relax for a few days when my father died at the age of seventy-two. After the funeral, we held a wake at his house on Harding, which was practically around the corner from the site of the incident on Kercheval, and the place was filled with relatives and friends when the phone rang. A policeman friend of mine was on the line, advising me to get everybody out of the house and clear the area because things could get ugly. I can still feel the rage I had toward the cop thugs as I ushered people away from my father's wake. When everybody was gone, I made some calls and pulled together a contingent that included Charlie Diggs, who'd become a U.S. congressman, and other elected officials, ministers, and community leaders, mostly black and a few white. Within hours, there were fifty or sixty of us marching arm in arm down Kercheval Avenue. As we walked, a cavalcade of tactical mobile units—police cruisers—pulled up alongside, rumbling along very slowly, bumper to bumper. The officers inside just glared at us, and before they moved on, one of them snarled, "You goddamn niggers get your black asses off the street."

The ratio of black officers on the force was beginning to increase measurably under Cavanagh, but not at a pace that kept up with the ostensibly changing times. For all of his progressiveness, the mayor was less diligent about appointing blacks as department heads. The effect was that whites maintained authoritarian control of the city even while forsaking it in staggering proportions, bailing out at the rate of about fifty thousand a year through the sixties. This came in a period when the Voting Rights Act of 1965, through advances in nondiscriminatory voter registration and election practices, was promising a new age of political empowerment for blacks, and the racially sensitive Great Society programs of LBJ and Robert Kennedy were supposed to be righting the wrongs of urban renewal and economic alienation. It was, if nothing else, a time of furious scurrying-about and much provocative ado.

The trappings of a new age were all around the city. In an inauspicious sound room on West Grand Boulevard, Berry Gordy, Jr., tapping into the indigenous rhythms and prodigious resources that enveloped him as Detroit evolved slowly into America's blackest major municipality, was remaking the image of the Motor City with sweet and funky urban music by the likes of the Supremes and the Temptations and the Four Tops and Marvin Gaye and Stevie Wonder. But the substance of the city bore little resemblance to its style. The irony was that a black man or woman could become a superstar in Detroit as nowhere else; but for the average black person looking for a place that would give him half a chance and a little

R-E-S-P-E-C-T (as C. L. Franklin's daughter so eloquently put it), Motown was no town to be stuck in. They still burned crosses in Detroit.

Of course, as a soul town, there was no other like it. At the Fox Theater on Woodward Avenue, the Temps and Little Stevie and some of the most popular recording artists in the world lit up the stage of the Motown Revue. At less glittery night spots, like the 20 Grand Club, which included a motel and a bowling alley, you might get lucky and catch an act on the order of Martha Reeves or Smokey Robinson; and it was worth going to Reverend Franklin's church just to hear his girl sing with the choir. For these and other reasons, I spent as much time as I could in Detroit. It was a kinetic, stimulating city, and I tried to listen to it. But after I had been in office for a couple of years and was elected majority floor leader of the senate, I admittedly and regrettably lost some of the closeness I'd had with my constituents.

The new position was a party job, not a people job. I was responsible for keeping the Democratic senators apprised of the party's positions on all the bills in progress, for counting votes on the floor, for mediating disputes within our ranks. I still had my conferences with the citizens, but I don't think I knew them quite as well.

If I had, maybe I could have seen what was coming in 1967.

7

The Big Bang

The newsmagazines called Detroit a model city. They marveled at its strong chin and gushed over the heroic benevolence of Mayor Cavanagh, who had become the gallant knight of the War on Poverty by spearing forty-two million federal dollars for the city's poor people. Cavanagh was widely portrayed as a sort of Great White Sympathizer, and the fact is, he worked hard at maintaining a symbiotic rapport with black leaders. In that spirit, he had established an amicable relationship that led observers to think of Detroit as being immunized against the outbreak of inner-city rioting that had torn apart Watts in 1965, bloodied Chicago and Philadelphia, and in 1967 was sweeping the country at a rate that would produce 164 incidents, among them, major revolts in Cleveland and Newark.

Despite the mainstream feeling that it couldn't happen in Detroit (a sentiment that was not unanimously observed in the black community, where it was common knowledge that the mayor's goodwill had failed to impress his police officers), Cavanagh had taken the extra step of setting up an Early Warning Commission to alert him at the first hint of a disturbance. The only problem was that an urban riot is generally not an independent organism, welling up by its own exclusive devices, but entails an implicit partnership with an outside party. This is where the police come in.

What they did in the dark early morning of July 23, 1967, was raid a blind pig at 9125 Twelfth Street, near Clairmount, an inauspicious building with For Sale signs all around and "Economy

Printing" painted on the front. The second floor was an informal meeting place called the Community League for Civil Action, where, at 3:45 A.M. that sweltering Sunday, scores of neighborhood folks were enjoying themselves in honor of servicemen home from Vietnam. The celebration ended when the police entered uninvited, threw somebody down the stairs, beat up a few others, and arrested more than eighty people.

The number of arrests proved to be most inopportune, because it required that many in the crowd be detained while the paddy wagon and squad cars ferried their friends to the precinct station. As that protracted process was taking place, others in the neighborhood began to close in on the scene until a swarm of hundreds had gathered. They taunted the police for their bullyish presence, and when somebody smashed the window of a squad car with a bottle, the bell went off on what the *Washington Post* called "the greatest tragedy of all [in] the long succession of Negro ghetto outbursts." By the time the glass hit the street, the crowd had become a mob, spilling garbage and setting it on fire, heaving bricks through store windows, and enthusiastically appropriating the merchandise therein.

Although the next few days are historically referred to as the Detroit riot, those in the black community still refer to it as a rebellion. I choose to think of it as an explosion—a chemical reaction to the prevailing conditions. The flammable element was police brutality, and when yet another measure of it was dropped into the beaker on July 23, the city went bang. As it was, the police might have neutralized the effects of the first fizz by mixing in peaceably, but they elected to agitate. Knowing that Cavanagh would disapprove of a full-scale action to quash the uprising, the cops brought in extra cruisers and menacingly circled the area, virtually inviting the defiance of the looters.

I was home from Lansing at the time, and many hours before I would have gotten up—remember, it was Sunday—I received a phone call from Louise Tappes, the wife of labor leader Shelton Tappes and a prominent community figure in her own right. The Tappeses lived in the vicinity of the blind pig that was raided, and from their back porch they witnessed the genesis of what was—

prior to the Los Angeles rebellion of 1992—the most devastating week of urban violence in American annals. The first of sixteen hundred fires was set in a shoe store around 6:30 A.M. Later that morning, driving through the streets of west-central Detroit, I helplessly watched buildings go up in flames on Linwood and then on Dexter.

Just after noon, I was to attend a meeting with the mayor and other local leaders at Grace Episcopal Church on Twelfth Street, near the nucleus of the explosion. People were milling through the neighborhood in droves, and when I turned off West Grand Boulevard onto Twelfth, I came upon a crowd so thick it covered the streets and enveloped the church. Police lines prevented me from making it there. In fact, the meeting never came off, because none of the principals could get through. So I drove on and saw the destruction spread east to streets like Oakland and Clay.

As the city was pillaged and burned, it became graphically evident that the black citizens were hell-bent on destroying the artifacts of their own haunted fate. John Conyers, a newly elected congressman and the son of a former patron of Maben's barbershop, climbed up on a car to address the mob through a bullhorn, and they stoned him down. When Reverend Nicholas Hood, the city's only black councilman, tried to calm his constituents, they threatened his life. The insurgents were going to do with their neighborhood what they would, and to hell with anybody who got in the way. The city hastily assembled an all-black firefighting unit to work the riot area, but it was pelted with debris and run off the scene.

As I made the rounds that day, I looked down the barrels of two or three police guns. Finally, I decided it was prudent to retreat home and monitor the goings-on from the front lawn of my apartment on East Forest, about a mile southeast of the heaviest action. But when I pulled into the neighborhood, I discovered that a liquor store had been burned down a few hundred feet from my place, across a vacant lot, and the apartment building had been evacuated because the wind was blowing the fire that way. Firemen hosed down the wall of the building as a precaution, and when the flames subsided, I pulled up a lawn chair and became a nervous spectator. From where I sat, the most unsettling sight wasn't the fire down the street but the caravans of police cars that rolled by with shotguns sticking out of the cruiser windows and station wagon tailgates. A couple of the officers ordered me inside the building, despite its condition, and although my custom would be to press the point, I also made it a rule not to argue with live ammunition in the heat of a major riot.

Remarkably, nobody was killed the first day. In that regard, the contrast with the 1943 riot was distinct, the earlier one having started and ended with white and black people murdering each other. The explosion of 1967, unlike the one twenty-four years before, was not a race riot. To be sure, most of the participants were black, and there were unmistakable racial implications, as suggested by the words "Soul Brother" and "Afro All the Way" painted on store windows by merchants who hoped that their businesses would be passed over by the looters. That strategy might have bought the owners an extra day or so, but it failed to spare them indefinitely, because the uprising was not a color dispute. A television cameraman took pictures of the looting of an A&P store on Trumbull, and there was racial unity up and down the goddamn aisles of that place. Blacks and whites were helping each other carry out cases of canned goods in complete harmony. Later, a survey was taken of those arrested during the week, the vast majority of whom were black, and in answer to a question about whether their actions were antiwhite in nature, ninety-one percent said no.

It could be argued that the rebellion—specifically, the pillaging part of it—was as much about consumerism as about race, a revolt of underprivileged, overcrowded, hot, and irritable citizens who were fed up with having their meager economic means exploited by the privileged and finally had a chance to be the takers. I'd be surprised if there was a television left in any store in the inner city when the week was over. In fact, TV was a vital two-way player in the brutal game being carried out in the streets. For a week, people had been watching and getting ideas from TV coverage of the riot in Newark. They'd seen clips of similar events in Memphis and Milwaukee and Boston and Tampa and Cincinnati and Buffalo earlier in the summer. In that sense, TV represented the riot textbook.

And on the other end, a television was the consummate looting item—an expensive, useful thing that could be carted off conspicuously. One of the most ironic and revealing snapshots of the week came when a looter was asked by a reporter how he liked the television he stole, and replied, "Not so good. The first thing I saw on it was me stealing the damn thing."

The looting was a cooperative effort in more than the racial context. Some observers testified that it was also government-assisted in a fashion, reporting National Guardsmen among those making off with merchandise. The Guard's ultimate role in the explosion, discharged with jitters, inexperience, and common bigotry, was to keep the fuel coming. Between the Guard and the police, authorities did their damnedest to turn the affair into a race riot, the operative word on their part being "nigger." Witnesses and photographs implicated police and Guardsmen in a horrific litany of offenses, among them: stabbing their arrest victims—many of them bystanders—with bayonets; fondling women's breasts; burning initials into a prisoner's back with a cigarette; and fire-bombing an Afro-American bookstore. The police attitude was aptly illustrated by an incident in which a black officer, Ike McKinnon, was driving home after a tense twenty-four-hour shift on the first day of the explosion. A white cop in a cruiser pulled him over for no discernible reason, and when the patrolman approached, McKinnon said, "Hi, police officer here." The other officer responded by shouting, "Get your black ass out of the car." When McKinnon showed his badge, the cop shot at him, fortunately missing.

If the insurrection of Detroit in 1967 must be called a riot, let it be recorded as a police riot. This is not to say that the citizens of Detroit were justified in destroying their own community, or that the police should bear all of the blame; only that there was a principal object of the rebels' vengeance, and it was not the generic white man (though he was on the list), and it was not the white man behind the counter (though he was high on the list); it was the white man in the blue uniform.

When they understood the mess they were in, the police set up a riot command post at Herman Kiefer Hospital, between Twelfth and the Lodge Freeway. I can't tell you what went on there. In fact, the government's strategic process as a whole was something of a riddle—particularly the deliberations of Governor Romney, whose indecision and political machinations resulted in deadly delays. Romney was quick enough to declare a state of emergency and to order in state police and National Guardsmen, but it was immediately obvious that they only quickened the prevailing anxieties. The situation clearly called for federal troops (an assessment that places me in the uncomfortable role of agreeing with Walter Reuther, who appealed to the governor to place the order), but for some reason which defies any explanation save that of political posturing, Romney was reluctant to request them. It was well-known that Romney was positioning himself for a run at the presidency in 1968, and if he were to succeed in winning the Republican nomination, which was not an outlandish prospect, he would presumably find himself pitted against President Johnson. As a candidate, he shrank at the prospect of appealing to his opponent to bail him out of an ugly problem in his own territory. In turn, Johnson was not above manipulating the situation to his political advantage.

By Sunday night, the inner city had become an open wound and the raw spot was spreading west to Grand River and Livernois and east to Mack Avenue while the governor fucked around with protocol and face-saving language. At three A.M. Monday—nearly twenty-four hours after the first salvo—Romney mustered a call to Attorney General Ramsey Clark, asking for federal assistance. But he was still limp on the details, and it was eleven o'clock before Johnson sent in 4,700 paratroopers. Even then, the political pussy-footing had only just begun. Instead of sweeping straight into the raging city, the soldiers put down at Selfridge Air Base, forty miles from downtown. Late Monday evening, after the second and worst day of rioting, help moved a little closer when three units from the 101st and 82nd Airborne arrived at the state fairgrounds on the northern extremity of Detroit, Woodward and Eight Mile. At midnight, the President went on national television to explain the federal state of emergency that had necessitated military action, making numerous references in the course of his address to Romney's inability to handle the crisis with state and local resources. Finally, at three A.M. Tuesday—two full days after the riot had started and twenty-four hours after Romney had summoned the wherewithal to ask for troops—Airborne personnel in full battle dress checked into Southeastern High School to defend the east side of the city, which they proceeded to do skillfully.

The pre-established police concentration on the west side, near the center of the explosion, dictated that the paratroopers be deployed on the opposite part of town, which proved to be an uneven and unfortunate arrangement. On the west side, the community was virtually under siege. The state police and the National Guard were lily-white at the time, or damn near; and combined with the racist Detroit police, the effect was like a white army of occupation on both sides of Twelfth Street. The jackboots of the authorities were on the necks of the black community, and the community was squirming violently to get free. The parameters were confrontational, fostering a winless situation in which peace would represent surrender. It was no coincidence that most of the violence occurred in that vicinity. By contrast, the paratrooper outfits were thoroughly integrated, right up through the officers—quite a change from my Air Force days—and they were able to bring the east side under control swiftly and firmly with a light touch. They made it clear, with little more than professionalism and an attitude, that they were in place to protect the citizens, not to punish them. After two or three days, there was an air of fraternization on the east side completely unfamiliar in the oppressive police climate of Detroit.

But the federal troops had arrived much too late to do anything about a tragic Monday, when an awful outbreak of fires accounted for more than six hundred alarms and the riot took its first victim, a white man who was shot while running from a store that had just been looted on Fourth Street. There would be forty-three people killed in all, thirty of them by law enforcement officials, and more than seven thousand three hundred arrested. In excess of four hundred buildings were destroyed, including twenty percent of the ones on Twelfth Street around Virginia Park. The riot hardly let up the whole damn week. Looting and sniping continued until Friday, and their side effect, price gouging—some of the stores that survived took advantage of the situation by charging up to four times the normal rates—was so rampant that the city council was required to pass an emergency ordinance to control it. Meanwhile, prisoners filled the state and federal penitentiaries, the county jail, the police gym and garages, and the bathhouse at Belle Isle, which looked like a goddamn war camp.

As the city quieted down, I became concerned that the police department might be overstepping its bounds in the effort to apprehend and punish those involved in the uprising. My fear was that we would see a repeat of what had occurred in Newark, where the police department had obtained a list of registered guns in the city, broken it down by precinct, and stormed through the neighborhoods kicking down doors and seizing legal weapons. Such an authoritarian tactic was a flagrant violation of civil rights and a frightening sign of oppression. To my knowledge, there was no comparable list circulating in the Detroit Police Department, but there were a disturbing number of reports about doors being kicked in. In reaction to those reports, John Conyers and I established a forum for citizens to air their complaints, setting up informal hearings at the Amalgamated Clothing Workers Hall, Twelfth Street and West Grand.

At one of the meetings, a young black man stood up and requested that we help his brother get out of jail to attend the funeral of another brother who had been killed in an incident at the Algiers Motel, a manor house on Woodward at Virginia Park renowned for its low-life activities. It was known that three people had been shot and killed at the Algiers during the rebellion, but the deaths had been reported as the result of violence initiated by guests at the motel.

When the young man began to tell an entirely different story, we realized that it was very hot stuff and advised him to say no more. We then interviewed him more privately at the Guardian Building law office of John's brother, Nathan Conyers, and followed up by bringing in additional witnesses. The result was a grisly, horrifying tale of wanton executions perpetrated by a combined force of city, state, and federal law-enforcement officers. Instrumental in reconstructing the events of the day were two white girls from Ohio, high school dropouts who had come to Detroit seeking adventure. They were very naive and soon found themselves in much faster company than they were prepared for. I don't think the girls were prostitutes, but no doubt some of the guys they were involved with were pimps who would have liked to turn them out. In the meantime, the girls were letting their hair down in the sort of activity that was common to the Algiers, and when the cops arrived in response to false reports of sniping at the motel, they apparently went nuts at the sight of white girls in the company of black men. According to the survivors, the lawmen busted in, rounded up everyone on the premises, and proceeded to brutalize the entire party with a twisted "death game" in which they ordered each person into a separate room, one by one, and fired shotguns to make the others believe—sometimes accurately, sometimes not—that he or she had been killed. In the process, three innocent people were shot dead for the hell of it.

When we fully comprehended the scope of what we were hearing, Conyers and I decided to call in the Justice Department. You can imagine how distasteful that was for me, given my history with the Justice motherfuckers; but it was either them or the police, and we sure as hell couldn't trust the police. The newspapers and the county prosecutor joined in the investigation, and the case against the officers made it to state court on charges of second-degree murder. It was a sensational, highly publicized trial, during which it was revealed that there had been no exchange of fire at the Algiers, and that the victims had been shot at a range so close that there were powder burns on their flesh and shotgun shells embedded in their wounds. Despite all of that, the jury, acting upon the judge's charge that the officers had to be found innocent unless it could be proven they had "killed with malice and premeditation," allowed the defendants to walk free. Nobody was ever convicted for what happened at the Algiers Motel. I issued a press release that said, "This latest phase of a step-by-step whitewash of a police slaying demonstrates once again that law and order is a one-way street. There is no law and order where black people are involved, especially when they are involved with the police."

It apparently took a rebellion and a major controversy for Cavanagh to recognize that the defining whiteness of the Detroit

Police Department—in both numbers and mentality—left it ill equipped to maintain order or represent justice in the inner city. When he did, he established a committee to address the matter of affirmative action in the department. I was appointed to the committee, but soon found that I was butting up against the hard heads of the law enforcement establishment, which was loath to integrate the department in the equitable proportions advocated by me and the black citizenry. The police unions were politically powerful—they could make or break an elected city official—and Cavanagh yielded to their pressure, backing off from any substantial affirmative-action initiatives. He and I fell out over that. When Jerry sided with the police, I felt I had no alternative but to publicly resign my committee position in protest. Before the riot, many blacks had been willing to give Cavanagh the benefit of the doubt, presuming that he had no control over the actions of individual police officers; but when he had the perfect opportunity to change the complexion of the department by administering bold affirmative-action measures, he faltered conspicuously. With that, the black community began to perceive the mayor as an uncertain trumpet, and he lost a lot of constituents because of it. Ultimately, Cavanagh became another casualty of the rebellion.

The heaviest casualty, however, was the city. Detroit's losses went a hell of a lot deeper than the immediate toll of lives and buildings. The riot put Detroit on the fast track to economic desolation, mugging the city and making off with incalculable value in jobs, earnings taxes, corporate taxes, retail dollars, sales taxes, mortgages, interest, property taxes, development dollars, investment dollars, entertainment dollars, tourism dollars, and plain damn money. The money was carried out in the pockets of the businesses and the white people who fled as fast as they could. The white exodus from Detroit had been prodigiously steady prior to the rebellion, totaling twenty-two thousand in 1966, but afterwards it was frantic. In 1967—with less than half the year remaining after the summer explosion—the outward population migration reached sixty-seven thousand. In 1968, the figure hit eighty thousand, followed by forty-six thousand in 1969. The flight of business and businesses was just as dramatic and even more devastating. Over the next quarter-century, the number of manufacturing and retail establishments in the city would be reduced by half while steadily increasing in the suburbs. In just ten years immediately following the rebellion, Detroit lost more than 110,000 jobs. As a result, we were losing Detroit.

As he played out the last years of his second term, there was not a hell of a lot Cavanagh could or would do at the administrative level to arrest the fervent racial antipathy that was tearing apart Detroit. Instead, he turned to the private sector and helped establish the New Detroit Committee, of which I became a member. Advertised as a think tank for urban race relations, New Detroit sponsored a gamut of programs intended to reform the racial attitudes of the city and the suburbs; but its preoccupation with the abstract turned off both the pragmatists and the militants and divided the effort. In 1970, another private committee emerged, under the name of Detroit Renaissance, a coalition of business and industrial elite led by Henry Ford II and committed to reversing the flight of commerce from the city. The advantage of Ford's group was money, which it used for a brick-and-mortar redevelopment of the downtown riverfront, the area designated as the starting point for Detroit's renaissance. Another impetus that Renaissance had going for it was desperation. So much blood had been sucked from Detroit that even the penthouse people grudgingly realized they had damn well better do something to save their city. It would take money, and nobody else had any. As Chrysler president Lynn Townsend put it at the time, "We'd better make an extra effort. Detroit is the test tube for America. If the concentrated power of industry and government can't solve the problems of the ghetto here, God help our country."

While Detroit was set into motion by the '67 rebellion, the response to it was not confined to the city. The national implications of the riot were certified immediately by President Johnson, who set up a National Advisory Commission on Civil Disorders to study it. The President's commission, whose membership included the likes of Massachusetts senator Edward Brooke, Roy Wilkins of the NAACP, and New York mayor John Lindsay, was popularly referred to by the name of its chairman, federal judge and former Illinois

governor Otto Kerner. In March 1968, it produced a candid, startling report that remains a primary reference in urban analysis.

The passage of the Kerner Report cited most often after more
than two decades is the prophetic observation: "Our nation is moving toward two societies, one black, one white—separate and unequal." That commentary was predicated upon profound racial
disparities in such essential areas as housing and education. At the
time of the riot, Detroit schools were spending five hundred dollars less per student than their counterparts in the near suburbs,
and the dropout rate was at fifty percent. The Kerner Commission
argued that the most pertinent single factor in the perpetuation of
family poverty was the head of the household's failure to graduate
from high school. It also recognized that suburban migration was
isolating the poor in pockets of the nation's big cities, twenty-five
of which have since become home to half the country's black population. A stark example of this punishing pattern was the Twelfth
Street neighborhood that produced the 1967 explosion, where
twenty-one thousand people were being overcharged to squeeze
into a square mile in which nearly half the buildings were below liv-
able standards. "What white Americans have never fully understood—but what the Negro can never forget—is that white society
is deeply implicated in the ghetto," the Kerner Commission alleged. "White institutions created it, white institutions maintain it,
and white society condones it."

One of the red-flag conditions with which the commission implicated the white establishment was the urban temperament that
made the riot inevitable. Formalizing what was painfully and un-
mistakably apparent to those of us who knew Detroit, it reported:
"We have cited deep hostility between police and ghetto communities as a primary cause of the disorders surveyed by the commission." It almost sounded as if the government was coming around.
Taking the theme further, the Kerner manifesto concluded that
the accumulated effects of time-honored discrimination, segregation, deprivation, and racial paranoia had collaborated powerfully
against an equal-opportunity society, and that bold interventions
were necessary to arrest the trend. It recommended such solutions
as public jobs and job-training programs, free child care, educa-

tional parity, and guaranteed income. Hell, the Kerner Report read like something Haywood Maben might have written between haircuts.

The only problem with the damn thing was that it came out in an election year. Because of that, it was shortchanged by the media in favor of campaign coverage, dismissed as politics, and ultimately ignored or rejected by the voting public. When the country elected Nixon, it effectively brushed off the findings of the Kerner Commission, going merrily about its business as if there had never been a problem in the first place.

I HAD THE PRIVILEGE of being teargassed at the 1968 Democratic convention in Chicago, and it drove me back to smoking. My caucus was meeting in a stuffy hotel room next to the park where cops were spraying Mace at the demonstrators wreaking havoc for the city and the convention, and the damn stuff was drifting through the window and getting in my eyes and mouth. Smoking seemed to help, which was all the excuse I needed to take it up again. After the meeting broke up, I was riding off in a convertible and got caught in a traffic jam on Lakeshore Drive, where the air was so thick with Mace that tears were streaming down my face. A rich Republican in a black limousine saw the anguish I was in and invited me over to join him in air-conditioned comfort. At that moment, we achieved unity between the parties.

I was at the convention as the national committeeman from Michigan, the first black in the country to be elected to such a position in the party. Actually, the distinction was merely a matter of timing, because several other blacks joined the committee later in the year. But it was sort of a big deal when it happened. I was becoming pretty goddamn legitimate.

My vote at the convention went for Hubert Humphrey in deference to a nice man and a nice letter he had written urging my support. But had he survived the bullet of Sirhan Sirhan after winning the California primary, my first choice would have been Robert Kennedy. I felt a kinship with Bobby Kennedy from the moment I saw that he referred to liberals as "sons of bitches." He and I seemed to agree that liberals are basically in the way of the people who would take on the world. Those people are radicals, which is what I consider myself. I don't know if Bobby Kennedy would have been at home in Maben's barbershop or if he would have been bounced by Walter Reuther or outlawed by the attorney general— hell, he *was* the attorney general—but I do know that in 1968 he and Martin Luther King were murdered for what they courageously represented.

Pushed by King's charismatic leadership and Kennedy's community action programs, the civil rights movement and the mutually inclusive War on Poverty had gathered a head of steam by that time, and it would not be stopped by the bullets of assassins. A concerted effort of the American public and bureaucracy was required, and by electing Nixon and then electing him again, the nation demonstrated that it was up to the task.

Even in Detroit, where the influence of black citizens far exceeded the national norms, there was still organized resistance to civil rights. In May 1968, a month after the assassination of Dr. King, the Poor People's Campaign of the Southern Christian Leadership Conference arrived downtown by caravan, and when one of the cars stalled in the service drive to Cobo Hall, police gathered around and aggressively ordered the procession to move along. This attracted a group of SCLC folks, who sat on their hoods singing protest songs until more than a dozen mounted cops charged in, swinging billy clubs and chasing people from the scene. I wondered if they would ever learn. In a letter to Cavanagh, I told him, "This is the stuff of which riots are made." A year later, a regrettable confrontation between police and a group of black nationalists at New Bethel Church resulted in a more serious incident—one policeman dead and hundreds of blacks arrested. Once again, Cavanagh's response was hollow. George Crockett, from his position on the Recorder's Court, took hold of the situation by releasing most of the prisoners, which appeased the angry citizens of the black community and galvanized their opposition to the mayor who had once been their great white hope. It was a mayoral election year, and in June, Cavanagh announced that he would not seek another term.

I wasn't sure if the city was quite ready for a black mayor, but I was damn tempted to find out. I *was* sure, after checking to see how the wind blew, that the state was not ready for a black governor, and the prospects were equally unlikely for a U.S. Senate seat. I was and remain somewhat bitter over the fact that white contemporaries of mine have been elected to higher offices for which I could have never been a serious candidate (Carl Levin, for instance, was president of the Detroit City Council in 1978 when he was elected to the U.S. Senate, where he has served three terms); but my consolation, in 1969, was that city politics were becoming a different matter in the face of changing demographics.

When I first decided to run for mayor, the problem was not entirely electability. It was eligibility—specifically, a misunderstood constitutional provision concerning a state legislator's freedom to pursue another public office. According to article 4, section 9 of the Michigan constitution, "no person elected to the legislature shall receive any civil appointment within this state from the governor, except notaries public, from the legislature, or from any other state authority, during the term for which he is elected." As I read the law, it meant that a legislator could not *be appointed* to another office and that there was no conflict concerning an *elected* office. But that was not the traditional interpretation, and when I attempted to file as a mayoral candidate, I was denied on the grounds that the office of mayor was regarded as a civil appointment. I was still hopeful of having my eligibility upheld in court, but the circuit court ruled against me, and there wasn't enough time to see my case through to the state supreme court. I resolved to initiate the process a year in advance of the next mayoral election.

There was, however, a strong black candidate in 1969, a Constitutional Convention colleague of mine and future Michigan secretary of state, Richard Austin. His opponent was Roman Gribbs, a former Wayne County sheriff who pulled out the election by one percent. In retrospect, Austin's excruciating defeat was of more historic relevance than the scant victory of Gribbs, who in later years conceded that his role was one of a transitional mayor serving out the short years between Cavanagh and the city's first black administration—which, he well knew, was surely only a term or two away.

The intervening years would not pass quietly. While in Detroit the street war dragged on between black citizens and police—some people have advanced the idea that the riot never really ended, it just slowed down—racial unrest became the rule on college campuses around the state and much of the nation. In the spring of 1969, at Ferris State University of Big Rapids, Michigan, three hundred blacks were arrested by state police following an incident that began when two thousand white students ripped through the campus shouting about white power while flaunting bows, arrows, and knives. Several black students were Maced by whites wearing sheets, and scores of them were so frightened by the mob that they spent a night huddled together in the library. Basil Brown and I requested an inquiry into why no whites had been arrested in the unrest, but we got nowhere. A couple of months later, the senate was visited by about seventy representatives of the Black Student Alliance, who were protesting the arrest of fourteen black youths at Eastern Michigan University. The students assembled in the balcony, and when they stood up with their fists raised in the air, I returned the greeting. However, another senator, Robert Huber—an archconservative from Oakland County who once proposed a resolution to investigate my activities—reacted differently, mumbling, "I'd better get my gun." I did not take this as an idle remark, since he was known to pack one.

In 1970, the trouble spot was Northern Michigan University, where white students passed out cards inscribed "Nigger Hunting Permit." (The small type noted that there was a five-nigger limit.) Six people were arrested as a result, all of them black students who had staged a sit-in protest. I took up their cause on the senate floor and tried to expand the issue, arguing that we would be getting somewhere when the percentage of black students at Michigan State was commensurate with the black casualty rate in Vietnam.

I would ultimately serve three terms in the senate, and I considered them productive. Surprisingly, I was not alone in my assessment, for a change. The *Detroit Free Press*, so wary of me for so long, actually endorsed me in 1970, going so far as to call me a "skillful, pragmatic legislator and effective spokesman for Detroit." To this day, I'm not sure where I went astray.

It helped that the worm turned as my tenure began, and I chanced into being part of Michigan's first Democratic legislature in more than thirty years. Reapportionment had increased the number of black legislators, and several of the white ones—fellows like Roger Craig and Sandy Levin, the majority leader—were kindred spirits. We worked together successfully in such areas as workmen's compensation, unemployment insurance, senior citizen relief, urban education, and, inevitably, busing.

I sort of pulled a fast one on busing. A bill was on the table outlawing the busing of city kids to predominantly white schools, and for tactical purposes I threw in with the antibusing side. In the course of the debate, I suggested that we not only prohibit urban busing but go the distance and outlaw all school buses in the city and throughout the state. That killed that bill. And although my proposal was deliberately overstated, the fact was that the state operated its school transportation system with an untenable inequity, spending $20 million on rural bus service and a fat zero for the same thing in Detroit.

The restructuring of urban education was still in its formative stage then—perhaps it lingers there even now—and much of our workload in the statehouse dealt with it. Among the measures I managed to pass was one that decentralized Detroit's school system, dividing the district into subregions in which, unlike the all-white school board, there was black representation. But as partial as I was to matters of special urban concern, I liked to think that there wasn't an issue about which I was incapable of producing legislation. One of my bills made it a misdemeanor to advertise a product as kosher if it did not satisfy Hebrew religious requirements. On a broader level, I succeeded with proposals to increase Aid to Dependent Children benefits and Detroit income tax, to regulate bail bonds, to facilitate urban renewal relocation, and to institute no-fault insurance legislation that became a model for other states. I regret that I also succeeded in seeing through compulsory binding arbitration for police and fire departments—the infamous Act 312, which provided collective-bargaining leverage that those municipal unions have since turned against me to great and troubling effect. I came up short with a bill to legalize dog racing, but in the effort was rewarded by the development of a long-lasting working relationship with the Republican leader, Emil Lockwood. And although I wasn't the sponsor, I worked hard, if fruitlessly, on a bill to establish a prochoice Michigan abortion policy, which was ultimately determined by *Roe* v. *Wade*.

It seemed that I spent most of my Lansing years writing and lobbying for legislation that should have been part of Con-Con's revised constitution in the first place. As governor, Romney was less of an impediment than he had been as the kingpin of Con-Con, and I had a little better luck in the senate. In all, I managed to get nearly twenty-seven percent of my bills passed while I was in Lansing, compared to a legislative average of about twenty percent. I thought this was pretty damn good, considering that I fired them off in record quantity.

At one point, when Sandy Levin and I were working on an urban package, I carried a stack of 117 bills from my basement office to the senate chambers on the second floor. My pile included measures that would, among other things, liberalize workmen's compensation; limit wage garnishments; provide for a housing court to protect the rights of tenants; and establish community housing authorities and civilian police review boards. As soon as I plopped down my load of legislation—the largest the senate had ever seen—Levin came behind me lugging a complementary stack of bills that concentrated on education. The whole caboodle represented some serious senatorial work, but I don't deny there was a little grandstanding involved. We hoped that if nothing else, our efforts would call attention to the worsening urban predicament.

Levin, who ultimately became a U.S. congressman, left the state-house in 1970 to undertake an unsuccessful campaign for governor, leaving open the position of minority leader (the Republicans having regained control of the senate). In the normal course of things, I would have moved up from my role as floor leader; but, for reasons owing more to public relations than prejudice, the Democratic caucus preferred not to place a black senator at the head of the party. Instead, it delivered the job to George Fitzgerald, an eloquent attorney—he had been Jimmy Hoffa's chief legal counsel—and a veteran legislator who spent about half the year at his condo in Lake Worth, Florida. Under that arrangement, a white man could hold the title while I did most of the work. Fitzgerald was a solid senator and friend, and we conferred amiably about positions that I would then execute at the capitol.

I continued to split my time between Lansing and Detroit, heading home on the weekends for entertainment and poker. It was about the worst period of poker I ever had, because people kept distracting me with their problems; but that didn't keep me out of the neighborhoods. I particularly appreciated the company at a barbershop on Joseph Campau, which took up, more or less, where Maben's left off when it was bulldozed for urban renewal. We'd sit around and bullshit, and eight or nine of us would throw in a dollar to get some liquor. We'd supply an extra cup for the runner, but the rule was that all the stockholders would get a drink before the runner was permitted one. If there was any whiskey left in the bottle and all the stockholders agreed, some other motherfucker might get a slug, too. But if you weren't a stockholder, you had a better chance of getting an argument than a drink.

I don't believe that a good, lively argument occupies the favored position on the entertainment spectrum that it used to. Many of my fondest memories have to do with disagreements, such as one I had at the barbershop with a schoolteacher named Ralph who thought he knew everything and loved to share his wisdom. One night, we were sitting around doing a lot of nothing and Ralph said, "I'll tell you one goddamn thing. I want some action, and that's a verb." I said, "Ralph, that's a noun." The argument ensued. I had a little money in my pocket and Ralph had his paycheck, but that wasn't enough to cover the action (that's a noun) we worked up. He put up fifty bucks plus his paycheck, which was around four hundred, and I answered it with a check. Then we dispatched the barber, Sonny, to get a dictionary, except that Ralph didn't know I had Sonny in the bag. If I was wrong, Sonny was going to come back and say, "I can't find no damn dictionary." See, he had about ten dollars of his own riding on the side. Everybody had something down. It was a hell of a bet, because how were those guys going to choose between the schoolteacher and the senator? Anyway, when Sonny came back with the word, I thought Ralph was going to cry. He was afraid his old lady would put him out if he came home without his paycheck, so I gave him back the check and he told me he could pay me the next week, which he did. Served his ass right. Don't think I was always so omniscient, however. I got taken plenty of times. Some motherfucker would start an argument about Heinie Manush's batting average in 1932 and then go pull the *Baseball Digest* out of his trunk.

I suppose I ought to make it clear at this point that not all of my extracurricular activities revolved around hustling. I also tried to stay busy with social issues. If you consider the ladies to be a social issue, so be it, but I'm talking about the subjects that were dominating the country during that period—Vietnam and civil rights. America hasn't been in a military conflict that I didn't vigorously oppose since World War II, but in the case of Vietnam, for once I was in the majority. In Detroit, the Vietnam protest was spearheaded by DAM, the Detroit Area Mobilization committee, on which I teamed with Congressman Conyers, Reverend Hill, a liberal white social worker named Maryann Mahaffey, and a black nationalist, Reverend Albert Cleage, who was the guru of an up-and-coming organization known as the Shrine of the Black Madonna. On the national level, I joined up with Julian Bond from Atlanta, actor Ossie Davis, and other black leaders in the Hemisphere Conference to End the War in Vietnam.

In 1972, there was a high-profile civil rights event about which I was very hopeful. It was a convention in Gary, Indiana, called the Black Political Caucus, organized by my congressman friend and neighbor, Charlie Diggs, and the black social poet and activist LeRoi Jones, otherwise known as Imamu Amiri Baraka. The caucus was much anticipated, bringing together black politicians and writers and religious leaders from all over the country for the purpose of drafting a platform that would unite us as a political coalition. It was a grandiose idea, the problem being that the platform was already put together by the time we got to Gary. After some inane discussion, we were handed a black agenda, as the Baraka people called it—a document about the size of the New York *Daily News*—

and told that we had two hours to digest it before the vote. I maintained that if they wanted us to consider their proposals seriously, we should take them home and study them for a couple of weeks, then come back, have some more discussion, and vote. The Baraka gang refused to allow that, which made it clear to me that they were trying to ramrod the thing through. That's about the only way it would get through, because, as a political monograph, the platform was completely off-target and unacceptable. It was a blatantly separatist document, the obvious work of Baraka, the misguided ramblings of a so-called artist who would be dictator. It consisted of bullshit like taking over five states for black people. Baraka wanted to impose his will on every black person in America, and I, for one, wasn't buying it. I refused to surrender the belief that any black solution will derive from unity between the races, and maintained, then as now, that separatism is asinine and suicidal. You don't have to be too damn good at arithmetic to figure out that a party with a small percentage of the population and even less of the money is not well advised to strike out on its own in pursuit of equality. Besides that, I didn't have much use for Baraka. I made him mad when I told him that behind that fancy-ass name he was still LeRoi Jones to me, a half-assed poet in a flowing gown and patent-leather shoes.

That more or less marked the time for me and my 245-member Michigan delegation to leave the premises. Baraka's henchmen tried to prevent us from going, but we were strapped down pretty well and showed them enough artillery to make it out of there. We closed ourselves off in our section of the hotel, and I contacted some trade union guys from Chicago who brought us some additional firepower under the cover of darkness. It was a tense and volatile situation—Baraka's followers were zealots, and he had brought a lot of muscle from New Jersey—but violence never broke out.

The people who stayed behind eventually voted in the black agenda, but it had lost any guise of unanimity. Poor Charlie Diggs didn't know what to do. He felt committed to the caucus as one of its organizers, but he had obviously been misled by Baraka. Taking note of his ambivalence, I used the occasion to say, "Charlie, I always told you I'd never run against you. But if you're going to run as part of this black political party, let me know, because I'm interested in being the Democratic candidate for Congress in your district." I didn't want to be any goddamn congressman; I just wanted to shake Charlie up, which I did.

As opposed to the dogmatic approach toward the black agenda that was promoted in Gary, I generally favored schemes that were more subtle and systematic. When the dispute over busing dominated the floor of the Michigan legislature, for instance, and the conservative wing of the Democratic Party was recalcitrant about recognizing urban concerns, I had been tempted by the notion of pulling all the black senators and representatives out of the party in protest—a radical ploy that had not been proposed by me, much as I'd like to claim it, but by Representative James Bradley, the dean of the black caucus.

For the most part, I can't kick about the politics of the rural Democrats, because we were a very active legislature. In fact, there was an unusual spirit of bipartisan cooperation in the senate, encouraged by Romney's Republican successor as governor, Bill Milliken, and necessitated by important issues that required compromise solutions. In the process of enacting a state income tax, Democrats and Republicans met regularly over coffee at the Olds Hotel across from the capitol and thereby established the Breakfast Club, which was effective for many years as a sort of doughnut coalition. Some of my best work came out of negotiations with constructive Republicans like Emil Lockwood and his successor as party leader, Bob VanderLaan. This is not to suggest, however, that there wasn't a good bit of the traditional bickering between parties, exacerbated by the fact that the Republicans had been accustomed to having their way with Lansing before reapportionment and the Barry Goldwater backlash evened things out. At one point, it got so silly that the Republicans ordered me, Stanley Novak, and Roger Craig to vacate our tiny statehouse office so that it could be taken over by television crews. We refused to move and defended our quarters by padlocking the door.

I regarded that sort of thing as obligatory political jockeying, the fun and games of public service, and chose to reserve my spite for more genuinely damnable enemies. Among those, the Detroit Police Department continued to top the list into the early seventies, as it had for the better part of a decade. You might say I carried on a crusade against the police department.

My grievances were legion. I lashed out at the special intelligence unit, the Red Squad, for its Big Brother style of surveillance; I kept up a constant criticism of the search and seizure techniques the department employed with virtual impunity; and I hammered away at its racial hiring practices. At my urging and others', Bill Cosby was brought in to work with the city on recruiting minorities. In the legislature, I led the discussion that produced the first black officers in the state police, and I called for state subsidies to cities whose police forces reflected the black percentage of their populations—essentially a quota system, which Michigan wasn't ready for. Outside the legislature, I co-chaired, with John Conyers, the Michigan Committee Against Repression as a protest against vicious police harassment of the Black Panthers and other activists.

Even more objectionable than their treatment of racial protest groups was the consistent manner in which Detroit policemen showed their disregard—even contempt—for the average black citizen, as manifested in countless beatings that predated the Rodney King case by twenty years and more. One that came to my attention involved a woman named Starmina Burgess, who in 1971 was arrested for a traffic violation and referred to by a police officer as a "nigger bitch." She responded by calling him a pig, for which she was choked, beaten, and taken to the precinct, where she was beaten again.

During Roman Gribbs's four years as mayor, which started in 1970, a substantial portion of the police atrocities were perpetrated under the auspice of a special unit known as STRESS, which stood for Stop The Robberies, Enjoy Safe Streets. STRESS was created as a decoy squad whose purpose was to apprehend street thugs by luring them into attacking police officers in disguise, but its scope and reality far exceeded the advertised design. The cowboys in the posse turned the thing into a goddamn shootout. Their activities were accompanied by an alarming rate of black deaths. STRESS, it seemed, facilitated the cops by providing an official vehicle for killing black people in the alleged line of duty. In less than three years, twenty-two citizens died after being shot by STRESS officers, twenty-one of them black. The black community referred to the decoy team as "the execution squad." It single-handedly put Detroit at the top of the country in civilians killed per capita by police. Versatile in its role as the agent of urban terror, it was also responsible for an estimated four hundred police raids without warrants.

In my campaign to stop STRESS and the type of police work that it personified, I had lobbied hard for the creation of a civilian police review board made up of one elected representative from each precinct in the city, with full authority to administer disciplinary action in response to citizen complaints. As might be expected, this was not a popular proposition in the circles of city administration, and I was unable to get it placed on the ballot as a referendum. I also fell short in my attempt to establish the review boards at the state level.

There was no shortage of other causes to take up on the police issue, however. Frustrated by the political bulwarks the department had built around itself, I argued that the partisanship of the policemen's union was making elected officials increasingly beholden to them and was marching us briskly into a police state. All around the country, law enforcement personnel were virtually taking control of their cities as the "war on crime"—i.e., the police assault on the black community—escalated. In response, I stepped up my push for fair racial representation within the departments, seeing that as the only way to fend off the police encroachment. Despite his unfortunate sponsorship of the monstrous STRESS, Gribbs performed significantly better than Cavanagh as a minority hirer; but the basic bigotry of the police department forged ahead nonetheless. The police union newspaper still referred to black citizens as "jungle bunnies."

The department's—and Detroit's—unyielding racial antagonism made it apparent that another collision lay ahead and that the status quo inevitably would be shattered, one way or another. Demographics would see to that. The black population of Detroit had reached fifty percent, and white people were still speeding out of the city with their windows rolled up. In 1971, at a meeting of the Committee to Defend the Detroit Fifteen—a group of blacks charged with conspiracy to murder a white patrolman named Glenn Smith—I stated, "We are looking into the face of the last white mayor in this city. The next mayor will be black."

Around the same time, there were efforts under way to alter the basic bureaucratic administration of Detroit by revising its charter. The administration felt handicapped by mayoral restrictions in the old charter and had formed a committee to draft a new one. Zeroing in on the same target from a different angle, a group of my constituents had determined at one of our monthly community conferences to draw up a "people's charter" that would make our public servants more accountable. Among those on the "people's charter" committee were George Crockett, Reverend Nicholas Hood, and Maryann Mahaffey. It was an influential lobby, and when the voters ultimately approved the formation of an official charter commission, our group was able to gain the sympathetic ear of its chairman, former city official Bernie Klein, and elected members. We naturally pushed for a civilian police review board, but the committee, realizing that such a polarizing measure might doom the charter's approval at the ballot box, instead wrote in a civilian police *commission* that would examine the overall performance of the department and include the review of grievances within a broader purview. I was quite satisfied with that. The new charter would also dole out substantially more clout to the office of mayor, giving him budgetary and appointment jurisdiction that had previously belonged to the city council. The matter of the charter's adoption would be put to the voters at the November election.

This, of course, did nothing to dissuade me in my ruminations about running for mayor. I was mightily tempted, but there were a couple of legal complications to consider first. One was the fact that the law still prevented me from filing for mayor as long as I remained a state senator. I had vowed to challenge the circuit court ruling of 1969 and win the right to run, but in the meantime I had been knocked off balance by an unexpected government hassle over a barbecue joint I was trying to open with my brother Charles.

My cousins had prospered with a place called Young's Bar-B-Q. When it was put up for sale, I tried to buy the rights to their operation or at least their barbecue sauce recipe, which was a combination of vinegar and paprika and some other things that nobody else has ever duplicated, although Heinz showed interest in it for a while. Young's slow-cooked their barbecue in a pit, and it was easily the best in town, but for some reason the wife of one of my cousins didn't care about us taking over the business. So we set out to open our own restaurant and bar. Previously, I'd attempted to buy a neighborhood hangout called Coleman's Bar on Joseph Campau, but that didn't come off. Anyway, Charles and I figured that the barbecue place was the ticket. We applied for a Small Business Association loan of just over $100,000 and made plans for our own Young's Bar-B-Q on Linwood.

The process dragged on for months, and when the SBA finally got back to us, it was to tell us that the loan had been denied on the grounds that it was not in the best interest of the federal government. Although it shouldn't have, considering my history with the feds, the decision surprised me, because I hadn't been aware of any problems between me and the Justice Department since my files were leaked to the Municipal Credit Union League when I applied there ten years earlier. (In fact, when I later received my FBI records, I noticed that I had been deleted from the Security Index classification in 1972 "because of diminished subversive activities and influence.") I really didn't think the government cared about me anymore. And I couldn't imagine that it would give a damn about a barbecue joint on Linwood—or perceive it as a threat to the very United States of America, for God's sake. I had some contacts in Washington who made some calls and finally got the loan granted, but by then the SBA had screwed around for so long that I had moved on to more important things and never had the opportunity to get involved in the management of the place, which didn't last long. I eventually defaulted on the loan and had to pay the federal government a settlement of $60,000. We never had a prayer. There were rumors of dope trafficking or something or other at Young's, and the FBI had it wiretapped shortly after it was opened. I wondered how the rumors started and attributed the attention to the government's renewed interest in my activities—resulting, no doubt, from the fact that I had become a legitimate candidate for mayor of Detroit.

When I initially filed to enter the mayoral race in December of 1972, my petition was refused by city clerk George Edwards, who again cited the state law against civil appointments. I mounted another legal challenge, and this time the case made it to the state supreme court, which ruled unanimously in my favor. But the decision was not forthcoming until May of 1973, the election year, which was awfully late to start up a campaign for mayor. On the other hand, the time was not entirely lost, because the rhetoric that would define my candidacy was scarcely different from that which I'd been putting forth for the past several years. My theme was the state of Detroit police, which made for an interesting campaign in light of the fact that one of the leading candidates going into the nonpartisan primary was Gribbs's police commissioner, John Nichols.

The initial favorite was Richard Austin, who had been elected Michigan's secretary of state after the 1969 mayoral race. However, that early sentiment was based upon the presumption that Austin would run again. I was among the many who eagerly awaited Austin's decision, although my interest was more personal than most people's. Given my high opinion of Austin as a public servant and a candidate, his entry into the race was the only thing that could keep me out of it once my eligibility had been established. When he opted to remain in his state position, I not only had my opening, but also inherited Austin's influential campaign director, Robert Millender—my old Army accomplice at Fort Huachuca—who had come to be regarded as the foremost political strategist in the black community. Even so, I was still a long, long way from home. Other formidable candidates included Mel Ravitz, a classic liberal who was president of the Common Council, and Edward Bell, who had resigned his position on the circuit court a year in advance to campaign for mayor.

I was a distant fifth in the first poll, pulling all of five percent, but I expected to come into a large portion of Austin's constituency. It was likely that a black candidate would take the race to the wire, because the racial balance of the city had finally tipped, if ever so slightly. Ironically, the political hope of the black community was vested in the same inexorable process that was putting the city in economic peril—the unremitting flight of white people. Joseph Hudson of the department store chain said it well on the occasion of the fifth anniversary of the 1967 riot: "The black man has the feeling he is about to take power in the city," Hudson observed. "But he is going to be left with an empty bag."

That pretty much described the bag I was holding in the early stages of the campaign. I started off with twenty-five dollars handed to me while loitering in front of the statehouse cigarette stand by Tom Ford, Vice-President Gerald Ford's half-brother and a state representative, when it was announced that the state supreme court had upheld my candidacy. By midyear, I still didn't have much more than those twenty-five bucks, the right to run, Lucky Millender, and a couple dozen friends, who agreed to co-sign a $25,000 loan for my campaign fund. We put in long hours kicking around strategy at the apartment of Georgia Brown, one of my energetic supporters, and ultimately agreed that I should take the money and plunge headfirst. Realizing that I had to enter the race with a splash, I bought a half-hour of television time on NBC affiliate Channel 4, reasoning that if I could come out of that with a pulse, I'd be all right, and if my campaign was going to bomb anyway, I could bomb coming off the blocks and get it over with. I also figured that the best strategy was basically to keep my mouth shut—to make a few opening remarks, say what I had to say, and then open it up to questions from the press.

What I had to say dealt a little with economic development, which I intended to pursue more aggressively than most of the other candidates, and a lot with law enforcement. I said that we needed a people's police department, and that law and order— with justice—could not be imposed without the cooperation and confidence of the community. When my thirty minutes were over, I had survived to say the same things another day, another way. I said, over and over during the next few months, that for all of Detroit's celebrated lawlessness, its criminals on the streets were seriously rivaled by the ones in squad cars. I said that we needed to wipe out spying, finking, and wiretapping, and put our officers back on the pavement to fight crime and assist the citizenry. I said that the police domination of our city was tantamount to a black-jack rule of terror. I said that if there was one thing for which I could be counted on as mayor, it would be to straighten out the Detroit Police Department. When asked by the press what I would do first, I said I'd fire John Nichols, as police commissioner.

But before I could do that, I had to beat candidate John Nichols, who took over as the front-runner by outdistancing the pack in the primary. Under Detroit's nonpartisan mayoral election system, the top two primary finishers meet in a runoff, and Nichols's preliminary victory put him in the lead heading into the November election. More unexpected than his strong showing, however, was mine. I managed to stay alive by finishing second in the primary.

With the field narrowed to Nichols and me, the election was reduced to a showdown over law enforcement policies. I regretted that insufficient attention was being paid to the matter of Detroit's reconstruction, but was pleased to have the battle waged over an issue I felt so strongly about. Nichols and I held a couple of highly publicized debates that inevitably centered around the role of police, which was evolving as a political focal point not only in Detroit but around the country. In reaction to the riots of the late 1960s, there had developed a distinct nationwide trend in which former police chiefs were being elected as mayors, the immediate example having been Frank Rizzo in Philadelphia. Even in advance of electing their own in city government, police departments had been accumulating political power through the partisanship of their unions. They were fast becoming a self-perpetuating bureaucracy, stomping the souls of cities like Detroit. I genuinely believed that a victory by Nichols would deliver a troubling, oppressive message to the rest of the country and goose it along toward a coast-to-coast police state. Somebody had to stop the cops.

At street level, the campaign boiled down essentially to one question: Should white officers be allowed to continue to kill black people in the name of law enforcement? The dialogue was about police, but by extension, and by all accounts, the race was about race. Everybody in the city was aware of that, despite the fact that Nichols and I tried to hold our tongues when the issue turned to color. For me, it was only prudent to assume a conciliatory tone, because the white voters seemed to harbor a preconception that I would run them off with guns or spears or something and turn the city into a black empire. To assuage those fears, I assured them that my hiring practices would reflect a fifty-fifty racial balance.

That's not to say that there wasn't a conspicuous color separation in the campaign. While the usual white suspects fell in behind Nichols, my camp included the likes of John Conyers, Charlie Diggs, and Reverend Cleage—now known as Jaramogi Abebe Agyeman—whose Shrine of the Black Madonna had become a political force. Out-of-town support arrived from Julian Bond and Fanny Lou Hamer, the Mississippi activist. Ray Charles raised money for me by performing at Cobo Hall. We asked Jesse Jackson to come to Detroit and lead a voter registration drive, but he demanded $50,000 in return, and I didn't have $50,000 for Jesse Jackson.

Frankly, there weren't a hell of a lot of white people behind me. Ted Kennedy gave me his blessing but didn't actively campaign on my behalf. I had token support from Henry Ford II, who also contributed to the Nichols campaign. I told Ford that he'd be wise to put most of his money on me because I was going to win, but he laughed and gave us the same amount. Maryann Mahaffey, who had been on my side through many previous issues and campaigns, was with me again at the outset of the race, but she was a candidate for city council and consequently coveted the endorsement of the United Auto Workers. Despite my split with Walter Reuther and the rocky private history that had ensued, I had gotten along splendidly with the UAW while I was in Lansing; but the union hierarchy elected to play it safe in the mayoral race by backing Mel Ravitz. When Maryann came to me and reported that she had a chance to receive the backing of the UAW, I predicted that the union would ask her to repudiate me in favor of Ravitz, which it did—and she did. I could only be grateful that a few bold dissidents and the Trade Union Leadership Council, led by Buddy Battle, saw fit to buck the UAW and support me anyway. When Ravitz dropped out of contention after the primary, I naturally picked up a lot of votes from the UAW rank and file—no thanks, of course, to the union itself.

On election day, I became the goddamn mayor of Detroit. There wasn't a single precinct in the city that was close—Nichols took the white ones and I took the black ones—but the final count fell within four percent, with 234,000 votes for me and 216,000 for the commissioner. To top it off, my victory was accompanied by that of my running mate, the new city charter.

Afterwards, I was hard-put to place the day in perspective. On one hand—the hand in which I gripped memories of the Boblo guide who turned me away from the park, the Catholic school priest who tore up my application, Tuskegee, Freeman Field, Walter Reuther, Ike and Mike, the FBI, the Un-American Activities Committee, the attorney general, and all the jobs I had lost over the years—it was a preposterous, impossible dream come true, an only-in-America kind of thing. On the other hand, I knew that this had only happened because, for once in my life, I was in the right place at the right time, and that my fortune was a direct result of my city's misfortune—of the same fear and loathing that had caused all of my problems and Detroit's problems in the first place. I was taking over the administration of Detroit because the white people didn't want the damn thing anymore. They were getting the hell out, more than happy to turn over their troubles to some black sucker like me.

The fact is, I didn't have much of a chance to think about perspective, anyway, because there was much celebrating to do. Diana Ross sang for us at Cobo Hall, and then the blacks, radicals, and assorted leftists of Detroit partied for four days and nights, pausing only for my acceptance speech.

My theme in the speech—as it had and has been all my life—was unity. I urged it between white and black, rich and poor, suburbs and city. I also talked about law and order, issuing a warning "to all dope pushers, to all rip-off artists, to all muggers . . . It's time to leave Detroit," I said. "Hit Eight Mile Road. I don't give a damn if they're black or white, or if they wear Superfly suits or blue uniforms with silver badges. Hit the road."

I thought that was innocent enough. I was the new marshal telling the bad guys to get out of Dodge. But some of the folks in the
suburbs didn't see it that way. They were aghast, shrieking that the
militant black upstart mayor had ordered a virtual armed invasion
of the outlying areas, dispatching his hellions over the border to
prey upon the wealthy white neighbors.

It was beginning.

8

The Friends Among Us

To this day, a lot of folks in the suburbs believe that I've been waging war on them since the moment I moved into the mayor's mansion, if not before. Many suburbanites, most of whom came from Detroit, subscribe to the notion that their former city is now their archenemy, and that I am, too, for that matter, Detroit and I being virtually interchangeable terms in their view. It doesn't matter that I've been preaching racial unity since Maben trimmed around my ears. It doesn't matter that I championed the slogan "Black and White Unite to Fight" forty years ago, or that my basic modus operandi as a labor official and politician and mayor has been to build coalitions that bring together the parties, the classes, and the races in a common self-interest. It doesn't matter that I established a regional council of mayors to address our mutual problems in concert, or that I've urged city and suburban cooperation in speech after speech and gone out into the suburbs to make the point in person (although I can't recall anybody from the suburbs coming to the city for that purpose). What matters—I'm referring now to the perceptions of the white people who despise my city, which I shouldn't have to clarify but feel that I must—is that upon the election of Detroit's first black mayor, the city effectively became a black enclave. Given the tradition of separatism in the vicinity (ours being the most segregated metropolitan area in the country, according to recent demographic studies), this meant that Detroit, in the minds of many, split off as a sovereign nation virtually overnight.

For the record, I would much prefer that this not be the case. If the city coexisted in harmony with the suburbs, we would have had rapid transportation in Detroit for quite a while now. Countless corporate headquarters and white-owned companies would have remained in Detroit, bolstering our tax base, and in turn improving our education and police protection and other basic services. The Lions and the Pistons probably wouldn't have moved to the suburbs, and neither would a few hundred thousand middle- and upper-class taxpayers. The local media would treat us as their city, as opposed to an unfamiliar place in which it is their apparent misfortune to work. The rest of the country would not be terrified of Detroit.

During my first term as mayor, I received a copy of a memo circulated in the editorial offices of the *Detroit News*. This was before the *News* and the *Free Press* entered into a joint operating agreement, and the competition between the two was openly vicious. The memo, written to reporters by news editor Michael McCormick, outlined a news-gathering strategy that isolated the booming suburbs as the paper's targeted audience. "Keep a lookout for and then play—well—the stories [aimed] at this group," the memo said. "They should be obvious: they won't have a damn thing to do with Detroit and its internal problems." According to the communiqué, the game plan was to seek out lurid and sensational tales about the depraved condition of the city, titillating and shocking the white readers in the tested tradition of cheap tabloids:

A fine example is [Pete] Waldmeir's column [about an incident downtown in which a black man assaulted a white couple and raped the woman] on the bottom of 1A Monday. I think it should have been at the top of 1A. While it dealt with Detroit and its horrors, it went beyond that. It was an example of just the horrors that are discussed at suburban cocktail parties. Notice I said suburban—that's the $18,000 plus and 28–40 group. Go through the last few weeks of the Early Edition and you'll see what I want: "Nun charged with killing her baby" . . . "They chummed together—and died together."

So there we had it: the paper's reporting about Detroit would aspire to the level of nuns killing their babies. When the memo became public, the *News* ran a page-one disclaimer, but its news columns have substantiated the message over the past two decades. Both papers, in fact, have reported copiously—even gleefully— upon the spectacular aspects of Detroit's troubles, real or rumored, while exercising noticeable restraint in their attention to the more salutary angles of daily life in the city.

This has naturally left Detroit with an image problem. I don't dispute the gravity of Detroit's problems. They are basically the same problems that beset every American city, except that they are magnified by the fact that modern Detroit was built around the auto industry, which has been losing blood for two decades, and the accompanying reality that white flight, industrial and social, has left Detroit with the damnedest demographics in America. It doesn't take a five-term mayor to recognize what's wrong with Detroit. But it's a life's work to get the right people to recognize and comprehend the real problems. They see only the public image. They think that the basic problem with Detroit is that it's dangerous.

That, of course, is inherently an outsider's perspective. The outsider, which in this case might be a synonym for a familiar sort of suburban white person, regards the city by his standards and according to his level of comfort. It has been my experience that many white people get very uncomfortable when they are not in control of a situation; when they slip into a minority position. White people not only have lost control of Detroit, but find it, as a rule, racially foreign and consequently frightening, and identify it in those terms. On the other hand, the typical resident of the city, to whom the condition of Detroit matters the most, is naturally concerned about the safety issue but not preoccupied with it. The citizens of Detroit are more concerned with the prospects of securing a job for themselves and an education for their children. Crime is an issue, indisputably, but not in the proportion that public image would place it.

When I took over as mayor of Detroit in 1974, the black citizens of the city considered the local police to be every bit as dangerous

and threatening to their welfare as crime. In that spirit, my inauguration remark about the bad guys (including the police variety) hitting Eight Mile Road was a law-and-order statement and nothing
more, although my antagonists, setting the tone for what would become a tiresome pattern in the years ahead, were determined to
misunderstand. Rather than siccing our criminals upon the suburbs, I was merely expressing my intention to rid the city of the
many and various thugs in our midst, inasmuch as Detroit led the
nation in crime at the time—and (unofficially) in police community antipathy as well. In terms of priorities, crime ranked no
higher in my estimation than the state and nature of the Detroit
police, which dominated my attention. I had campaigned on the
law enforcement issue and was prepared to go at it full-bore.

My first order of business, as promised, was to oversee the abolition of STRESS and reduce the violence level in the city. Detroit
was known at the time as the murder capital of America, and I
staunchly believed that the disrespect for human life that was all
too prevalent in our city was, to a significant degree, a reflection of
the attitude demonstrated by our police department. We had to
make the cops stop shooting everybody. STRESS was gone within a
few months, but by that time I'd already stood in frozen cemeteries
for three or four police funerals. With the streets cleared of the
gun-happy plainclothes militia, it would be many years before we
had another.

The fundamental challenge before me—and one that still confronts many of America's major cities, as demonstrated by the Rodney King incident in Los Angeles—was to reorder the police
department so that it was perceived as a sympathetic agency of the
community and not as a cocked pistol. Don't misunderstand me—
"sympathetic" should not be confused with "soft." I don't countenance crime any more than John Nichols did, or Daryl Gates (the
notorious former Los Angeles police chief), but I believe that law
enforcement can and must be effected in a manner that respects
the innocent citizen, because protection is its inherent purpose.
We have seen, in riot after riot, what happens when the police and
community perpetuate an adversarial relationship. They ought to
be partners. That's what we had in mind when, shortly after

STRESS was shut down, we initiated a city-wide program of neighborhood mini-stations.

The first of these was in the old Black Bottom area, and we eventually expanded to fifty-five, although public demand suggests that we would do well to double the number if we had the resources. The success of the mini-stations lies in the fact that they have reestablished the concept of the beat cop and introduced a more benevolent police presence in the neighborhoods. To complement the mini-stations, we also established workshops on topics such as drug awareness; a Neighborhood Watch network that is the largest in the country; regular meetings between citizen groups and the Civilian Police Commission; and a Senior Call system, in which a representative of the police department will make regular telephone checkups with every senior citizen in the neighborhood. You could almost see the atmosphere changing before your eyes when these programs were implemented. We've had law enforcement officials from four continents visiting Detroit to study our community police programs. What they see is nothing more than a concerted, diligent effort to involve the neighborhood in its own defense against crime. Even now, after twenty years of experimenting, we're continuing to look for ways to accomplish that: training young people as police cadets who assist the officers in activities such as overseeing the streets as kids walk home from school; calling on civilian volunteers for crowd control; and relying upon a CB radio patrol to help us monitor the neighborhoods.

As we redefined the police force, however, it was important for the department to demonstrate that it would still not be reluctant to assert its muscle against those who would prey upon the neighborhoods. We had a gang problem when I became mayor, and resolved to take it head-on with a specially created gang squad that was prepared to meet intimidation with intimidation. There is no gentle way to handle urban bullies, and the gang squad literally hit the streets and reclaimed them. Detroit's streets might not be as warm and fuzzy as small-town America's, but they are no longer dominated by gangs like those of comparable large cities.

When I assumed office, I had a pretty clear model in my mind of the kind of police department I intended for my administration;

but for all of the theorizing and planning and policymaking, a police department's profile is usually chiseled out in moments of crisis. My first one occurred in 1975 on Livernois Avenue—in the neighborhood of my ill-fated barbecue joint—after a black teenager named Obie Wynn had been shot in the back and killed by a white man who owned Bolton's Bar and claimed to be defending it.

The situation blew up instantaneously. Black protestors looted the bar and set fire to the carpet before they were run out. As soon as I heard about what was happening, I ordered the police chief, Philip Tannian, to call every black officer in the department to the scene, the idea being to merge them with white officers and make a show of racial unity on the street. Tannian said he had no way of knowing which of his officers were black. Bullshit, I said. In about an hour, they were all there.

I joined them with a line of community leaders and clergymen. Our presence did not have an immediate effect, and I decided to fight attitude with attitude. To that end, I climbed up on a car and spoke to the people as angrily and sternly as I dared without turning them against me, figuring that the only way to check their mood was with a passionate petition of reason. I said that Detroit was their city and they should not tear it apart; also, that there was a difference between justice and vigilante violence and that I, like them, was interested in the former. When other black leaders had stood on cars during the 1967 uprising, the community had shouted them down; but this time was different, because the crowd knew that my words were more than rhetoric: I was the goddamn mayor. I guess they figured they owed me one chance to prove myself. It probably didn't hurt my case when somebody threw a rock at me, which earned me some sympathy points. The people understood that I was putting myself on the line up there. We all knew that they could have blown my ass off that automobile at any point.

I had averted further violence for the time being, but the people were still hot. In fact, we were getting it from both sides. Long after the crowd had broken up, I was standing on the street talking to some police personnel when three white officers drove by in a cruiser and tossed a smoke bomb under a car next to me. I jumped into the car of a sympathetic inspector and we chased them for a while, but the patrol car had too much horsepower for us.

Back on Livernois, meanwhile, angry blacks regrouped and tried to ram their way into the bar and pull the owner out. They were unsuccessful, but the situation intensified when the mob stopped a car driven by an innocent Polish baker on his way home from work, dragged him into the street, and stoned him to death. In retrospect, we were probably on the verge of another major riot at that moment. But it never materialized, and I firmly believe that it was our community presence which ultimately saved the day—the cooperative effort of neighborhood leaders and black and white police officers. If we had gone about cracking heads in the Detroit tradition, there would have been hell to pay. It was a trial by fire for our police reforms, and thank God they worked.

Of course, the black citizens were not the only party that had to be appeased. The Poles are not a passive group in matters of turf, but they are a parochial one, and I recognized the need to bring the parish bishop into the crisis from the other side, along with Polish community leaders. They sat down with the black leaders and ministers and established a tone of conciliation. I also visited the widow and the mother of Obie Wynn, assuring them that justice would be vigorously pursued. All the while, the black and white police officers—including some of the newly hired women on the force—were performing in a very professional manner despite extreme provocation in the form of bricks and the like. They were able to restore order without a single shot being fired.

That may have been the first time in Detroit history that black officers had been called upon for emergency police work. In his term as mayor, Roman Gribbs had moderately increased the percentage of black officers on the force, but they had not been legitimized by deployment. Traditionally, the assignment of the black officer was to "walk the triangle," which meant patrolling the three streets that came together around Eastern Market. In rain, snow, and ridiculous weather nobody was fool enough to be out in, the black cops would still be faithfully walking the triangle. The basic concept was to give them assignments that were god-awful enough to make them quit. Few actually did.

The percentage of black officers on the force was still under ten when I was elected, and my pledge was to bring the figure up to fifty percent within four years on the way to achieving the same ratio throughout the administration. I arrived at fifty percent because that would very nearly reflect the proportion of black residents in the city, and also to demonstrate that I did not intend for my administration to approximate a black empire. It was important, I believed, to manifest this commitment conspicuously. When I hired two secretaries, I made sure one was white and one black. When I was accompanied by two security guards, one would be white and one black. My insistence upon a fifty-fifty administration was so visible and unyielding that it frustrated many of my supporters, who asked why I didn't turn the tables entirely in racial hiring. I replied that those of us who have been victims of discrimination for so long should be the last ones to practice it. Affirmative action is about justice and equity, not revenge.

Given the community tension that had characterized its recent history, the police department was the perfect vehicle through which to make a statement about racial unity. Understandably, though—I shall never fail to recognize that people act in their own self-interest—there were many in the department who didn't see it that way. The two white-dominated police unions, the Detroit Police Officers Association and the Lieutenants and Sergeants Association, rebelled against our affirmative action programs at every turn. As the issue played out, the battle was joined over two policies we instituted in order to bring parity to the racial balance of the department and make it more community-oriented.

First, we began to enforce the city's residency rule, under which it was mandatory for police officers and other city employees to live within the city limits of Detroit. The rule had been on the books since 1914 but was largely winked at by administrations prior to mine. Given the prevailing "us versus them" law-enforcement climate in Detroit, the residency rule was vital to our efforts to increase the community element in the neighborhoods. Consequently, we stuck with it in spite of vehement objections from the veteran cops.

After establishing our position on residency—in all departments of the administration—we then went to work on the existing police promotion procedures. At the time, the DPD based its promotions on testing that I maintained was culturally biased and effectively discriminated against black officers. Without ripping apart the system, we profoundly modified it by establishing two lists of test scores—one for white officers and one for black. After a qualifying mark was established as a cutoff for eligibility, promotions were made alternately by selecting the officer with the highest score from the white list, then the officer with the highest score from the black list. Contrary to scuttlebutt, we have never promoted black officers unless they have passed the test. In fact, records show that in the oral-board portion of the test, black officers on the average have scored higher than white. We also used a similar strategy to ensure that women, who constituted only one percent of the department in 1974, were hired in far greater numbers.

The white officers responded to the two-list strategy by filing suits against me and the city to challenge our promotion policies, charging, among other things, that our affirmative action measures amounted to reverse discrimination. My attitude was, You're damn right—the only way to arrest discrimination is to reverse it. It was little known that the revised city charter of 1974 mandated the elimination of racial discrimination, of which the police department was a time-honored practitioner. The abundant evidence of discrimination in the department's past and present included the letter C, for "colored," marked at the top of application forms submitted by blacks.

The courts duly took note of the department's bigoted tradition. In the suit challenging our use of affirmative action in the promotion of sergeants to lieutenant, we lost the case in the lower court but won twice on appeal. The final round, resolved ten years after it was filed, was heard by the United States Supreme Court, which upheld the appellate court's decision that our policies constituted "a valid and permissible remedy" for past discriminations.

A parallel Detroit Police Officers Association suit, contesting the promotion of officers to sergeant, went our way through three appeals that encompassed nearly twenty years—the final ruling, from the Sixth Circuit Court of Appeals in Cincinnati, being delivered

THE FRIENDS AMONG US

late in March 1993. "Today," I said to the local media upon learning of the decision, "after twenty years of pursuing a persistent program of affirmative action, fighting with one hand in the courts all the way, for the first time we can say we have reached our goal. The department is truly fifty-fifty, both across the board and in the command ranks, including sergeant."

At the moment in 1993 when the federal court upheld our affirmative action program, the personnel roster of the police department showed 303 white sergeants, 302 black sergeants, four Hispanic, two Asian-American, and two American Indian. About two-thirds of our police hirings had gone to blacks, Hispanics, or females. Along the way, we had to do some active recruiting in the neighborhoods—literally sending cruisers into the streets in search of civilians who would be cops—to surmount the deep-rooted skepticism with which the minority citizens regarded the police department. In the first two years of my administration, the ratio of black applicants rose by more than twenty-five percent.

The response of the people and the favorable judgments of the judicial system notwithstanding, the implementation of affirmative action has been a wearisome struggle. Legal triumphs have at times proven perfunctory in the absence of a budget to promote, hire, or even maintain positions on the force. Testifying before the United States Senate in 1975 on the urban economic crisis, I said, "This time I will state the stark, blunt, and inescapable fact that Detroit is in the strangling grip of a major depression." Largely due to the oil embargo and the attending automotive slump, Detroit was suffering from an unemployment rate of more than twenty-three percent (the figure was nearly fifty percent among young blacks), compared with the national rate of less than nine percent. As a result, the city's budget deficit was approaching $100 million, and we were mandated by the state constitution to balance it. Unwilling to defer the problem by borrowing, as New York had, we couldn't avert a series of layoffs of city employees, including police officers.

The untimely layoffs not only undermined a beleaguered police department that was contending with the nation's most celebrated crime rate, but also created a delicate predicament concerning affirmative action. If we followed custom and laid off the last policemen hired, it would negate the gains that we had already achieved. Thankfully, District Judge Ralph Freeman had relieved some of the burden on us by ruling in the DPOA suit that the city was forbidden to lay off the 275 blacks and women whose positions were federally funded through CETA (Comprehensive Employment Training Act) grants. With that decision in place, our tack was to begin the layoffs—which would ultimately exceed eight hundred and could have reached twice that number—with those officers who were not in compliance with the residency rule.

Virtually all of the nonresident policemen were white, of course, and when I started to lay them off, it prompted a blue flu strike from the DPOA and a protest rally of a thousand white cops that ended in the brutal beating of a black officer. Fully aware of the risk, I nonetheless threatened to lay off 550 additional white officers if they would not participate in a compromise. Ultimately, the police officers' union agreed to wage concessions in lieu of additional layoffs.

Over the kicking and screaming of both police unions, our affirmative action initiatives have pushed ahead as the most aggressive in the country, and despite budget restrictions, we emerged as the only major city whose programs were not mitigated by the courts. We eventually attained the highest percentage of blacks and women among the nation's major police departments, and both groups were acutely instrumental in changing the demeanor of our force. The presence of black officers reduced the antipathy and distrust between police and black citizens, and women introduced a civilizing agent to the department's chemistry. Crime dropped by more than thirty percent in Detroit over just two years at the end of the seventies, and at times the city led the country in crime reduction, much of which I attribute to the influence of female officers, who have come to represent twenty percent of our ranks. To me, it's not difficult to understand the success of women in law enforcement. Contrary to the old tradition in Detroit and the ongoing tradition in some other cities, a police officer's job is not to kick ass. He or she is most effective when employing reason to enforce the law, and women—at least in Detroit's experience—seem to be more adept at that than men. We have consistently found that where women are present, there is far less likelihood of police brutality and, consequently, of an explosive incident.

Had it not been for the diligence with which Detroit has pursued affirmative action, and its broad if belated endorsement by the courts, it's doubtful that we could have made a dent in the mail-coat disposition of the DPD. The department was very much a fraternal order under previous administrations; and in the tradition of most fraternities, it zealously protected both its exclusivity and its customs. I realized going in that we were threatening all of that and could expect resistance. In retrospect, we might have had a better understanding with the veteran cops if we had spoken their language—that is, if we had gone in kicking down doors, figuratively, instead of changing procedures. I don't believe the veterans ever took us at face value, because they were unaccustomed to our methods and as a result didn't trust us.

It's evident, looking back, that the chief, Philip Tannian, certainly distrusted me. Tannian had taken over late in the Gribbs administration when Nichols ran for mayor, and he had a fair record of minority hiring. Although he was a former FBI agent, which was reason enough for me to be queasy about him, I thought it prudent to keep an apparently competent white chief in place for the transition and had no intention of replacing Tannian. But he wouldn't believe that. A veteran black officer, Frank Blount, had been promoted to executive deputy chief, and Tannian was convinced that he was going to be sacrificed in favor of Blount. As a result, he carried on an openly antagonistic relationship with Blount that ultimately escalated into the first in a series of police and, by extension, personal controversies that have undermined my terms.

Tannian's fear of Blount showed through in a pact he made with the federal government in an effort to indict the deputy chief for accepting payoffs from drug dealers. The scheme was publicly played out in a deplorable drama one September afternoon in 1976, commencing when Tannian ordered Blount and others to remain in their offices while the chief and Drug Enforcement Agency personnel raided Blount's home in front of television cameras. I found out about the raid coincidentally when a call came into my house for Blount's son, Mike, who was a member of the

Manoogian Mansion security force, from his wife. Deputy Chief
Blount rented upstairs living space in his son's house, and Mike's
pregnant wife had been home when hell broke through the front
door. Obviously terrified, she reported to her husband that cops
were crawling all over the place. When he heard that, Mike tore
out of the mansion with blood in his eyes—angry, armed, and one
of the best pistol shots in the country. When he arrived home,
Mike went straight for Tannian, but fortunately he was grabbed
and bear-hugged by a cop friend.

I was as livid as Mike was. Not only had Tannian pursued a weak
case by questionable means, but he had collaborated with the feds
while failing to notify me. He went so far as to bring in the media
while still keeping his boss in the dark. I'm sure Tannian anticipated the Blount raid as his triumphant moment, and wished for
all of Detroit to witness it. Tannian loved to see himself on television. Earlier, he had tipped off newspapers and TV stations about
a major raid he had planned at a candy store on John R and
Erskine where dope was sold in the open. He led a damn caravan
from the police station to the candy store, which naturally alerted
the dealers, who were gone by the time the circus arrived. The media dutifully reported on a colossal fuckup orchestrated by the police chief.

Although it was perceived differently and had a far longer reach,
the Blount raid amounted to much of the same. The feds and
Tannian confiscated boxes and filing cabinets that allegedly related to felonious payoffs, but there was not a damn thing in them
that criminally implicated Frank Blount. This little detail was not
sufficient to salvage Blount's integrity or his career, however. Despite the fact that neither he nor any other police officer was indicted in the case—four civilians ultimately pleaded guilty to
narcotics charges—Blount was effectively tried and convicted by a
damning drumbeat in the local press, which, in a fashion that I've
come to regard as customary, eagerly seized upon specious information provided by the federal authorities. Blount took a leave of
absence when the case broke and never returned to the force, retiring the next spring and accepting a job as chief of security for
Detroit public schools. Recently, after his retirement from that

post, I appointed him to a newly created position as chief of security for Detroit's public housing developments. I still regard Blount as one of the finest law enforcement officials I've known.

Blount was not the only casualty in the investigation. Nine days after the raid, an implicated deputy chief named Reggie Harvel committed suicide over the pressure of the feeding frenzy. But neither Harvel nor Blount nor any of those indicted was the principal target in the case. Even Blount, who says he still doesn't know what the events of that unfortunate autumn were all about, is convinced that the whole thing really wasn't about him at all—it was about me. For Tannian, perhaps, the chance to bring down Blount in the investigation represented a compelling opportunity; but for the Justice Department, the real objective was a renewal of the case that the feds had been trying to develop against me for more than thirty years. Former Justice Department officials have since indicated that they were concerned at the time about the DEA's enthusiasm for bringing me into the Blount investigation, which, despite the elaborate public facade, was internally referred to as "the Young case." In the later stages of the case, a newspaper reporter was told over lunch by an FBI agent that the Bureau was interested in any information the reporter could supply about the Young administration.

Some might say I'm paranoid about the feds, but it doesn't require much imagination to conclude that they were out to nail me one way or another. A few months after I took office, the Justice Department, for no apparent reason, subpoenaed records of a HUD apartment in which I had invested as a rehab project. Roger Craig, my attorney and former roommate in Lansing, turned the records over to the U.S. district attorney, who kept them for a year in the desperate hope of finding something.

It was shortly after that case turned up empty that the Blount affair broke. It became another example of the cruel and unscrupulous manner in which the government consistently runs roughshod over the lives of innocent people. Several of my relatives and in-laws were publicly implicated in the case and damaged by it, despite the fact that there was no goddamn evidence to indict any of them. I was enraged by that and by the general manner in which the Justice Department manipulated the media by leaking damning and unsubstantiated information about the implicated principals. The newspapers brought me into the loop by regularly describing Blount and me as old friends, which we were not, even though I respected him and he had supported my election. I considered the whole scheme to be a form of collaborative harassment and demanded that the government come forth with specific evidence from its investigation, which of course it was unwilling and unable to do.

Given the spurious nature of the Blount case, it quickly became obvious why Tannian had not familiarized me with it. Electing not to pardon him on the grounds that the feds were after my ass, I fired his and replaced him with an experienced black officer named William Hart. With that, I figured we could put scandal behind us and get on with police work.

Hell, I was still new to the job.

I PICKED a fine time to take over the administration of Detroit. This is not to imply that it was a coincidence, by any stretch, because I know damn well that if the city had been white and prosperous at election time, it would have run me out of the race before either one of us broke a sweat. Detroit was the fifth-largest city in the country, but it was leaking both people and money at a prodigious pace. The same thing was happening to other cities, although not with the same blinding speed. Several of them—some of the worst cases—had been put into the hands of black mayors. I was the fifth, taking over around the same time as Tom Bradley in Los Angeles and Maynard Jackson in Atlanta. The consensus was that the black mayors, with rare exceptions, had been drafted as caretakers for cities in critical, probably terminal, condition.

When I was inaugurated as mayor of Detroit on January 2, 1974, automobile production was at its lowest level since 1950. The city was already staggering when the oil embargo kicked us in the gut. Then the Japanese danced on our head while the local manufacturers and the remaining white people tiptoed past the prostrate body on their way out of town. I felt helpless. When American Motors announced that it was moving its headquarters from Detroit to the suburb of Southfield, I couldn't do anything about it except make a show. Reduced to symbolism, I ordered a change in the bidding specifications for city vehicles so that they excluded AMC. It wasn't much, but it felt good.

What didn't feel good was laying people off. It was damned impossible to find a job in Detroit as it was, and I was forced to aggravate the unemployment epidemic by sending city employees to the streets by the thousands. My second budget eliminated four thousand city jobs. With local industry on its ass, the nation in recession, and a foreign-policy Republican in the White House, there wasn't a lot of compassion—or revenue—being spread around. My job was to find some money under some rocks. (When one of our downtown landmarks, the Book Cadillac Hotel, was in danger of going under, a potential buyer from New York appeared on the scene. I understood that Jimmy Hoffa knew the guy, and to get a report on him I set up a meeting with Hoffa in the Book's presidential suite. Our meeting was around noon on July 29, 1975, and Hoffa, a stocky man whose directness I admired, was helpful, hale, and hearty. The next day, Hoffa disappeared from the Machus Red Fox restaurant parking lot in Bloomfield Hills, never to be seen again. Nothing came out of our conversation that would have given me any insights into what might have happened to Hoffa, but I've always found it strange that the FBI never questioned me about the meeting or about my connection to him. It certainly wasn't due to any reluctance on the part of the feds to draw me into a case. The only thing that makes sense to me is that, somehow or another, they figured they had a fix on it. Hoffa's recommendation of the New York buyer, incidentally, proved to be regrettable, and the Book eventually closed down.)

As a dramatic means of injecting money into the city, I suggested that we legalize gambling, but the voters and naysayers wouldn't have it. By hook or crook, though, we needed help, and I didn't give a damn who it came from. When I was struggling for the privileges of black workers in the union movement, I gave no consideration whatsoever to the color or the politics of the person at my side, and the same applied here. If the devil himself wanted to help Detroit and its people, then God bless the devil.

Short of negotiating with the devil, hard times have a way of encouraging a mayor's trust in bipartisan coalitions. Although it startled many of the radicals with whom I came through the political ranks, I had to deal immediately with Republicans or watch my city fade from the map, block by forsaken block. I also had to deal with the state of Michigan, because it was obvious that Lansing would have to participate somehow in the recovery of Detroit. Fortunately, the governor of Michigan at the time was the finest and fairest the state has had, despite his party affiliation. Bill Milliken was not your typical Republican. As the complaining conservatives were quick to point out, Milliken's social policy more closely resembled a Democrat's—which is to say that he had one. It included affirmative action in state government and an active urban agenda. What's more, as I knew from my days as a state senator, Milliken was a guy who would at least step into the ring with you on issues that many Republicans ducked.

We both knew that the city had something coming from the state. There had been little equity in the relationship between Detroit and Michigan. For years, Detroit's health department, not Michigan's, had conducted milk inspections throughout the state's Lower Peninsula. At the same time, the state police had no presence in Detroit whatsoever, although they covered the rest of the state with the help of Detroit tax money. Despite these obvious imbalances, however, there was little sympathy around the state— particularly in Lansing, which at times has reeked with racism—for anything that might help Detroit. Detroit had become a code word for black, and in turn my name became a code word for Detroit. It was not politically expedient for Milliken to work closely with me, but he had enough integrity to screw the politics and get on with what was right and necessary.

He wasn't going to make it easy for me, however. I had to prove to him that I could land a punch, and he had to identify a compelling rationale for giving me money. We zeroed in on the fact that Detroit had been completely underwriting the cost of a number of major institutions that were enjoyed by the entire state, such as the Detroit Zoo, the Detroit Public Library, and, most significant, the Detroit Institute of Arts. To compensate Detroit for those invaluable services, we agreed upon an "equity package" that eventually brought $35 million into the city.

After that gratifying initiation, Milliken and I felt so comfortable with each other that we would sit at the table without any staff around and address our common problems. We got so much business done together that the press referred to us as "the odd couple." I suppose we were. Milliken was a wealthy moderate from a rural background that did not share a social hemisphere with Black Bottom. He was originally elected to the state senate from a district that didn't have a single black voter. When he ascended from lieutenant governor to governor in 1969 upon George Romney's appointment as HUD secretary in the Nixon cabinet, I had little reason to believe that Milliken would depart from the course of his right-wing predecessor. But I've never had a more productive relationship with a public servant. In addition to the little bit of capital that I was able to pry out of his fingers, Milliken, who was well respected in the corporate and Republican world, provided me with accelerated credibility and entree. He certainly didn't hurt my case with the vital, unrelated Fords, Henry and Gerald.

I happened to catch Henry Ford II at the right moment. Hank the Deuce, as I called him—and as the guys at the plants called him (when a group of black Detroiters honored Ford with a party at the mayor's mansion, we had "Hank the Deuce' matchboxes printed up)—was the grandson of the original Henry Ford and a whimsical industrial leader who, to the good fortune of Detroit, felt that he owed the city a signature landmark. He had already started construction on the Renaissance Center when I became mayor. It was to be the pièce de résistance for Detroit's riverfront and the cornerstone from which the reconstruction of Detroit would emanate—five cylindrical towers that included offices, more than a hundred upscale shops, and the world's tallest hotel. To finance the Ren Cen—the largest private investment made in any city in the United States—Ford had put together an unprecedented consortium of fifty-one local banks and corporations, most of which found themselves in recessionary straits by the middle of the decade and unable to muster up their share of the construction costs. That left Hank the Deuce with one dwarf tower and a very large memorial hole between Jefferson Avenue and the river.

Timing, of course, is a major player in the art of power brokering; and at that moment Ford, like me, needed an ally. I asked him if the process had reached the point of no return, and he answered that it had: it would actually be cheaper for him to proceed with construction than to cut back or scrap the whole development. Recognizing that we had to go forward, I did what I could to keep the project alive by getting on the phone with CEOs all over the city and persuading them that between Ford, me, Detroit, and the Renaissance Center, they had a good bit at stake in the big hole on the riverfront. At a dinner meeting in my office to save the Ren Cen, oil and real estate baron Max Fisher, probably the most influential businessman in Detroit, suggested that we form a committee for that purpose, to which I replied, "We *are* the damn committee." With that, Henry Ford stood up and said, "I'm here to support Coleman." He meant it, too.

The irony of being in bed with a Ford was not lost on me—I never dismissed the ugly vision of Harry Bennett or put away the humiliating memory of being twice fired—but I think that Hank the Deuce and I recognized a similarity in each other as mavericks from adjacent worlds. For him, getting chummy with me was not the traditional or safe way to go. But it helped him finish the Renaissance Center, which opened in 1977 to the exponential benefit of our tax base. For me, the relationship with Ford meant a lot, personally and especially politically. When I gained Henry Ford II as a friend, I gained a good and worthy one. At the same time, I remained very aware of our fundamental differences. I was never comfortable at the sort of social gatherings frequented by Ford and his fellow industrialists, and on the rare occasions when I attended, it only served to remind me that we inhabited different universes. I recall one dinner party, for instance, when Ford and I were arguing the merits of capital punishment. "Henry," I finally said, "when's the last time someone with your money went to the electric chair?" He was simply the wrong class and the wrong color to understand.

Nonetheless, there were those—a few of my oldest radical friends among them—who were disenchanted with my new associations, reasoning that one cannot be pure if he does business with the rich and powerful. I still haven't convinced some of my old leftist cohorts that the day a black man became mayor of Detroit, everything changed. We had become so accustomed to a mentality of us versus them that some people have never come to terms with the acquisition of power. I recognize, of course, that holding an office doesn't mean any damn thing unless its political power rests upon and gathers strength from a substantial economic base. I've never been anything but a pragmatic radical, pursuing the best way I know to get what's coming to me and mine as first-class citizens, and I simply don't understand the wisdom of allowing ideology to stand in the way of getting what you're after. Hell, ideology *is* what you're after. As mayor, I want the same things I wanted as a disenfranchised radical—equality in jobs, education, housing, and social environment for the people I represent—the difference being that I'm enfranchised now and have a more effective way of attaining them.

To that end, I joined Ford, Fisher, and Milliken as part of an overtly bipartisan group of civic and labor leaders who banded together for a trip to Washington in 1975 as representatives of the Move Detroit Forward committee, our purpose being to lobby as a diverse but united front for everything from social services to rapid transportation. With magnates and influential Republicans and a large city of registered voters on my side, I felt sufficiently empowered to ask President Ford about a fixed rail system for Detroit. The timing was right, inasmuch as we were entering into an election year and the President was rather interested in carrying his home state. With due consideration given in the areas that mattered, Ford eventually pledged six hundred million federal dollars for a Detroit subway. The pledge has been carried forward from administration to administration and remains on the books to this day.

The President's promise notwithstanding, I wasn't entrusting the city's future to the Republicans. That wasn't part of the deal. But I needed to decide whom to support among the possible 1976 Democratic presidential nominees, who included Morris Udall,

Jimmy Carter, and Hubert Humphrey. There was a pilgrimage of candidates and lobbyists to my office, including Udall and Ted Kennedy, but I was intrigued by Carter. He was a little-known southern governor, which made me very wary, but I had visited with Andrew Young in Georgia before the primaries and received a favorable report about Carter's performance there and his positions on human and civil rights. Daddy King, Martin's father, was in his corner also, which said a lot. Carter had courageously advocated the Civil Rights Act in front the Georgia legislature and appointed blacks to important positions in his administration. He had also fought for blacks to be accepted as members of all-white Baptist churches in his hometown of Plains. I did some more research into his record, listened to his speeches, and decided to cast my lot with the governor, advising those around me to get on board because the train was leaving the station. My faith in Carter was reinforced when he spent a night as my guest at the Manoogian Mansion during the campaign, impressing me with his sensitivity toward urban problems and with the way his mind worked.

Not long after that, Carter came out with his infamous remark about ethnic purity. In an interview with the New York *Daily News,* he commented that he saw "nothing wrong with ethnic purity being maintained. I would not force the racial integration of a neighborhood by government action. But I would not permit discrimination against a family moving into the neighborhood." Coming from a southerner, and taken out of context, the quote smacked of segregationism; but I was pretty sure that wasn't what Carter meant. He was merely presenting a snapshot of America as a melting pot with multifarious cultural communities and saying that he would not use government authority to impose integration upon a neighborhood that was ethnically distinct. Since he was careful, at the same time, to denounce discrimination, I had no problem with Carter's remarks. The ethnic communities that remain in cities like Detroit (where the Italian and Polish neighborhoods have scattered to the suburbs, leaving the Chaldean district in the northern sector as the only significant nonblack ethnic enclave) have immeasurable historic value, and their cultures contribute uniquely to the compound culture of America. From my experience, I only wished that the ethnic purity of Black Bottom had been preserved instead of bulldozed.

Anyhow, the liberals had Carter for lunch on that one. He was assailed by the press, the civil rights leaders, even Andy Young, who said that Carter's statement sounded like "something out of Nazi Germany." As a result, the Carter campaign was swiftly degenerating into one protracted apology, which, as I saw it, was hurting Carter even more than the original remark. His candidacy had reached the crisis point. He needed a friend.

Although I was confident that I knew what Carter had meant by "ethnic purity," I wanted to hear it from him. He wanted me to hear it from him, too, and he called to clarify himself, just as he was calling other black leaders throughout the country. I found his explanation to be satisfactory, as expected, and recommended that he get up off his knees and stop apologizing. Actually, I told him something my granddaddy used to say—that if you stay on your knees long enough, somebody is bound to take indecent advantage of you, or more graphic words to that effect. I suspect that Carter, being a very religious and decent man, might have been a little uncomfortable with my use of the language sometimes, but we became close nonetheless. If I can believe what I've heard secondhand, Carter once said that aside from Daddy King and Coretta and Andy Young, he never had a closer friend, black or white, than me, which I humbly accept as a pretty remarkable statement from a Southern Baptist who blushed at four-letter words.

Anyway, Carter got my grandfather's message, picked himself up, and beat the ethnic purity controversy by sticking to his principles. In the end, it was urban America that elected him, and we all knew it. That is, we in the cities—the mayors—knew it, and, most important, Carter knew it. It was a perfect scenario for the population centers, which, in their economic free-fall, were in desperate need of a champion in the White House. We—the mayors—knew that, too. The problem was, we didn't have anything to present to the President; we didn't have a program.

So we wrote one. The Conference of Mayors, for which I was chairman of the urban economic policy committee, called an emergency meeting at the O'Hare Hilton in Chicago right after the election for the purpose of pulling together a national urban policy. Informally, we had been working on an urban policy every time we met, and commonly presented a united front in behalf of the cities. With Henry Maier, the feisty mayor of Milwaukee, I had testified in 1975 before a Senate subcommittee on countercyclical urban fiscal assistance—federal aid in hard times. I also had gone to Washington with Richard Daley, whom I admired as a bottom-line politician who had the guts to stick his neck out and do what was best for Chicago, to lobby President Ford about federal dollars for urban mass transit—an initiative that appeared to bear fruit when Ford granted the $600 million for Detroit's subway. Daley and I also caucused in Detroit about a federal jobs program. But for all of our policymaking efforts, the mayors had never packaged their concepts in the form of a position paper.

It was a stirring few days in Chicago. I argued with mayors from the Sun Belt, which was common; paced incessantly, fidgeted, and started several small fires by inadvertently setting paper on my cigarette butts. We knew that we might well be banging out the immediate future of our cities. By the time we caught our return flights out of O'Hare, we had put together a multidimensional urban blueprint that included public works programs, job training, countercyclical assistance, and a National Urban Development Bank. We also had a meeting set up with the President-elect. We presented our program to him in Atlanta the next weekend, and he received it warmly.

By the time Carter had assembled his transition team and begun piecing together his programs, it was evident that our urban policy had essentially become his urban policy—with the notable exception of the Urban Development Bank, which I regarded as the key to the entire program. I never knew why he eschewed the bank, and could only assume that it got lost in the labyrinth of advisers he had around him. At any rate, the cities were in no position to complain. Urban America was obviously one of Carter's principal priorities—and one of his principal resources as well. With my blessing, he dipped deeply into Detroit. Our Washington lobbyist Chester Davenport was appointed as head of the team dealing with housing and transportation issues. Another lobbyist from Detroit, Carl Riedy, was assigned to assist Davenport and ultimately became an important aide to HUD secretary Patricia Harris. My finance director, Dennis Green, took a prominent position as associate director of the Office of Management and Budget, and my right-hand man, Bill Beckham, was named assistant secretary of treasury and then deputy secretary of transportation. I felt like part of the administration myself, conferring regularly with Stuart Eizenstat, Carter's domestic advisor, and the President. There were rumors that Carter offered me a cabinet position, but it never came up, and I wasn't seeking one. When a member of Carter's administration, my friend Moon Landrieu, asked me about serving in the cabinet, I told him (jokingly, of course) that I wasn't interested in being a cabinet member, just in owning one. Carter did make me vice-chairman of the national Democratic Committee.

Riedy's work at HUD became the basis for the UDAG (Urban Development Action Grant) program, which was probably the most original and significant aspect of Carter's urban policy. UDAG money was offered for development incentive at a rate of about a dollar for every six or seven private equity dollars committed. Detroit received $107 million in UDAG grants—more than any other city—for sixteen development projects, many of them along the riverfront, which I had pledged to redevelop from bridge to bridge. The riverfront plan, in fact, was a major reason why we got as much federal help as we did in the Carter years—we simply submitted better requests than other cities. Given the devastation inflicted upon Detroit by white flight and the automotive recession, it was hard to match our case. When Patricia Harris visited one time and I walked her through a tour of the wasteland that had once been my old Black Bottom neighborhood, she awarded $80 million in HUD money on the spot as mortgage guarantees for more than two thousand housing units.

By the midpoint of Carter's term, Detroit's piece of the pie was $500 million, and our proportion of federal money to locally raised revenue was the highest of any major city in the country. Consequently, my campaign slogan in 1977 was "Bring Home the

Bacon." Because I had been able to do that so noticeably with Carter in office, the election was one of my easiest.

My opponent, a black councilman named Ernest Browne, was a conservative candidate—the first black White Hope, I called him—who couldn't argue with my economic performance and went after me on the basis of my language, street values, Caribbean vacations, and lifestyle as a single. Long before George Bush traveled the same road, Browne campaigned on the issue of family values, implying that I lacked them. During a debate at the Detroit Economic Club, I answered that if being married was a qualification for mayor, then my record made me twice as qualified as he was. In the meantime, my endorsements ranged from Jesse Jackson and Coretta King to Henry Ford and the president of General Motors, Tom Murphy. Even the UAW was behind me by this time. It's amazing what a little legitimacy can do.

While Jimmy Carter dollars continued to stream into the city after my reelection, we also began to reap the benefits of the Renaissance Center. Within four years of its completion, property value increased by three hundred percent along the riverfront. It was a vital improvement, because the riverfront had become a regional disgrace.

By every practical and historic measure, the setting of the Detroit River should reflect its station as the city's greatest natural resource, its link to the Great Lakes and the Atlantic, a unique waterway wide enough to accommodate oceanfaring cargo ships and sufficiently handsome to dignify the breach between two great countries. (The Detroit River, incidentally, is the only boundary across which one can look south from the United States into Canada, as I do from my office in the City-County Building.) The riverfront was the original Detroit, which began to take shape after French commander Antoine de La Mothe Cadillac came ashore in 1701 and swore to defend his new settlement against the British. But through the years industry had sullied the riverfront and abandonment had disrobed it. It had become a tumbleweed row of peeling paint and broken windows. In my first campaign, I had stressed that the strip from bridge (Ambassador) to bridge (Belle Isle) had to be the starting point in the rebuilding of Detroit. Over the next two decades, more than a billion dollars would be invested along the river.

Unquestionably, the Renaissance Center was the inspiration that renewed the city; but to me, the piece that actually did most to advance the development process was the informal open space just down the street—Hart Plaza, thirteen acres of sidewalks and promenades and easy landscaping along with an amphitheater. The plaza had been discussed by several previous administrations, and it was my good fortune—and Detroit's—to get it built in the atmosphere of Renaissance and Jimmy Carter. Our key decision was to make it a people place as opposed to a formal garden. Hart Plaza provides a brown-bag lunch spot on the weekdays, and on weekends we've had all manner of ethnic and music festivals there over the years, from polka to soul to bluegrass. Not only did the plaza humanize the area, but the city's commitment to it encouraged private developers to venture along the riverfront. Max Fisher took note of the UDAG grants being made available and dragged his very reluctant friend, Al Taubman, the real estate baron, warily into riverfront housing. A HUD study had indicated that the downtown area could accommodate no more than fifty units of housing per year, but Taubman and Fisher, flying in the face of even their own skepticism, defied the timid projections with a twenty-nine-story, six-hundred-unit, twin-tower high-rise called the Riverfront Apartments. It was received so well that they put up a third tower, which is now fully occupied.

In Detroit, when Fisher and Taubman invest, others respond in kind. Carter's pump-priming money didn't hurt, either, nor did our city tax abatements, which served as incentives to private developers. Across from the Renaissance Center, the construction of the Millender Center—the first building of its kind in America named for a black civic leader (Robert Millender)—added apartments, shops, restaurants, another hotel, and an enclosed, connecting skywalk over Jefferson Avenue. The riverfront boom continued into the eighties and nineties, stretching east along Jefferson nearly to the Grosse Pointes.

The critics, mostly bleeding-heart liberals, typically had and still have a problem with all of this development. These incessant naysayers—several of whom, led by Maryann Mahaffey (my former campaign worker) and Mel Ravitz, have occupied seats on the city council for nearly my entire tenure as mayor—can find fault with most anything I do as an economic activist; yet I seldom hear much from them in the way of solutions. For five terms now, they've complained that we've spent all of our money along the river and downtown at the expense of the deteriorating neighborhoods. First of all, this is patently untrue, inasmuch as four out of every five of our development dollars have gone into neighborhood projects, such as residential complexes and recreation centers. Furthermore, I have no goddamn idea how they propose to maintain their new and improved neighborhoods without jobs and a tax base, and as far as I can tell, they don't, either. But the knee-jerk liberals are so blinded by the fear that we're subsidizing industry and wealthy developers—helping the rich and ignoring the poor—that they've lost sight of reality. The reality is that if you have a billion dollars to spend in the city and spend every penny of it rebuilding the neighborhoods—giving people brand-new or refurbished houses—and *they don't have jobs,* within five years the goddamn place will be a slum again. Because without a job, there is no rent or mortgage money. Without a job, there is no hope for the future. Without a job, there is no pride.

On the other hand, if the billion dollars is used, like we used our Jimmy Carter dollars, for pump priming—as incentive money to bring in private capital—then it has begun to multiply and serve the city by creating and maintaining jobs. A city bereft of jobs is a city bereft of commerce and hopelessly removed from prosperity. That's the reality that any development plan must address in Detroit, where only 49.6 percent of the population participates in the civilian labor force, the lowest rate among major U.S. cities and fifteen points below the state and regional percentages. Detroit's epidemic joblessness is naturally reflected in its median income level (just over $19,900), the nation's lowest among major cities. In turn, the city's per capita outlay for retail sales (around $9,000) is even further in arrears, which points up the fact that unemployment is exponentially debilitating to the local economy. This is further demonstrated by the following bottom-line statistic: as Detroit's unemployment rate has more than doubled in the past twenty years, the total comparative value of property in the city (the sum of residential, commercial, and industrial real estate, plus personal property) has plummeted by two-thirds, a decline of $3.6 billion. The number of citizens paying municipal income tax in Detroit has decreased by a quarter-million in that period. As applied to urban development, the obvious lesson is that a community will flourish only when its residents have access to jobs. This bleeding-heart bullshit about building communities without a job base is like building on quicksand.

To strengthen the job base necessary for a strong urban community, it is imperative that we put aside our idealistic philosophies and practice economic activism. No private developer is going to risk a hundred million dollars on housing or community buildings for Detroit just because it's the right thing to do. But if we prime the pump for him—add ten million to his hundred—to develop a plant or a hotel or an office tower, then he's building up the community out of his own self-interest. When you can achieve a confluence of your own self-interest with somebody else's, then you've got a deal. That's a very basic dynamic that the bleeding hearts, by stubbornness or stupidity or both, refuse to recognize—a fact that has annoyed me for most of the last twenty years. Frankly, it offends the hell out of me that I'm charged by the pansy-ass liberals with ignoring the poor folks—i.e., the black folks. For God's sake, I've spent a lifetime fighting for the black man's privileges and standard of living! It's what I do. And I firmly believe that by stimulating the redevelopment of Detroit with federal and private money, I've done it damn effectively.

Although you'd never know it by listening to the naysayers, the neighborhoods have been part of it from the beginning. When I assumed office, Black Bottom and Twelfth Street still lay wasted from urban renewal and the rebellion, respectively. My plan was to complement our new commercial development by rebuilding the neighborhoods in the approximate sequence of the bulldozer. We used Jimmy Carter dollars and HUD money for several classes of housing in Black Bottom, converting eighty acres of the Lafayette Park and Elmwood Park neighborhoods into one of the largest, most socioeconomically diverse and integrated communities in the city. We were also able to improve the neighborhoods in numerous ways through Carter's $2 billion public works program, as prescribed by the Conference of Mayors, in which he was passing out block-grant money at $5 million a pop to build something. We obliged him with the Coleman A. Young Recreation Center on Chene and did the same thing on Twelfth Street—now called Rosa Parks Boulevard—with the Joseph Walker Williams Center.

That area, dismembered in 1967, has been resurrected with an architecture known locally as "riot renaissance." At the heart of the riot scene, the Virginia Park neighborhood on Rosa Parks now features more than a thousand new housing units, some of which represent the first single-family new housing that went up in Detroit in several decades. Despite its economic liabilities, Detroit is not an apartment-and-tenement town. We are essentially a settlement of displaced peasants, whether from Poland or Italy or Alabama, and consequently we tend to be house-and-fence people, which is why Detroit has the highest percentage of homeowners among the country's major cities. The neighborhood adjacent to Virginia Park, New Center Commons, boasts of some of the finest old homes in Detroit, many of which have been restored as part of a $50 million effort that General Motors put into the blocks surrounding its headquarters. Needless to say, that type of corporate commitment might not have been plausible without the federal incentive programs that ran parallel throughout the city; and by the same token, the government initiatives would have been stillborn without the willing response of private developers.

Since 1974, more than fifteen thousand units of new housing have been constructed in Detroit's neighborhoods, much of it with Carter dollars. But at the same time, Carter's public works money was extremely versatile, and we were on something of a crusade to explore the outer reaches of its application. With $5 million Detroit received in the fall of 1976, I decided to begin construction on an indoor stadium next to Cobo Hall. There were many who thought—and I can't reasonably blame them—that I'd lost my marbles, inasmuch as both our hockey team, the Red Wings, and our basketball team, the Pistons (whose home court was Cobo), had made it abundantly clear that they would not play in any new facility the city might conjure up. Our football team, the Lions, had already ditched us for the Silverdome in the Oakland County suburb of Pontiac, and the Red Wings and the Pistons were obviously captivated by the vision of parking lots and white people. The Red Wings, in fact, who were eager to move out of their city home at Olympia Stadium after two murders occurred nearby, were all set to relocate in a new arena that was being planned in Oakland County not far from the Silverdome. Fed up with seeing Detroit played as the patsy—and unable to abide it economically—I felt that I had to answer the suburban initiative in a decisive manner. As a second-generation poker player, I was betting that if I opened with $5 million in federal money, Oakland County might stay in the game for a while to see if I was bluffing but would fold the minute we put a shovel in the ground.

We couldn't afford to wait for a commitment from a tenant before we started digging, because the delay would cause us to lose our leverage and our federal money, which came with a deadline attached for beginning construction. Speed was of the essence, so I forged ahead in defiance of the technical challenges (little things like financing, land acquisition, and the actual function of the building) that we hadn't worked out quite yet. This confounded the press, which was unanimous in its disapproval, and played uneasily upon the business leaders with whom I had formed a working relationship. They were not falling in line, apparently hung up over the facts that we had no tenant and no goddamn idea where the money would come from to finish the construction once we started it. At one particular meeting, after this theme had been advanced various times by the parties in attendance, I stood up and said, "Look, I've got five million dollars to dig with, and if nothing else, we'll have the biggest fucking hole in the state of Michigan!"

There were the usual complications in securing approval from the likes of the city council and the Michigan Municipal Finance Commission, which balked over our request to raise money for engineering studies by selling $1.5 million in general-obligation bonds but ultimately granted it. A suit by a suburban citizen group to halt the bond sale (on the basis that the project had been falsely described—i.e., referred to as a stadium as opposed to an arena) was another impediment, keeping us occupied in the courts while critical time passed. As a countermove, we filed an action against the proposed Oakland County arena, Olympia II, on the grounds that it would remove jobs from an economically depressed area. The suits were a wash—ours against the Oakland County group was rejected, and the state supreme court upheld Detroit's bond sale.

Meanwhile, amidst all of the political and legal dickering, the owner of the Red Wings, Bruce Norris, sent me a long letter detailing all of the reasons why he was not interested in a downtown arena. He wrote, among other things, that the team's fans were overwhelmingly suburban and that "if we move our operations, they should be moved to the suburbs." Norris's letter was distributed widely and held up as another prime exhibit in the case of the mayor's runaway lunacy. But I thought the letter was promising. Why would he bother to spell out his objections if he had no interest in negotiating with the city? Sure enough, at the urging of a couple of local businessmen, retailer Max Pincus and Fisher Theater owner Joey Nederlander, a Red Wings executive, Lincoln Cavalieri, finally called my office one morning to request a meeting.

That afternoon, we sat down and agreed to terms that kept our hockey team in Detroit. It was a unique contract in which the Red Wings formed a corporation to lease and book events for the new arena and Cobo Hall. The city would receive a surcharge on each ticket and collect parking receipts, which would go a long way toward paying off our revenue bonds.

Of course, there was still the small matter of raising money to build the damn thing. Tapped out at the city level, we were able to triple our original grant through the U.S. Housing and Community Development Act, passed in 1974 under Nixon (who doesn't look so bad after twelve years of Reagan and Bush) and borrow another $38 million against block grants that would be issued to the city in the future. When the arena was finished—before the approval of all of our federal loans actually came through—the naysayers whined that we had built it with smoke and mirrors. What the hell else did we have?

I named the place for that great hockey player from Black Bottom, Joe Louis.

9

The Reason We Exist

"**F**undamentally, modern Detroit exists to build and sell motor cars," wrote historian Arthur Pound in 1940, "and once it quits doing that it will lose its chief reason for existence."

Without attempting to be melodramatic, I can avow that we were about to tumble headfirst into that very scenario forty years later, when the Chrysler Corporation was on the brink of bankruptcy. As it was, auto jobs had been skulking out of Detroit for more than a score, each and every job carting off a little more of the Motor City's chrome and a working part or two. Industrial employment in the city decreased by thirty percent in the seventies alone. Detroit's proportion of Michigan's assessed property value was in the process of dropping from thirty-seven percent to only five percent in the forty years following World War II, and the local unemployment rate was on its way to twenty percent. The situation was pretty well summed up by a popular bumper sticker that I might have found morbidly amusing if it hadn't been so goddamn appropriate: DETROIT—WILL THE LAST ONE TO LEAVE PLEASE TURN OUT THE LIGHTS? By the end of the seventies, it had just about reached that point.

With austerity and a little economic creativity, we had survived the fiscal tremor of 1975, only to find chasms in the road ahead. As we contemplated the financial abyss into which we would free-fall without Chrysler, Detroit had just been hit with an $80 million contract arbitration award to the police and fire unions, one of a series of arbitration decisions that reflected an incredible and utter disre-

gard for the city's ability to pay such awards. At the same time, we
were attempting to raise funds for a new city trauma center called
Receiving Hospital (which has since been sold by the city and become part of the Detroit Medical Center) and to pull money out of
thin air for Joe Louis Arena—all of this despite a drop in our bond
rating begotten by the auto crisis engendered by the oil embargo.
It was no time to lose the city's biggest employer.

The importance of Chrysler's survival was not universally understood. The general feeling around Detroit—and, more pertinently,
around Washington—was that Chrysler was Lee Iacocca's predicament: he was the miracle man the company had brought in to set
things straight, and if he was half as smart as he and everybody else
seemed to think he was, he could somehow figure something out
on his own. From where I stood, however, Chrysler was the nation's
predicament, Detroit's predicament, and very much my predicament.

To the extent that I drink from the cup of free enterprise—and
there is a limit to that extent—I would never push the argument
that the government is obligated to perpetuate Chrysler or General Motors or any major corporation for that corporation's sake. I
would argue to the death, however, about the government's obligation to sustain the working people of America—particularly when
the specific America in question happens to fall within the boundaries of my executive authority. I have taken it as my solemn duty
to never let Washington neglect its obligation to the city of Detroit. If Chrysler had to be bailed out in the greater interest of
Detroit, then God save Chrysler. To me, it was incidental that tens
of thousands of jobs would also be spared in other cities around
the country. I had my hands full trying to keep Detroit working.

Although it was not unprecedented for the government to supply emergency aid to big business—Lockheed and American Motors were just a couple of the precedents—there didn't seem to be
a lot of sympathy for Chrysler on Capitol Hill, perhaps, in part, because Iacocca appeared to be going it alone in the beginning. In
order to intervene, Washington had to be convinced that this was
not just a corporate problem but a regional and national emergency. However, the automobile industry, separated into conti-

nents by the gulf between management and labor, was not in the practice of putting up united fronts. Therein lay my challenge.

Since the company and the UAW had no forum for exchanging ideas that did not relate specifically to collective bargaining, and since the Chrysler offices and the union's Solidarity House were partisan corridors, I invited the concerned parties to meet on the neutral turf of the mayor's office. Iacocca was there, along with Doug Fraser, my old CIO ally, who had risen to president of the UAW, and Marc Stepp, head of the union's Chrysler division. It helped that Fraser was familiar with my union roots and could therefore be confident that, despite my obvious preoccupation with keeping Chrysler alive, my instincts were on the side of labor. Everybody at that table stood to lose and lose big if Chrysler went under, so it was in everybody's best interest—including the union's—to give a little to avoid losing a hell of a lot. But the thing was, the UAW had never given back anything it had won from a manufacturer and, as a matter of self-preservation, had long ago fallen deaf to the wolf cries of the auto companies. My charge was to convince the union that this time the big bad wolf had its fangs in Chrysler's backside and that the company—and all those UAW jobs—could not be saved without labor in the rescue party. I went so far as to suggest that the union indulge its skepticism by looking at Chrysler's books, which it did for the first time, thereby satisfying itself that the crisis was genuine. Once the UAW agreed, out of necessity, to give back a load of concessions for which it had fought long and hard, the union and the company were in the same choir, with Fraser and Iacocca—and me, if you can excuse the image— singing out of the same hymnal.

Fraser, whose invaluable connections included Vice-President Walter Mondale, was a vital and unrelenting lobbyist for the Chrysler bailout. I spoke to the President about it and made several trips to Washington to buttonhole Stuart Eizenstat, impressing upon them in no uncertain terms that my city was at stake here. I told them, as I've often said, that when the auto industry catches a cold, Detroit develops pneumonia. This was a serious case, and we wouldn't be able to keep the city on its feet without federal doctoring.

I also testified before a Senate subcommittee, representing both Detroit and the Conference of Mayors. I stressed that the closing of Chrysler would have a devastating impact not only on Detroit but on several pockets of the country—that, for starters, St. Louis would lose more than twenty-five thousand jobs, that unemployment would be doubled in the Wilmington area, and that forty percent of all the jobs in Kokomo, Indiana, would be affected. Chrysler was the tenth-largest industrial corporation in the country and by far the largest employer in Detroit. The thirty-seven thousand Chrysler employees in Detroit represented seven percent of the city's work force. It did not escape my attention—or, when I was finished, the Senate's—that of those thirty-seven thousand workers in Detroit, twenty-five thousand were black. In terms of annual revenue from various corporate and personal tax sources, the city would stand to lose $30 million if Chrysler went under. We would consequently be forced to lay off city employees, including police officers, at a time when unemployment and desperation would no doubt accelerate the crime rate. All things considered, it was easy to see that however much the government risked by providing temporary emergency relief for Chrysler, it would be in much deeper financial peril—the demands upon it for aid would be immeasurably greater—if Chrysler were to shut down.

It was fortunate that our ad hoc Detroit coalition had myriad friends and contacts in the administration, among them Moon Landrieu, the new secretary of HUD, who, as former mayor of New Orleans, had been an ally of mine as well as the boss and close associate of my new community and economic development director, Emmett Moten; and Secretary of Transportation Neil Goldschmidt, whose deputy was my former top aide, Bill Beckham. Our reach, however, did not embrace Secretary of the Treasury William Miller, who had gone on record as saying that the economy, like a pair of kidneys, needed to be purified, that purification consisting of the disposal of unprofitable companies. At a subsequent cabinet meeting, the President went around the table soliciting opinions on the Chrysler dilemma, at which time Goldschmidt strayed from Miller's philosophy by urging that the government give every consideration to the company's request. Then

Carter came to Landrieu, under whose jurisdiction Chrysler was beginning to fall. The way I've heard it, Landrieu turned to the President and said, "Who's going to pick up the phone and call Coleman Young to tell him we just purified the economy by eliminating his number-one employer?" He also asked who was going to call organized labor to say that the government had just purified the economy by putting more than a hundred thousand auto workers on the street. You can see why I've always maintained a high regard for Moon Landrieu.

Washington turned in our direction after that, and the loan guarantee, controversial as it had been, passed Congress with relative ease. Chrysler proceeded to make the most of its second chance, ultimately paying back the entire loan seven years early. To his credit, Iacocca read all of the charts correctly and did a masterful job of navigating a very perilous interlude. I believe that he carried Chrysler with the sheer force of his personality, but I also believe that he emerged from the ordeal with an acute case of myopia. In the glow of triumph, he seemed to lose sight of the efforts of Doug Fraser and Moon Landrieu and many others who put themselves on the line for Chrysler. In his autobiography, Iacocca dismisses me, "the black mayor of Detroit," with one obligatory paragraph. I resented the kiss-off and frankly can't explain it. But I don't regret a single minute I put into saving Chrysler, because I wasn't doing it for Iacocca. I was doing it for Detroit.

While it's no scoop that the Chrysler recovery yellow-flagged the flight of jobs from Detroit and perpetuated the level of competition within the automobile industry, it could be argued as well that the partnership between the union and the company opened up a new era of cooperation in American auto plants. The innovative aspects of General Motors' Saturn, wherein the workers participate in the design and decision-making and even the profits of the car, represent a natural extension of the labor-management coalition fostered by the Chrysler crisis. The Chrysler episode was also a historic success and an enormously profitable venture for the government. In retrospect, Chrysler's comeback marks one of the better stories of the period. Jimmy Carter has ranked it among the proudest accomplishments of his presidency.

The financial rehabilitations of both Chrysler and Detroit over those years were products of a federal sense of responsibility that was sorely missed as soon as Carter was voted out of office. Neither of his Republican successors so much as discussed an urban policy. Even Carter, despite his courage in the Chrysler crisis and for all his sensitivity in the areas of human rights, was not without serious conflict when it came to the needs of the cities. He was a champion of the mayors' recovery program for as long as the money held out, but when the fiscal net began to tighten, he reverted to his basic economic conservatism. He and I had some pretty sharp discussions when he was dismantling the urban program, and he reluctantly reconsidered some of his initial cutbacks. The Chrysler deal, for instance, went against his fiscal instincts. Although it wasn't easy for him, I can proudly say of my friend Jimmy Carter that, on balance, he allowed his humanitarian side to win out.

E DUCATION, DRUGS, homelessness, unwed mothers, crime, you name it—to varying degrees, every social issue is about jobs.

If I could have brought enough jobs to Detroit, I would have gone down as the greatest mayor the world has ever seen. The same could be said for mayors of New York or Cleveland or Buffalo or Los Angeles or Philadelphia. The problem is, there's only so much a mayor can do about jobs. He can use federal grant money for incentives, he can offer tax abatements, he can buy land, he can recruit and solicit and lobby; but he can't keep a factory from folding and he can't change his climate and he can't control wages or utility bills, and as much as he might like and try to, he can't make another man's decisions.

When the matter of jobs for the city comes down to another man's decision, the best a mayor can do is hope for someone he can work with—a man like Tom Murphy, the former chairman and CEO of General Motors. Thomas Aquinas Murphy, I called him, in honor of his character. Murphy was a man of his word, and because of it the face of Detroit was changed historically in 1980.

Although I respected Murphy and he had supported my reelection, my encounters with him during the late seventies had not been propitious. He was an outspoken opponent of the Chrysler deal and had exacerbated the local job problem by moving a Cadillac transmission plant from Detroit to the suburb of Livonia. By law, I could have prevented GM from receiving tax breaks in Livonia or any other location in Michigan, but I figured that if the plant was going to leave Detroit anyway—and hell, they all were—it would be better off in Livonia, where at least some Detroiters could hang on to their jobs, than in Indiana. Besides that, I didn't see much purpose in alienating the nation's largest employer for nothing more than spite. And I did get one little thing out of Murphy: I got him to promise me that the next time GM planned to build a new plant, he would give me time to come up with a site. His practice, like Ford's and Chrysler's, had been to notify me that the company had decided to relocate and that he would be happy to consider a site in Detroit if I could show him a suitable one—say, three hundred acres, rectangular, with access to highways and rail lines—within, say, twenty-four hours.

In deference to the impossible time parameters that the auto industry was wont to impose upon us, I lobbied Lansing for an unusual special provision within the state's eminent domain law. Eminent domain is the government authority by which private property can be taken over for public use, as commonly defined by public works projects such as highways and dams and occasionally hospitals. My contention was that rampant unemployment—which by 1980 had reached more than twelve percent in Michigan, eighteen percent in Detroit overall, and thirty percent in Detroit's black community—constituted a public emergency in the state's industrial cities, and I intended, at some undetermined but propitious moment in the near future, to push the argument that eminent domain could and should be utilized for the unprecedented purpose of providing jobs in such cities. Even if the state would buy into my unusual interpretation of the law, however, there was a critical aspect of eminent domain that had to be addressed in the meantime if it was to be of any use in securing an automobile plant. The problem was that eminent domain tended to be a very slow legal process, consuming precious time that the manufacturers would not be willing to sacrifice. In order for the courts to approve an application, it was necessary first to establish whether the takeover was constitutional in terms of the public-use requirements; then the matter of compensation had to be resolved. That was commonly a thankless and contestable procedure which delayed eminent domain projects by years upon years. The automobile industry could not possibly operate under that sort of timetable. So, determined to have my ducks in a row the next time a new plant was up for grabs, I petitioned the state legislature for a "quick-take" statute which would enable municipalities to acquire the title to property and take possession of it under the eminent domain law *before* a purchase price was negotiated with the previous owner. When it passed in April of 1980, Michigan's quick-take law became the only one of its kind in the country.

At the time, I could not have known that we would be breaking the maidenhead on the new law so soon. I did know, however, that quite a bit of land was becoming available in pockmarks throughout the city—the residue of white flight—and that we had to be creative and speedy if a situation presented itself. As it happened, the occasion developed within a month after the legislation passed, when Murphy came to me and said that General Motors had made a decision to spend $40 billion on retooling and rebuilding production facilities in order to modernize its cars. Part of that package was a state-of-the-art Cadillac plant, for which GM had several potential sites in mind. I believe that Murphy was looking at the new plant as a way for GM to establish itself in the Southeast, but he had promised me that he would give Detroit a chance, and was loyal to his promises. So he strolled into my office one spring morning and said that our chance would last for exactly one year—beginning today.

GM needed a whopping five hundred acres for the new site, which was designed to occupy a perfect square nearly a mile on each side. As a rule, that sort of space is simply not available in fully developed urban areas, as Murphy knew damn well. Detroit doesn't make the short list when corporations go out in search of green fields. Despite that, we showed General Motors about ten sites, some of which were not the proper shape and some of which were too far removed from the lines of transportation and some of which required too much relocation. To a lesser degree, we'd been through the same drill with the Cadillac transmission plant. At that time, we'd determined that one of the most suitable sites was the area around and adjacent to the old Dodge Main plant, which amounted to 144 acres in Hamtramck, an enclosed city surrounded on three sides by Detroit. Dodge Main—which began producing cars in 1914, once employed as many as forty thousand people, and had historic significance as the first plant under whose roof an entire automobile was made—would be closing a few days after New Year's, 1980, putting its remaining three thousand auto workers out of jobs and idling thirty-seven miles of conveyor belts.

To the city, there were obvious advantages in maintaining an industrial site at Dodge Main, one being that 144 acres could be purchased from Chrysler for a buck and nobody had to be relocated—reasons don't come any more compelling than that—and another being that Hamtramck was severely depressed and in desperate need of the jobs, without which it could become a costly ward of Detroit. The problem was that the blocks surrounding Dodge Main in both Hamtramck and Detroit represented a compact residential neighborhood, ensuring that—under the traditional legal parameters—purchase of the property and the subsequent relocation process would be a tedious and protracted ordeal.

But the quick-take law changed all of that. All we had to do to acquire the land under eminent domain—and I don't mean to underestimate the complexity of this challenge—was demonstrate that the jobs created by a new General Motors plant responded to a public need. If we could pull that off, we could immediately condemn the land and evacuate the area to clear and prepare it for the new plant—provided, of course, that GM approved the site. That was not a given by any means.

Because of the 144 acres that the Dodge Main site brought to the table, GM had an inherent interest in the land encompassing the plant. But after examining the acreage closely, company engineers decided that it wouldn't work. Its rail line was curved (the blueprint called for a straight rail line); it was dissected by a historic boulevard (East Grand); and even if the neighborhood could be cleared, which was sure to be a controversial proposition, there was still a cemetery at the edge of the property. It was the best we had to offer, though; and when GM turned it down, it looked as though it was time to fold. My point man on the project, Emmett Moten, called me one night to say that he had nowhere left to turn. I told him to get a good night's sleep and we'd talk about it in the morning.

Rather than sleep, however, Emmett called GM's point man, Stu Hockman, and arranged one last-ditch meeting to see if there was any way that Dodge Main could work. Hockman brought along the chief engineer of the project, who was full of reasons why the area was all wrong. In its retooling campaign, GM had designed plants on a cookie-cutter concept, as if they were McDonald's franchises. There was no way that the cookie-cutter plant could be rolled out of Dodge Main. But on the other hand—and the more they examined it, the more they realized it—there wasn't another site in the world that could match Dodge Main in terms of access, infrastructure, and a trained, ready, and willing work force. And despite what the cynics said and still say, there was a strong and genuine interest on Murphy's part to be loyal to the city of Detroit. With all of that in mind, Hockman turned to his cookie-cutter engineer and said, "Look, I'm not going back to Tom Murphy on some bullshit that we can't make this work because engineering refuses to redesign the site." He told his engineer in so many words to screw his perfect square, because the plant would work on Dodge Main if they would only try to make it work.

And by God, they did. It cost them a hell of a lot of money, because they had to redraw and reorder and flip things around, but they committed themselves to making it work. I'm convinced that if Hockman hadn't spoken up that night—and if he hadn't understood the depth of Tom Murphy's loyalty to his word and to Detroit—GM would have put its new Cadillac plant in Alabama.

Of course, there were people in the neighborhood who would have preferred it that way. The new plant was not a unanimously popular item, which I, as a sentimental former resident of the much-lamented Black Bottom, could certainly appreciate. To compensate for the very real loss of home that many of the community members would involuntarily suffer, the city extended relocation terms that were very generous. To homeowners, many of whose houses were so deteriorated that they were worth only $2,500 to $5,000, we we offered market value and moving expenses plus $15,000. Renters received a $4,000 moving allowance. Since liability lawyers had wormed their way into the writing of the quick-take statute, the city had to tack on an additional one-third of each settlement cost for attorney fees. This didn't affect the negotiations with the residents, however; and given the blatant decline of the neighborhood, most of them couldn't settle fast enough. Still, a small percentage—to be precise, about three hundred out of forty-two hundred—refused to come to terms with the city. The holdouts were mostly elderly, first-generation Polish-Americans who had lived in the area since coming over from the old country. To capitalize on their ability to elicit public sympathy—as if the little old ladies in black dresses and babushkas weren't enough—the bleeding-heart activists in the area organized an opposition group and began very effectively referring to the neighborhood by the deliberate misnomer of Poletown, falsely implying that the neighborhood, as a whole, had been preserved over the decades as a quaint ethnic treasure.

As I understand, there was, some years before, a neighborhood known as Poletown in that vicinity. But the real Poletown had been a turn-of-the-century enclave south of the Dodge Main area, on the other side of what became the Edsel Ford Freeway. The suddenly reincarnated Poletown was actually an ethnically diverse neighborhood that reflected the work force of Dodge Main—black, Appalachian, Arab, Albanian, and, of course, Polish. Many of the Polish-American families had moved into the district from the original Poletown when blacks began to locate on their streets. Over the years, the black population of the entire area had become so significant that I suggested the neighborhood would be more accurately described as Afro-Poletown, although that didn't seem to catch on.

The resistance organized itself into the Poletown Neighborhood Council, which drew attention to the human and community sacrifice that would be exacted in the name of industrial development. I was familiar with that sort of thing, of course. I'm still angered by the utter contempt with which the federal government eliminated the blocks where I grew up; and back then, there was no industrial development in store for Black Bottom, and there were no neighborhood councils coming forth in its behalf. There was, in fact, little similarity between the whimsical destruction of Black Bottom, which lay barren for years afterwards, and the essential conversion of Poletown into a job-providing automobile facility. I viewed the GM plant as a community project of grand and urgent proportions. As it was, the immediate and greater communities were slipping fast. Poletown (I'm loath to use the name but lack a better one) had become an economic microcosm of Detroit, where industrial abandonment had put a quarter of a million auto workers out of jobs. The *Free Press* had published an article about the Dodge Main neighborhood shortly before the GM issue broke, portraying it not as a tight-knit Polish settlement but as a vanishing community in which property value had declined so sharply that the area had become a disinvestment. Poletown, like Detroit, was looking like a disposable city at the throwaway end of its life cycle.

The alternative for the city, as I saw it—the only alternative presenting itself, and one that we couldn't afford to let pass—was to retool Detroit, to build a new industrial town within the sagging boundaries of the old one. Such a thing had not happened anywhere else in the country, but it was in Detroit's tradition to be on the leading edge of industrial evolution. We had an opportunity not only to maintain an automotive foothold in the city, but to do so with a state-of-the-art facility that would place Detroit back in the industrial vanguard, where it belonged. On top of all that, Murphy had told me that the plant could create as many as six thousand jobs. He had said the magic word.

But nothing would happen without bold initiatives on the city's part and GM's. We knew we would be taken to task by the nearsighted liberals, who were certain to dramatize the destruction of the neighborhood. I'm the first to admit that the condemnation process, which I had to sign into action, was damn dramatic. I would never trivialize the loss involved in clearing out three hundred urban acres. Although the site required less displacement than any other we could have come up with in the city—and that was first among all considerations—it was still a staggering proposition, the largest urban condemnation in history. The city attempted in vain to renegotiate the dimensions of the project, angling for less parking space, utilization of the Dodge Main buildings (which GM intended to raze), etc.; but every time we tried to modify the specifications, GM insisted that it needed every inch on its blueprint and that there were cities in other states eager to accommodate the requirements of the plant. We conducted an independent study which verified that the company did indeed need all of the property. There was no way around it: to make room for the Central Industrial Park, as we called it, we would have to buy and bulldoze 1,300 houses, 16 churches, 2 schools, a hospital, and 114 small businesses. In all, the city acquired nearly two thousand pieces of property and relocated more than four thousand people. It was an undertaking so formidable and unique as to become the example of eminent domain taught at Harvard Law School. We were treading on virgin legal territory.

The Poletown Neighborhood Council, however, would not allow us to forge ahead uncontested. It took us to court to challenge our standard of public purpose. I testified that the plant was not only in the public interest but "beyond doubt the most important single program that has been undertaken since I became mayor." To back up that claim, I was armed with a barrage of information about the declining job base not only of Detroit but also of Hamtramck, and about the rest of the urban economic complex that was being sucked down by the whirlpool of unemployment—city services, bond ratings, welfare rolls, etc. The circuit court judge considered it all and approved our application of eminent domain, noting that unemployment in Detroit had reached "calamitous proportions." The state supreme court upheld his decision by a 5–2 vote in March of 1981.

By April 1, we had purchased the first parcel for the Central Industrial Park. Between us, Detroit and Hamtramck had to raise more than $200 million to clear the site, the catch being that Hamtramck was basically broke—it lost $2.6 million in property taxes when Dodge Main closed—and ineligible for federal aid because of a suit against it. But we were not without places to turn. The Detroit Economic Growth Corporation, established early in my administration for just this sort of thing, did an amazing job of rallying funds from a diverse spectrum of public and private sources, including HUD, UDAG, and even EPA grants, Carter's auto recovery package, industrial revenue bonds, a consortium of local businesses and banks, state road and rail funds, and on and on. The effort was complicated by the changeover in administrations, but Governor Milliken was very successful in lobbying Reagan on our behalf. As the package took shape, federal officials said that they were awed by the unprecedented magnitude of the venture.

Demolition began in May, but despite the judicial endorsement and inspired financing, our opponents were not quieted. On the contrary, they were emboldened by the touching down of Ralph Nader and his youthful flock of guardian carpetbaggers. Being a consummate button-pusher, Nader set up headquarters in the basement of Immaculate Conception, a decorative old church that had become the symbol and centerpiece of the campaign to save Poletown. John Cardinal Dearden, head of the archdiocese, had endorsed the demolition of the church—its congregation had dwindled to a faithful few—but its pastor, Father Joseph Karasiewicz, had unexpectedly stepped out in defiance of the cardinal, GM, and the city of Detroit. An unobtrusive, sincere man, Father Joe was the champion of the babushka crowd and the nightly news, the ultimate martyr. It was the perfect setting for a publicity-grubbing little prick like Nader.

The irony of being on the big-guy side was not lost on me. It was a peculiar position, but one that I wasn't inclined to compromise, considering the stakes. Without intending to be flip, I commented that you had to crack some eggs to make an omelette—or starve. My city was figuratively starving, and I'd crack eggs until the hen keeled over if I had to. Somebody had to take a stand for Detroit, goddamnit, and Ralph Nader sure as hell wasn't the guy.

Nader's purpose, as I saw it, was to orchestrate another lawsuit. That's what he does, as I explained to the media: he swoops in, he sues, he leaves. In the meantime, he might meet with the grass-roots folks a time or two, which qualifies him as an expert on that particular situation. If General Motors is involved, Nader also makes it his business to froth at the mouth whenever the company's name comes up.

The suit he drummed up, meanwhile, had to do with environmental controls. It sought to stop our bulldozing on the basis that the federal government had awarded Detroit an emergency waiver of our Environmental Impact Statement so that we could receive federal funds without delay and proceed with land acquisition. We had to shut down the equipment for a while as the suit traipsed through the courts, during which time we bought Immaculate Conception from the archdiocese for $1.2 million. In reaction to that news, parishioners carried signs in front of the church saying, among other things, "Saint Peter Will Want to Know Why." Others camped out in the basement of the church, setting up vigils so that somebody would be there when the wrecking crew arrived. We were cleared to move ahead when Nader's appeal failed in federal court. In the decision, a judge called the expedited Poletown process—as far as I could tell, we had broken all the speed records for this sort of thing—"a most impressive display of government efficiency."

In the course of all the legal deliberations, Tom Murphy had retired as chairman of GM and been succeeded by Roger Smith. I was concerned that Smith might not support the project with Murphy's fortitude, and in fact wondered if, deep down, Smith wasn't silently pulling for Nader's injunction to be upheld so that he could take the plant somewhere else. In terms of GM's commitment to the city, we had nothing more than Murphy's word. It was a tough spot for Smith. He immediately became the object of abuse from the Poletown protesters, who picketed outside his house and smashed an old GM car in front of company headquarters.

Smith was not immune from the passions we'd raised. He became emotionally involved with the clearing process and especially Immaculate Conception, which dominated public attention. Lost in the hullabaloo over Father Joe and his flock was the fact that the rest of the neighborhood churches, including several Catholic and nearly a dozen that were predominantly black, had settled without much of a fuss; but that didn't soften the Immaculate Conception situation. Although it smacked of grandstanding, it was heart-rending nonetheless, and one morning Smith rode around the neighborhood at five A.M. in search of solutions to the church quandary. Later, he came upon a man who had relocated another Catholic church and with that information hastily called together his staff to propose the idea of moving Immaculate Conception brick by brick at GM's expense. When the news circulated, the church bells rang for two hours. But Cardinal Dearden would have none of it. When Immaculate Conception was sold to the city, it had been deconsecrated. As far as the archdiocese was concerned, there was no church there. Catholics were rapidly evacuating De-troit, and the last thing the archdiocese needed was another old, nearly vacant church. There were already four Polish-oriented churches within a short distance, and they, too, were struggling, each having lost at least half of its congregation. A few years later, the archdiocese would close more than a third of its churches in the city—forty-three in all, the largest shutdown the church has ever overseen in the United States.

Although Cardinal Dearden was solidly in line with us, he, too, stepped down before the clearance was completed. Before he did, I asked him if he thought his replacement, Archbishop Edmund Szoka, might modify the position of the archdiocese regarding Im-maculate Conception. Cardinal Dearden dutifully pointed out that he couldn't speak for his successor, but then he smiled knowingly and assured me that the new archbishop was well aware of the cost of heating an empty church.

The wrecking ball came in July, as protesters carried their signs ("GM: Mark of Destruction" and "Sold for Thirty Pieces of Sil-ver"), chained themselves to the fence around the church, and prayed on their knees with Father Joe. The crew was under orders to begin the demolition after the eleven o'clock news and have it finished within twenty-four hours. Four months later, we had fin-ished clearing all 462 acres, which we turned over to General Mo-tors at the rate of $18,000 each—a process that without the quick-take statute would probably have been wrapped up about the time the plant ultimately opened in July 1985.

When it did, it actually put three thousand people back to work, half as many as I had optimistically hoped for but more than enough to make the effort worthwhile. In the times when GM runs two shifts at Poletown, which it began to do permanently in June of 1993, the facility employs four thousand. That's strictly a bonus to me. I'd said in court that I would have done it all for two thousand jobs. I knew all too well that the new-age, high-tech auto industry would never again supply jobs in the numbers it generated for Detroit in the 1950s, when as many as forty thousand worked in one plant. Regardless of the numbers, the important thing was to keep making cars in Detroit—to preserve the Motor City's "chief reason for existence," as Arthur Pound put it. I was a proud mayor the day that first Cadillac rolled off the line. To me, it made up for nearly every goddamn person, plant, and corporate headquarters that had hightailed it to the suburbs over the previous twenty years.

The flak we received for buying up the neighborhood was a small price to pay for the benefits of one of the world's greatest automotive facilities. Despite the vast attention given to the Poletown protesters, I held firm in the knowledge that they represented only a minuscule minority of those in the neighborhood. I regarded the quick acceptance of our purchase offer by most of the residents as a community plebiscite showing overwhelming favor for the Central Industrial Park. As I read it, the people were voting with their feet. This conclusion was borne out a few years later when the city hired a University of Michigan research team to survey the relocated residents of Poletown about the moving process. An overwhelming majority, eighty-four percent, reported that they were satisfied with their new accommodations, and the percentage was even higher among senior citizens, the group that had elicited the most sympathy. Furthermore, the poll showed that most of the residents felt they had benefited from the move and had been treated fairly by the city. Only eight percent believed that they had not received adequate compensation for their homes.

Even so, the book on Poletown has not been closed and will not be for a very long time. There are ways in which the effects of a plant like that can be measured—jobs and property taxes, for instance (studies have shown that every single job in the auto industry generates an additional six)—and ways in which it can't. There is no telling how many ancillary businesses have gained a life because of Poletown, either directly, by contracting with the company, or indirectly, by catering to its employees. There is no telling how much the local hotel and travel industries have benefited from the plant, or to what extent its presence has influenced other companies who have located or remained in the city instead of flying to the suburbs. But we do know, unequivocally and with profound satisfaction, that our considerable efforts on the Central Industrial Park cleared the way not only for General Motors but also for the huge Chrysler plant that followed shortly thereafter on the east side of Detroit.

The city was in an enviable bargaining position with Chrysler. The Poletown episode had demonstrated to the auto industry that when it came to the commitment and wherewithal required to build a major production facility, Detroit could get it done like no other place. GM, meanwhile, had shown that an investment in the Motor City returned both practical and civic benefits. On the spot for having closed down several plants in the city, Chrysler had no excuse not to consider Detroit this time. Besides that, after we'd gone to bat for Chrysler over the bailout package, the company owed us one.

I was not reluctant to bring this to Iacocca's attention, or to stress the moral points at issue. It wasn't necessary, but it didn't hurt. The situation was that Chrysler needed a new plant to replace its old, obsolete operation on East Jefferson Avenue, and the reality—as Iacocca and I both knew—was that he could build it cheaper and pay less for his labor somewhere else. But nowhere else did he have a comparable obligation. And nowhere else could he save millions of dollars in retraining costs by inheriting a skilled work force of men and women who had spent their adult lives making cars.

In 1986, less than a year after the Poletown plant went on line, the city bought 380 acres adjacent to the old Chrysler site and commenced to relocate nearly a thousand families in deference to another cutting-edge production facility, this one designed to turn out Jeep Grand Cherokees. By then, it was general knowledge that the settlements with the Poletown people had turned out favorably, and as a result the clearing of the Chrysler neighborhood never veered off into public dispute. We had also learned a little from Poletown about the value of communication. To keep the residents informed about the Chrysler situation, the city published monthly newsletters and distributed them throughout the neighborhood as the process unfolded. We hardly heard a peep of protest, and it was interesting to note that half of the renters whom the city relocated from the Chrysler area found that the settlement money was sufficient for a down payment on a house.

The only significant controversy surrounding the Chrysler plant concerned an unfortunate overpayment of around $25 million, for which I must take a measure of responsibility. Included in the property we had to purchase were some warehouses filled with industrial equipment. The owner of the warehouses would not allow the city to inspect the contents, and since we were under very severe time pressure from Chrysler, we signed a contract agreeing to pay an amount to be determined by an independent appraiser. The appraiser, an experienced professional whom both sides approved, came up with a price of around $40 million for what turned out to be some rusted old machinery. We suspected at the time, of course, that the figure was ludicrously high, but we had signed a contract and had no legal recourse. When the overpayment was exposed, there was much speculation that the deal had been a Mafia production—the owner of the warehouse was the son of a well-known local mob figure, which caused many to wonder whether the Mafia had influenced the appraiser—but a grand jury investigation resulted in no indictments. It couldn't be denied, however, that the city had fucked up by agreeing to abide by the opinion of only one appraiser, and as head of the executive branch of city government, I had to be held accountable. Inasmuch as the legislative branch—the city council—approved the contract, it was also accountable in part. The deal got past two levels of government, which, although there is no excuse for it, is an example of what can happen when operating under excessive demands for speed.

While I wish to hell that the overpayment had been avoided, the Jefferson Avenue Assembly Plant was nonetheless a major coup for the city of Detroit. Not only did it take up where the Central Industrial Park left off in terms of reindustrializing the city, it also firmly reestablished Detroit's previously precarious position as the heart and leader of the world's automotive community. There is not another city in America, for instance, with one state-of-the-art automobile plant, much less two—to say nothing of the numerous manufacturing locations and technical centers that have proliferated as a result. There can be no dispute that the parlaying of Poletown and Chrysler Jefferson has grandly preserved Detroit's tradition as the Motor City.

The North American International Auto Show is testimony to that fact. Detroit has had an auto show for as long as there have been auto shows, but until 1989 it wasn't much different from any of several others around the country. It so happened, though, that the construction of the two new auto plants roughly coincided with the expansion of Cobo Hall, which doubled the size of the building and created more contiguous exhibition space than in any other convention center in the country. With all of those pieces in place, it was natural that somebody—in this case it was German-born industrialist Heinz Prechter, a Detroiter who had become a major player in automotive circles through the development of sun roofs and other automotive conversions—would come to me with the aggressive notion of escalating the auto show to a grandiose, global level. It made sense that the automobile people would want to congregate where the technology is concentrated so that they could examine innovations manifest in Detroit's plants, technical facilities, and university laboratories. After years of mediocrity, the Detroit show now dwarfs any other in the United States, with more than eight hundred cars from virtually every automaking country in the world on display each January. As an international attraction, it speaks eloquently to the incalculable benefits derived from the perpetuation of modern industry in a city's midst. Whether the naysayers will admit it or not, goddamnit, Poletown and Chrysler Jefferson reinvented Detroit.

It can be seen very tangibly how Chrysler Jefferson remade its own neighborhood. While Poletown revitalized a moribund section of the city, in the vicinity of the Chrysler plant we had the opportunity to reconstruct the surrounding area with new housing that would serve both the plant and the greater community. I called it "a new town in town," and frankly, I don't believe it has received the public attention it deserves. In modern Sun Belt cities like Houston and Phoenix and San Diego, new development goes with the territory, insofar as most of the goddamn city is new; but you don't see much of it in Cleveland or Philadelphia or Chicago, obviously, because the northern industrial cities have been built up for the better part of a century. What we did just isn't done very often.

A notable segment of the reconstructed Chrysler Jefferson neighborhood is a 155-home development called Victoria Park, the first subdivision built in Detroit in forty-two years and the site of the first Homearama (a new home show popular in many metropolitan areas) ever held in an urban setting. One of the local financing companies told us that Victoria Park was the most successful subdivision ever started in the country, meaning that the homes sold at a record pace. I point this out to offer a contrast to the war-zone image that has unfairly attached itself to the city most closely associated with black America. It is additionally satisfying that the subdivision, like most market-rate new housing in Detroit, is integrated at very nearly fifty-fifty. At that, it constitutes but one part of a very diverse new town in town, taking its place alongside subsidized housing, senior citizen housing, and market-rate townhouses and condominiums.

None of the new housing would exist, of course, without the Chrysler plant, which opened ahead of schedule in January of 1992 with a work force whose carmaking experience averaged twenty-six years. For all of their tenure, however, most of the auto workers had never set foot in a place like Chrysler Jefferson. Warmed by the new climate in company-union relations that had moved in during the bailout negotiations, Chrysler had rolled up its sleeves and invited labor into the decision-making environment, much as Saturn had done. The result was the new Grand Cherokee.

Not so coincidentally, the first one rolled off the line just as the auto show was setting up. The president of Chrysler, Bob Lutz, called to ask if I would like to ride in it with him to Cobo Hall, where it would promptly be put on display. I honored the occasion by wearing the Stetson I had won from Dallas mayor Steve Bartlett when the Lions beat the Cowboys in the NFC playoffs (the Lions, mind you, win playoff games about as often as Chrysler opens Jeep plants on East Jefferson) and strapped in for an eventful ride. Lutz is a former fighter pilot, and he takes no prisoners behind the wheel. In that spirit, it was to his mischievous advantage that the Grand Cherokee is a four-wheel-drive vehicle. With the media observing closely, he drove down Jefferson Avenue to Cobo, up the concrete steps to the arena, and through a plate-glass window into the main concourse.

As the glass popped and shattered all around me, I realized why Iacocca had elected to pass up this particular photo opportunity.

10

Buzzards Overhead

We were in the nitty-gritty of the Poletown travail when the Republican convention came to town in 1980 after some ardent lobbying and a substantial onset of skepticism on the part of those who doubted that Detroit had a best foot to put forward. It turned out to be a smashing success that lavished praise on our redeveloped downtown and facilities, climaxed by a fifteen-minute closing tribute to the city by ABC-TV. It was a great moment for Detroit.

I was proud and pleased to bring in the Republicans, and impressed by the efforts of those like Max Fisher and Governor Milliken who went the extra mile to pull it off. Although Detroit was and is an overwhelmingly Democratic city, and although I have traditionally been at cross-purposes with the prevailing ideology of the Republicans, as a champion of the United States Constitution and the spirit of bipartisan cooperation, I fully supported their right to assemble and spend lots of money in our hotels, shops, and restaurants. I also appreciated what the national exposure could do for the city's image, which was still characterized by the '67 riot and out-of-date murder charts. And I thrilled to see Joe Louis Arena enjoy such a conspicuous and honorable christening. At the same time, the convention was an event that I find difficult to index historically. To this day, it sticks in my craw that Ronald Reagan was nominated in the damn building that I put myself on the line for.

Detroit and other American cities would suffer unceasingly and unconscionably during the Reagan and Bush years. It was a bleak period of neglect and retrogression on the urban scene. For twelve years, the nation completely kissed off such basic civic concepts as entitlements, governmental responsibility, and social sensitivity. Behind Reagan's lead, middle-class white Americans were encouraged to feel comfortable with their racial prejudices. The bipartisan coalition that had been developing nationally under Carter and Ford was completely undone by the Reagan administration's social and economic backwardness. At the citizen level, the average income of black college graduates dropped by more than ten percent under Reagan—in no small part because of the reduction in government hiring—while the average income of white college graduates increased by more than ten percent due to the emphasis on the private sector.

As the rich prospered from their tax cuts, Detroit strained to meet its expenses, with fewer and fewer of its tax dollars being returned in federal funds. After receiving federal revenues of nearly $400 million at the end of the Carter administration, a figure that comprised more than a quarter of the city budget, Detroit's slice of the pie by the end of the Bush administration was down to just over $160 million, covering eight percent of the city budget. Like all big cities, Detroit took a severe hit when the Republicans discontinued federal revenue sharing and countercyclical funding and made deep cuts in countless areas of urban priority, such as job training, community development, housing subsidies, pollution control, mass transportation, and health services. Developers who had been lining up in our hallways in the seventies were never seen again after the Reagan administration shut off the incentive programs by which Carter, Ford, and even Nixon had stimulated urban reinvestment.

Reaganomics clipped the knees of a city that was desperately trying to manufacture jobs even as local industry was being hauled out of town piece by piece on federally built highways. Old Pruneface, as I was fond of calling him—it was nothing personal, of course; just a way of calling attention to Reagan's age during the campaign—abused Detroit for eight years before yielding to his heir. And while Reagan slapped us around from the supply side, we were being clobbered from behind by the goddamn state-appointed arbitrator.

For this, I can blame myself somewhat. When I was in the state senate, I sponsored a law that established an experimental system of compulsory arbitration to settle disputes between city governments and their police and fire unions. The purpose of Act 312 was to provide police and fire departments with a reasonable degree of negotiating leverage, since, by state constitution, they did not have the right to strike—a law that had been occasionally defied, with dangerous consequences for the municipality involved, a scenario that Act 312 was devised in part to avoid. It has apparently been lost on the state government, however, that Act 312 was intended to be experimental, because the experiment has failed, and in the meantime compulsory arbitration has never been reviewed by the legislature.

The failure of compulsory arbitration lies in the unbridled power of the arbitrator. Michigan's law, for instance, like a similar one in New York, requires that the arbitrator take into account a city's ability to pay. But in Detroit, the arbitrators have ignored that consideration and have operated as a law unto themselves. Such reckless exercise of authority presents a colossal problem for city governments, who simply cannot meet the unrealistic financial demands imposed by the arbitrator without severely cutting back public services somewhere down the line. It has also undermined collective bargaining to the degree that the unions can negotiate with utter disdain for the city's position, knowing they can fall back on arbitration—which they nearly always do. The habitual tactic of the uniform unions has been to stall until the civilian unions settle their contracts, then work those numbers to their advantage. The spirit of give-and-take has effectively been eliminated from the working relationship between the cities and their vital public servants. And most regrettably, compulsory arbitration has wreaked havoc with fiscal management in the cities. In Detroit, it precipitated nothing short of a major fiscal crisis at the outset of the 1980s.

Talks between the city and the police and fire unions had broken off in 1977 with two years left on the contracts, and the arbitra-

tor screwed around for all that time before rendering an award
that Detroit could not afford to pay. If he had honored our offer to
the unions, Detroit's policemen and firemen would have been the
most generously compensated in the country in both base salary
and fringe benefits. If he had made his decision more promptly, we
might have been better prepared to accommodate it. But we
couldn't possibly ready ourselves in advance for a judgment as ludi-
crous as the one he belatedly granted the unions, which was based
upon an irrelevant cost-of-living formula that gave them a thirty-six
percent increase over three years—three times more than that received by any other Detroit city employees. The arbitrator's determination meant that through and beyond the 1980s, Detroit would
pay more per capita for police services than any comparable city in
the country. This was despite the fact that the auto industry had
pummeled Detroit's economy, Uniroyal had just shut down a local
tire plant that employed five thousand, and Parke-Davis had closed
a pharmaceutical factory, putting another two thousand out of
work. Hudson's, our commercial anchor downtown, was about to
close its last department store in the city, and Stroh's brewery was
ready to pull up stakes. At the time of the award, the economic situation was so depressed throughout Detroit that churches were
passing out cereal and canned goods, and welfare dependency was
at an all-time high. What's more, the city had been laying off policemen by the hundreds, which would have indicated to most
semiconscious people that we didn't have a lot of loose cash to be
doling out for personnel increases. In the face of all that, compulsory arbitration saddled us with an obligation of $80 million that
we simply didn't have. We challenged the ruling in court on
grounds that Act 312 was unconstitutional and that we were financially unable to meet the arbitration terms, but in 1980 the state supreme court upheld the arbitrator's decision. It was a judgment
that created an emergency condition with our 1981 budget, and a
jolt from which the city never really recovered.

It was impossible to predict where the next blindside blow would
come from. As we tried to make it through arbitration and Reagan,
the 1980 census undersold us in population by 180,000, a difference that stiffed Detroit with a shortfall of nearly $400 million in

state and federal funds over the course of the decade. I sued the government to get what was coming to us, and we won in district court. The appeals court agreed that Detroit had been under-counted, but ruled that nothing could be done about it, saying, in effect, "Yep, you've been screwed—tough break." (By the time the 1990 census came around, we were prepared and mobilized. The Census Bureau issued a preliminary count for Detroit's 1990 population at 970,000, but we then went on the offensive by canvassing door-to-door with copies of the form the bureau uses to record un-counted citizens. In a concerted campaign that we called "Come to Your Census," we collected more than 88,000 forms representing 154,000 Detroiters who had been missed by the federal government—about a third of the nationwide total of those re-ported as uncounted. The Census Bureau added 47,000 of our names, plus another 10,000 of its own, for a final tally of 1,027,000.)

The little things we could do to conserve money were effective but inadequate in the context of Detroit's monstrous economic li-abilities. I was particularly proud of the efficiency demonstrated by our Public Works Department in the collection of garbage. We were the first city in the country to adopt a system of one-man au-tomated trucks. Our innovations in garbage collection expedited service, cleared out packs of dogs and rats, and saved us about $150 million in the first decade. What's more, the automated trucks gave us unprecedented bargaining leverage with the union, and every job that we eliminated meant, roughly, that we didn't have to lay off another policeman.

Unfortunately, by 1981 our problems went much deeper than curbside garbage. My charge was not only to pull us out of finan-cial peril, but first to convince the public and the power brokers of the gravity of the situation. It could hardly have been more serious. In 1981 and the years just prior, we had to lay off nearly five thou-sand city workers in all departments. Our income was virtually level while inflation was eating us up at about twelve percent. I stressed to the press and public that our fiscal situation was potentially more severe than it had been during the Depression, when the city paid off its personnel in scrip.

To give credibility to my petitions, I sought input from an ad hoc blue-chip civic committee chaired by Fred Secrest, a retired Ford executive, and headlined by the top gun of urban finance, Felix Rohatyn. Although Rohatyn was regarded as something of a wizard in the field after having spirited away disaster in New York, Cleveland, Chicago, and Washington, it wasn't only his expertise that I was interested in acquiring; it was also his name. The mammoth task that lay ahead of us would require trust, participation, and sacrifice at all levels of the city, a comprehensive coalition of local people following the same pillar of fire. If the citizens wouldn't take my word about Detroit's crisis, maybe they should hear it from the man acclaimed as an urban savior by both Wall Street and Washington. I told the press, "The iceman cometh. Maybe now the people will believeth."

Rohatyn's best contribution to Detroit's recovery may have been his initial evaluation of our condition, which he described as being "between extreme pain and agony. Detroit has more of the really basic, core problems of older cities than any other major city," he said. "There is an ongoing survival crisis caused by the city's requirement to reduce its services as a result of the general economic decay of its basic industries." Rohatyn's representative in Detroit, Gene Keilin, reinforced that theme when he opened a presentation to local business leaders by passing out a Xerox sheet that said: Detroit's budget and financial problems are:

- Real
- Serious
- Not Temporary
- Not Solvable by Conventional Means.

The Secrest committee predicted a city deficit of $132 million by the middle of 1981 and proposed a three-part program that consisted of a tax increase, short-term borrowing, and employee wage concessions. Rohatyn agreed that the arbitration award had been murderous and that any package must include givebacks from the municipal unions. The problem was getting the unions to agree. The grand plan also required the sale of bonds, the catch there being that our bond rating had taken a hit and it wouldn't be easy to find a buyer. Raising the city income tax, meanwhile, would present multiple problems. It was already at the highest level allowable in the state, which meant that the legislature had to grant approval before we could even place the increase on the ballot in an emergency referendum. Then we'd have to persuade our already overtaxed population to assess itself at a level unprecedented in Michigan. We were facing the ultimate exercise in politics.

I thought of the package as a three-legged stool, and without any one of the legs we would be on our ass. Others preferred to think of it as crazy. Our political consulting firm out of Boston advised me that the referendum—in fact, the whole goddamn package—amounted to political suicide and that it couldn't possibly be pulled off. Of the three legs, the tax increase was clearly the shakiest and most controversial. Behind Reagan, the country was riding the rapids of antitax fervor, and we were swimming against them with one arm.

If we failed to reach the shore in any of the three recovery phases, we ran the risk of being rescued by the state and taken in as a ward. For its own financial stability and bond ratings, Michigan could not allow Detroit to fall into bankruptcy, although from my point of view that would have been preferable to state control, which would effectively have left Detroit without authority in its own affairs. Antipathy toward Detroit ran high in the state legislature, and I was loath to put my city's fate into the hands of such a demonstrably unsympathetic body.

To wit, there was a screaming suburban protest—a blatantly racist response—regarding the concept of additional nonresident tax revenues being assessed for Detroit. The increase we proposed would raise the tax of Detroit residents from two to three percent and the tax of nonresidents from one-half to one-and-a-half percent. Rohatyn noted that no other city in the country had such a disparity between resident and nonresident income tax, and further remarked that a significant aspect of Detroit's problem was the drain of suburbanites "who don't put back into the city what they take out." I had been saying that for years, only to be labeled a racist. Rohatyn, however, had the advantage of being white, wealthy, and eastern. To correct the imbalance between the city and the suburbs in the long term, he recommended a formula that would establish a metropolitan base in which revenues were shared throughout the region, as is done in some Sun Belt cities; but Michigan would not even contemplate a plan so apparently pro-Detroit as that one. It was all we could do to convince the state to let Detroit tax itself.

My staff and I spent a lot of time in Lansing stumping for the referendum. Among the other influential lobbyists were Doug Fraser and Tom Murphy, who addressed an unusual joint session of the legislature on our behalf; but one of the more persuasive arguments on the floor came from a conservative Detroit bank president who pleaded for the state to allow him, as a voting citizen of the city, to determine his own economic fate at the ballot box. Governor Milliken did us proud, too.

It was taken for granted that the suburban legislators weren't going to cut us any slack on the income tax, which meant that our support would have to come from rural and small-town Republicans. Milliken was crucial to the cause of lining them up on our side. I appreciated his efforts, although I mistakenly thought, at one point, that he might be proceeding a little too deliberately. Impatient, I remarked to a group of reporters that the motherfucker wasn't moving fast enough for my purposes. The governor was duly informed that his pal the mayor of Detroit had just called him a motherfucker, which precipitated a little to-do in the media. Milliken knew me well enough not to take it personally, but I nonetheless felt obligated to call him the next morning and explain that "motherfucker" is a word of myriad connotations, at least a few of which can be construed as amiable. He stuck with me, and together we got the referendum voted onto the ballot in Detroit.

By the time the legislature cleared the way for the special election, we had less than a month to campaign for the income tax proposal. It was a challenge I was eager to undertake, however, because my instinct has always been to appeal directly to the community in a time of trouble. I believe that if you are honest and forthcoming with people—tell them exactly what you need from them and why—they'll understand. Of course, the whole package wasn't exactly that simple. While burdened with the monumental task of convincing poor people to raise their own taxes, we also had to push around some mountains to sell $125 million worth of bonds and to somehow persuade the municipal unions to reach into their pockets.

The bonds were necessary to forestall our looming deficit and represented a strategy that I regarded as much more accountable and self-sufficient than New York's reliance upon government loan guarantees, which Rohatyn had engineered out of necessity. The bonds were a tough sell for us, though—for a city with fleeing industry and declining federal support—and to get around the obstacle of our fallen bond rating, we turned in large part to the pension funds of state and city employees as prospective buyers. The entire bond process was a logistical juggling act, with lawsuits and legal questions and membership votes all in the air at the same time; but when the cymbals crashed, everything was in place.

The wage concessions presented an even thornier problem, because they were unprecedented and completely out of character for the municipal unions—police and fire, in particular. While I had used gentle persuasion to sell the bonds, I played hardball with labor, indicating to the DPOA, for instance, that I would have to lay off another thousand policemen if they refused to cooperate with us. The cops refused anyway, at first—over the objections of most of their black members. Fortunately, the other city unions were quicker to grasp the realities of the crisis and negotiate a solution, led by the biggest, the American Federation of State, County, and Municipal Employees. They all agreed to wage freezes in return for guarantees that there would be no additional layoffs, leaving only the police and fire unions as holdouts.

Meanwhile, our campaign for the income tax increase—"Vote Yes"—was proceeding at full speed. I spoke at rallies and churches around the city and on the three largest local television stations, appealing to the civic and personal pride of our citizens. We all knew damn well that the survival of Detroit was above all a race issue—that the rest of the state and country was watching closely to see if a city run and mostly populated by black people would have the gumption and wherewithal to step up and save itself. In a situation like that, I don't see any purpose in sugar-coating reality. "Are we going to do what we have to do to guarantee that the city continues to move forward and our destiny remains in our own hands?" I asked the people. "Or will we do what thousands of bigots hope we'll do—vote no and the state takes over? We stand to lose just about everything." At the same time, I was compelled to stress that decent people of all races and situations applauded the pursuit of self-determination. "If I believed that most whites in this city or state or nation don't want blacks to live their lives in dignity, I'd quit being mayor and grab my gun and get ready for the next great race war," I said, meaning every word. "But I don't."

For visual effect—and for the benefit of our union employees—I held up a scrip issued in 1933, during the Frank Murphy administration, and mentioned that I had no aspirations to be the second Detroit mayor this century to put pieces of paper into the pay envelopes of city workers. The point was that the people, and only the people, had the power to save Detroit. It was a bitter truth, I told them, but one they had to come to grips with, because there would be no more rabbits and no more hats.

Then, two days before the referendum, I pulled one more rabbit out of one more hat. The hare assumed the form of Dave Watroba, the president of our longtime nemesis the DPOA, who appeared with me at a press conference to announce that the policemen had finally agreed to the same deal signed by the other municipal unions—wage freezes in exchange for job guarantees. The main point we conceded in the trade-off was a twenty-five-years-and-out clause that eliminated the previous stipulation whereby an officer had to have twenty-five years of service and also be sixty years old before he could retire with full pension. Although the deal was negotiated by the DPOA, the Lieutenants and Sergeants Association was also included by virtue of a me-too clause in its contract, as were the city firefighters. With the cops and firemen in the fold, we had secured two of the three legs needed to solidify our recovery.

In the context of the election, the DPOA announcement couldn't have been more fortuitously timed. It sent an eleventh-hour message to the voters that if the cops were willing to take a hit—the very union that had been bleeding us dry—the times must truly call for drastic measures. But while the DPOA agreement was hailed as the miracle we needed to have a prayer in the referendum, in truth I had liked our chances all along. I've always maintained that the essence of politics is the ability to count votes in your head, and it's an instinct that I believe has pulled me through many sticky situations. It's essentially a matter of knowing when to call for the showdown, of being patient and staying with the program until the moment is right for the vote.

In the case of the income tax vote, some thought that our timing could not have been worse. There was vigorous antitax sentiment rippling through the country. California had just passed Proposition 13, which was an assault on property taxes, and Milliken had recently failed, by two to one, to win a proposal that would have raised state income tax in exchange for cutbacks in property taxes. But I had no other choice; and besides that, I trusted in the people of Detroit to do what was necessary. On that trust I had placed my political future. I was well aware that the election, in addition to its definitive impact on the future of the city, was also an advanced plebiscite on me as the incumbent mayor. This was an election year, and the Vote Yes campaign was also my mayoral campaign. I felt pretty good about that, really, taking consolation in the knowledge that if I was to go down, I'd be going down with my ship.

I intended nothing of the sort, however, and the people of Detroit bore out my confidence on election day, defying the skeptics by voting yes with a thunderous majority. The most remarkable aspect of the election was that black voters approved the tax increase by an astonishing eighty percent. Goddamn, I was proud. With the exception of my initial election as mayor in 1974, I've never had a more thrilling victory in public life. It's rare that a public official is able to share his triumph with an entire city—or vice versa. "There can be no doubt," I told the voters, "that we have a special kind of city here in Detroit. We have been willing, in the face of a so-called national tax revolt, to step up to the window in Detroit and pay the price to buy a ticket on the train of progress and freedom."

I honestly believe that we saved our city from disaster with that election. So many other cities have awakened in the emergency room, it's hard to believe anything else; and none of them had Detroit's disabling particulars. There isn't an urban area in the country—in the world—that has had to deal with the commercial, industrial, governmental, and social abandonment that has been tearing at Detroit's flesh since the end of World War II. Yet, by the resilience of our people, we have managed to survive where others have failed. Two years after the fiscal crisis of 1981, Detroit was actually showing a surplus. At the end of the decade, we balanced five consecutive budgets.

It was no coincidence that the 1981 mayoral election, held less than five months after the tax referendum, produced my easiest victory ever. My opponent was a little-known white accountant named Perry Koslowski, who received thirty-seven percent of the vote, a significant minority which apparently represented the portion of Detroit that would not support me if my opponent were a trained (or hell, untrained) monkey. To this day, anyone who runs against me starts with a hard core of what I refer to as the ABC coalition—Anybody But Coleman. They're mostly conservative ethnic whites, with a few bleeding-heart liberals sprinkled in. Since 1981 and Perry Koslowski, I have always estimated their percentage to be in the neighborhood of thirty-seven.

I WAS RIDING HIGH for a month or two, anyway, before the federal government and local media, in a tacit but enthusiastic partnership, moved to take me down with an elaborate program of eavesdropping, entrapment, innuendo, and collusion.

Actually, although the media entered the campaign early in 1982, by that time the FBI was already two years into an incredibly expensive and screwed-up sting operation concerning the legitimacy of a city contract that in fact had been awarded to the only qualified bidder. It would use more than a hundred agents, accumulate six thousand hours of furtively acquired tapes, and spend millions of dollars in the effort to catch me—or at least someone close to me—in a compromising position. By the time the media jumped into the investigation with both left feet, it had become known as Vista, the name of a sewage-sludge disposal company around which the case revolved.

The Vista mess began in January 1980, when a felon named Jerry Owens moved to Detroit from Mississippi, where he had been convicted for defrauding a government food program, to become president and part-owner of a newly formed sludge-hauling concern. His partner in Vista, although few knew it at the time, was a highly successful real estate broker named Darralyn Bowers, who, by her own vulnerability and the contrivance of federal agents, would become the central figure in a protracted and very celebrated bribery case involving a large city contract for removing raw sewage from the west side.

Now, if one were inclined to be suspicious about such an unlikely alliance as that of Owens and Bowers—and far be it from me, of course—I suppose he might wonder if there could possibly have been a little third-party orchestration by which such a partnership had so curiously come together. He might wonder, for instance, if by some remote chance it could have been encouraged by someone or some agency with an independent agenda. This is just idle rambling, of course, but perhaps, in a moment of wild imagination, the FBI might even come to mind.

Strangely enough, it was the FBI to whom Owens reportedly confided concerning a plan he and Bowers had devised to secure the contract. If it seems a little out of the ordinary for a criminal to tell the FBI about an illegal scheme he was in the process of pulling off, one might also wonder if there was any relevance to the fact that Owens, as a token of appreciation for his invaluable cooperation in the Vista investigation (which was conceived with the information he so selflessly shared), received a reduced sentence for his Mississippi fraud. Standing back to see the big picture, one's curiosity might take root in the original question of how a welfare thief from Mississippi landed in the presidency of a Detroit disposal company in the first place.

I had known Bowers for several years as a businesswoman and political supporter, having met her and her husband at their real estate firm during a fund-raising campaign in the mid-seventies. We had developed a casual friendship, and from one of our subsequent conversations I had come to assume that she was the sole owner of Vista, which was indeed a serious bidder for a big cleanup job that Detroit badly needed. Sludge was being dumped directly on the ground on the west side, stinking up the neighborhood and creating an environmental emergency as the discharges made their way into the Detroit River. In deference to the pressing need to clean up the area, Federal Judge John Feikens had appointed me the receiver of the Water and Sewerage Department. In effect, I was the shit czar. It was my responsibility to get the sewage out of there as quickly as possible. The first step was to hire somebody to haul it.

It was not at all unusual for me to take an active role in the matter of city contracts for companies like Mrs. Bowers's. My interest was in seeing that, if they were fully qualified, black-owned businesses were given the full consideration that they had been systematically deprived of in the years before I became mayor. This did not preclude the observance of city procedure, however, which in Vista's case required Mrs. Bowers to contact Charlie Beckham, who was the director of our Water and Sewerage Department.

I stayed in touch with Mrs. Bowers, having renewed our friendship, and the conversations that ensued between us over the next several months, both social and professional, proved to be of monumental interest to the FBI. In order to hear them, the Bureau wiretapped Mrs. Bowers's home and office telephones and my goddamn townhouse. I used the townhouse for both business and relaxation, but the FBI was not discriminating in its waste of tape. I'm told that the recording procedure alone cost the taxpayers over a million dollars and that the Bureau used more tape in the Vista case than in any other in history with the exception of a huge Teamsters investigation in Chicago. Its operatives spent fruitless hours on the other side of my wall, monitoring the sophisticated electronic equipment set up in the adjacent townhouse. The agent whose purpose in life was to bring federal charges against me, Virgil Woolley—I believe he might have traded his mother for my indictment—set up camp there. I can just picture him and Old Blue Eyes, U.S. attorney Leonard Gilman, with their headphones on, salivating at the thought of nailing my black ass.

Meanwhile, Beckham was taking charge of the Vista contract, bringing it before the city council for approval. The council was dragging its feet, as it ordinarily does, which compelled me to exercise the authority bestowed upon me by Judge Feikens. Inasmuch as Vista was the only qualified bidder on the contract—none of the competing companies had twenty-four-hour access to a landfill—and the health risk was ongoing as long as the sludge stayed on the ground, I used my federally mandated authority to circumvent the council delays, expedite the contract procedure with Vista (which would ultimately receive $3.7 million from the city for its disposal services, paid over a nine-month period ending in January 1982), and get on with the cleanup process. Beckham maintained communications with the Vista people as this unfolded. All the while, federal agents were following and taping his comings and goings. One of the tapes showed him accepting an envelope in Bowers's office.

About two and a half years later—after volumes of vilification in the newspapers and a couple of grand jury investigations—bribery charges were filed in federal court against Beckham, Bowers, and four others. The government prosecutor sought to involve me as an unindicted co-conspirator, but there was no basis for it, despite all the goddamn tape that Lenny Gilman and the FBI henchmen had piled up. If the judge had not disallowed it on the grounds that the conversations on the tapes were completely immaterial, the prosecutor—whose arguments were publicly championed by the newspapers, which were licking their chops at the prospect— would have played every irrelevant goddamn minute, knowing that, with my liberal proclivity for referring to people as pricks and motherfuckers, I wouldn't have a political friend left in the city.

The cheap and personal nature of the case made it apparent— from my perspective, anyway—that the government was reaching beyond the pertinent facts, and that, as in the Blount affair, others were being victimized in the attempt to get to me. For example, if the feds were so sure there was money in the envelope Beckham received—they charged that it contained $16,000—then why the hell didn't they stop him right there and open it? There are two plausible answers to that question. One would be that they didn't want the trail to end; they wanted it to lead to me. The other would be that they *weren't* so sure there was money in the envelope. The allegation was, in fact, discredited in courtroom testimony from Vista people who said they had never seen or heard about Beckham taking money, despite the transparent efforts of the government to entrap him. On the witness stand, Beckham testified that the envelopes—he actually received two of them from Vista people—contained a letter concerning details of the contract and a reading from Bowers's water meter. (He was looking into a problem she was having with her bill and had been unable to straighten out through ordinary channels.) The only thing of material value that Charlie took from Vista was a sport coat he was given on his birthday by Jerry Owens, which is not my idea of a blockbuster federal bribery case—besides which, how do you reject a birthday gift? The damn FBI supplied Owens with the coat and gave him specific instructions to wish Charlie a happy birthday as he presented it.

Charlie handled himself extremely well on the stand, to the extent that I, along with nearly everybody else following the case, was very confident of his innocence and the acquittal it seemed to guarantee. I should have known better. The feds can't come up sucking air after spending millions of dollars on a highly publicized investigation. Somebody had to take a fall—even if it wasn't the guy they were really after. When the jury returned a guilty verdict on Charlie, I felt like I had been kicked in the stomach.

The four white defendants—Michael J. Ferrantino, owner of Michigan Disposal; Joe Valentini and Sam Cusenza, owners of Wolverine Disposal; and lawyer Charles Carson—were found guilty of conspiracy (the other disposal companies participated in the Vista scheme as subcontractors) and pleaded guilty to bribery charges. Bowers and Beckham, the only black defendants, received the stiffest sentences, four years and three, and were the only ones to actually serve jail time. It wasn't easy for me to come to grips with my miscalculation of Bowers (whose improprieties, in my view, were severely mitigated by the fact that she was set up by Owens and the FBI), but I can deal with that. On the other hand, I'll never get over what was done to Charlie. He had been a victim on every level—of deceit by the Vista crowd, of entrapment by the FBI, of persecution by the media, and finally of injustice by the courts.

And I knew, also, that the only reason he was going to jail was that he had been perfectly positioned as a scapegoat, a convenient foil for the federal government in its obsession to bring me down. To this day, it baffles me that the jury accepted the word of a desperate thief like Jerry Owens over that of Charlie Beckham, a public servant who had taken a leave from his executive position at General Motors to come work for the city.

Most disturbing to me in the grand scheme of things—aside from the perpetuation of the federal vendetta that was pursuing me into its fifth decade—was the large-scale, all-embracing collusion between the government and the media. While the press was running amok with specious and fabricated leads, it was caught in the eye of the real story, to which it was nonetheless blind. I appealed often to the media to turn the microscope on itself and examine the most newsworthy aspect of the Vista case—the government manipulation of the media.

While casting itself as the watchdog of government on the city level, the press was systematically being used as a communications organ for the federal agenda. The real story of Vista was of a government-manufactured scandal, abetted and legitimized by public reports. It was the moles in the FBI and U.S. attorney's offices leaking bogus evidence to the newspapers, poisoning the waters of public information. It was a multilevel network of entrapment, Judge Feikens authorizing wiretaps so that Lenny Gilman could invade my privacy and feed immaterial trivia to the voracious media. It was sealed grand jury information—including transcripts from wiretap tapes of my private conversations with Darralyn Bowers—showing up on the front page. It was the media itself, sending up trial balloons for the feds. It was the tunnel-vision reporting that, for example, profiled Jerry Owens as a convicted criminal while neglecting his much more pertinent role as a government informer. It was letters that we couldn't find at City Hall showing up in the hands of the FBI. It was a staggering waste of tax dollars. It was a reluctant internal investigation into the grand jury leaks that resulted in the sanctions of two FBI agents (a development, it should be noted, that was *not* leaked to the press). The real story was the ethics of the government and its shameless fabrication—through the willing media—of a high-profile federal case.

The result of this calculated flow of information was that the truth of the Vista case bore scant resemblance to the sensational speculation that ultimately defined it. Darralyn Bowers was portrayed as the mastermind of the contract scheme when in actuality she was being used by Owens and the FBI. Charlie Beckham, a conscientious public servant, was viciously misrepresented as an eager accomplice, and the government and media managed also to implicate me in spite of the facts. They got a lot of mileage out of the $17,000 that Bowers put up for me as a down payment on a townhouse, presuming it to be a bribe when in fact the transaction occurred long before I ever heard of Vista. The grand jury tried to take that one to court, but the district judge laughed off the motion. Even so, the papers continued to harp on my relationship with Bowers. The *Free Press* referred to her as "a major contributor" to my reelection fund on the basis of a thousand-dollar donation. I don't mean to sound cavalier, and I'm certainly most appreciative of the support, but with a war chest of three or four million, I don't regard somebody as a major contributor at a thousand bucks.

The taint of Vista stays with me to this day. There are those—and their numbers are considerable—who are determined to dispute my integrity, and I know I'll never convince them otherwise. A person doesn't come through an ordeal like Vista unaffected. Most regrettably, I can't give back the years that Charlie Beckham had to pay because he worked for me. And I'll never enjoy my townhouse again. I don't even go there anymore, because it always feels like there's a motherfucker under the bed.

The reels of worthless tape, incidentally, didn't faze the Justice Department a bit. If I've learned anything about the feds after fifty years of harassment, it's that they don't give up easily. Even as they were drumming up the Vista scandal, government officials were pursuing a grand jury investigation in yet another overblown hubbub known as the Magnum case.

Unlike Vista, however, Magnum was not entirely a federal production. It began with a city auditor general, Marie Farrell-Donaldson, who claimed that the Magnum Oil Company had overcharged Detroit $250,000 for bus fuel that it provided under a $6 million city contract and had also received an illegal city loan of a million dollars. The press took it from there, rabidly pursuing the assumption of wrongdoing while foregoing the alternative explanation that there might have been, at worst, an incidence of innocent incompetence.

The quarter-million at issue represented a price increase that was not recoverable according to the contract and was occasioned in part by purchasing difficulties Magnum encountered as an upstart black-owned company in a traditional white-dominated industry. I would have been hard-pressed to object if the newspapers had reported the additional payment as an honest procedural error in the negotiation of the contract. In fact, I publicly conceded that there were screwups beyond compare in the handling of the Magnum contract.

The basic problem arose from the fact that oil prices were rapidly increasing at the time the contract was let, and as a result it contained no de-escalator clause, meaning that our price would not be reduced if oil prices in general came down. Given the trend of the times, we were much more concerned about protecting ourselves against price increases, and considered it a coup to negotiate a fixed-rate deal that would protect us from inflation in the oil industry. When oil prices surprisingly dropped, we were stuck paying an unnecessarily high rate. It was obvious, then, that we had botched the negotiations.

The local papers eschewed this unspectacular possibility. Nor did they see fit to examine the role of the city council in awarding the contract. The council, in fact, was addressed as the guardian and savior of the public interest, as well as a friendly, authoritative source of information. In kind, sanctimonious council members—led by one of my former mayoral opponents, Mel Ravitz—were among the most vocal accusers of the administration, calling for an outright termination of the Magnum contract, which was a hopelessly inefficient option that would have cost the city additional millions.

The reality is that Magnum Oil charged us considerably less than it could have, and less than other companies probably would have. The million-dollar prepayment, in fact, was made to facilitate Magnum's practice of spot-purchasing oil at the best available prices. Despite raging publicity that suggested otherwise, the prepayment was not illegal, and it was reimbursed in full, with interest.

Also lost on the press was the fact that the city, by the dictates of our charter, was legally mandated to honor Magnum's bid, which represented the lowest acceptable one among the six firms that responded to our bus-fuel advertisement. That notwithstanding, the media did their damnedest to portray a personal-interest relationship between me and Magnum, implying that the company had received preferential treatment in the awarding of the contract. Whereas in the Vista coverage I had remained more or less a looming peripheral presence, I was placed front and center in the Magnum reporting. The charges, as they concerned my involvement, were based on unrelated and coincidental information—for instance, that one of the partners of Magnum happened to own a store that was located about two blocks from my townhouse, and that I'd once hired and received campaign contributions from the secretary-treasurer of Magnum, prominent Detroit attorney Allen Early, who was a friend of mine.

That sort of innuendo placed me in ninety percent of the articles written about the Magnum investigation—a figure determined by a study my office later commissioned from Ohio State University. The OSU report counted an incredible five hundred stories on Magnum in the two Detroit newspapers, twenty-nine of which featured my picture. That was for an investigation that resulted in absolutely nothing—a total of three misdemeanor indictments (of the president of Magnum Oil and two city officials) by a county grand jury, all of which were thrown out in pretrial proceedings by a district court judge who described the charges as ridiculous.

Investigations by both a county and a federal grand jury had been requested by a couple of city auditors who worked for the auditor general and were well known as my political opponents—Gerald O'Neill and my personal favorite, the embodiment of the ABC coalition himself, former mayoral candidate Perry Koslowski. The federal case came under the auspices of my Vista nemesis, Lenny Gilman. I have to say of Old Blue Eyes that, for all of the time and effort he directed my way in the Magnum and Vista investigations, the Justice Department's chronic vendetta was not his baby. Over the years, there were those in the FBI who dogged my cases with a vengeance that exceeded the professional norm, but with Lenny it was nothing personal. Nonetheless, he spent nearly a year on the Magnum investigation before declaring that there wasn't a damn thing there to warrant a federal indictment.

The absence of wrongdoing never slowed down the local press, however, which indulged in a feeding frenzy that was insatiable and totally indiscriminate in its selection of news fare. As a media event, Magnum exceeded even Vista. The newspapers magnified every twist and nuance of the Magnum contract, despite the city's legal obligation to award it. While the press enlarged its nonstory to epic proportions, creating a scandal in the public perception, there was never a point at which the city had a viable alternative at its disposal—or, for that matter, a compelling reason to reverse its position in the Magnum matter. It should be noted that with Magnum supplying the fuel, our buses never ran short; the company delivered every last gallon for which we contracted.

By and large, the city was well served by the Magnum contract, to the extent that when it had run its course and we looked back at the carnival of controversy it had brought to town, it was damn hard to understand what all the fuss was about. But knowing the dynamics of Greater Detroit as I do, I can't believe it was a coincidence that Magnum, like Vista, was the first minority company to win a city contract in its field. It seemed that whenever we broke the color line with a pioneer contract, trouble was at our heels. I also can't and won't believe that the investigations were unrelated to the desire of the suburban municipalities to take over Detroit's water-sewerage and transportation systems. Over the years, the suburbs have worked studiously to that effect both behind the scenes and publicly, angling unsuccessfully for state legislation that would allow them to pull our strings.

Whatever the personal and political machinations behind Magnum and Vista, the bottom line, in every respect, has been the concerted and collected aggression against a black administration. Regardless of the whys and hows and wherefores, the historic relevance of the various investigations that have conspired to scandalize my terms as mayor has been the effective sabotage of the general welfare and good government of the city of Detroit. The perpetrators of public scandal have staged an unrelenting assault on the fabric of the city, sniping from our institutional rooftops and blowing up our political bridges. In that regard, the gratuitous drain on our time and money is only a flesh wound. The heaviest casualties hit the areas of public trust, which are so vital to the operation of a city with the deep-seated, complicated problems of Detroit.

At the personal level, the attack on my character has been unremitting since the Magnum and Vista stories. I've remained under federal investigation almost continuously in recent years, as reflected by the headlines. Although I suspect that the particulars are largely incidental—the feds and the media are committed to keeping me on the hot seat one way or another—much of the attention has resulted from a protracted case that began in 1986 with a former civilian deputy police chief and con man named Kenneth Weiner.

Before the police department hired him, first as a consultant and then as a civilian deputy, Weiner had been a criminology professor at the University of Michigan and Wayne State University in Detroit. He was a man with a lot of dazzle and a lot of ideas, some of which related to private investments and sounded pretty damn good—good enough, in fact, that as I got to know him, I consented to venture with him into a couple of business deals. I trusted Weiner in part because I knew and trusted his father, Doc, a pharmacist from the east side who had briefly been my stockbroker and who impressed me by remaining in the neighborhood after most white merchants had fled to the suburbs. Like his father, Weiner was known as Doc; but that's about the only way in which he resembled the man.

Weiner's access to me—and his willingness to abuse it with deceit—ultimately became the only thing standing between him and federal prosecution for securities fraud in Oakland County, where his scam had been a Ponzi scheme (a pyramid investment setup) in which several wealthy suburbanities were bilked. Pardon me if this sounds like Jerry Owens redux, but Weiner, who was a hell of a con man, managed to convince the feds that if they kept him out of prison, he could deliver me to them. A good con man always capitalizes on the other party's weakness, and Weiner knew the FBI's. He promised my head on a platter, and they gave him the platter. Actually, they gave him a briefcase with a hidden microphone.

To impress the federal authorities with his connections to me, Weiner had played tapes of some of our private conversations that he had surreptitiously recorded. Taking the bait, the feds allowed him to tape another seventy-five hours with that goddamn hidden microphone, and once again someone at the federal level leaked the juiciest parts simultaneously—and unlawfully—to the grand jury and the media, despite the fact that nobody could attest to their veracity. Along the way, Weiner tried to trip me up by linking me to South African Krugerrands, which was not illegal but would have been tantamount to investing in the South African government, a very untenable situation for someone in my position.

He and I were to be partners in a high-tech-security-system business, which was ostensibly his specialty, and Weiner set the Krugerrand trap by coming to me with the story that he had sold a large system to Sony. He also said that in the absence of available cash, Sony was paying off with gold pieces. When he asked if I wanted to see the gold, I said no, just take it to our lawyer, convert it to cash, and deposit it into our business account at the bank. All of this was recorded on tape, of course, along with remarks from me that I wanted everything to be done aboveboard. The FBI, apparently electing to disregard the latter, followed Weiner to a safe deposit box, where he showed them Krugerrands that he claimed were mine. In fact, they were coins that he had gotten his hands on in some suspicious manner about which I can only speculate— maybe from the goddamn FBI itself. I certainly can't put that past the feds, knowing that they set the crook at liberty for the express purpose of victimizing me in the first place. There was no reason for the Bureau to even be concerned about the Krugerrands, since possession of them was not a federal offense; but, as my bitter experience repeatedly and damnably confirmed, it was in the steeped tradition of FBI agents to at least embarrass their targets if they couldn't indict them. Anyway, the fact of the matter regarding the Krugerrands is that I wouldn't have known one if it got stuck in my teeth.

When it finally dawned on the authorities that Weiner was conning them the same way he conned everybody else, they blew the whistle and belatedly indicted the motherfucker for his Oakland County hustle. He was convicted, but that wasn't the end of it. While behind bars, Weiner was indicted again for embezzlement and tax evasion. The weasel was embezzling from a police fund at the very time he was being excused from prison in order to entrap me for the FBI. He was stealing with a goddamn license handed to him by the federal government to deviously bring me down. I still feel a sense of outrage whenever I think of the avalanche of damning publicity that was shoved on my head throughout the Weiner case and of the incredible fact that the government, meanwhile, has never been called to task. Once again, the press was not the least bit interested in the real story. Not once did anybody from the media stick a camera or a tape recorder in the face of the U.S. attorney or the chief of the local FBI to ask about their disgraceful participation in the crimes of Kenneth Weiner.

There was another distasteful element to Weiner's embezzlement case, and it involved my police chief. William Hart was a career cop who had done an exemplary job since taking over after the Frank Blount affair; but eventually, in much the same manner as Darralyn Bowers came under the crooked influence of Jerry Owens, he fell prey to the tempting, persistent wiles of Weiner. An eighteen-month federal investigation implicated Hart, along with Weiner, in the misuse of two-and-a-half million dollars from a secret police fund designated for undercover operations. From grim experience, I knew that, despite the considerable efforts made to ensnare the chief, any investigation in such close proximity to me was not coincidental, and that Hart was not the only or even the primary target. I didn't know all the facts of the case; but out of loyalty to Chief Hart and my fundamental disregard for the methods of the Justice Department, I stood by him as the investigation unfolded with the generous assistance of premature and prejudicial information reported in the newspapers. My refusal to take the feds' bait and turn against Hart during the investigative stages of the case was apparently frustrating to the U.S. attorney, Stephen Markman, who accused me of putting up "legal roadblocks and obstacles." I sure as hell wasn't going to make it easy for a government official who was doing his damnedest to link me to the embezzled money and anything else that his criminal informant, Kenneth Weiner, might have cooked up. Hart's conviction didn't satisfy the feds. To this day, they're still trying to trace that money to my door.

Hart was the third high-ranking city employee—following Frank Blount and Charlie Beckham—to be victimized by a plot that revolved around me. It was a demoralizing pattern, and one that unquestionably influenced my attitude toward representatives of both the Justice Department and the media, which I ultimately came to regard as another prosecutor with the power of indictment, however unofficial. The papers and the talking heads have been my confirmed accusers for twenty years, and damned if I will cooperate with them. I'm all for freedom of the press as a sacred American privilege, but I will not abet its wanton misappropriation by playing along as a source for the type of feckless reporting that Detroit has so wearily endured; nor will I pardon the incrimination and compromise of due process that has been perpetrated ad nauseam in my city. I won't put up so much as an amiable pretense toward an institution that has been so profoundly detrimental to the well-being of Detroit. The aspect of it all that really boils my blood is the manner in which the newspapers set themselves up so high-mindedly as the purveyor of information that the public needs and deserves when the fact is that over the past decade, their presentation of so-called news has been one of the most wickedly destructive forces to the condition of the city.

The weapon they have often used in this campaign is the Freedom of Information Act, through which they can accumulate all the available government data and then pick and choose what to print for public consumption. By that process, the papers presume to decide what the people ought to know and what they ought not, and it's a process in which I will not participate. As a result, I have stubbornly and purposefully withheld information from the media, inviting them to exercise their constitutional recourse and challenge my position with a lawsuit, which they periodically do. Midway through my fourth term, for instance, the *Free Press* issued an FOI request for a list of all city-owned property, which I was unwilling to surrender because such information would present a blueprint for speculators, who could use it to purchase certain parcels that might put us at their mercy someday. Emmett Moten of the Community and Economic Development Department represented our position on that one, and when we refused to comply with the court's order to supply the records, Emmett went to jail. He was there about half a day, making calls all the while from the phone in his cell. I was in London at the time (laying over on my way back home from a trip to South Africa for the ceremony in which Desmond Tutu was elevated to archbishop), and negotiating for Emmett's release by long distance. We agreed to turn over the material if the *News* would agree not to print it until I returned to Detroit and spoke to the editors. That way, the paper at least had to hear me out before rushing ahead without consideration of the city's interests. On another occasion, Don Pailen, the head of the city law department, served three days in jail after he would not provide the *News* with files from the Chrysler land deal. The files had been submitted to the grand jury, and since a grand jury investigation is not public, our position was that we would withhold the information from the press until the grand jury was finished with it. Once again, our cause was a losing one, the consolation coming in the statement we made.

I know I'm a pain in the ass to the local media, but goddamnit, somebody has to make them face the music. When I purport to act in the public interest as mayor, my performance redounds to a show of support or rejection at the polls every four years. But who makes the newspapers accountable? They might say that their readerships do; but, hell, we all know that the readership to which they appeal is not located within the limits of the city they're fucking with. The papers charge that I run the most uncooperative administration in the country, and I say, so be it. Given our relationship—or lack of it—they would prefer even that I argue with them on a regular basis; but it would be foolish for me to imagine for a moment that I could enter into a fair editorial dialogue with an adversary that buys ink by the barrel.

At the same time, I would not paint all reporters with the same brush. There are some—such as former *Free Press* political writers Remer Tyson (who now covers South Africa for the paper) and Kirk Cheyfitz; former *News* reporter Bob Pisor (whom I hired as my press secretary in the seventies); national correspondents like R. W. Apple of the *New York Times* and syndicated columnist Jules Witcover; and popular radio personality J. P. McCarthy and the late radio newsman Bill Black of WJR in Detroit—who exercise objectivity and responsibility in their work. There also are some, such as the legendary Bill Bonds of WXYZ-TV, with whom I frequently spar but whom I still grudgingly admire. I credit Bonds, for instance, with caring deeply for the city of Detroit, which he first proved to me in his sensitive coverage of the 1967 riot. He is also mercurial and pugnacious, and our conflicts were dramatized in 1989 when he challenged me to a benefit boxing match at the Palace in Auburn Hills. I prudently declined.

There are those in the press, however, regarding whom I would not be so circumspect. I believe a proper flogging is in order for the entire staff of WXYT radio in Southfield, which merchandises racism over the airwaves; I have little regard for the tediously conservative house columnists of the *News,* such as George Cantor and Bill Johnson; and I am continually amazed by the obsession that *Free Press* editor Joe Stroud seems to have lately developed toward me. Stroud gets a lot of mileage out of the theme that I have become old and ineffectual; and yet on occasions such as the defeat in 1993 of Proposal A, which would have redirected certain personal property taxes to sales taxes at the state level, he switched horses long enough to blame the outcome on my power and arrogance. To columnists like him and Pete Waldmeir of the *News,* objective reporting means objecting to everything I do or say. Waldmeir, who is perhaps my most ardent adversary in the media, once followed me to Jamaica to investigate my goddamn vacation. As I told the press at the time, I wish the motherfucker had caught me. I'm mayor of nothing down there; we'd just be two crazy old Americans rolling around in the alley.

11

In the Best Interests

My city received quite a bit of notoriety in the 1980s for trying to burn itself down every year around Halloween. The tradition is called Devil's Night, and although we seem to have it under control now—the number of fires the past couple of years has been fairly normal—it was a vision from hell for a while there. In 1984, when it peaked, there were more than eight hundred fires in a three-day period at the end of October.

For decades, it had been local custom to perpetrate a little devilment on the night before Halloween. When I was young, a lot of kids soaped windows, and the really rotten ones used wax. In the late seventies, vandals carried the mischief a step further and began setting fire to dumpsters. It's not hard to see how from there, Devil's Night escalated into an urban inferno. Detroit's unemployment rate was the highest in the country. That was the match. White flight had left thousands of old houses abandoned throughout the city. That was the wood. All that remains is the motive, and there is no shortage of possibilities from which to choose.

Some of the data that contributed to the *Brown* vs. *Board of Education* decision in 1954 demonstrated that isolationism and racism can lead to self-hate and self-destruction—attitudes that seemed to be conspicuously manifested by some Detroiters late in October. With unemployment and its sidekicks, desperation and depression, also conspiring against it, the city predictably—although not excusably—turned inward and joined the ranks of its enemies in a blazing fashion. It should be understood, however, that even at its worst, Devil's Night was a spectacle, not a suicide. To a unique degree, Detroit had buildings to burn.

The arson rate dropped sharply after we undertook a program of razing the abandoned houses and stores. We ultimately managed to turn Halloween week into something of a civic rally, firing up the citizens to defend their town against the Devil. As they had in the referendum of 1981, the people of Detroit answered the call. The community began to respond in 1985, and by the early nineties, Detroiters were turning out forty thousand strong on Devil's Night to keep watch over their neighborhoods. It was an inspiring example of cooperation between local government and its citizens. We set up a command center for volunteers with CB radios and car phones; and for street patrols we used every available city vehicle, from police cars to garbage trucks. As an extra preventive measure, we even prevailed upon the local cable TV company to unscramble the Pistons game and the other premium channels to keep people home. After a few raging years, the show was over.

Strange as it sounds, some misguided people were actually disappointed to see it end. Devil's Night had become something of a tourist attraction, with visitors coming from as far away as Texas and New Jersey to warm themselves in our misfortune. It was also one of the few occasions of the year when suburbanities deigned to visit the city. This was a phenomenon that I found to be every bit as provocative as that of a city burning itself. The concept of Detroit on fire was irresistible to some of our suburban neighbors, a few of whom have privately expressed the urge to do the deed themselves. For certain displaced and disaffected Detroiters, Devil's Night was watching the object of their fear and loathing go up in flames; it was witnessing the contemptible ghetto people burning down their own neighborhoods. To this day, I believe, there are suburbanities who like to think of their old city in either of two ways—the way it used to be, or on fire.

This suburban antipathy toward Detroit is not imagined, and, contrary to popular belief, it has not been promulgated primarily and spitefully by me. It has been fostered by the anxieties accompanying a large neighbor city where upwards of eighty percent of the residents are black, including the outspoken mayor; by the resent-

ment of what is perceived as a foreign occupation of one's home-
land; by the same sort of factionalism and provincial racism that
has embattled the Middle East and Eastern Europe and South Africa.

It would be difficult to overestimate the depth of racial tension
surrounding Detroit. Southeastern Michigan is well known as a
hotbed of the Klan, some of the largest and liveliest congregations
being located within thirty miles of the blackest city in America.
Cross burnings are commonplace in towns like Gregory, Howell,
and, appropriately, Hell, where bumper stickers make the rounds
with messages like DON'T SHOOT JESSE JACKSON . . . WE DON'T NEED AN-
OTHER HOLIDAY. Closer to the city, Warren turned down a hunk of
HUD money in the fear that public housing would attract blacks.
Southfield, which has become the most commercialized of the suburbs and the most integrated of the many municipalities outside
Detroit, has undertaken a program to limit its percentage of blacks
by offering to find housing for them in alternative locations.
Grosse Pointe, the wealthiest community in the metropolitan area,
tried to build a flood wall between itself and Detroit and for years
used a point system for prospective newcomers that effectively kept
out blacks and other minorities. Macomb County, a largely blue-
collar region just north of the city, attained political significance in
1972 when it rallied behind George Wallace, who played effectively
upon its prejudices to carry the Democratic primary there—and
the rest of Michigan as well—on the day after he was shot in Mary-
land. It was an extremely embarrassing development for the Democratic Party, and one upon which Reagan shrewdly capitalized
eight years later, campaigning in Macomb County with a purposefully antiurban agenda and thereby creating the prototype for the
Reagan Democrat. After Pruneface twice won Macomb, the *Free
Press* reported on a study authorized by the Democratic legislators
in the statehouse to determine why the county's Democrats were
switching parties. The reason they discovered was a literal hatred
of the city of Detroit—i.e., of blacks and all of their affiliations. Bill
Clinton, well-informed and seeking to reclaim Macomb County for
the Democrats in 1992, visited in March of 1992—just before the
Michigan primary—with the message that he couldn't restore the

spirit of America "until all of you folks decide that race is not the problem." He said the same thing at a black Baptist church in Detroit the next morning, and the day after that, I endorsed him.

Clinton's trenchant racial remarks echoed a declaration that five years before had come out of an ambitious local consortium called the Detroit Strategic Plan, which was formed with a broad charge of isolating the problems most critical to the city's future. After I intervened to see that blacks were appropriately represented on the various committees, the local leaders of the Detroit Strategic Plan had examined the nuances of Detroit's predicament and concluded that race relations were the most troublesome issue facing the city. This was not news to me, of course; but I was happy for the metropolitan area to hear it from another source, because a lot of the white people still seemed to think that the problem was in my head.

On the other hand, I think it's in theirs—cultivated, if not planted, by the media. I recognize that to a large degree, the suburban rancor toward Detroit is driven not by overt racism but by fear for personal safety. I also understand that to a large degree, the fear is a function of sensational and exaggerated reporting. To many, for instance, Detroit has retained the image of the murder capital of America, even though we happily surrendered that title more than a decade ago. By 1985, in fact, Detroit had been honored by the International Society of Crime Prevention Practitioners for having the best crime-prevention program in the country. By 1990, our murder rate was dropping by 6.7 percent at a time when national figures were showing a 10 percent increase, and Detroit's mark of 56.6 homicides for every hundred thousand people was decidedly lower than Washington's of 77.8. While a hot town like Atlanta ranked first in the country in serious crime, Detroit was far down the list at twenty-fifth and dropping fast.

In reality, it simply doesn't work anymore to attribute suburban hostility to Detroit's crime rate; nor does it work to argue for gun control that is restricted to the city of Detroit, as many of the local liberals have done, to my considerable irritation. The city gun control discussion is one on which I've been rampantly—and perhaps deliberately—misrepresented, the myth being that I'm stocking up for some sort of metropolitan Armageddon.

It was an incident in 1986 that firmly established my regrettable reputation as the agent of hostility between the city and the suburbs. During an interview with the Canadian Broadcasting Corporation, I was asked what would happen if somebody went door-to-door collecting guns. I reiterated that I'd have no problem with a nationwide system, like Canada's; "but I'll be damned," I said, "if I'll let them collect guns in the city of Detroit while we're surrounded by hostile suburbs and the whole rest of the state . . . where you have [the Ku Klux Klan and] vigilantes practicing in the wilderness with automatic weapons. I am in favor of everyone disarming. I'm opposed to the unilateral disarming of Detroit." Can you guess which phrase was lifted from that answer, magnified in the headlines, and yodeled through the white communities? "Hostile suburbs" became the rallying cry for those who would hold me responsible for the region's racial antagonism.

My reference to hostile suburbs—out of context, of course—was also a theme for a one-dimensional, injurious book on Detroit named after Devil's Night (which says all you need to know about the book's objectivity). Some of the most distorted portions were excerpted in a *New York Times Sunday Magazine* cover story, which only served to promote Detroit's inaccurate image as America's urban wasteland and war zone. Other national media swooped upon the story like buzzards, led by the television show "Prime Time Live," one of whose researchers was a former Detroit newsman who called several times to commiserate about the misleading *Times* piece and let me know that ABC intended to show the other side of the city. The "Prime Time" reporter, Judd Rose, also assured me during the interview that "this is going to be a very balanced portrait of Detroit, with the good and the bad." That quotation didn't air, of course; nor did much semblance of the good to which he referred.

I have sixty-three pages of transcript from Rose's interview, and about sixty-one pages of it never aired. Pictures of burning and abandoned buildings aired. A crack raid aired. A mother mourning her slain son aired. A fool saying that a job at minimum wage was beneath him aired—although not the part where the young man, after making a string of positive comments about Detroit, was told, in effect, that he needed to show a little more attitude if he wanted to get on national TV.

Since "Prime Time" purported to be putting together an objective story, I tried to explain to the interviewer about the dynamics of white flight, about the economic forces impacting upon Detroit, about the principles of urban development, about the crippling effects of federal policy, and about my efforts to bring together the city and the suburbs. None of that aired. What aired was Rose interrogating me about allegations of corruption in my administration without any evidence whatsoever, and me cursing at him, and him asking, "Why do you get so defensive?"

"I'd be a goddamn fool," I said, "to discuss with you, on television, an allegation, which would be the same as taking the goddamn stand. And who the fuck do you think you are, to come in here and cross-examine me?"

"It's a question. And a valid question."

"Yeah, you're out of line. And as far as I'm concerned, the interview is concluded."

And so the country watched the defiant black mayor of a bleak, blighted city tearing into the humble reporter at the very mention of corruption that had been so profusely alleged by the media. As you might imagine, this, too, did wonders for the image and recovery of the city of Detroit. There wasn't a single word in the story about solutions, or hope, or the unbroken spirit of our people. The "Prime Time" segment ended with the mourning mother sobbing over her son's grave, one of a series of poignant shots that were portrayed as extemporaneous but which many people felt were contrived.

Unlike a network journalist, I don't have the luxury of writing my own ending to every story, then packing up my equipment and moving on to another one. While the staff of "Prime Time" was creatively editing in New York, I still had to deal daily with kids being killed, with joblessness and despair, with dope and dopes, with allegations, and, fundamentally, with the racist underpinnings that perpetuate all of it. My charge was and is to call attention to the problem—nobody disputes that I've done that—and pull together a way to solve it. The operative phrase there is "pull together." I know damn well that I can't do it alone. That's why the media's proclivity to inflame my words—along with the white public's eagerness to receive them into an atmosphere of enmity—has been so damaging. I need to be and would like to be the emissary of conciliation in my part of the country, but the prevailing winds of bias blow the other way. Few choose to hear my petitions in the healing spirit.

A notable exception, and the type of young politician who gives me cause for optimism, is the new mayor of Dearborn, Michael Guido. For much of my lifetime, Dearborn has been known as a citadel of racism, owing largely to the separatist efforts of former thirty-year mayor Orville Hubbard, who espoused that integration would lead to intermarriage and mongrelization. For a time, Dearborn closed its city parks to outsiders, for reasons that are not hard to guess. It and Detroit were uneasy neighbors. But Guido has managed to see past all of that and identify the need to reconcile with Detroit. He and I had a chance to stand in each other's shoes on Mayors' Exchange Day, upon which occasion Dearborn actually held a parade for me. That was a day I would have never imagined back in the fifties, when I was spending the afternoon in Orville Hubbard's jail for collecting coins in a can.

I've tried hard to establish the same sort of relationship with other regional leaders that I've developed with Guido. It is generally agreed that the city and the suburbs are mutually dependent; and to provide a forum for exchanging ideas on issues that affect the entire metropolitan area, I organized a committee known as the Big Four, consisting of myself and the executive heads of Macomb, Oakland, and Wayne counties. I've taken the Big Four a step further by suggesting that the mayors within those areas (the Detroit area would include the mayors of Highland Park and Hamtramck) form a loose federation for dealing with regional affairs. I am a strong proponent of this type of coalition, having demonstrated in twenty years as a mayor that coalitions get things done. It is time now—high time—to move beyond the bipartisan public-private coalition that developed Detroit in the seventies and expand to an even broader partnership that is geographic in scope.

The power of unity was political lesson number one for me, and I take umbrage at the charge that I stand for anything but. In my inaugural speech of 1990, I said, "It is absolutely essential that we have cooperation across the board and also across Eight Mile Road. I am sincere in that. I don't think we can afford the luxury of throwing rocks at each other in this metropolitan area, acting like a bunch of crabs in a barrel while cities all around us, and the metropolitan areas all around us, move forward. I extend the hand of cooperation to our suburban neighbors." In general, I can't say that they've taken it.

If the people of the suburbs don't always accept the words that I have for them—there is a general suspicion of most of what I have to say, and a substantial rejection of some—at least I can't complain about their level of interest. I seem to set attendance records about every time I venture beyond Eight Mile for a luncheon or something. I consider it incumbent upon me to find a use for the apparent fascination the suburbanites seem to have for me and Detroit, however perverse. In that spirit, I've pushed, among other cooperative efforts, for a combined city-suburban marketing scheme. At one black-tie affair, for instance, I commented at some length about the outflux of jobs from our area, noting that Japan and Mexico and even Ohio had been stealing us blind, and concluded that "we've got to stop fighting among ourselves and go out and steal from Ohio."

Often as not, when I have a captive suburban audience, I use the opportunity to advance the ongoing dialogue about rapid transportation. As far as I'm concerned, some form of fixed rail or light rail system ranks at the top of the priority list for the development of the Detroit area, and has since the Ford administration; but the suburban insistence on controlling everything—or, at the least, not letting Detroit control anything—has kept us bound and gagged in the dark ages of transportation. Detroit is the only city in America with a population anywhere near a million and no subway or light rail. It's a disgrace, and the most disgraceful thing about it is that there was a rapid transportation package all wrapped and waiting for delivery, with Detroit's name on the tag; but the city and the suburbs argued so long about who would get to open and operate the damn thing that before we knew it, Christmas was over. Santa Claus might still be holding something for us—the $600 million that President Ford pledged for a Detroit subway in 1976 is still being carried on the Department of Transportation's agenda—but first we've got to show that we can stop fighting with each other long enough to agree on what to do with it.

At least fifteen cities have received rapid transportation since the letter informing us of the federal pledge arrived from my old Air Corps buddy, Transportation Secretary Bumps Coleman. In no other instance has a metropolitan area been so divided as to blow the whole deal; but in Detroit's case, it seemed that the state and the suburbs were intent upon it.

To create an administrator for the construction and operation of the subway awarded to Detroit, the state legislature mandated a merger between the Detroit Department of Transportation (D-DOT) and the Southeast Michigan Transit Authority (SEMTA), which includes the city in its jurisdiction but is dominated by suburban representatives. Considering that ninety percent of the people in the metropolitan area who use public transportation live in the city of Detroit and ride D-DOT buses, I had a hell of a time justifying a partnership between us and the domineering suburbs. And given the general suburban disposition toward Detroit, it was an arrangement of which we were very wary going in.

The suburbs' drive to control Detroit is an impetus that we've had to continually resist. Oakland County has pushed relentlessly for ownership of Detroit's very efficient water system, which the city has managed for more than a hundred years, never failing in all that time to furnish the outlying areas with water and sewers. Recently, some folks in the suburbs have been maneuvering to annex our crown jewels, the Detroit Institute of Arts and the Detroit Zoo, throwing around buzzwords like "regionalization" and "privatization." Our budget problems have led the newspapers and some metropolitan leaders to the opinion that we ought to strongly consider such an arrangement, but I'd rather ride out the storm than toss the valuables overboard. The suburbs have also tried to take over our park system, which is bigger than all of their park systems put together, and our bus system, even though the satellite municipalities pay nothing for the buses we send their way. I'll be damned if we will hand over our assets to the suburbanites just because they want them. Detroit is not a sharecropper.

When we sat down at the table to arrive at a subway plan, it quickly became obvious that SEMTA didn't place the same priority on rapid transportation that we did, or that the federal government apparently did. In fact, the suburban interests didn't really want it at all. Without a subway, Detroit remained pretty much the way so many suburbanites preferred us—isolated and underdeveloped. Despite the fact that the money was specifically granted for light rail in Detroit, there was even a movement in Oakland and Macomb counties to use the $600 million for a suburban bus system. I urged that the city and the suburbs work together to define the most favorable transportation system for the entire metropolitan area and then present a united front to Washington—which was all we needed to do to have the cash in our hands. But there was no reciprocation. SEMTA insisted on dictating the terms and logistics of any regional plan, and that was a deal breaker for the city. We couldn't make any headway in the negotiations because SEMTA was completely indifferent about advancing the process. It was no damn way to run a railroad.

The years we wasted squabbling over the subway were particularly critical in light of the fact that Carter was in the White House and our chances of grabbing anything for Detroit would never be better. Reagan's victory in 1980 persuaded me that it was time to reassess our position on light rail. So to salvage something before Carter left office, I opted to eschew the $600 million in credit and take what, with a considerable amount of concentrated effort, we could manage to get immediately—$120 million for an elevated track called the People Mover that would ring the downtown district. With the People Mover in hand, I'd save the subway battle for another day.

Planning for the People Mover was complicated by the same state conditions that had stymied the subway, and the suburbs once more controlled the fate of the project by holding down eleven of the fifteen positions on the SEMTA board. The suburban authorities had no qualifications for that sort of responsibility, however, and screwed it up colossally. By nothing more than mismanagement and gross incompetence, they were $10 million over budget before ground was broken. Ultimately, through a complex negotiation process involving the governor and the federal government's Urban Mass Transit Administration, the city put SEMTA out of its misery by taking over the People Mover and getting it on track. When completed—for less than the projected cost, and with the worst of SEMTA's overruns eliminated—the system provided 2.9 miles of downtown transportation, accessible at thirteen stations embellished by artwork, and linking, among other stops, Cobo Hall, Joe Louis Arena, the Renaissance Center, and the popular Greektown district. The People Mover has done much to pull the city into the modern era, but I hold out hope that it is only the beginning of a comprehensive network of light rail in Detroit.

With each day, it becomes increasingly essential for Detroit to connect with the suburbs, both geographically and socially. The social part is a misty, multidimensional proposition, but rapid transportation is clearly the most efficient and palpable way to do it geographically. Although light rail is traditionally identified with bringing commuters into the city, in Detroit's case it would also serve the crucial function of carrying city residents—many of whom are currently unemployed and cannot afford an automobile—to where many of the jobs have gone. Decentralization and white flight have systematically separated Detroit's black people from their jobs, which have been removed to suburban places like Southfield and Troy and Farmington Hills and Livonia, and the time is long past to rejoin them systematically.

More than anything else, rapid transportation is about jobs. Most of the pertinent economic studies indicate that a subway or elevated train system, through the creation of jobs and the encouragement of commerce, would stimulate economic development exponentially in a city like Detroit. Detroit's opponents argue that the city does not have the ridership base—i.e., the job base—to justify light rail; but if that's the case, then why the hell *don't* we? One good reason might be that there's no way for people to get to the damn jobs. How is it that Detroit has not received federal money for rapid transportation when San Jose and Buffalo have, along with every other city the size of Detroit and many smaller ones? What's different about Detroit that could explain why it has not been modernized and facilitated like every other major city in America? The answer has deep roots.

Inevitably and soon, if it's not too late, the government and the suburbs and the rest of the white establishment will realize that it's in their best interest to stop screwing Detroit. Of course, self-interest is the only reason anybody ever does anything, anyway. In this case, it is blatantly against the country's best interest to permit the socioeconomic condition of the cities to become malignant; nor can the suburbs skip along merrily with disease at their core. They cannot prosper in the company of economic despair. The suburbs were created in great part by white people who didn't want blacks for neighbors, but Detroit is Warren's neighbor and Grosse Pointe's and Southfield's, and it is not conceivable that the standard of living in those places can be unaffected by Detroit's. The social maladies of the city will not be contained by an artificial boundary like Eight Mile Road. Whether the problem is communicable disease or crime or drugs, it has been proven time and again that city limits don't limit anything.

Suburbs, which by definition lack the density of the inner city, can only expand so far before they become an amorphous, clumsy, unmanageable mass without advantages of proximity or communication. In the Detroit area, the only spot within easy reach of all of the suburbs is the center of the city, where the expressways come together. Yet many of the suburbanites who have fled the city—by those very expressways—would prefer to live their lives as if it were not even there, as if the urban center were a large concrete wasteland between shopping centers. It occurs to me that people outside Detroit like to think of the metropolitan area as a doughnut, with the suburbs as the sweet meat and the city as the hole in the goddamn middle. I say that we need to go back to the bakery and come out with a jelly roll.

It's mind-boggling to think that at mid-century Detroit was a city of close to two million and nearly everything beyond was covered with corn and cow patties. Forty years later, damn near every last white person in the city had moved to the old fields and pastures—1.4 frigging million of them. Think about that. There were 1,600,000 white people in Detroit after the war, and 1,400,000 of them left. By 1990, the city was just over a million, nearly eighty percent of it was black, and the suburbs had surpassed Detroit not only in population but in wealth, in commerce—even in basketball, for God's sake.

As I viewed it, the departure of the Pistons was much more than a team moving to a new facility; it was a symbolic gesture, a prime example of another group of suburbanities contriving to create a new center for the metropolitan area. It was further evidence of the suburban raid on Detroit, the looting of the old community in the interest of the new. It disturbed me when the Lions moved, but the Pistons really pissed me off. I'm a basketball fan, and I enjoy my friendship with Isiah Thomas and other Pistons, but I've never been to a game in Auburn Hills. I felt so strongly about pro basketball belonging in Detroit that I came damn close to bringing in the Milwaukee Bucks after the Pistons walked out on us. I actually thought the deal would get done.

The Pistons have been very successful in Auburn Hills, but there isn't a doubt in my mind that with a decent team they would have done just as well downtown. In the twenty-one years they played in Detroit—the last seventeen at Cobo Hall—the club had exactly three winning seasons. The Tigers, meanwhile, have attracted a consistent gate over the years despite a rickety old ballpark on the fringe of downtown; and the Red Wings—an unlikely draw in a city that is three-quarters black—fill up Joe Louis Arena with a hockey clientele that is overwhelmingly suburban. While swearing that Detroit can support any major team, I don't dispute for a minute that we require plenty of involvement from the suburbs to do it. It's obvious that we need a metropolitan partnership, not only to remain in the big leagues of sport and commerce but to compete with any pretense of parity in the modern economic society. We need the suburbs' dollars, their jobs, and, mostly, their cooperation. We need them—I'm not ashamed to say it—every bit as much as they need us.

Despite the misperception of hostility attached to my remarks over the years, I'm honestly not dumb enough to tell the suburbs to fuck off. I've never lost sight of the fact that they possess many of the resources we need to make a full comeback. In point of fact, they possess the resources that once were ours—an updated, metropolitan adaptation of the process by which white people came to occupy the land that was my family's in Marengo County, Alabama. As that unnatural evolution was fundamental to the sociology of the South, the northern corollary is a key consideration in understanding Detroit. The redistribution of economic assets in Greater Detroit has been unprecedented at the big-city level, reflecting a reconfiguration of people, jobs, and money unlike anything else in history. No comparable urban community that I'm aware of in the nation or the entire world has lost population at the rate that Detroit has in the past forty years. Nowhere else has white flight been as dramatic as it has been in this city. I ask you: Is it so damn hard to recognize the unique circumstances that have heaped upon Detroit an inevitable surplus of lost souls and wasted neighborhoods?

At the same time, how could America—Reagan-Bush America, that is—go so damn long without acknowledging the federal and state commitments that these kinds of circumstances demand? In that regard, the nation miserably failed Detroit and its urban counterparts for most of two decades. Government amounts to a public pledge of accountability, and the Republican administrations of the eighties, perpetuating a position established in the fifties, ignominiously betrayed that pledge. It's disgraceful and unconscionable that the leadership of the United States of America operated for so long without an urban policy—with hardly a pretense of a plan for urban jobs, urban development, urban education, urban health care, urban social services. Our cities are wracked with poverty and crime and drugs and unemployment and disease and bad schools and infrastructures that are falling apart, three-quarters of the American people live in these cities, and the federal government didn't have a goddamn policy to deal with it all.

It's a rather incredible thing to contemplate. Here were the major social problems of our time all percolating together in one pot, and Washington couldn't even smell the coffee.

■

F OR ALL of the election-year rhetoric about the federal deficit, the issue that dominates the contemporary domestic dilemma—that speaks to our times as the social legacy of Reagan and Bush—is one to which Bill Clinton is clearly sensitive but, for obvious political reasons, was not able to articulate at great length during the 1992 campaign. It is the responsibility of federal and state government to the disenfranchised.

The Republicans summarily rejected the concept that the American public has certain implicit and constitutional rights that would pertain, directly or indirectly, to standard of living: the right to work, for instance; the right to a competitive education; and if necessary, the right to adequate public assistance. Washington instituted massive urban cutbacks during the Reagan-Bush years, simultaneously pulling back on social spending and increasing the outlay for war materials. As a result, the government's responsibility toward its urban constituents fell to the states, which had no available means by which to meet such a formidable obligation. (In Michigan, our Republican governor, John Engler, just trimmed eighty thousand people from the welfare rolls—most of them, naturally, from Detroit and the other large cities.) The states in turn shifted social responsibility to the cities, whose people and jobs and tax dollars had bolted to the suburbs.

In my estimation, the election of Clinton was the first signal of a massive, decisive, inevitable backlash to the federal philosophy that was carried to extremes by Reagan and Bush. Americans will not continue to tolerate the deprivation of their inherent rights. The United States Constitution is a contract between the people and the government, and by the spirit of that contract, the people have a right to expect certain things from their government. Reagan and Bush—and to a lesser extent, Ford and Nixon before them—operated under the premise that there are no entitlements for those individuals who do not have the independent means of seizing them: i.e., senior citizens, minorities, and people in the impoverished inner cities. The Republicans defied American tradition in the matter of the huddled masses, and they got away with it for a

long damn time. What happened to the working class, the poor?
Even the Democrats lost touch with them.

Through the years when we were losing to the Republicans, and
even in the course of the 1992 campaign, some Democrats were
pinning their hopes on what they called the great middle class; but
I'm frankly at a loss to identify what the hell the middle class is anymore. The line between the working class and the middle class has
become blurred by unionism to the extent that the contemporary
middle class embraces virtually anybody who works for a wage that
has been collectively bargained. It has been redefined according to
income rather than one's relationship to the means of production.
There is a blue-collar middle class and a white-collar middle class,
an urban middle class and a suburban middle class, a black middle
class and a white middle class, a Democratic middle class and a Republican middle class. Reagan understood this better than anybody else and rode into Macomb County and western Wayne
County to successfully convert the unionists whose suburban life-
styles and federally approved racial views had left them estranged
from the Democratic Party. They, more than any other group in
any other part of the country, had come to symbolize the modern
middle class, which seems to include everybody except the privileged and the underprivileged.

The entitlements of the underprivileged formed the bedrock of
the Democratic Party, and it is they, represented most visibly by the
urban disenfranchised, who will spearhead the coalition that has
begun to effect a comprehensive political turnover in this country.
The traditional underprivileged will be joined by farmers who have
lost their jobs because of subsidy cuts and laborers who have lost
their jobs because of foreign trade agreements. I'm convinced that
this broad, inevitable alliance will constitute an ideological union
of the new working class and set the agenda for the Democrats in
years ahead. In order to stay atop the political wave that they have
ridden to the White House, it is imperative that Democrats everywhere cease trying to out-Republican the Republicans and return
to the party's fundamental principles.

The specific mandate before the American government at this
moment is to assume responsibility for the welfare of its people. I

have never advocated federal handouts as dividends toward any sort of artificial prosperity or nationalized standard of living, but I do maintain that the government is charged with providing essential services such as mass transportation, and I do believe that it is called upon to supply work for citizens who have no other means of attaining it—to step forward as the employer of last resort. It is crucial that the federal government become vigorously and wholeheartedly involved in the creation of jobs.

Franklin Roosevelt found himself in the same sort of situation, and it is worthwhile to note, in that respect, that Roosevelt followed a succession of Republican presidents—Harding, Coolidge, and Hoover—whose ideological bearings were not unlike those of their modern counterparts. It was Roosevelt's destiny, as a result, to pull us back from the brink of a social revolution with a recovery program pinned on the notion that citizens have basic economic entitlements, including the right to a livelihood. Confronted by an epidemic of unemployment, he cured with jobs. That's what the Works Progress Administration (WPA) and the Civilian Conservation Corps (CCC) and all the other alphabet programs were about. Today's conditions cry out for a similar response.

Roosevelt's New Deal innovations ultimately did as much for the national character as they did for the economy. The CCC camps, for example, provided an atmosphere removed from urban despair where kids were disciplined to get up in the morning and undertake a task, to work hard and respect the job at hand and be rewarded for the effort. I can't imagine a program that would better serve as a model for the modern city kid. If a young person is being compromised by a troubled household in which violence or neglect or crack or alcohol plays a part, he or she ought to be separated from that environment and placed in a healthier one. Conservatives balk and squawk at the expense of such a thing, but I prefer to look at the savings. By providing a productive setting for youths who might otherwise lack one, we would save the cost of incarceration that awaits so many city kids from broken homes; we would save the victims of the crimes those kids might commit under different circumstances; and we would save the kids themselves. It might not be practical to replicate the rural logistics of the CCC camps; but as the requisite skills of the work force evolve from blue-collar to technical, it would be eminently advantageous to effect the same sort of program for job training or retraining.

Those who matriculate at the august school of skepticism will disagree by trotting out the traditional patter about blacks not being interested in jobs or jobs programs. That, of course, is pure bullshit. The media likes to sensationalize the issue with stories about rich pimps too proud to pump gas and skewed young men like the guy on "Prime Time" who claimed—for the benefit of the camera—that flipping hamburgers was beneath him because it didn't pay enough to spit on. But the fact is that black people have proved time and again that if a job is available, they will line up for it. Hell, that's how the cities became overcrowded in the first place. That's why the percentage of blacks in the military service is twice the percentage of blacks in the civilian work force. The myth about blacks not wanting to work is as old as Reconstruction. It usually plays alongside the old saw that black people prefer a welfare life to a working one. That fable is refuted by the fact that there has been no relationship in recent years between the relative value of welfare and the number of black people on its rolls. If welfare were regarded as a career alternative, its enrollment would rise and fall with its worth.

One of my favorite mayors in the history of Detroit, Hazen "Potato Patch" Pingree, demonstrated a hundred years ago that unemployed people are generally eager to get busy at whatever opportunity comes their way. During the hard times of the 1890s, he instituted a program in which the city turned over its public park land and owners of vacant lots donated them for vegetable gardens to be planted and maintained by the unemployed. Pingree's potato patches involved nearly half of all the local families on relief.

That wasn't the only thing about Pingree that made him a man and mayor after my own heart. I can fully appreciate the manner in which he feuded openly with the conservative newspapers that did not objectively state his positions, repudiating them to the point of posting his own alternative bulletins on the door of City Hall. Politically, meanwhile, Potato Patch, like yours truly, was a staunch progressive who pushed for public works programs as an antidote to unemployment. What's more, his opening remarks to the city council were delivered in support of an electrical system of rapid transit. Back then, Detroit was still using horses at a time when much smaller cities had already converted to electricity. Some things never change.

It escapes me why rapid transportation for Detroit would not rate with the highest domestic priorities of the federal government. On a broader scale, the construction and repair of urban infrastructure throughout the country would go a long way toward strengthening the economic condition of the cities. Over the past forty years, the federal government has spent billions of dollars on highways systems to connect the cities and circle the cities and exit the cities and, in effect, carve up the cities, often at the exclusion of badly needed urban transportation systems. As a result, black neighborhoods—and in many cities, Hispanic neighborhoods as well—have been cordoned off from the mainstream suburban economy, rendered, for practical purposes, forbidden zones, the collective inner continent of America.

Because of the myriad ways in which they benefit the cities and the job market, urban transportation systems and other public works investments were fundamental to the urban program that the Conference of Mayors presented to Jimmy Carter in 1976. In 1988, the Commission on Cities also recommended that the creation of jobs be the top government priority for socioeconomic rehabilitation, with an emphasis on infrastructure work as the means of generating employment and direct consumer dollars. Government data shows that an infrastructure investment carries with it an income multiplier (a statistic used to estimate the economic stimulus derived from various expenditures, as measured by the recirculation of dollars) of 3.0 to 3.5, as opposed to alternatives like unemployment compensation, which has a multiplier of just over one. Particularly in times of economic recession—like these—it seems unpardonable to not invest in urban infrastructures.

Nonetheless, the Republican administrations of the eighties adopted a hard-line resistance to public works expenditures, apparently forgetting that the nation was built on federal subsidies.

The railroads were subsidized by enormous land giveaways. Most of the country west of the Alleghenies was settled on land grants. Our competitors are currently prospering by government participation in the economy. The Japanese have open collaboration between the government, unions, and business, including tax fixes; and if that system is so problematic, how in the hell have they managed to run us out of half the world markets? Why is their education system so much better than ours? There's a stubborn arrogance about supply-side economics that simply isn't justified by historic or modern reality.

The ideological right has forever been paranoid that subsidy programs might bring us dangerously close to communism, but what the hell—I've been accused all my life of being a Communist. As practiced in Europe and Asia, the Communist system is obviously flawed; but as the Russians and other former Soviets are surrendering to Western economic principles, perhaps we should not be so quick to dismiss the ones by which they achieved so much this century. We haven't figured out all the answers for health care, for instance. America hasn't coped well with decentralization and the cycles of industry. I don't believe the world has yet stumbled upon the perfect system of government, but maybe it's an amalgamation of capitalism and socialism. That seems to be the direction in which all the signs are pointing.

There can be no question, at any rate, that the American government must somehow dedicate itself more responsibly to the basic human needs and present deficiencies of its citizens, urban or otherwise. The fact is—and this is one of the great tenets of good government, as far as I'm concerned—that you can't separate the human condition from the economic. The programs that will serve the people of the cities are the same programs that will stimulate the national economy.

Because of the personal tragedies that are being played out in every city in America, we commonly think of rebuilding the urban centers as a human concern, and we should; but I'm perfectly willing to play along with the conservatives and put the discussion in economic terms, because I believe that's where it has to take place. Some people are so romantic that they would remove economics from the conversation, but that's an irresponsible, utopian style of pseudo-political thinking. Play that with violins and serve it up with white wine. I believe fervently in committing our resources to the underprivileged and disadvantaged people of the cities, but it should not and cannot be done with a bleeding-heart disregard for pragmatic realities. The truth is that the cities are pulling away at the fabric of the country, and what is good and necessary for the cities is good and necessary for America.

Construction of a rapid transit system for Detroit, for instance, would not only unify the metropolitan area and dramatically upgrade the physical condition of an ailing city whose demise would have dire consequences for the region and nation; it would also fuel the local economy by putting the monies immediately to work through the production of the system itself and through the consumer activity of the laborers for whom jobs would be created. Money circulates much quicker in the possession of poor people, who require it for necessities, than rich, who can afford to stash it away.

Reagan and Bush gave lip service to the creation of jobs whenever they reduced taxes for big business, ostensibly observing the jaded commandment of conservatism which states that tax cuts stimulate commerce and expand the work force. But it flatly didn't work. It has been amply demonstrated that corporate tax cuts do not quicken employment in a manner that compares with public jobs and public works programs. According to a study by the Congressional Budget Office, a billion dollars spent on public service employment will generate three times as many jobs as a billion in income tax cuts.

It was no coincidence—and poetic justice—that the economic decline that was Bush's undoing paralleled the urban decline that he didn't seem to care about. By the same token, the economic recovery programs on which Clinton campaigned were actually urban recovery programs under a more marketable label. They bore a striking resemblance to the suggestions delivered to him by the Conference of Mayors in 1992, which bore a striking resemblance to the suggestions we delivered to Jimmy Carter in 1976.

The dollar amount that Clinton initially settled on for his economic package, twenty billion, happened to be the very same amount we suggested to Carter sixteen years earlier. Clinton also picked up on our call for an accelerated public works program to create jobs—with a premium placed on infrastructure repair and construction—and a countercyclical fiscal assistance provision that would kick in to benefit the neediest cities when unemployment reached a designated level. Additionally, Clinton's proposal and the mayors' shared features on national health insurance, on job training, and on a peace dividend to adjust the balance between military and domestic funding. Unfortunately, the President's comprehensive urban policy hit a slick spot when it ventured out of the campaign and into Capitol Hill.

The Senate's opposition to Clinton's jobs bill has been a slap in the face to the cities and, to me, an amazing perpetuation of the Republican insensitivity that has had such tragic consequences for urban America. I look at Bob Dole, the minority leader, and my mouth slackens. How can so many of our federal officials continue to brush off progressive, aggressive solutions to our urban and economic emergency? Optimistically, I'm beginning to think that perhaps they can't. In the House, the black caucus has attained such numbers that it is now damn near as powerful as the old Dixiecrat alliance used to be. Meanwhile, the intransigence of Republicans like Dole has begun to outrage the black legislators, who are rising up in unison. The problem is that Clinton hasn't proven strong enough to take advantage of it. But while I believe the President has been too eager to please and too quick to sell out on many positions, he at least earns points for trying. His economic package was thoughtfully designed to bring fast relief to the places that most desperately require it, and at the same time make some headway against the federal deficit. To wit, a one percent increase in national employment would reduce the deficit by $30 billion. A raise in gasoline taxes is another city-sensitive measure that addresses the deficit. The government could collect an additional $100 billion through gas taxes and still leave the prices far lower than Europe's, at the same time restoring some equity between the cities and the suburbs in consideration of the fact that suburbanites typically do the most driving.

The debilitation of the cities has been hastened by the fact that over the last few decades many public works projects—even those dealing with infrastructure—while creating jobs, have inequitably benefited the suburbs. Whereas black urbanites have been the first to suffer in periods of recession and budgetary cutbacks—a disproportionate number hold government jobs that are sacrificed when the federal monies dry up—they have often been last to prosper from new public construction undertaken in the far reaches of metropolitan areas. Even worse, corporate relocation has moved millions of jobs from the cities to the Sun Belt. Through this process, the urban infrastructures have been forsaken by the American obsession to spread out. Meanwhile, many of the booming areas of the Southwest have never paid their dues in terms of infrastructure. Unlike older cities that have been maintaining their infrastructures for decades, they have no investment in sewers and roads, etc.; yet they expect the federal government to jump in and pay for new roads and sewers on an eighty-twenty basis. Please try to understand where I'm coming from on this. Why the hell should my tax dollars be used to build roads and sewers for Houston and San Antonio and Santa Fe while Detroit limps along with century-old systems that are inadequate to service our established population? It's a reckless replication of infrastructure—building more when there's plenty out there that needs to be repaired.

Conservative Republicans argue patriotically that, in the sacred tradition of capitalism, the flow of the market dictates where the money is spent; but no matter what semantics they use, it's still a case of screwing the Detroits. Going with the flow of the market, Reagan and Bush permitted the number of urban poor to nearly double during their terms. In the name of Reaganomics, they artfully reshaped poverty into a big-city, central-city phenomenon. The self-righteous, simplistically patriotic excuse the Republicans used—letting the marketplace rule—in reality amounts to little more than taking care of your own and leaving the poor huddled together in their hovels. It's an utter breakdown of governmental responsibility, a pitiful rationalization for an attitude that can only divide a great nation: God for us all and devil take the hindmost and fuck you; I got mine, you get yours. That's the Republican philosophy that we lived with for most of two decades, and it has left us with the two societies—black and white, separate and unequal—that the Kerner Report predicted twenty years ago. Meanwhile, Reaganistic Americans everywhere have done their part, picking clean the likes of Detroit—there are probably half a dozen cities around the country on the verge of bankruptcy—and then turning to each other and saying, indignantly, "Look what the niggers did to our city!"

The alternative, of course, is to stop economically pillaging the cities and reconstruct them instead. It would mean the building and repair of streets, highways, and sewers in the decaying population centers instead of in the sprawling suburbs and freshly paved fields; the emphasis on urban-friendly public works instead of environmentally destructive dam projects; the development of transportation systems that would modernize the old neighborhoods instead of extending the new. It's a matter of spending on the necessities instead of the amenities; on the struggling and stranded instead of the advantaged and mobile.

For Detroit, specifically, my priorities include not only an urban rail system, but a bullet train that would connect us with Chicago in two or three hours. I don't try to delude anybody with the notion that the fares would pay for the trains, but there's hardly a transportation system in the world that's self-sufficient. They're public services. And if it would require a tax raise to build one in a city, like Detroit, that sorely needs the public service, then goddamnit, raise taxes. They have to be raised anyway. The Republicans have been making noise for years about balancing the budget and lowering taxes, but it's obviously not going to happen that way.

As one of the few city-sensitive economic proposals that were even discussed in the Republican years, the concept of the urban enterprise zone (an impoverished inner-city area where lower tax rates and other incentives are put in place to attract businesses), as advocated by former HUD secretary Jack Kemp, has received considerable publicity, and it has merit. But the mechanism that I've firmly advocated since the seventies is referred to by the Conference of Mayors as the Urban Investment Bank. It appeals to my coalition instincts because it would involve the private sector in the process of urban development by purchasing stock in local businesses and offering low-interest loans to firms that would invest in city-approved projects. Although Carter never incorporated it as part of his urban program, the Urban Investment Bank would operate in the same sort of pump-priming role as his public works money (of which Detroit took such enthusiastic advantage), encouraging the cities to develop themselves.

As I view it, that sort of public-private partnership is the only plausible way in which cities and city people—blacks and other minorities—are going to gain any semblance of economic parity. It is essential that the government and the business community practice nothing less than economic activism, which is a matter of affirmative action all along the commercial front. Working in concert, we need to create an urban climate in which opportunity will flourish for everybody—a state of affairs I haven't seen in Detroit since we shot craps at the cleaners and bought bootleg at the sweet shop. Only by an unswerving, cross-sectional commitment to the creation of jobs will there emerge a significant class of black entrepreneurs and black professionals, a black middle class. Only by the same means will there emerge a significant Hispanic middle class, and, more generally, a significant inner-city middle class.

Equity in the workplace, moreover, must encompass promotion as well as placement. With comparable education, the average black man earns about three-quarters the wage or salary of the average white man. Black Americans have made encouraging progress in terms of political power, but it's obvious that our economic progress has not kept up. When the subject turns to economic power for blacks, the conservative pundits are fond of saying that we should pull ourselves up by our bootstraps; but the fact is, the motherfuckers stole our boots. As economic activists, we need to go out and get them back.

To that end, no national policy is more vital than affirmative action. Minorities—and their ranks most certainly include Native Americans, who have been economically abused on a level comparable to blacks—will never assume their rightful place in the job market until affirmative action is undertaken broadly, aggressively, and without legal impediments. The Reagan and Bush courts, however, battled affirmative action down the line, as Detroit learned the hard way in our effort to bring racial parity to the police department. The Republican administrations attempted over and over to thwart affirmative action by classifying it as reverse discrimination and more popularly—and perplexingly—as a quota issue. Much of the nation seems to have developed a phobia over quotas, which strikes me as a damn curious thing in light of the fact that quotas have been fine and dandy throughout most of American history, set for black people at zero. Any black person of my generation—and you don't have to be that old—is all too familiar with the tradition of quotas in this country. My whole life, I've been the first black person to do this and enter that—one of the first blacks in the Catholic school, one of the first blacks to venture into the white officers' club, the first black official in the CIO, the first black mayor of Detroit, the first black member of the Democratic National Committee—and every time, I was merely raising the old quota by one. We need to continue raising it. If quotas are the only way to keep the white folks honest, let there be quotas. Let us build on their long and revered heritage in this country, to which I can personally attest. Put in the historical context, it's obvious that all the carrying-on about quotas really isn't about quotas at all; it's about turf. A lot of white folks don't want to give it up. And if they must, which they know they ultimately will, they're not going to give it up any quicker than they have to.

To a great extent, I regard the civil rights slowdown of the last two decades as a predictable middle-class, Republican reflex to retard the reform movement that swept them off their feet in the sixties and early seventies. When the black and other politically enlightened communities set out to reverse Jim Crow, the results (the Great Society programs, antidiscrimination laws, and especially affirmative action) were assailed as merely Jim Crow of a different color—which of course they were. But I have a problem with anybody who has a problem with any type of legislation that might try to atone for the generations of suppression and indignity systematically inflicted upon a race of people. Our sluggish white friends have to understand that aggressive measures like affirmative action are the only way to make up for the deep-seated wrongs of the past.

On that point, the common response from many white people these days is that they've personally done nothing to keep the blacks down; but the fact is, they've all benefited incalculably from the discrimination and inhumanity imposed by their ancestors. Affirmative action does not ask white society to pay for the social crimes of its ancestors, only to give back what has been wrongfully obtained and passed down. If the hypothetical sale of my great-grandfather, for example, brought five hundred dollars on the auction block, he was a form of primitive capital with which a landowner improved his property and net worth. Although recent generations of white people claim to have had nothing to do with that transaction, in many cases they have knowingly and willingly accepted the fine house and land that was secured with the currency of slaves and handed down.

The sale of slaves is not required for this argument, however. Regardless of whether a person is traded as capital, if I do a hundred dollars' worth of work every week, and you take fifty of it (would that the slaves had it so good!), the fact is that after ten years you owe me about $25,000. Now I'm coming to you and saying that you owe me the $25,000 that I have advanced you, and you're saying, "Coleman, I'm sorry, I'm not going to steal from you anymore." That's wonderful, but in the meantime, you've got my $25,000 and you're using it in a way that puts me at a further disadvantage. You've bought a nice house outside the city alongside other people who have taken money from my friends and used it to buy nice houses outside the city. Since you have money to spend—my money—shopping malls have sprung up in your neighborhood, which has prospered as a result. There is very little evidence of hopelessness or desperation where you live; very little crime, drugs, social decline. Your children have gone to safe, well-funded schools and then to college. Meanwhile, my neighborhood has been abandoned and neglected. There is little money with which to improve our situation, and few businesses are interested in moving into an area that they consider blighted. Many of the men can't find jobs and have turned to other things—degenerative things—leaving the women and kids to fend for themselves. Some of the best teachers don't want to teach in our schools because many of the fatherless kids lack discipline. College is a dream. Prison is almost as likely. And we want our money back. . . . That's affirmative action. The bottom line is that much of what the white folks have, acquired in an environment of slavery and double standards and unequal opportunity (and in the case of the Native Americans, by trespass and force), doesn't rightfully belong to them; and ultimately it has to be in their best interest—the country's best interest—to give it up and restore the natural order.

If you don't give us our money back, then we live in a very unbalanced society, which can be neither secure nor salutary for either side. For as long as affirmative action is resisted at any level, none of us, rich or poor, will be immune from the ravages of discrimination and disfranchisement and desperation. On the societal level, as well as the personal, affirmative action is the imperative campaign to make amends for an exclusionary, divisive situation in which generations of a people have been expressly and actively relegated to an inferior station. The central struggle here is the one I embarked on more than half a century ago with the union movement—to establish unity and parity between the races in the workplace. There will not be significant progress until that is achieved.

Nor will economic improvement be meaningful without the underpinnings of solid education—particularly in our high-tech society, in which an increasing percentage of jobs require specific expertise. The public school systems around the country have been set up in the most discriminatory manner that it would be possible to conceive for city students. What could be more inequitable than funding schools by property taxes in every district? Given the federal and commercial assault on urban economy—directly reflected in property value, of course—such a prejudicial custom smacks of an unsubtle conspiracy to undereducate the ghetto children of America. Inasmuch as those are predominantly black children, this represents a tradition with very deep roots in certain parts of the country. The prevailing method also violates the lawful obligation of the state to provide for a system of free public education.

The Michigan constitution, for instance, does not say that the various districts shall provide public schooling based on the relative resources of their tax base; rather, it places education under the purview of the state. The legislature's failure to meet that requirement impacts profoundly upon Detroit. Although the public schools do not fall under my jurisdiction as a mayor (their autonomy traces back to the 1787 ordinance establishing the Northwest Territory, which set aside one section of each township for education), I can't divorce the welfare of my city from the multifarious ramifications of education. Inadequate schools not only put their students at a competitive disadvantage; they do the same for the city at large. Realtors will attest to the fact that the quality of the local school district ranks at or very near the top of the list of considerations for prospective homeowners. A city like Detroit will not attract young professionals in substantial quantity until its schools can compete on even terms with those in the wealthier suburbs.

Only very recently has there been a dawning awareness around the country that the state—every state—must, at the minimum, guarantee an equal amount of money to be spent on every schoolchild. It's indefensible that students in some school districts can have $8,000 spent on their education while in another district the figure is $3,000. Detroit is the most highly taxed city in Michigan in support of education, yet our kids receive about half of the amount that is spent on students at the top-level public schools in the state, such as those in East Lansing and Okemos or suburbs like Troy and Birmingham and Bloomfield Hills. This is despite the fact that inner-city kids, who commonly enter school at a disadvantage, obviously require a greater allocation. (As a way of isolating and addressing some of the social problems inherent with city schools— i.e., of separating the boys and the girls, and moving past that implicit distraction—the Detroit school board recently established a brace of male academies as elementary alternatives. The ACLU, in the tradition of bleeding-heart liberals and with a perspective that I suspect was highly suburban, sued on the basis that gender segregation is discriminatory. The result is that the academies, though permitted to operate, have been watered down and the experiment remains inconclusive at this point.)

Although many of Detroit's economic and social problems are unique, the same cannot be said of our education predicament. We're certainly not the only district being shortchanged. I would strongly recommend that Detroit and other systems inequitably provided for—both urban and rural, in and out of Michigan—join in a coalition and demand that the state governments live up to their educational mandates. In Michigan, the issue ought to be addressed at the next Constitutional Convention, where the question of authority can be reconsidered. One solution, which I wholeheartedly advocate, would be to place city schools under the auspices of municipal governments instead of the state. The cities, after all, have much at stake in the education of their young citizens.

As a method of approximating parity between rich and poor school districts, Michigan does have a municipal overburden formula, providing a vehicle whereby needy districts—those which, because of low property values, must assess exorbitant millage rates to generate adequate revenue for education (a levy of ten mills in Detroit, for instance, will produce about the same dollar value per pupil as a single mill in a suburb like Birmingham)—can be partially compensated by the state, which (in theory) recognizes their efforts to raise money for schools and their resulting overburden. It's a start, but the problem lies in the fact that the state of Michigan has demonstrated an overwhelming indifference toward putting money into the overburden pool, funding it at around one percent of the amount required to meet the full obligation of the formula. Detroit has commonly received ten to fifteen million dollars a year from the overburden formula when it would be eligible for about seventy-five million if the pool were funded at a ten percent level, and about 750 million if it were fully funded. To me, that's unconscionable, raw-ass racism, a matter of the state legislature effectively and diabolically ensuring that Detroit's school system remains inferior.

In the final analysis, the educational disparity between the cities and the suburbs leaves the urban student severely disadvantaged on a basis that is significantly racial—especially as it pertains to a city like Detroit, where the average student attends a school that is only nine percent white. As might be expected, there have been attempts to better integrate Detroit's schools through busing, and in 1974 the case reached the Nixon Supreme Court, where, by a 5–4 decision, the justices reversed the lower court's ruling, which had stated that the existing segregation resulted from a history of unconstitutional local and state actions and that there was no other remedy for a city as overwhelmingly black as Detroit except to desegregate the districts.

Our schools have never recovered from the high court's final disposition of that case. As a result, they're probably among the worst in the state of Michigan—which is a far cry from what they were when I attended them. When I was at Eastern High, our quality of education was the best in the state—so good, in fact, that kids were bused in from Grosse Pointe. Curiously enough, there was no public uproar over busing when it was used that way.

12

If It Could Happen
Here . . .

In the interest of equal time, and in light of the fact that I've now been enumerating the nocuous predilections of the federal government for several chapters, I ought to take this opportunity to note that Washington cannot claim all of the credit for the urban predicament. Pertaining to the case of Detroit, I should like to call special attention to the tireless efforts of some of our knee-jerk liberals on city council.

Together with assorted bleeding-heart newspaper types, they have managed, or at least attempted, to sabotage just about every proposal for economic growth that has come out of my office. They've made it very clear what they oppose—the motherfuckers are against everything—but I've yet to figure out what they propose. They were against the Poletown plant and the Chrysler plant and Joe Louis Arena and expanding Cobo Hall and City Airport and replacing city-owned, closed-down Ford Auditorium with a major office tower—which was a strange one. Actually, council voted at first to raze the auditorium, and we were all set to redevelop the site, but then the losers of the council vote sued the other members over the outcome. They lost the suit but managed to petition the issue onto the ballot in 1991 as a referendum, whereupon the approval for the new development was overturned.

I was shot down three times on referendums to bring gambling to the city, and finally decided to hell with it. The opposition was so damn righteous that I was punishing myself. Of course, it didn't

seem to matter to the do-gooders that we already had gambling in
the form of the state lottery, not to mention the bingo games on
every other street corner, many of them sponsored by churches.
Nor did it seem to matter that gambling in the city would ultimately provide thousands of jobs. I challenged my antagonists to
come up with an alternative plan that would provide as many jobs,
but, typically, they had no response. Then, no sooner had I given
up the cause than it began to take on a life of its own. First, the Canadian government decided to put a casino across the border from
us in Windsor, and then a local developer came up with a plan to
place one in Greektown under the auspices of the Chippewa tribe,
which would assume ownership of the land and thereby be exempt
from local regulations.

For a long time, I've regarded gambling as a creative way of revi-
talizing Detroit. Maybe it has to do with my memories of St. Aubin
and Hastings streets; but I get excited about the thought of what
first-class gambling would do to stir the economy and remake the
image of a city like ours. One way or another, it will take our collective imagination to replace the automobile jobs that have been
forever lost. No longer dominated and fed by a mammoth, sugar-
daddy industry, we will have to somehow redefine Detroit; and if I
were to author the new definition, gambling would be an integral
part of it. Among other advantages, it would allow us to develop a
new regional identity in concert with our Canadian neighbor, toward whom we've been much too indifferent in the past. It would
also capitalize on the unparalleled convention resources of Cobo
Hall and the prolific tourism trade that otherwise just misses us,
whizzing through Detroit bound for the lakes upstate or the Ford
Museum and Greenfield Village in Dearborn, the most popular
indoor-outdoor historical site in North America.

In addition to the moral arguments, which to me weigh very
lightly against the economic considerations, the naysayers will say
about gambling, as they say about nearly every project I get behind, that it does nothing for the neighborhoods. That's been
their response every time I've turned my attention to the riverfront, or bought up some land for an auto plant. Rather than
spend our block-grant money for development projects, these

"poverty politicians," as I call them, would prefer to hire community planners at $50,000 and $75,000 a throw. That's one of the best ways I know of to jettison your cash. Unless we succeed in using our available dollars in a manner that will replace the jobs that have left the city, there isn't a neighborhood in Detroit that can be saved by any goddamn community planner.

The neighborhood approach to rebuilding a city is a matter of the liberal coaxing the tail to wag the dog. Neighborhoods develop organically from the socioeconomic soil from which they spring, not vice versa; and I can't imagine that even my harshest critic or the bleedingest-hearted liberal on city council would deny that I've done all that could be done to fertilize the commercial turf of Detroit in the interest of nourishing our socioeconomics. Even in the merciless Reagan years, the inadequate federal development dollars that came our way exceeded those received by any other major city except New York. Not only has the riverfront been reborn, but the ripples of renaissance have spread grandly to the Woodward Avenue corridor. When Mike Ilitch, the dynamic and daring (which is exactly what we need) pizza mogul who was rated by *Detroit* magazine as the most powerful businessman in the city, moved his Little Caesar's headquarters from the suburb of Farmington Hills to the old Fox Theater building—a neglected local landmark whose glory days of the sixties featured Stevie Wonder, Diana Ross, and the second-largest pipe organ in the world—it marked the first time in thirty years that a major corporation had elected to locate in Detroit. He also refurbished the Fox in lavish rococo detail, which brought renewed attention to the downtown theater district and touched off its revitalization. Numerous new and restored restaurants and theaters (among them the State and the Gem, which present musical shows) now appear up and down Woodward Avenue, from the Fox to the renovated Orchestra Hall a mile and a half down the street. It's not unlikely that Ilitch, having recently added the Tigers to a sporting interest that already included the Red Wings, will ultimately bring baseball and hockey downtown as well, freeing up Joe Louis Arena for a world-class aquarium and environmental center while creating an urban entertainment complex that would be unmatched by any other in America. Needless to say, I believe that gambling, in Greektown or anywhere else in the city, would be a perfect complement to the new dynamics of downtown, completing the symbiotic transformation of Detroit's image and economics. That's the most important thing that could be done for our neighborhoods.

I'd be lying to say that I haven't been frustrated by the number of my ambitious and perhaps unconventional development projects that have been squelched by one voice of negativism or another. The revised city charter, while increasing the authority of the mayor in some respects, disabled me in other ways. Detroit's nonpartisan system of electing councilmen-at-large—designed in reaction to the Democratic machines that Richard Daley and other city bosses built around ward systems by which municipal voting patterns can be localized and manipulated through the partisan efforts of city employees—has come to mean, in effect, that we have an extra nine would-be goddamn mayors sitting up there in the City-County Building. Some of our councilpeople feel so empowered that they even draw up and present personalized city budgets. With each council member having his or her own city-wide electorate, the mayor is unable to generate the sort of leverage that can be achieved by putting together territorial political units and coalitions within the framework of the municipal government. Despite the charges of bossism in Detroit—the Big Daddy image I've been carrying around in recent years—we do not and cannot have a spoils system in this city, and consequently cannot put together a political machine on any scale comparable to the old one in Chicago. I don't control tens of thousands of jobs as Daley did, and don't have the power to reward and punish as he did. I wish I did. Although it may not have been the purest form of local government, I'm not reluctant to say that I envied Daley's machine. He had the ability to do whatever he thought was necessary for his city. When Chicago needed him, he was there. No mayor can ask for a better epitaph.

As for me, I think I've done pretty damn well with what I've had to work with. The media is constantly after me to evaluate my performance in terms of whether the city is better off than it was when I became mayor, but that's an absurd and blatantly prejudiced way to look at it. Hell no, I don't think Detroit is better off now than it was when I became mayor. The auto industry certainly isn't better off than it was in 1974. The job market certainly isn't better off than it was then. How the hell could Detroit be better off? But I damn sure think it's better off for me *becoming* mayor. I'd hate to think of the shape my city would be in right now without the Poletown plant and without the Chrysler plant and without Joe Louis and without a bigger Cobo Hall and without the highest income tax in the state and without a mayor who will take on any motherfucker who tries to mess with Detroit.

I also believe that, despite the efforts of the media, the people of Detroit agree with me that the city is better off than it would have been if I hadn't become mayor. They've elected me five damn times.

MY ADMIRATION for Joe Louis was not passed on automatically to his relatives. His nephew, an accountant named Tom Barrow, twice tried to knock me out of office, both times making it through the primary to oppose me in the general election.

I was able to put him away in 1985 without much effort, thus becoming Detroit's first four-term mayor. The emphatic show of approval should have been enough to make me feel roundly accepted within the city, and to a large extent it did; but something had come to my attention during the campaign that tainted the moment for me. Our election committee had held a fund-raiser in the backyard of a friend who lived in a house overlooking one of the fairways of the Detroit Golf Club. Previously, anyone who lived in that proximity to the golf course had automatically gained membership in the club, but the policy curiously changed when my friend and a few other blacks moved in. Another club tradition that had apparently been discontinued was the one whereby the mayor of Detroit was given a complimentary membership. In three terms, I'd received no such thing. In fact, although Detroit was seventy-five percent black, there wasn't a single black member of the Detroit Golf Club. Naturally, I applied. There was quite a bit of publicity attending the situation, and the club had little choice but to approve my application. Since then, other blacks have become members. I only hope they get more use out of the club than I do. To this day, I've never played a round of golf there or anywhere else.

There were no such distractions in 1989, and thankfully so, because the campaign itself was more challenging. The field included not only Barrow but also John Conyers, the Black Bottom native who had been in Congress for twenty-five years and with whom I had worked on behalf of countless causes. His obvious rapport with the voters—he had been elected thirteen times—gave Conyers a little more weight than my customary opponents. He chose to throw this around, claiming as he announced his candidacy, "It's all over, Big Daddy." Like hell. Conyers kept expecting Jesse Jackson to breeze into town on his behalf and turn the campaign upside down, but it didn't work out that way. The congressman never made it out of the primary. I got fifty-one percent of the primary vote—enough to preclude the final runoff in many cities—and that was despite a tabloid-style scandal that hit me early in the year and festered through most of the campaign.

It was headline news in Detroit when a report came out that I was the object of a paternity suit filed by a former city employee named Annivory Calvert, who, with the considerable aid of her lawyer, proceeded to play the local media in a manner that I can only envy in retrospect. She had decided to move to California and was on her way there when the story broke, but all the while she remained in touch with her attorney, who supplied the media with the phone numbers of the motels where Ms. Calvert stopped en route. I was taken aback by the whole development and the feeding frenzy that ensued, because, although I'd had a relationship with Ms. Calvert, I did not believe I was the father of her child. It took me by surprise when blood tests revealed that her six-year-old son, Joel, was indeed mine. I had always wanted a son, and it was one of the great disappointments in my life that I didn't have one—in which context I received the news as very welcome. I've since had Joel out to Detroit for a visit, and I keep up with him at birthdays and holidays. He is a fine, loving boy, and well provided for.

Meanwhile, my opponents jumped all over the paternity situation as a character deficiency that made me unfit to be mayor. It was not the thing, however, with which to bring down a seventy-one-year-old four-term mayor. I'd never concealed the fact that I enjoyed the company of women, and if anything, the episode proved that I was a hell of a lot more fit than many people might have thought. If they were going to call me Big Daddy, I might as well live up to the name.

Anyway, its author, Conyers, was out of the race, which focused attention on Jesse Jackson, who had a decision to make. Barrow figured that he had a lock on Jackson's endorsement, and not without reason, since it was well known that Jesse and I were not bosom buddies. I've always considered him a friend, and our goals are similar, but we've generally taken different roads to reach them. When Jesse ran for President in 1988, I had a tough call to make and ended up supporting Michael Dukakis for pragmatic reasons, although I turned loose my troops to vote for Jesse with my blessing if they wished. But I didn't think he could win, and after eight years of Reagan's vicious negligence toward the cities, I reasoned that we couldn't afford a symbolic endorsement. People speculated that I was getting even with Jesse for what had happened in 1974, when he refused to campaign for me unless I paid him, and I'll admit that I hadn't forgotten that; but I make my political decisions for practical reasons, not personal.

Fortunately, Reverend Jackson is just as practical as I am. In late October of 1989 he paid a timely visit, riding with me in my city Cadillac to Chrysler's old Jefferson Avenue plant, where we arrived just as the shifts were changing and shook some hands. Then we drove back to the mansion and held a press conference, which included all of the candidates who had lost in the primary, even Conyers. Jesse played a big part in forging that unity, and it, in turn, played a big part in the election. Later, on the last Sunday of the campaign, Jesse came back for a rally at New St. Paul's Tabernacle. Aretha Franklin joined us and sang "Precious Lord." It was enough to make a religious man out of a septuagenarian sinner. Then Reverend Jackson took the podium and said, "The blood of Malcolm and Martin brings us to an emancipation rally. When they were needed, they were there. And when the roll was called, Coleman Young was there. He answered, 'Present.' " Two days later, we won big.

In 1993, a flock of candidates filed for the mayor's race long before I had made up my mind whether to run. The first to announce was a state supreme court justice named Dennis Archer, whose candidacy disturbed me less than the person who introduced it. Calling Archer to the podium was my HUAC counsel and longtime ally, former congressman George Crockett.

Crockett and I had been estranged since his final race for Congress in 1988. He had come to me before the campaign and said that he wanted me to succeed him, but I replied that I didn't want to be a congressman, didn't consider it a promotion, and in fact didn't like a goddamn thing about Washington. I suspect Crockett may have been sore about that; and after the election, which he won, he claimed that I had supported his opponent, Barbara-Rose Collins, despite the fact that I told him otherwise. Collins had sought my endorsement, and since she was on city council at the time and I needed all the friends I could get on council, it would have been politically expedient for me to throw in with her. I later did support her when she won the congressional seat in 1990 (after Crockett retired), which put him and me on opposite sides, since he backed the other candidate. But in 1988, I honored my relationship with Crockett and made available to him my campaign fund and machinery, which had been building up formidably for fifteen years. Nonetheless, he was apparently persuaded by somebody—a political adversary of mine, I can only assume—and chose to believe that I had supported Barbara-Rose. I consider myself a man of my word, and by taking someone else's over mine, Crockett insulted my integrity, which is something I don't easily forget.

The split with Crockett was one of the major disappointments of my later terms, but it certainly doesn't stand alone. Chief Hart's indiscretions with Kenneth Weiner and the police fund hit me hard, and my inability to win a gambling referendum was of course a setback. But nothing knocked me cold like the police beating death of an unemployed father of five named Malice Green on the night of November 5, 1992.

I would have sworn—in fact, I probably had sworn—that it could never happen in Detroit. For nearly twenty years, I had emphasized a firm but respectful style of law enforcement. I had campaigned on that issue and fought over it with the veteran cops. The police department's attitude adjustment had been the first priority of my first term, and I was damn proud of the progress we had made since then in our relationship with the people, much of which could be attributed to the affirmative action measures we so diligently pursued for two trying decades. It was a struggle that could not have been won with a lesser commitment, or—I'd like to think—a lesser mayor. Despite staunch and collective resistance, my administration never gave up on affirmative action, and the reward was in the relative climate of harmony that prevailed between the police and the citizens of Detroit. Our reputation for improving police-community relations was such that the commission looking into the Los Angeles riot had expressly requested a member from Detroit. When Detroiters had watched the tape of L.A. cops bludgeoning Rodney King, we had taken consolation in the fact that, for all of our hardships, our city was long past that sort of thing. Or so we thought.

There had been a few incidents of racial cruelty in the Detroit area, but the most notable of them had occurred in the suburbs. A black kid in Bloomfield Hills was waiting for his mother in a parking garage when a fearful white doctor pulled a shotgun on him. In Birmingham, a black news anchor arrived home to find racial slurs painted on his garage door. But none of this enmity had been manifested on the streets of the city, between black citizens and white cops, until two plainclothesmen in a power unit, a pair well known in the neighborhood as Starsky and Hutch, approached the vehicle of Malice Green after he had dropped off a friend in front of a boarded-up hair salon and suspected crack house at Warren and Twenty-third, in the heart of the 1967 riot area. Starsky and Hutch—Larry Nevers and Walter Budzyn—told Green to let loose of whatever he was holding in his fist, and when he wouldn't, they pulled him out of the car and pummeled him with their flashlights. Then four more cops arrived, and the beating continued until Green was dead.

When I heard the news, I felt like the wind had been knocked out of me. It was my worst nightmare coming true. And the toughest part of it was that there was nothing I could do for Malice Green. Rodney King survived to get his day in court and to symbolize the tensions that tore up Los Angeles. He could be helped. But Malice Green was dead at the hands of cops—my cops. I say that with terrific difficulty, because I cannot for a second stomach what those policemen did. Nonetheless, I have to live with the fact that they were on the payroll of the city for which I'm responsible.

It's worth noting, though small consolation to me or the Green family or Detroit, that one of the officers, Nevers, had been a member of the pernicious STRESS unit, the police decoy squad that had perpetrated so much violence until I abolished it in my first few months as mayor. It was poignant and worth noting also, though small consolation, that Nevers admitted he must have done something wrong because a guy died. I don't doubt that he regretted the loss of life; but no matter how repentant, the white cop with blood on his hands was in no position to be the agent of solace. Nothing he could say would bring comfort and calm to Detroit. I had to do that, if I could.

In a statement the next afternoon, I said, "I am shocked and sickened at what I have learned regarding the incident that occurred last night involving several Detroit police officers that resulted in the death of a citizen of the city. I have ordered an immediate, complete investigation to determine exactly what happened. Every officer found to be guilty of any misconduct in connection with this tragic incident will be dealt with in the harshest manner possible. I have worked too long and too hard to build a community-based police department to have something like this happen. So long as I am mayor, we will not tolerate any mistreatment of the citizens of this city by the police department." In further comments, I mentioned Nevers and Budzyn by their street nicknames and vowed that city personnel would be all over the neighborhood listening to the people.

Then, in a later interview with "NBC Nightly News," I pointedly referred to what had happened as murder. It was the wrong thing to say, legally, and I was not surprisingly taken to task by the local media for my remarks. But as usual, they had their heads up their asses. Quick as they were to jump on the technicalities of my wording, most of the reporters and commentators didn't seem to have a clue about what I was up to. Did they think I didn't know about the legal proprieties? Did they think I was insensitive to the concept of convicting people in the newspapers after all the times it had happened so damnably to me and those around me? Didn't the motherfuckers understand that I had an angry city to consider? Whatever I had to say about the Malice Green incident, I had to say with the city in mind. The people of Los Angeles had just staged the most devastating riot in American history because they thought—and with damn good reason—that the authorities showed no remorse over what had happened to Rodney King, were not appropriately appalled, and did not object profoundly enough to renounce it or to take even symbolic action against the perpetrators. I couldn't let that happen in Detroit. I was in no hurry to win back the riot championship. My charge, consequently, was to convince the people of Detroit that I was on their side, and that I was just as outraged about what had happened as they were. My job was to learn from Los Angeles; to alienate myself from any official attitude against which the people of my city might revolt.

It was interesting that, around the country, Detroit was lauded for the sensitive manner in which we handled the Malice Green case and put off further violence. Many of the national stories made a point to note that the incident was an aberration for Detroit and that, in fact, our city had virtually written the book on healthy police-community relations. While the black citizens of the city seemed to recognize this, and that recognition undoubtedly held them in check when they might otherwise have lashed out in the fresh tradition of Los Angeles, most of the salutary and pertinent nuances were lost on the local media. They were lost also, I might add, on former L.A. police chief Daryl Gates, who, at a speaking engagement in Ann Arbor, said, "I did see that the chief suspended the officers before the investigation was completed. I think that is wrong. You may take them off the streets, but to suspend them is wrong. Then I read that the mayor said they were guilty of murder. I realize that they said this as a way to avoid a riot like in L.A. If they were being intimidated to do what is politically correct instead of what is right, I think that is absolutely wrong." The way I saw it, if we were being criticized by Daryl Gates, we must have been absolutely right.

The courts ultimately determined that Nevers and Budzyn *were* guilty of murder, in the second degree. Their conviction, however, was not the bottom line. The verdict I continue to hope for is that the country learned something from the beatings of Malice Green and Rodney King before him. I can only hope, also, that it learned something from Detroit in the way we responded to the tragedy at our doorstep and, more fundamentally, the way we averted even greater disaster by carefully cultivating our city's police-community relationship over the years. Maybe, from those lessons, America will pay more attention to us from here on out. As I see it, that's a worthy legacy for both Malice Green and me, as well as for our city.

While it was encouraging that Detroit was able to contain the community reaction to the killing of Malice Green, our tranquilizing efforts in general must now be joined by those across our boundaries, near and far. There isn't a single problem Detroit has that's going to stop here. The candidates for mayor have been spouting that the danger in our neighborhoods is the principal dilemma confronting Detroit, and while I disagree with the thesis—as I view it, street violence is but the bloodiest manifestation of a larger and deeper economic emergency—all of us should indeed be alarmed at the frightening phenomenon of kids killing kids. Murder occupies roughly the same station among our youth right now that drugs did fifty years ago, when they were considered to be a ghetto problem exclusively. By the sixties, drugs had swept through our college towns and the nation at large, and violence will follow the same pattern if we—all of us, together—don't arrest it soon by eliminating its provocation.

The lifestyle of the street is superficially a social condition, of course, but to search for its cause is to probe into the nation's economic anatomy. Urban violence, like poverty and infant mortality and so many of our civil maladies, is another conspicuous symptom of the despair and desperation and instability that accompany geographic and fiscal isolation. The cure requires nothing less than a comprehensive ideological and political rehabilitation, a basic recognition of where we've gone wrong and what we have to do to make it right.

On the metropolitan level, it is paramount that we come to grips in the years ahead with the concept of regionalization, ensuring that if it's undertaken, it's undertaken with a spirit of quid pro quo; that, as a fundamental component of any regional restructuring, the city will not be expected to surrender its majority interest in itself or its authority over its assets; that regionalization does not become simply one more way for white people to exercise control over blacks. If the suburbs are to receive urban-quality public transportation, for example, then the cities will have to receive suburban-quality education in return. Equity, in fact, won't cut it. The parity process will require affirmative action regionalization designed to compensate the cities for half a century of economic rape. It will require a way, for instance, to recompense Detroit for a network of services and infrastructure that was designed for two million people and is only serving one million. It will require a concerted initiative to carry city people to the jobs. It will require, above all, cooperation. The cities and the suburbs are going to have to do this together, I truly believe.

In my part of the country, specifically, any regional partnership will require a multilateral commitment to identify and deal with the circumstances that make Detroit unique—the blackest, most segregated, most isolated, most restructured, most abandoned, most disenfranchised, most detested, and possibly the most feared city in America. At the same time, we ought not to be characterized exclusively by our special problems, in consideration of the fact that our assets are equally defining. As a minority-dominated community, Detroit has achieved a level of autonomy and professionalism and peace with itself that no other city can match and that the white skeptics wouldn't have thought possible in 1974. That accomplishment should not be undermined by regionalization or any other kind of -ization that may come along before the century is out.

Perhaps our town's greatest accomplishment, however—and probably mine—is simply that we have survived this far into the century. In that spirit, I would also call Detroit the most resilient city in America, to which end I kind of like to think that it takes after its mayor of the past twenty years. We've been through a lot together, up to and including the unsubstantiated rumors of our demise. The critics have suggested several times that Detroit's was at hand, and mine more than once.

Actually, this has been a recurring theme in my experience. In addition to the political obituaries that have been circulated for me periodically, the issue of my health has seemed to captivate the media over the past couple of years, owing to the fact that I have a chronic respiratory condition that precludes cross-training with Bo Jackson and checks me into the hospital now and then. Every time I go, the papers launch into lengthy discussions and eager speculation concerning my mortality. They've written me off a few times, although never before with such finality as late in 1992, when word got around that I had been rushed to the emergency room in critical condition and failed to pull through. One of the local television stations went so far as to report me dead on the eleven o'clock news, which I was watching comfortably in my bedroom, playing solitaire.

This was a little disconcerting, I'll admit, and might have genuinely disturbed me had not various political misadventures left me considerably deader on any number of previous occasions.

Epilogue

In my heart, I had known for quite a while that I didn't want to run for a sixth term. Twenty years is enough.

But it wasn't that simple. It is not in my nature to abandon a task before it is completed (which mine, realistically, would never be); and as mayor, I had a duty to think foremost of the city. It was my sworn responsibility to do what I could to ensure the future of Detroit, whether I was running or not. So, as the candidates entered the race one by one and launched their campaigns, I watched them and I waited. For a vision. For a program. For a few good, solid ideas.

When those ideas were not forthcoming, I kept thinking in the back of my mind that maybe I'd have to crank up the old engines one more time, tired and creaky as they were. All the while, the newspapers kept pushing me to step down, attaining new heights in negativity and publishing polls that showed me hopelessly behind. If they wanted me to go gracefully into the night, that was precisely the wrong strategy.

I never doubted that I would win if I ran; I had trailed in the polls before. But the campaign was a matter that troubled me considerably. I knew I couldn't go all out as I had in the past. Many people approached with offers to lighten the load by actively helping me campaign, but that wasn't my style. And even if I made it through the campaign, I would still face the rigors of a very demanding office.

Without question, the most influential factor in my ultimate de-

cision not to run again was my health. For all of the media babble
to that effect, I knew better than anybody else that in my final year
or so as mayor, I hadn't been able to expend the effort to which I
was accustomed. I found I could often go full tilt for three or four
days, working late into the night and weekends, but then I would
have to slow down or withdraw for a spell. On top of the fatigue
that generally accompanies a man of seventy-five years, my respiratory problems persisted. There were two nighttime episodes, in
particular, when my emphysema made it a struggle to draw a
breath. Those incidents forced me to question whether my physical condition would allow me to function in the manner that the
mayor's office deserves. I didn't want to sleep through my last term
the way Ronald Reagan did.

And so I stepped down reluctantly, postponing the final decision
until the eleventh hour—actually, the day before the filing
deadline—in case I felt a sudden surge of energy and fitness. But
it wasn't there, and I knew, at last and without a doubt, what I had
to do. The next morning, June 22, I felt a powerful sense of confir-
mation when a front-page headline in the *Free Press* heralded the
resumption of a second shift at the Poletown plant, spotlighting
one of the great monuments of our struggle to rebuild Detroit and
giving me hope that things were in place for my departure. That
put me at peace with my decision, and at three-thirty in the afternoon, half an hour before the deadline, I met with my appointees
at the International Marketplace to give them the news first, as
promised. Then we sealed the room so that there were no media
leaks, and I held a four o'clock press conference in my office.

I had an agenda that afternoon, and it was not simply to announce my retirement as mayor. It still made me uneasy that none
of the candidates seemed to have a plan for Detroit, and I felt it incumbent upon me to leave the city with a working vision as I va-
cated my office. So, before I came out with the words that everyone
awaited, I talked about my blueprint-in-progress. I talked, as I always had and always will, about jobs for the city—about economic
development. I talked about affirmative action and minority contracts, mentioning the fact that before I was elected in 1973, Detroit issued less than $20,000 in minority contracts, and that since

1988 we had averaged more than $125 million, the most awarded by any city. I talked about the immense progress we had made in the police department, in both racial composition and community presence. I talked about the various modes of modern transportation required to make Detroit competitive.

Determined to press ahead with a program for the city, I noted that we needed, among other things, to construct a new railroad tunnel underneath the Detroit River; to acquire a high-speed rail line between Chicago and Detroit, extending to Montreal and Toronto; to develop an elevated train connecting downtown with the neighborhoods and suburbs; and to expand City Airport. I also remarked that with these immediate goals in view, Detroit's greatest days lie ahead.

Then, and only then, I said, "I shall not seek another term as mayor of Detroit."

I hope people understand that what I said was not calculated to call attention to my accomplishments or to salvage my pet projects, but to underscore the need for aggressive, specific, pragmatic solutions to Detroit's and the larger urban dilemma. It was no coincidence, either, that so many of my proposals, as related specifically to Detroit, had to do with transportation. We cannot forget that Detroit, like most major cities, developed because of its natural setting. Detroit owes its very existence to its strategic position on the Great Lakes and the Detroit River, and it retains that inherent advantage. It is the international gateway to the Midwest, and a unique location for the development of the state of Michigan. It has the setting, the water, and the work force required to regain the eminence it attained in the first half of the century, when Detroit was a promised land for job seekers. I have no doubt that we can continue the renaissance of that tradition. We need only the programs and the leadership.

For those programs to succeed, however, and for that leadership to be effective, there must prevail a spirit of unified cooperation between city and suburbs, city and state, city and country. There must be a widespread recognition of the fact that America can only be as strong as its most troubled areas—its cities. There must be a goal shared commonly between all jurisdictions and races, that being the achievement of full employment and equal opportunity for all.

I've done my damnedest, in the office of mayor, to carry forward the pursuit of unity on both the intramural and extramural levels. Inevitably, my most immediate, conspicuous opportunities have occurred through the vehicle of city hiring, and I have used, as my instruments in the campaign, racial balance and affirmative action, among other means. I endeavor to make the point about racial balance whenever I can—to the extent of going out in public with two security officers, one black, one white. Despite my record of fifty-fifty hiring, I have been boorishly charged over the years with "racial politics" and "playing the race card." I prefer to think of it as "equal opportunity politics" and "playing the equality card." I only wish that my fellow public servants in the suburbs were held to the same standards. To the contrary, I submit that many of them would severely endanger their reelection potential if they dared to hire on a fifty-fifty racial basis.

I'd like to think that Detroit has set the modern example for racial cooperation; but there was a prior embodiment of that commitment, which I was poignantly reminded of early in 1993. Veterans of the National Negro Labor Council gathered in Detroit for our first-ever national reunion, and while it was an emotional experience for those of us who participated in that noble and persecuted endeavor, the reunion served a greater purpose. It transported us back to the invigorating days when black and white people damned the odds and the feds and the conservative unions by laboring together on behalf of the disadvantaged worker. That's the attitude this country needs right now.

I can proudly say that I brought the spirit of the NNLC to the city of Detroit in my twenty years as mayor; and it has been gratifying, in the days since I announced my retirement, to hear others articulate their appreciation of my efforts. The usual dignitaries have publicly paid their respects, many of them spewing forth in uncharacteristically benevolent tones—mindful, of course, that I have finally loosened my grip upon the city's top office and no longer pose an institutional threat to their agendas. To me, though, the most flattering remark came from JoAnn Watson, the executive director of the Detroit chapter of the NAACP, who observed, "He's the only mayor I've known in my lifetime about whom the brothers stand out on the corner and slap hands and say, 'My man.' "

That comment was especially meaningful to me in view of the fact that it was the brothers on the corners of Black Bottom, myself among them, for whom I embarked on my life's work more than fifty years ago, and it was substantially with their modern counterparts in mind that, as mayor of Detroit, I bargained with Presidents and collaborated with captains of industry. If, as I suspect, those brothers slapping hands are young men out of luck, searching for human respect and a living wage—and Detroit is full of that kind, believe me—then hell yes, I'm honored to have been their man for the last two decades, and eager to continue in that capacity, however it might shake down in the years ahead.

Bibliography

Alderman, Ellen, and Caroline Kennedy. *In Our Defense.* New York: William Morrow, 1991.

Astor, Gerald. *And a Credit to His Race: The Hard Life and Times of Joseph Louis Harrow, a.k.a. Joe Louis.* New York: Saturday Review Press, 1974.

Boyle, Jackie, and Dennis Rosenblum, eds. *The Quotations of Mayor Coleman A. Young.* Detroit: Droog Press, 1991.

Carson, Clayborne, David J. Garrow, Vincent Harding, Darlene Clark Hine, and Toby Kleban Levine. *Eyes on the Prize.* New York: Penguin Books, 1987.

Chafets, Ze'ev. *Devil's Night.* New York: Random House, 1990.

DuBois, W.E.B. *The Souls of Black Folk.* A. C. McClurg and Company, 1903.

Eisenger, Peter K. *The Politics of Displacement: Racial and Ethnic Transition in Three American Cities.* New York: Academic Press, 1980.

Fine, Sidney. *Frank Murphy, the Detroit Years.* Ann Arbor: University of Michigan Press, 1975.

———. *Violence in the Model City.* Ann Arbor: University of Michigan Press, 1989.

Hacker, Andrew. *Two Nations.* New York: Charles Scribner's Sons, 1992.

Halberstam, David. *The Reckoning.* New York: William Morrow, 1986.

Halpern, Martin. *UAW Politics in the Cold War Era.* Albany: State University of New York Press, 1988.

Harris, Fred R., and Roger W. Wilkins, eds. *Quiet Riots: Race and Poverty in the United States. (The Kerner Report Twenty Years Later).* New York: Pantheon Books, 1988.

Hendrickson, Wilma, ed. *Detroit Perspectives.* Detroit: Wayne State University Press, 1991.

Holli, Melvin G. *Reform in Detroit.* New York: Oxford University Press, 1969.

Howe, Irving, and B. J. Widick. *The UAW and Walter Reuther.* New York: Random House, 1949.

BIBLIOGRAPHY

Iacocca, Lee, and William Novak. *Iacocca.* New York: Bantam Books, 1980.

Jones, Bryan D., and Lynn Bachelor. *The Sustaining Hand.* Lawrence: University of Kansas Press, 1986.

Komorowski, Conrad. *The Strange Trial of Stanley Nowak.* Detroit: Stanley Nowak Defense Committee, 1954.

Leggett, John C. *Class, Race, and Labor: Working-Class Consciousness in Detroit.* New York: Oxford University Press, 1968.

Lemann, Nicholas. *The Promised Land.* New York: Knopf, 1991.

Lincoln, James H. *The Anatomy of a Riot.* New York: McGraw-Hill, 1968.

Lochbiler, Don. *Detroit's Coming of Age.* Detroit: Wayne State University Press, 1973.

Nowak, Margaret Collingwood. *Two Who Were There: A Biography of Stanley Nowak.* Detroit: Wayne State University Press, 1989.

Phelps, Alfred J. *Chappie.* Novato, Calif.: Presidio Press, 1991.

Powledge, Fred. *Free At Last?* Boston: Little, Brown, 1991.

Rich, Wilbur C. *Coleman Young and Detroit Politics.* Detroit: Wayne State University Press, 1989.

Shogan, Robert, and Tom Craig. *The Detroit Race Riot.* Philadelphia: Chilton Books, 1964.

Stark, George. *City of Destiny.* Detroit: Arnold-Powers, 1943.

Terkel, Studs. *American Dreams: Lost & Found.* New York: Pantheon Books, 1980.

Wilson, Edmund. *The American Earthquake.* Garden City, N.Y.: Doubleday Anchor Books, 1958.

Woodford, Frank B., and Arthur W. Woodford. *All Our Yesterdays.* Detroit: Wayne State University Press, 1969.

Woodward, C. Vann. *The Strange Career of Jim Crow.* New York: Oxford University Press, 1974.

Wylie, Jeanie. *Poletown.* Urbana: University of Illinois Press, 1989.

Authors' note: In addition to articles from numerous newspapers (e.g., the *Detroit News, Detroit Free Press,* and *Michigan Chronicle*) and magazines *(Time, Newsweek, Detroit Monthly),* other source materials for this work included files from the Federal Bureau of Investigation, the Detroit Police Department, and the Reuther Archives at Wayne State University.

Index

INDEX